Law, Institutions and Malaysian Economic Development

T0345556

Law, Institutions and Malaysian Economic Development

Editors

Jomo K.S. with Wong Sau Ngan

NUS PRESS
SINGAPORE

© 2008 NUS Press
National University of Singapore
AS3-01-02, 3 Arts Link
Singapore 117569

Fax: (65) 6774-0652
E-mail: nusbooks@nus.edu.sg
Website: http://www.nus.edu.sg/npu

ISBN 978-9971-69-390-9 (Paper)

National Library Board Singapore Cataloguing in Publication Data

Law, institutions and Malaysian economic development / edited by
   Jomo K.S. with Wong Sau Ngan – Singapore : NUS Press, c2008.
   p. cm.
   Includes bibliographical references and index.
   ISBN-13 : 978-9971-69-390-9 (pbk.)

   1. Law and economic development. 2. Land tenure – Law and
legislation – Malaysia. 3. Finance – Law and legislation – Malaysia.
4. Malaysia – Economic policy. I. Wong, Sau Ngan. II. Title.

KPG970
343.59507 -- dc22   OCN166280532

Typeset by: Forum, Kuala Lumpur, Malaysia
Printed by: Vinlin Press Sdn. Bhd.

Contents

Preface   vii

1. Making Malaysia Legally   1
   Wong Sau Ngan and Jomo K. S.

2. The Political Economy of Post-colonial Transformation   22
   Jomo K. S. and Chang Yii Tan

3. Post-colonial Legal Developments   54
   Wong Sau Ngan

4. Financial Sector Legal Developments   80
   Wong Sau Ngan and Shanthi Kandiah

5. Colonial Land Law and the Transformation of   129
   Malay Peasant Agriculture
   Jomo K. S.

6. Labour Laws and Industrial Relations   156
   Jomo K. S. and Vijayakumari Kanapathy

7. Investment and Technology Policy: 177
   Government Intervention, Regulation and Incentives
   Jomo K .S.

8. Institutional Initiatives for Crisis Management, 1998   203
   Wong Sook Ching and Jomo K. S.

9. Corporate Governance Reform for East Asia   222
   Jomo K. S.

Glossary   240

Bibliography   244

Index   266

Preface

Interest in the relationship between the law and economic development has grown in recent years. This has been encouraged by several different academic developments especially growing interest in institutional economic analysis. To be sure, there are many different and competing strands of institutional analysis, with the very nature of academic competition encouraging differentiation and diversity of analyses. Similarly, there is no single school of "law and economics" as such, just as there are diverse approaches to the study of economic development.

Legal frameworks have been crucial for defining the "rules of the game" in the economy. They do not merely define what is legal or illegal, but influence what is considered legitimate or illegitimate, shaping the normative standards and not just the regulatory parameters inducing and deterring economic behaviour. If one were compelled to reduce highly complex relations to a circular chain of causation, it might look like the figure on the right.

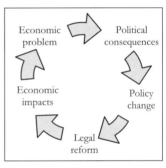

In other words, economic challenges have political implications, which can lead to new policy initiatives, often requiring legislative, administrative or other regulatory or institutional reforms to address perceived economic problems or their social and political impacts, and to induce desired economic behaviour in line with changing policy priorities. The newly induced behaviour may eventually lead to adverse undesired consequences, often contrary to the intentions of policy and lawmakers, which in turn brings about a new round of reform.

Hence, the dialectical relationship between economic and legal changes can also be seen as cyclical in the medium term. But, of course, such an account can be caricatured as overly Hegelian, if not somewhat functionalist. History is far more complicated than that, especially when one considers that the effects of particular laws have to be evaluated within context as it is often not the existence of law in itself which is important, but rather, the detailed legal provisions as well as the nature and consequences of their enforcement.

The late development of a few developing countries over the last few decades has drawn attention to the necessary and sufficient conditions for such accelerated economic progress. The late developers are different in some key aspects from the early developers, although similar in other regards. States seem to have crucial roles in ensuring high rates of investment and rapid technological progress. However, there is little agreement about the institutional, including legal conditions, economic policies and state role needed. For mainstream institutional economists, private ownership of assets and market coordination of all activities not organized within firms are considered necessary, if not sufficient for economic development, but the more recent revisionist literature on the developmental state suggests otherwise.

The recent experiences of late development in East Asia over the last few decades suggest important institutional differences between early and late developers, particularly the key role of the state in inducing large investments and rapid productivity growth in late developers. The conventional wisdom about how to induce development by creating market economies and enforcing property rights in developing countries persists despite the lack of evidence that they have been key for late economic development. Late development may require significantly different institutions and laws from early developers. Khan (2006) and others have pointed out that removing market restrictions is not sufficient, let alone necessary for accelerating investments and growth. Markets and even property rights have long existed without leading to rapid economic development.

The debate on how economic institutions should be organized to accelerate economic development has very significant implications. At least three trends of the growing political economy literature on the role of law in economic development have influenced this volume. Our collaboration began as a contribution to the emerging policy literature on legal systems, governance and economic growth, specifically to the study on law and the economy in six Asian countries published by the Asian Development Bank (ADB). However, several fundamental misgivings developed in the course of this work, resulting in the contrarian perspective in the last chapter of this volume on corporate governance reforms promoted in the wake of the 1997–98 Asian crisis. No serious study of the role of the state in Malaysia will reject arguments about "rule by law" through "regulatory states" (e.g. Jayasuriya, Rodan), and this volume is no exception. Chapter 5 about the transformation of the Malay peasantry due to colonial land laws is also likely to be identified with the institutionalist school of economic history *a la* Douglass North, although the analysis offered here comes to rather different conclusions about property rights.

Economic liberalization, with its focus on stable property rights and well-functioning markets, has clearly been the dominant strategy associated with the conventional wisdom. But while well-functioning markets and protection of property rights are now considered characteristics of an advanced economy, economic development may require substantial reordering of existing property rights and fresh incentives for investors to rapidly acquire new technologies. Stable property rights may no longer be appropriate (e.g. consider the East Asian land reforms of the early 1950s or the changing status of township and village enterprises in China), particularly since existing property rights and production are associated with low investments and productivity growth.

The developmental state literature (Woo-Cumings, 1999, and many others) shows that successful late development has required a range of novel institutions, laws and interventions. As Arrow (1962) famously noted, productivity was always initially low with new equipment, and only gradually improved with "learning-by-doing". Institutional arrangements to facilitate and subsidize such learning are necessary to induce investment in potentially high productivity activities. Thus, for example, effective protection conditional on export promotion has not only protected infant industries, but also forced new industries and firms to become internationally competitive as quickly as possible in order to export successfully. Hence, a key developmental challenge is to ensure that economic and institutional changes facilitate and induce investments as well as technological change through such learning.

Book Outline

The first half of this book reviews major changes in the Malaysian political economy and legal system from 1957 to the end of the Mahathir era, and at least five regimes with different visions of developmental priorities can be distinguished. During the late colonial period, 1950–57, in the face of a communist-led insurgency, the British colonial government had initiated social reforms, including rural development efforts to consolidate a Malay yeoman peasantry, protect labour and allow limited popular political participation through elections. This was followed by a dozen years of post-colonial economic diversification with very limited government intervention from 1957 to 1969. After independence, generally *laissez faire* policies were pursued, with "mild" import-substituting industrialization, some agricultural diversification, greater rural development efforts and modest, but increasing, ethnic affirmative action policies.

A period of growing state intervention followed from around 1970 until around 1985. The New Economic Policy (NEP) provided the legitimization for increasing state intervention and public sector expansion for inter-ethnic redistribution. Export-oriented industrialization policies succeeded in reducing unemployment, while increased petroleum revenues financed rapidly growing public expenditure. Counter-cyclical expansionary public expenditure from 1980 was followed by cuts from mid-1982, but government-sponsored joint ventures with the Japanese to develop heavy industries grew in the face of declining foreign investments. In this sense then, the Mahathir regime from mid-1981 had a different rationale for state intervention, moving from interethnic redistribution to industrial modernization.

Reforms from the mid-1980s can be attributed to the difficulties attributed to preceding state interventionist policies as well as new international pressures for economic liberalization. The slower economic growth of the mid-1980s led the Mahathir leadership to undertake reforms often described as pro-market, but probably more accurately characterized as pro-private investment. Massive ringgit depreciation and economic liberalization from the mid-1980s were accompanied by privatization, improved official support for the private sector, increased investment incentives and regressive "supply side oriented" tax reforms. Such measures favouring private investment continued until the 1997–98 regional financial crises which led to renewed state intervention for crisis management and economic recovery.

The survey of Malaysian economic and legal developments in this book will show that new economic policy initiatives have generally been accompanied by corresponding legislative and other regulatory reforms to create a legal environment deemed suitable or necessary for pursuing the new policies more effectively. The book also suggests that major legislative innovation has reflected policy changes coming about in response to economic problems or crises due to or associated with preceding policies.

The first four chapters offer general surveys of changes in Malaysia's political economy and laws. The first chapter captures the colonial heritage in the post-colonial order by concentrating the circumstances surrounding the creation of the nation. The second chapter reviews the transformation of the Malaysian political economy in response to political developments, policy initiatives and institutional transformations. The third chapter surveys major post-colonial legal innovations and their impact on Malaysia's economic development. The fourth chapter focuses on the legal reforms in the financial sector during the last two decades of the Mahathir era. The remaining five chapters examine selected issues in greater detail.

The significance of sequencing and "path dependence" emerges time and time again. The fifth chapter on the consequences of colonial land law for the transformation of the Malay peasantry underscores the significance of colonial legal innovation in the form of the Torrens land registration system — in sharp contrast to the *status quo ante* as well as the alternative of English land law with its strong feudal heritage, often seen as not conducive to modern capitalist agrarian relations. The peasant economy at the time of independence and since cannot be accurately characterized as traditional in the sense that it is a vestige of the pre-colonial economic relations. Rather, socio-economic relations involving the Malay peasantry were irreversibly transformed by the colonial impact in two profound ways, first, by integration into international markets as well as circuits of capital, and second, by the impact of colonial land laws.

The changing nature of Malaysian labour laws and the impact of such legislation and other institutions of industrial relations are the subject of the sixth chapter. The major labour legislation changed with overall employer needs and concerns as well as with significant political changes. For example, the laws were changed to facilitate import-substituting and, a decade later, labour-intensive export-oriented industrialization. Likewise, labour laws were introduced or amended in the face of imminent Japanese aggression before the Second World War, with the declaration of a state of Emergency against communist-led insurgents in mid-1948 and with the efforts to develop a new social contract following the May 1969 racial riots. It is also clear that union membership as well as industrial actions have generally been constrained by government legislation and policy from 1948 and again since the early 1970s.

Malaysia's changing industrial policy is reviewed in the seventh chapter. All the major industrial investment promotion legislation has sought to stimulate new manufacturing investments. The 1958 Pioneer Industries Ordinance sought to encourage import-substituting manufacturing investments with the use of import tariffs and other investment incentives after the colonial period favoured reliance on manufactured imports from the UK. The 1968 Investment Incentives Act responded to the decline of such investments and growing unemployment by encouraging labour-intensive export-oriented manufacturing investments; such incentives had to be supplemented by complementary legislation including the Free Trade Zones Act of 1972. The 1975 Industrial Coordination Act has seriously constrained the flexibility of industrial policy innovations since then — as became apparent in the government's responses to the mid-1980s' economic slowdown. Later, the 1986 Promotion of Investments Act sought to reverse the economic slowdown of the mid-1980s following a "second round" of (heavy industrial) import substitution from the early 1980s. This and other legislation and regulations were crucial in attracting Japanese and other East Asian investments and in efforts to raise the technological level and value addition of the new investments compared to the earlier labour-intensive export-oriented industrialization of the 1970s. Regulatory efforts since the 1980s also sought to enhance technological development and value added in the economy, while reforms after the 1997–98 crisis have sought to attract new foreign investment to the country in the face of adverse trends in the region.

The 1997–98 regional financial crises led to renewed state intervention for crisis management and economic recovery, including currency controls and "bail out" facilities for the banking sector and other politically well-connected businesses. Instead of the usual focus on the September 1998 measures, which were too late to stem the capital flight in the first 14 months after the crisis began in Bangkok in July 1997, Chapter 8 reviews the earlier mid-1998 institutional innovations often decried as involving "bail-outs" for politically well-connected cronies, which successfully sought to recapitalize banks and politically well-connected businesses which dominated much of the economy (Gomez and Jomo, 1999; Jomo [ed.], 2001; Wong, Jomo and Chin, 2005).

The final chapter revisits the claim that the East Asian crises of 1997–98 were due to failures of corporate governance. It considers the major claims to this effect and the conventional thinking then as to desirable corporate governance arrangements as advocated by the World Bank and the Organization for Economic Cooperation and Development (OECD). Besides rejecting the unsubstantiated claims that corporate governance failures caused the financial crises in the region, the chapter critically examines the claims that Anglo-American corporate governance arrangements are superior, and should therefore be introduced in the region for superior outcomes, particularly in terms of corporate performance.

CHAPTER 1

Making Malaysia Legally

Wong Sau Ngan and Jomo K. S.

Malaysia can be said to be a legal creation in at least two ways. First, like many other former colonies, the territory which constitutes Malaysia today was ruled by the same colonial power, Great Britain. However, the territory was never administered together by the British for various historical reasons summarized below. British Malaya included Singapore, an independent island republic since 1965, while Sabah and Sarawak on the north-western flank of the island of Borneo were administered quite differently.

Second, the Merdeka (Independence) Constitution, drafted by the 1955 Reid Commission, largely preserved the colonial legal framework, especially protection of the property rights of business interests associated with the departing colonial power. Besides providing for an ostensibly Westminster-style parliamentary system, the constitution has two other very consequential features. Firstly, it includes provisions for special privileges for "Bumiputera indigenes" by virtue of Article 153 of the Constitution, which "safeguards" the special position of Malays and later, the natives of Sabah and Sarawak. This includes ethnic reservations for positions in the public services and provisions which disallows Malay reservation land from being acquired by non-Malays. Secondly, the Constitution's federal structure provides for land and natural resources to be administered by the states.

Colonial Legal Heritage

Besides consolidating colonial property rights in the post-colonial period, for fear of capital flight (which had begun in the late colonial period in the 1950s following the Emergency from June 1948), the independent Malayan government also introduced legislation and new institutions in a broad range of areas to complete the transition to independence. For example, rural and regional development efforts were strengthened to secure Malay political support for the ruling multi-ethnic Alliance coalition.

The complex mélange of Islamic law and custom governing economic activity and relations in pre-colonial Malay society was eventually largely replaced by British colonial law. The Portuguese conquest of Malacca of 1511 and its subsequent Dutch capture in 1641 had limited legal implications. The establishment of the Straits Settlements from 1786 in the ports of Penang, Singapore and Malacca saw the imposition and development of laws and conventions facilitating "free trade" under the English East India Company, largely at the expense of its more mercantilist rivals.

Later, the expansion of British power into the peninsular hinterland from 1874 involved control over the actual production of raw materials, notably tin mining, and later, cash crops, requiring appropriate land law (the Torrens System of land registration developed in British colonies was alien to Britain itself). British Residents were appointed to advise British-recognized Malay rulers in tin-rich Perak, Selangor and Negeri Sembilan, and later, Pahang. In 1885, the Temenggong of Johor was elevated to the status of Sultan by the British. In 1896, the Federated Malay States (FMS) were formed from the other four Malay states already under British influence. Then, in 1909, Siam ceded the northern Unfederated Malay States of Kelantan, Terengganu, Kedah and Perlis, which accepted British "Advisors", thus extending "indirect rule" by the British over the rest of the peninsula known as British Malaya. With the availability of cheaper Japanese imports from the early twentieth century, free trade gave way to "imperial preference" protectionism. Colonial law thus developed to advance British economic and political interests, including pre-emptive legal provisions in response to real, as well as anticipated threats.

The Japanese invasion and Occupation of Malaya from late 1942 until August 1945 accelerated the end of the British imperial order despite the Allied victory. British Military Administration for a year from September 1945 barely stemmed the rising tirade of decolonization. In 1946, the British Malay Union proposal — including the Federated and Unfederated Malay States, Penang and Malacca — was rejected by ethnic Malay mass mobilization before the Federation of Malay was created in 1948 as a state of "Emergency" was declared to counter a communist-led insurgency.

The Federation of Malaya (now Peninsular Malaysia) obtained its independence from Britain and became a sovereign state on 31 August 1957. Before that, the colonial state had been fighting a communist-led insurgency from June 1948. In 1960, the independent Malayan government declared the state of "Emergency" — declared by the British colonial authorities to prosecute the counter-insurgency from mid-1948 — over. Comprising the eleven states of the Malay Peninsula, independent Malaya inherited a colonial economic structure, mainly exporting rubber and tin, with the majority of the population of 6.8 million involved in agriculture.

In 1961, the first Malayan Prime Minister, Tunku Abdul Rahman, endorsed the British plan to form Malaysia, which would include the 11 states of Malaya, Singapore, North Borneo (now Sabah), Sarawak and Brunei, i.e. all the former British territories in the region. The oil-rich sultanate of Brunei withdrew before the new federation was established. Before the Second World War, North Borneo had been leased from the Sulu Sultan and was run by a chartered company, while Sarawak was ruled by a family of white rajahs from the Brooke family. Even after the Japanese Occupation, they were administered quite separately from Malaya and Singapore. To entice the Borneo states to join, various concessions were made, including enhanced rights for the Borneo state governments over natural resources (e.g. forests) and immigration (from Peninsular Malaysia) as well as greater parliamentary representation.

Despite the serious difficulties involved, not least due to the contrived nature of the new nation, convenient mainly to the former colonial power, the formation of Malaysia was pushed through by the British. Thus, in mid-September 1963, the federation of Malaysia was formed with Malaya, Sabah (previously British North Borneo run by a charter company), Sarawak (previously a fiefdom ceded to the Brooke family) and Singapore. Barely two years later, in August 1965, Singapore seceded to form an independent island republic, leaving Malaysia's current borders and a shared colonial legal legacy. Hence, since then, Malaysia has comprised the eleven states of what was then called West Malaysia (later Peninsular Malaysia), and the two Borneo states of East Malaysia. In the early 1970s, after the secession of Bangladesh from Pakistan, the official terminology changed to Peninsular Malaysia for the old Malaya, and Sabah and Sarawak, instead of East Malaysia.

The country now known as Malaysia is a federation of 13 states and 3 federal territories.[1] The country, with a total land area of about 330,000 square kilometres, comprises two distinct regions: Peninsular Malaysia on the southeastern tip of the Asian continent; and Sabah and Sarawak on the north-west flank of Borneo island. It is an ethnically plural society, with a population of over 6.8 million in 1957, and a population of around 25 million today, comprising 65 per cent Malays and other indigenous people (together referred to as Bumiputera), 26 per cent Chinese, 8 per cent Indians and 1 per cent Others.

British Colonialism

For the better part of the twentieth century, economic growth was first regulated by the legal order imposed by British colonialism, and then, by the successor independent state. The relationship between economic transformation and the legal framework has been reflexive or dialectical. Like other former colonies, Malaysian history has also been shaped by the political and legal developments of the colonial era. Needless to say, the legal restructuring of the Malaysian economy has continued to the present.

The colonial authorities created the basic legal framework within which the Malaysian economy continues to function. Malay custom and Islamic Shariah law have been limited to matters of personal law (marriage, divorce, inheritance, etc.) and royal succession, though there has been a spate of new legislation passed by an essentially secular parliament enabling new ostensibly Islamic financial instruments as well as taxation measures since the 1980s. However, these continue to remain largely marginal to the main economic practices of the country.

The consequences of the property rights framework created by colonial laws were far-reaching. The land laws negated earlier usufructuary rights and enabled the stratification of the Malay peasantry by juridically separating land ownership from its cultivation. Together with the emergence and growth of credit and goods markets, colonial land law thus created new land property rights and markets (see Lim, 1977; Wong, 1975; Jomo, 1986).

Malaya's economic infrastructure (e.g. railways, roads, ports, utilities, etc.) — so crucial for profitable capitalist investment — was generally more developed than in most other British colonies. Such infrastructure, mainly using imported British materials, was paid for by taxes levied on the population by the colonial government. Colonial monopolies thwarted the development of a strong local capitalist class producing for the domestic market; instead, local investors found it more profitable to engage in production for export, commerce and usury. Malays largely remained as peasants in the countryside, marginal to growing capitalist activities, with the Malay elite integrated into the colonial state apparatus. On the other hand, the more urbanized and commercially better-connected Chinese took advantage of emerging business opportunities.

Much of Malaysia's uneven development can be traced to the crucial formative decades under colonial rule that shaped the economic structure. For instance, the differences between the East Coast and the West Coast can be traced to uneven regional growth dating back to the location of the early tin mines, colonial annexation and infrastructure development, as well as subsequent growth building upon existing advantages. Similarly, differences between the rice growing North and the rest of the peninsula are related to demographic history as well as the British policy of preserving Malay peasants as rice farmers, despite the rational peasant preference for rubber cultivation, which threatened British plantation interests. The urban-rural gap is, of course, related to the typical roles of town and country in capital accumulation, while the relative backwardness of the peasantry compared to plantations is only the most obvious of various differences in the rural economy. The uneven development of the colonial economy has been primarily perceived in terms of ethnic disparities that often coincided with class and occupational differences.

Late Colonial Experience

After their ignominious defeat by the Japanese at the beginning of the Pacific War in the early 1940s, the British returned to Malaya in 1945, only to face strong, but ethnically-based anti-colonial movements. The military repression of the communist-led armed insurgency from June 1948 was not especially successful in the early years until the British began to "win hearts and minds" from around 1951. The new strategy involved a range of political reforms to establish partially elected legislatures and municipal authorities for the first time, labour reforms to build and legitimize a "moderate" and "responsible" anti-communist trade union movement, and agrarian reforms to reduce rural exploitation and poverty in order to consolidate an ethnic Malay yeoman peasantry.

This period also marked the beginnings of pro-Malay ethnic affirmative action programmes. The colonial authorities reluctantly responded to the communist challenge by introducing rural development initiatives they had never previously considered and legitimizing reforms allowing greater popular participation in politics and trade unions, while economically "protecting" and "advancing" the Malay community at the same time. These reforms, in response to a major threat to the security of the late-colonial state, thus involved significant new land, labour and other legislation, with important developmental consequences. However, these reforms were circumscribed by the colonial government's over-riding concern with Britain's imperial interests.

In the decade after the end of the Second World War, Britain faced serious foreign exchange shortages and balance of payments difficulties that weakened sterling considerably, sealing its fate as an imperial power. Colonial Malaya, Britain's most profitable colony by far, contributed considerably towards alleviating these problems and strengthening the pound by increasing Britain's reserves in two main ways. Firstly, imports from outside the sterling area were curtailed and Malayan exports outside the zone were increased to improve the Empire's overall payments balance. Secondly, the British colonial government increased Malaya's sterling balances held in London by increasing public sector savings through maintaining a fiscal surplus.

During the colonial period, authority over plan formulation and implementation rested with senior British officials in the Treasury. Planning in the 1950s was confined by the colonial government's over-riding concern with Britain's welfare and underlying commitment to the predominantly British plantation and mining interests in Malaya. The colonial authorities, who generally considered the colonies as suppliers of raw materials and importers of manufactured goods, only allowed a few types of industries to develop. Most British-owned industries were set up to reduce transportation costs of exported or imported goods (e.g. factories for refining tin-ore and bottling imported drinks), while local capital manufactured other goods needed by the local population such as food products. These local industries developed most when economic relations with the colonial power were weak, e.g. during the Great Depression and the Japanese Occupation.

Colonial bias towards business interests was reflected in public development expenditure allocations. Public development expenditure heavily favoured export and urban interests, with priority for providing economic infrastructure — such as telecommunications, electric power, roads, railways and port facilities — to service the primary commodity export economy. The allocations for such infrastructure were consistently high during the 1950s. The colonial state also emphasized projects that yielded revenue, thus hoping to render such projects self-financing as far and as soon as possible. Conversely, the colonial government limited resources for social services that were considered consumption items incurring high recurrent costs that would reduce funds for economic investment projects.

Development planning reflected the interests and priorities of the colonial state, e.g. agricultural development expenditure under the Draft Development Plan (DDP) was mainly for the development of the new villages, set up to cut off supplies from Chinese rural residents to the communist-led insurgents. Under the First Five Year Plan (FFYP), public agricultural sector investment mainly involved the government-sponsored rubber-replanting scheme initiated in the early 1950s, which primarily benefited estates, rather than smallholdings. While estates — with their larger acreages — could replant in stages, smallholders usually had to replant their small farms all at once. Since smallholders had to forego their entire rubber income while waiting for their trees to be productive again, their lukewarm response to replanting reflected the higher opportunity cost of smallholders replanting. Subsequent reforms, especially after independence, did more for replanting in the smallholding sector, thus inadvertently consolidating the "involution" of peasant agriculture.

Sectoral targets and their attainment also reflected official priorities. Throughout the 1950s, the overall rate of target fulfilment in the economic sector was higher than for social services, with the exception of health during the DDP period (1950–55). During this period, the highest rates of target attainment were recorded for health (83 per cent) and agriculture (82 per cent), followed by infrastructure (68 per cent) and education (64 per cent). The highest rate of target fulfilment in health was due to the colonial government's efforts to eradicate malaria and other diseases in urban centres, plantations and mines, while the relatively low rate of plan attainment in infrastructure was supposedly due to the shortage of trained technical staff.

This situation was reversed during the First Malaya Plan or FFYP period (1956–60), when infrastructure development targets were exceeded, while only 25 per cent of the health allocation was spent. Over-fulfilment of infrastructure development targets reflected the emphasis on transporting primary commodities for export. For example, though Malayan Railways operated at a loss between 1957 and 1960, it was given substantial funds for modernization, thus effectively subsidizing its users, mainly primary commodity exporters. Project implementation was also effected by competing interests, e.g. the development of Port Kelang was delayed for several decades because of opposition by British interests in Singapore and Penang. Thus, planning during the 1950s was a relatively simple, unsophisticated process. In fact, the DDP and the FFYP were little more than programmes for public sector capital formation.

Following Malayan independence in 1957, the basic legal framework introduced under British colonialism was retained. New laws were soon promulgated with the establishment of an independent nation-state, especially after the first parliamentary elections in 1959, e.g. the Central Bank of Malaysia Ordinance, 1959, for the establishment of a central bank. The first dozen years after independence also saw the emergence of laws and other institutions to promote economic diversification. There have also been very significant changes to the personnel involved in the judiciary and the legal profession, including the government legal and judicial service.[2] Various politically motivated social reforms carried out from the early 1950s have also had important economic implications for labour, employers, peasants, and agriculture.

Federation of Malaysia

A substantial aspect of the amendments made to the Constitution in 1963 was to modify the constitutional provisions to provide for the establishment of Malaysia by the admission of new states, namely Sabah, Sarawak and Singapore.

The federation of Malaysia is an independent sovereign state which came into existence on 16 September 1963 with the merger of the Federation of Malaya, Singapore, Sabah and Sarawak.

Malaysia's constitutive legal documents comprise:

(1) An Act of Parliament of the Federation of Malaya — called the Malaysia Act, 1963 — which came into operation on 16 September 1963.

(2) An Act of Parliament of the United Kingdom — called the Malaysia Act, 1963 — which received the (British) Royal Assent on 31 July 1963 and came into operation on 16 September 1963.

(3) An Order in Council of the Queen of England — called The Sabah, Sarawak and Singapore (State Constitutions) Order in Council 1963 — which was made on 29 August 1963.

These enactments of the Federation of Malaya and United Kingdom Parliaments were the outcome of an agreement between the two countries that the United Kingdom would surrender sovereignty over its former colonies (Singapore, North Borneo and Sarawak), and that the Federation of Malaya would reconstitute itself as a new and larger federation — comprising its old territories, plus the three former colonies, as new States — which would call itself the Federation of Malaysia. This agreement was concluded on 9 July 1963.

The Federation of Malaya itself had been conceived in 1947 and established in 1948 after widespread, mainly ethnic Malay opposition to the earlier Malayan Union proposal. An independent nation with a Federal Constitution, came into existence on 31 August 1957. The constitution divides the authority of the Federation into:

(a) executive authority, vested in the Yang di-Pertuan Agong ("Agong") and exercisable by him or by the cabinet, or by any minister authorized by the cabinet;

(b) legislative authority, vested in Parliament; and

(c) judicial power, vested in the judiciary.

Malaysia is a constitutional monarchy. The Constitution provides for a "Supreme Head of the Federation", to be called the Yang di-Pertuan Agong (Article 32 (1) Federal Constitution). The Yang di-Pertuan Agong holds office for a period of five years, and is elected by the Conference of Rulers from among the nine hereditary Malay rulers, while the other four states each have a Yang di-Pertua Negeri (formerly known as "Governor"), appointed for terms of five years. It is said that "the traditional rulers continue to wield considerable political influence in their domains" (Jenkins, 1987: 29). Apart from exercising functions provided by the Constitution and the law, the Yang di-Pertuan Agong serves as the symbol for the nation. The Constitution has entrusted him with the responsibility for safeguarding the special position of the Malays and the natives of Sabah and Sarawak, and the legitimate interests of the other communities. He is also meant to be a symbol of justice and fair play, as it is he, acting on the advice of the Prime Minister and after consulting the Conference of Rulers, who appoints all judges of the superior courts.

Legislative power is held by both federal and state legislatures. The Malaysian bicameral parliament consists of two Houses of Parliament, referred to as the Senate (Dewan Negara) and the House of Representatives (Dewan Rakyat). Besides the parliament at the federal level, each state has a unicameral legislative chamber or Dewan Undangan Negeri.

A new federal Constitution came into effect on Malaysia Day, 16 September 1963, as did the Malaysia Act 1963. By the provisions of the Malaysia Act 1963, the judges of the Supreme Courts of the constituent States of the new federation became judges of the two High Courts for Malaya and Borneo respectively. The jurisdiction, procedure and practice of the High Courts were to be as previously exercised and followed in the Supreme Courts of the constituent States of Malaysia. Other provisions for the jurisdiction, procedures and practices of the High Courts were made by the Courts of Judicature Act 1964. Provision was made for the original criminal jurisdiction, original civil jurisdiction and other powers of the High Courts. With the formation of Malaysia, the judiciary was set to develop and expand. The High Courts of the two territories were soon established in virtually every major city and town. New subordinate courts were also set up in smaller towns to adjudicate claims of the rest of the population.

Federal-state relations in Malaysia are characterized by the high degree of concentration of powers in the federal government and the relative weakness of the states, which are fiscally incapable of sustaining the burdens of modern government. The Constitution provides that Parliament may make laws with respect to any matter enumerated in the federal or concurrent list, or as is otherwise provided for by the Federal Constitution. Matters in the federal list include external affairs, defence, internal security, civil and criminal law and procedure, administration of justice and citizenship, commerce, finance, trade and industry. Matters on the state list include Muslim law, land, agriculture, forestry, local government, and turtles and riverine fishing. Matters in the concurrent list include social welfare, scholarships, protection of wild animals, and town and country planning. In the case of the Borneo states, matters on the supplementary list include native law and custom, and native courts are deemed to be on the state list. The central government has vast powers to legislate and act, even in exclusive state spheres, in order to implement treaties to promote uniform state laws and national economic development programmes in case of emergency.

It has been said that the relationship between the states and the federal government is an unequal one, for there is a clear preponderance of power vested in the hands of the federal government. For example, the power to amend the Federal Constitution belongs to the federal legislature, which does not have to consult or procure the consent of the states in order to make amendments. With a virtually permanent two-thirds majority, the ruling (federal government) coalition has long had in the Parliament, it is in a position to effectively curtail many rights originally granted to the states.

Legal Institutions and Processes

Administration of Justice

Prior to 1957 in Malaya and 1963 in Sabah and Sarawak, the development of the court structure was shaped by the politico-legal status of the States, i.e. the Straits Settlements, the Federated Malay States (FMS), Unfederated Malay States (UFMS), Sarawak and North Borneo (now Sabah). The first Supreme Court of the Federated Malay States (FMS) was set up on 1 January 1906, headed by a Chief Judicial Commissioner and assisted by a number of Judicial Commissioners. The title "Judicial Commissioner" was dropped in favour of "Judge" in 1925. From 1948, the structure of the Supreme Court of the Malayan Union (from 1946) remained, except for a change of name to the Supreme Court of the Federation of Malaya. However, the Subordinate Courts were reorganized as Sessions Courts, Magistrate's Courts and Penghulu Courts, with each having its own defined jurisdiction.

Before British intervention, many of the Unfederated Malay States already had their own Islamic courts. However, the British replaced Muslim court judges with legally trained English officials. Lay magistrates holding other administrative posts were also appointed to administer justice in these states. Sarawak and North Borneo, together with Brunei, shared a combined judiciary for the three territories, consisting of a Court of Appeal and a High Court. The system continued until 1963, when North Borneo (renamed Sabah) and Sarawak merged with Malaya and Singapore to form Malaysia.

Superior Courts

After independence on 31 August 1957, the right to appeal from the Federal Court to the Privy Council was retained and embodied in Article 131 of the Malayan Federal Constitution. When Malaysia was formed on 16 September

1963, the Constitution continued to preserve the right. The Constitution circumvented the possible anomaly of having appeals originating from Malaysia — as an independent, sovereign country — heard by judges in England by providing that all appeals from Malaysia were addressed not directly to the Privy Council, but to His Majesty, the Yang di-Pertuan Agong, who would in turn refer the matter for advice to the Privy Council. The Courts of Judicature Act 1964 was enacted to make detailed provisions for reference by appeal to the Privy Council.

From 1963, the judicial power in the new federation was vested in three new High Courts (i.e. the High Court of Malaya, the High Court of Singapore, and the High Court of Borneo), the Federal Court and such inferior courts as might be provided for by federal law. The Lord President presided over the Federal Court, and a Chief Justice presided over each of the three High Courts. With Singapore breaking away from Malaysia on 9 August 1965, the High Courts in Malaysia were reduced to two. There was no change in the structure of the Federal Court except that the Chief Justice of Singapore and the Federal Court judge from Singapore were no longer members.

In 1975, by Act of Parliament (PU[A] 320/75), Federal Court decisions in criminal cases tried under the Essential (Security Cases) Regulations of 1975 could no longer be appealed to the Privy Council. This was followed in 1978 by the abolition of appeals to the Privy Council in all criminal and constitutional matters. Finally, in 1985, with the establishment of Malaysia's Supreme Court as the highest court of the land, Malaysia's long standing judicial association with the Privy Council finally came to an end.

Presently, the superior courts of Malaysia comprise the Federal Court, the Court of Appeal and two High Courts, one for Peninsular Malaysia (Malaya) and one for Sabah and Sarawak (Borneo). With the elimination of the right to appeal to the Privy Council, the Federal Court is the highest court of the land. At the apex of the organization of the court structure is the Federal Court (up until 24 June 1994, it was called the Supreme Court), which is now the highest court and final appellate body in the country. Next in status and jurisdiction comes the established Court of Appeal, which in turn is followed by the High Courts.

The Federal Court has three jurisdictions: original, consultative and appellate, but it does not cover those matters under the jurisdiction of the Shariah Court. The Federal Court's original jurisdiction gives it the exclusive power to deal with constitutional issues raised under Article 128(1) and (2) of the Federal Constitution, to determine whether a federal or state law is invalid. Its consultative jurisdiction allows it to determine any question referred to it by the Agong. The Federal Court also has the jurisdiction to hear civil and criminal appeals from the Court of Appeal. However, appeals to the Federal Court are not as of right; leave of the Federal Court is required.

The Federal Court consists of a total of ten members, including the Chief Justice (formerly known as Lord President), the Chief Judge of Malaya, the Chief Judge of Sabah and Sarawak, and seven Federal Court Judges. The Federal Court normally sits with a quorum of three members. However, in cases where there are serious issues of public importance, the Federal Court may sit with a quorum of five members; in any event, the quorum should be of an uneven number.

Next in status and jurisdiction comes the Court of Appeal, followed by the High Courts of Malaya and of Borneo. The Court of Appeal was established on 24 June 1994. It is headed by a President and has ten judges. In terms of seniority, the President of the Court of Appeal stands immediately below the Chief Justice. With the establishment of the Court of Appeal, the three-tier appeal system, eliminated with the abolition of appeals to the Privy Council in 1985, was eventually restored.

The High Courts consist of two Chief Judges, one in Peninsular Malaysia and one for Sabah and Sarawak. At present, there are 57 High Court judges. The Constitution provides for 47 judges of the High Court of Malaya and 10 for Sabah and Sarawak. It also provides for the appointment of Judicial Commissioners for a specific period or purpose, who have the same powers as High Court judges. In recent times, there has been a trend to increase appointments of Judicial Commissioners (who hold office typically for two-year tenures) to preside in High Courts.

The civil procedure practised in the courts in Malaysia mirrors that of England since the procedures are adopted from the English Rules of Supreme Courts. Under these procedures, matters can only be set down for trial if the parties have completed all pre-trial requisites such as exchanging Affidavits of Documents, Notice to Admit Documents and the Agreed Bundles of Documents. This probably contributed to the huge backlog of cases in recent decades with a large volume of such cases still left pending despite some progress in recent years.[3] The courts now claim to be using new procedures to cut down unnecessary wastage of time in getting cases to trial.

Subordinate Courts

At the lowest level was the Penghulu Court, presided over by a Penghulu, or headman, appointed by the State Government for a *mukim* (district). The Penghulu Court has very limited jurisdiction and operates in Peninsular Malaysia only. Although the Court possessed criminal and civil jurisdiction in the *mukim*, it seldom tried cases, mainly because the Penghulu settled disputes informally, wherever possible. The Penghulu was empowered to try civil disputes where the subject matter does not exceed RM50 in value, and to impose a fine not exceeding RM25 in criminal matters. In criminal cases, an accused could elect to be tried by a Magistrate's Court. An appeal against a decision of the Penghulu's Court could be made to a First Class Magistrate, but this rarely happened. The Penghulu Courts were established to provide an avenue for villagers to seek legal redress when roads to the major towns and cities, where most Magistrate's Courts were located, were still poor. As a consequence of developments following the Second World War, the need for Penghulu Court dwindled and it has since become non-functional.

The Small Claims Tribunals within the Magistrate's Courts are available for claims which do not exceed RM5,000. This Tribunal is intended to simplify the collection of small debts in an informal atmosphere. Legal representation by advocates and solicitor is not allowed in the Small Claims Tribunal and the parties have to represent themselves. As companies are required by law to be represented by solicitors in all Court proceedings, the Small Claims Tribunal does not entertain claims by or against companies. The trial is held in a relaxed and informal manner. Although the normal rules of evidence do apply, the Tribunal is unlikely to allow technical procedural arguments. The trial is normally conducted in the Malay language before a Magistrate. If necessary, the parties may apply for the proceedings to be conducted in English, or for an interpreter to be present for testimony or submissions to be delivered in the Chinese or Tamil languages. At the end of the trial, the Magistrate makes an order, which stands as an enforceable judgement.

The Magistrate's Court, which used to be presided over by either a First Class or a Second Class Magistrate, deals with both civil and criminal cases. The First Class Magistrate has more extensive jurisdiction than the Second Class Magistrate. For civil cases, his jurisdiction is limited to subject matters not exceeding RM25,000. In criminal cases, he may pass any sentence allowed by law not exceeding five years imprisonment, a fine of RM10,000, whipping up to 12 strokes, or any combination of these sentences. Most of the Second Class Magistrates were lay magistrates who were previously court interpreters. The Juvenile Court is for offenders below the age of 18. The Court is presided over by a First Class Magistrate assisted by two lay advisers.

The highest of the Subordinate Courts is the Sessions Court, presided over by a Sessions Court Judge. Its criminal jurisdiction extends to all offences other than those punishable by death, and it may pass any sentence allowed by law other than the sentence of death. Its civil jurisdiction is unlimited in actions involving motor vehicle accidents, landlord and tenant disputes, and distress applications for non-payment of rent. Other than these, civil suits are confined to disputes not exceeding RM250,000. Matters relating to probate and administration of estates, divorce, bankruptcy and immovable properties are normally excluded from its jurisdiction. However, the court may adjudicate over matters involving the title of any immovable properties if all parties interested consent.

The jurisdiction of the Subordinate Courts, in particular, the Magistrate's and Sessions Courts, has undergone many changes, with their jurisdiction further enhanced over time. Besides the superior and subordinate courts, there are also the Shariah Courts and the Industrial Court that both come under different administrations from those of the civil courts stated above. Shariah Courts have jurisdiction over the nation's Muslim population in family and religious issues, while the Industrial Court deals with industrial relations disputes. In the states of Sabah and Sarawak, Native Courts deal with indigenous matters.

The Special Court was established in 1998 and is provided for under Article 182 of the Federal Constitution. The Special Court hears all offences committed by the monarchical heads of the component states of the Federation of Malaya, including the Yang di-Pertuan Agong, including all civil cases brought by or against them. It is chaired by the Chief Justice of the Federal Court who is assisted by four other members, namely, the two Chief Judges of the respective High Courts and two other persons appointed by the Conference of Rulers.

The Industrial Court is an arbitration tribunal and is not regarded as a civil Court. The Industrial Court is constituted and empowered by the Industrial Relations Act, 1967. The function of the Industrial Court is to arbitrate disputes between employers and employees arising from alleged unjustified dismissals in which the employee seeks to claim for reinstatement or damages in lieu of reinstatement. An award by the Industrial Court will be enforceable in the same manner as a Court order. Decisions from the Industrial Court may be quashed by way of an application for certiorari to the High Court.

The Shariah Court only hears matters pertaining to Islamic law and family law of persons professing the religion of Islam, including Islamic law relating to succession, testate and intestate. However, the Shariah Court is not allowed to exercise jurisdiction over any offence punishable with imprisonment for a term exceeding three years and/or any fine exceeding RM5,000, or whipping exceeding six strokes, or any combination thereof. The Shariah Court is not open to all advocates and solicitors of Malaysia. The Court admits only Shariah lawyers, who are persons deemed to have sufficient knowledge of Islamic law.

"Indigenous" Sources of Law

Malaysian laws can be classified into two general categories: written and unwritten law. "Unwritten law" refers to laws which are not enacted by the legislature and which are not found in either the Federal or State constitutions. This category of law derives from cases decided by the Courts and from the application of local customs, which is otherwise known as "common law".

The written laws are much influenced by English laws as the Malaysian legal system retains many characteristics of the English legal system. However, these laws have also been influenced by Australian and Indian laws. "Written law" refers to the laws contained in either the Federal or State Constitutions, or codified or enacted as statutory legislation. At the apex of written laws is the Federal Constitution. The Constitution of 1957 basically preserved the pre-existing legal framework put in place by the British, especially for the protection of property rights besides incorporating unique elements relating to the sultanates, Islamic religion, Malay language and Malay privileges.

For example, Article 152 of the Constitution states that the Malay language is to be the National Language of the Federation. By designating the Malay language as the National Language, it has become the language to be used for all official purposes. Though they can be taught and learnt, all other languages can only be used for purposes "otherwise than for official purposes". This was a response to the imposition of the English language during the colonial era. In spite of the Constitutional position of the Malay language and its usage for official purposes, the English language continues to be used, even today.[4]

Another noteworthy feature is the special privileges conferred on Malays by virtue of Article 153 of the Constitution, which safeguards the special position of Malays and natives of Sabah and Sarawak. This includes making ethnic reservations for positions in the public services, government scholarships and grants or other public educational facilities, as well as permits and licences required for business and trade operations. Also included among Malay privileges are provisions relating to Malay reservation land which disallow such land being acquired by non-Malays.

With regard to governing economic relations and business transactions, it can be said that only statutes, court decisions, and bureaucratic guidelines and rules are significant. "It is clear that as the law is developed in Malaysia through legislation and court decisions, there will be less and less need to rely on English law to fill the lacuna in the law" (Ahmad Ibrahim, 1971: lviii).

The five main indigenous sources of law in Malaysia are:

(a) customary law;[5]
(b) Muslim law;[6]
(c) Malaysian statutes;
(d) Malaysian case law; and
(e) bureaucratic law.

Malaysian Statutes

Malaysian statutes include:

(i)   the Federal Constitution;
(ii)   the State Constitution of each of the 13 States of Malaysia;
(iii)   Federal Acts of Parliament;
(iv)   State Enactments of State Assemblies (including Ordinances of the Straits
        Settlements, continued as existing law under Article 162 of the Federal
        Constitution of Malaysia); and
(v)   subsidiary legislation made pursuant to (iii) and (iv).

Malaysian Case Law

Past decisions of Malaysian courts constitute an important source of law in
Malaysia. Court decisions interpreting and applying the laws constitute a body
of jurisprudence that is truly voluminous. Decisions of the Federal Court,
in particular, are studied closely, for Malaysia adheres to the doctrine of *stare
decisis.*

        Despite the development and advent of statutory laws, the Civil Law Act
1956 allows the filling of "gaps" with English common law to supplement
local laws. The Civil Law Act 1956 provides for the application of certain
English common law and equity as of 7 April 1956 in Malaya, and as of
December 1951 in Sabah (including English statutes), and as of 12 December
1949 in Sarawak (including English statutes). In particular, it stipulates that
the law to be administered with regard to partnerships, corporations, banks
and banking, principals and agents, carriers by land and sea, marine insurance,
life and fire insurance, and commercial law more generally shall be "the same
as would be administered in England in the like case at the corresponding
period", unless other provisions are made by statute. Courts in Malaysia
have, in many instances, invoked this provision to import commercial law as
practised in England.

        There are also various other provisions which provide for the reception
of English law. For example, in regard to the law relating to bills of exchange,
the law of England shall, "save in so far as they are inconsistent with the
express provisions of the Bill of Exchange Act 1949", apply to bills of
exchange, promissory notes, and cheques. As regards matters of criminal
procedure for which no special provision has been made by the Criminal
Procedure Code or by any other law for the time being in force, the law
relating to criminal procedure for the time being in force in England shall
be applied in so far as the same shall not conflict or be inconsistent with the
Criminal Procedure Code.

Bureaucratic Law

Parallel to the regulatory frameworks created by custom, Islam, court decisions and legislation in Malaysia, there is a wide range of administrative policies and procedures which have been put in place either to govern the exercise of broad executive powers conferred by statute or to implement the government policies of the day. Bureaucratic law became more significant in the 1970s, when they served as important tools in an economy with growing state intervention.

Where considerable governmental powers are exercised under specific legislation, there exist some limits on how discretion or power is exercised in certain cases, but the possibility of discretion being exercised remains. The bases for many decisions are often neither transparent nor known to the affected parties. Legal enforcement sanctions exist for any breach of the legislative framework. In theory, the Minister responsible is accountable to Parliament for the exercise of such discretion.

Where government policies are implemented in the form of administrative guidelines, such impositions on legal economic relations between legal entities, arguably, have no force of law. No formal legal sanctions exist for any breach although indirect governmental sanctions may be imposed.

Substantive Economic Laws

Malaysia's economic system is essentially based on private enterprise with its legal system rooted in common law.[7] Nevertheless, statutes have always been an important source of law defining and governing economic interests and business relations in the country. Even prior to independence in 1957, there was already a body of statutes that dealt with a wide range of affairs including much of what was relevant to the colonial economy. It can be said that most basic economic laws were already in place to support and facilitate resource use, property rights, primary production, and commerce of the day. Brief descriptions of some of the principal economic legislation at the time of independence and their subsequent reform follow in Chapter 4.

However, laws on manufacturing, industrial development, and those in relation to securities markets and the financial system were not yet put in place. Of particular significance were laws governing access to markets and other private economic activities, and laws relating to agriculture and natural resources. Colonial statutes included the Mining Enactment 1914, Bills of Exchange Act 1949, Contracts Act 1950, Specific Relief Act 1950, Bills of Sale Act 1950, Employees' Provident Fund Act 1951, Exchange Control Act 1953, and the Rent Control Act 1954. Most of these laws were based on the English legal framework. However, there was more innovation with land legislation in the colonies owing to the strong feudal heritage in English land law.

The Federation was part of the sterling area with its currency arrangement and sterling payments system. The Exchange Control Act 1953 was modelled after the English Exchange Control legislation. Exchange control restrictions during the colonial period related to capital transactions with a non-sterling area country. No direct restrictions were imposed on the current account or on capital receipts and payments from and to others in the sterling area, or even on non-sterling area transactions.

Legislative and Administrative Procedures

Legislation has played a crucial role in regulating economic interests and business relations in the country. Prior to independence in 1957, there was already a body of statutes dealing with a wide range of affairs, including what were considered relevant to the needs of the economy then. After independence, there were frenetic efforts to introduce legislative programmes in response to a post-colonial economic development programme emphasizing economic diversification and industrialization in the 1960s.

In order to promote agricultural diversification and to move away from the colonial emphasis on rubber, mandatory cultivation conditions for land were changed. To encourage import-substituting manufacturing, new laws were enacted for the protection of "infant" pioneer industries. In addition, investment and labour laws were introduced to provide incentives to investors and to minimize the potential for industrial unrest respectively. During this period, the legal framework and other colonial institutions that existed prior to independence were not only maintained, but also strengthened and developed.

Notes

1. Peninsular Malaysia consists of nine sultanates (Johore, Kedah, Kelantan, Negeri Sembilan, Pahang, Perak, Perlis, Selangor and Trengganu), two states headed by governors (Malacca and Penang) and two federal territories (Putrajaya and Kuala Lumpur). What used to be called East Malaysia consists of the states of Sabah and Sarawak and the federal territory of Labuan.

2. Prior to 1954, the Malaysian superior judiciary consisted entirely of expatriate judges. It was only in 1955 that the first Malayan (Tan Sri Abdul Hamid Mustapha) was appointed High Court Judge. When the country attained independence in 1957, there were only three Malayans presiding in the High Court. In 1967, when the last expatriate judge left the superior bench, the entire superior judiciary was Malaysianized, as were the subordinate courts. In order to Malaysianize the judiciary, many promising civil servants and court officials were sent to England to qualify as barristers. It is presumed that when presiding over cases, Malaysian judges would be more sensitive to Malaysian conditions and sentiments.

Data on the number of practising lawyers in this period are not available. From an interview with a former senior lawyer, Ms P.G. Lim, it appears that most lawyers then were trained in Britain and had their practices in major towns such as Kuala Lumpur, Penang and Ipoh. According to Suffian (1976: 212), up to the early 1960s, the Bar was dominated by expatriates. Even after the Bar was Malaysianized, members of the Bar were still predominantly non-Malay. Meanwhile, the number of practising lawyers in Malaysia has increased manifold in recent decades.

The Judicial and Legal Service Commission appoints Sessions Court Judges, Magistrates, and Deputy Public Prosecutors. The Commission comprises the Chairman of the Public Service Commission, the Attorney General, and judges and former judges recommended by the Chief Justice. It was formerly known as the Colonial Legal Service, staffed entirely by expatriates under British administration. After the formation of the Federation of Malaya in 1948, the Colonial Legal Service began to admit locals. The Service trained its cadets for a wide variety of governmental, legal and judicial positions. Many members of the Superior Bench were selected from this service.

The last expatriate Lord President of the Federal Court (who retired in 1966) then commented that almost all government lawyers (those who work in the Attorney-General's Chambers) were Malays, while almost all non-government lawyers were non-Malays. He observed that if this imbalance was not corrected, there would be an unhealthy ethnic polarization between government and non-government lawyers. Suffian later noted that the perceived polarization between government lawyers and members of the Bar was partly due to the fact that members of the Bar were never asked to assist the government in undertaking prosecution or litigation, as in England. He felt that there was often unfriendliness and even animosity between government lawyers and private practitioners because of this very marked ethnic division of labour. However, Ms P.G. Lim has noted that the relationship between government lawyers and private practitioners then were cordial, where all were respected for their competence and professionalism.

3. For example, in the period 1972 to 1983, the total number of cases registered was 313,740, with civil cases constituting 95.5 per cent of the total number of cases, and criminal cases constituting a mere 4.5 per cent. This shows that the bulk of the workload in the High Courts during the period were civil cases. In comparison, the total number of civil cases disposed of by August 1983 was 199,020, which formed 66.4 per cent of the total number of civil cases registered.

4. The policy of using Malay in the courts was introduced in the 1980s, but not earnestly pursued until the early 1990s. Since the 1990s, arguments in the subordinate courts have been conducted in Malay. Arguments in the superior courts, though, are still largely made in English after perfunctory introductions in the Malay language. The primary language of commerce and business is English. Statutes passed by Parliament are always given in both the National (Malay) and English languages. By virtue of the Interpretation Act 1949, the definitive text for purposes of statutory interpretation is the National Language text. In practice, however, the English text is primarily used. In spite of the Malay language being the official language by statute, it is believed that the pragmatic approach adopted by

the authorities, business community and Malaysians to the usage of other languages, in particular the English language, facilitated business.

5. Malay customary law includes: (a) a patriarchal system of customary law known as *Adat Temenggong* — in operation in most States, except Negeri Sembilan; (b) a matrilineal system of customary law known as *Adat Perpateh* — in Negeri Sembilan and parts of Malacca (see *Anyam v. Intan* [1948–49] *MLJ Supp* 13); and (c) native laws and customs among the natives of Sabah and Sarawak. By virtue of the Native Courts Ordinance of Sabah, a Native Court has jurisdiction in cases arising from the breach of native law or custom. In one court decision (*Haji Laungan Tarki bin Mohd Noor v. Mahkamah Anak Negeri Penampang*), the Supreme Court of Malaysia held that it was not for the Native Court to assert jurisdiction over offences against the Federal Penal Code or to impose a sentence of imprisonment. This decision may perhaps be taken as an indicator that the Supreme Court is not anxious to see the enlargement of a Native Court's jurisdiction. There seems to be a perception that customary law is too vague and the procedure of the Native Courts too informal to be compatible with the modern system of jurisprudence now in operation in Malaysia. The importance of customary law and Native Courts will probably continue to decline.

Chinese and Hindu customary laws, brought to Malaysia by Chinese and Indian settlers, mainly apply in the areas of personal law, e.g. marriage and family law. Chinese customary law covers issues of divorce, charitable trusts and adoption, while Hindu customary law extends to family matters and chettiar money-lending practices. In earlier times and even now, tradition and custom would often be invoked for resolving business disputes among Chinese. Merchants would seek amicable settlements based on advice given by leaders of business associations they were affiliated to, rather than resort to legal channels. Over the years, there seems to have been a change in perception that Chinese merchants would first seek legal redress in court, while seeking an amicable settlement by informal means through a mediator, who may or may not be a leader of their business association. However, there is no systematic data to substantiate this view. There are also no data available to indicate the significance of customary laws governing economic relations and business transactions among Chinese and Indian merchants in Malaysia. While recognizing the existence of chettiar money-lending practices, and allowing them to operate within a business framework identified by the community itself, the legal characteristics of such customary practices are still determined by reference to the yardstick of the common law.

6. Muslim or Islamic law — especially on family and religious matters — is an integral part of the law for Muslims. Only persons professing the religion of Islam are under the jurisdiction of the Shariah Courts. Islamic law, a matter for the State legislatures and not the Federal Parliament, is administered by Shariah Courts. The jurisdiction of these courts is set out in some detail in the Constitution. The ordinary civil High Courts have no jurisdiction in respect of matters within the jurisdiction of the Shariah Courts, including the Islamic law on matters affecting the family, succession, titles and religious matters. The Muslim Courts (Criminal Jurisdiction) Act 1965 confers criminal jurisdiction on the Shariah Courts

for offences punishable by up to three years' imprisonment or a fine of up to RM5,000, or whipping of up to six strokes. In one case (*Che Omar bin Che Soh v. Public Prosecutor*: 55), the Supreme Court was faced with the argument that the death penalty for drug trafficking was unconstitutional because it was against the precepts of Islam, which the Constitution deems the official religion of the Federation. However, the Court held that the term "Islam" or "Islamic religion" in the Constitution only refers to such acts relating to rituals and ceremonies. The judgement of the then Lord President contained enlightening remarks concerning the British colonial attitude towards Islam and the place of Islamic law in Malaysia. This decision effectively put a brake on the movement to inject Islamic principles into the law through the courts. It seems that efforts in that direction are now being pursued by other means such as the political arena. The question now being asked by legal scholars and others is "to what extent will there be Islamization of the law"? A number of developments may be briefly noted. First, Islamic commercial laws have been enacted, for example, the Islamic Banking Act 1983 and the Takaful Act 1986. Secondly, on 9 June 1988, the Federal Constitution was amended to provide that High Courts shall have no jurisdiction in respect of any matter within the jurisdiction of the Shariah Courts. This has enhanced the status of the Shariah Courts and freed them from any interference by the civil courts. See also Article 121 (1A) of the Federal Constitution, which provides that the courts shall have no jurisdiction in respect of any matter within the jurisdiction of the Shariah Courts. See *Nor Kursiah bte Baharuddin v. Shahril bin Lamin & Anor*. The High Court, under Article 121 (1A) of the Constitution, has no jurisdiction to question the validity of an order made in respect of a matter obviously within the jurisdiction of the Shariah High Court. The way in which Art 121 (1A) operates was made clear in the case of *Lim Chan Seng v. Pengarah Jabatan Ugama Islam Pulau Pinang*.

7. Here, the principle of *stare decisis* applies.

CHAPTER 2

The Political Economy of Post-colonial Transformation

Jomo K. S. and Chang Yii Tan

This chapter offers a review of Malaysia's economic growth and structural change over the last five decades since Malaya gained independence in 1957 and the formation of Malaysia in 1963. Specific emphasis is given to the economic role of government, particularly in terms of public finance and state expenditure to complement and provide background to the attention to policy, institutional and legal reforms in the rest of this volume. This should make clear that Malaysia's generally impressive post-colonial economic development has been largely due to appropriate government interventions and reforms, rather than a simple reliance on market forces, as often suggested in some of the literature on the country. And while some government interventions and policies have had adverse consequences for development, either from the outset or eventually, as conditions changed, the ability of the government to reform policies and legislation, has greatly enhanced its ability to overcome constraints, including those unwittingly self-imposed. At least five regimes with different priorities can be distinguished in Malaysian economic development from 1957 to the end of the Mahathir era in late 2003.

Independence in 1957 was followed by a dozen years of post-colonial economic diversification with limited government intervention until the post-election "racial riots" of May 1969. Generally *laissez faire* policies were pursued, with some import-substituting industrialization, agricultural diversification, rural development and ethnic affirmative action efforts. A period of growing state intervention followed. The New Economic Policy (NEP) legitimized increasing government intervention and public sector expansion for inter-ethnic redistribution and rural development. Export-oriented industrialization also generated considerable employment, especially for women, while increased petroleum revenues financed rapidly growing state expenditure.

Counter-cyclical expansionary public expenditure from 1980 continued after Mahathir became Prime Minister in mid-1981. However, expenditure was cut from mid-1982, but government-sponsored heavy industries grew as other foreign investments declined. Thus, the Mahathir regime had a different rationale for state intervention, shifting from inter-ethnic redistribution to industrial modernization. From the mid-1980s, the economic slowdown and massive foreign debt build-up led to massive ringgit depreciation and economic liberalization accompanied by privatization and improved government support for the private sector, including new investment incentives and regressive tax reforms. The new measures favouring private investment resulted in a decade of rapid growth until the 1997–98 financial crisis led to renewed state intervention for crisis management and economic recovery, including currency controls and bail out facilities for the banking sector.

During the colonial period, authority over plan formulation and implementation rested with senior British officials who were mainly concerned with Britain's imperial interests and committed to protecting the predominantly British plantation and mining interests in Malaya. Colonial bias towards these interests was reflected in public development expenditure that prioritized economic infrastructure to service the primary commodity export economy. As Britain's most profitable colony, Malaya provided much of the export earnings that financed British post-war reconstruction. Legal developments, especially in the area of property rights, during this era played an important role in shaping and developing Malaya. During the early and mid-1950s, the colonial government initiated reforms, including rural development and affirmative action efforts. (For an alternative view suggesting that colonial and post-colonial governments have been mainly concerned with ensuring social and political stability, rather than advancing expatriate corporate interests, see Drabble, 2000.)

The Alliance Phase (1957–69)

With the attainment of formal independence in August 1957, the Alliance, a coalition of the political elite from the three major ethnic groups, formally took over state power and political jurisdiction in Malaya. Not unlike other newly independent countries, the post-colonial government embarked upon a programme of economic development emphasizing economic diversification and industrialization. In preparing for this political transition, the British had ensured that the leftist forces that threatened their economic interests were curbed, while ethnic elites committed to protecting their interests were cultivated to eventually inherit state power in 1957. A basically *laissez faire* development path for newly independent Malaya was thus assured. The post-colonial government continued to promote private enterprise and encourage foreign investment inflows, while the economic interests of the ex-colonial power were protected.

The Alliance government's economic development strategy reflected the class interests represented by the major parties in the ruling coalition and the political compromise among their leaders. Consistent with this compromise, the state pursued a basically *laissez faire* development strategy with minimum state interference except in ensuring suitable conditions for rapid capital accumulation. The post-colonial government was committed to defending British business interests in Malaya, which also enabled the predominantly Chinese local businesses to consolidate and strengthen their position.

Development policy during this phase was therefore profoundly influenced by such interests. The essentially *laissez faire* strategy precluded direct government participation in profitable activities, such as commerce and industry, which were left exclusively to private business interests. Hence, a relatively low proportion of public development expenditure — never exceeding 3.3 per cent throughout the 1960s — was allocated to commerce and industry. Within this overall strategy, the government made some highly publicized, but nonetheless feeble attempts to promote the interests of the nascent Malay business community, while also undertaking rural development programmes to consolidate rural Malay electoral support.

The increased allocations for social services, particularly education, partly reflected the increased commitment to utilize educational expenditure to create a Malay middle class besides meeting the human resource requirements of the rapidly growing and modernizing Malaysian economy. The government increasingly regarded educational expenditure as an investment that would yield returns in the form of increased output from a more productive labour force, rather than merely as a public consumption item. Government agricultural development policies were essentially conservative. Rural development efforts were constrained by the government's reluctance to act against politically influential landed, commercial and usurious interests. The main thrust of rural development efforts involved new land development by the Federal Land Development Authority (FELDA), other measures to increase agricultural productivity and rural incomes, as well as greater provision of rural facilities such as roads, schools, clinics, irrigation, etc.

During the early years after independence, the major physical development initiatives in the country were reflected in the annual and economic budgets of the five-year Malaysia Plans. Almost all the infrastructure developments undertaken during this period (before the late 1980s) were financed by the government, averaging about a third of overall public expenditure. Private sector involvement in infrastructure was largely as a service provider (e.g. construction activities) and did not involve financing or collecting revenue from such developments.

At the time of independence and even in the late 1960s, the private sector was largely confined to local Chinese capitalists and the generally larger and more powerful foreign investors. While the Chinese were mainly in retail and wholesale trade, rubber plantations, tin mining, domestic transport, small-scale manufacturing and some banking, foreign interests dominated the formal economy, such as the large plantations, trading agencies, tin dredge mines, bigger banks and financial institutions (e.g. insurance), and manufacturing. Malay business interests were often initiated by the government through agencies such as Mara and the state economic development corporations (SEDCs), with a few well-connected individuals spread out over many boards desiring them for their purported political influence (Tan, 1982).

Policy in the 1960s also saw two other major changes from the 1950s. Firstly, the state was increasingly willing to incur budget deficits, especially for development expenditure. This resulted in increased borrowing from both domestic and foreign sources to finance rising public sector development expenditure. Secondly, more sophisticated planning techniques were adopted, e.g. the Harrod-Domar growth model, which was used to estimate the investment rate required to attain certain income and employment growth targets. Policy in the 1960s generally emphasized growth, assuming that its benefits would trickle down.

After independence, and especially during the 1960s, Malaya — and from September 1963, Malaysia — achieved impressive growth, with considerable infrastructure development, although economic diversification in both agriculture and industry was limited. Planning grew in sophistication in terms of information gathering, preparation and implementation. Alliance ministers, senior Malayan civil servants and American advisers participated in the increasingly complex planning process, involving more bureaucratic organs.

During the early years after independence, the government carried out economic diversification efforts to reduce Malaya's over-reliance on tin and rubber. Diversification was pursued on two main fronts. Firstly, plantations were encouraged to grow other crops, particularly oil palm, and an increasing number of Felda-sponsored schemes were also planted with palm trees. Secondly, the state encouraged manufacturing by offering incentives, and providing infrastructure and other supportive economic measures.

The government placed emphasis on moderate import-substituting industrialization, passing the Pioneer Industries Ordinance and creating institutions to facilitate this policy emphasis. However, due to the limited size of the domestic market, growing unemployment and other problems, the government gradually shifted to export-oriented industrialization. The Federal Industrial Development Authority (now the Malaysian Industrial Development Authority, or MIDA) was established to encourage industrial investment, and the Industrial Incentives Act of 1968 was enacted, offering incentives to attract more labour-intensive export-oriented industries.

Helped by favourable commodity prices and some early success in import-substituting industrialization, the Malayan and then, Malaysian economy sustained high growth with low inflation in the 1960s. Official statistics for 1957 and 1970 — though strictly non-comparable for methodological reasons — suggest a worsening income distribution over the 1960s, including a growing gap between town and country. Inequality within the Malay community increased most among all major ethnic groups — from least intra-ethnic inequality in 1957 to greatest inequality in 1970. However, this growing inequality did not only result in growing inter-class tensions, but was primarily perceived in racial terms, not least because of widespread political mobilization along ethnic lines. Hence, Malay resentment to domination by capital was primarily expressed against ethnic Chinese, who comprised the bulk of businessmen, while non-Malay frustrations were directed against the Malay-dominated post-colonial state, widely identified with UMNO, the dominant partner in the ruling coalition.

Even though the economy sustained reasonably high growth with low inflation in the 1960s, income disparities increased, especially between those in the urban and rural areas. Inequality within the Malay community increased most among all major ethnic groups.

Such popular ethnic perceptions resulted in widespread racially-inspired opposition to the ruling coalition of ethnic parties in the Alliance in the 1960s. The decade had been marked by import-substituting industrialization, which generated relatively little employment and petered out by the mid-1960s, and rural development efforts that emphasized productivity increases, while avoiding redistribution in favour of the poorly capitalized, land-hungry peasantry. Following the May 1969 general elections, the ruling coalition's grip on power was significantly challenged by non-Malay as well as Malay-based opposition parties. The incumbent Prime Minister's position was further undermined by his critics within the ruling party who supported his deputy following ethnic riots probably initiated by the youth wing of the ruling party led by a State Chief Minister whose own position was threatened by the election results.

The poor electoral performance of the ruling coalition was probably the result of continued economic deprivation, growing unemployment, and inter-ethnic disparities despite creditable economic growth. The general election results and "racial riots" of May 1969 thus reflected some ethnic dimensions of the new post-colonial socio-economic order. Meanwhile, the emerging Malay middle class, who had nominal political control, feared the gradual decline of British economic hegemony would give way to Chinese ascendance. This "political-bureaucratic" faction, which had become more assertive from the mid-1960s, succeeded in establishing greater dominance after May 1969.

The First New Economic Policy Decade (1970–80)

The New Economic Policy (NEP) was announced in 1970 by the late Tun Abdul Razak, who was then Deputy Prime Minister and Director of the National Operations Council (NOC), which was set up during the state of Emergency after the events of May 1969. The NEP sought to create the socio-economic conditions for "national unity" through massive economic redistribution programmes to achieve its twin prongs of "poverty eradication" and "restructuring of society". The NEP's first Outline Perspective Plan for 1971–90 (OPP1) envisaged the incidence of poverty declining from 49 per cent in Peninsular Malaysia in 1970 to 16 per cent in 1990.

"Restructuring society" efforts sought to reduce inter-ethnic economic disparities, as the NEP tried to "eliminate the identification of race with economic function". OPP1 also sought to raise the Bumiputera share of corporate equity from 2.5 per cent in 1970 to 30 per cent in 1990, ostensibly through growth, rather than redistribution of existing wealth. Through ethnically differentiated financing of, and controlled access to tertiary level education, the NEP tried to reduce inter-ethnic disparities in the professions and other lucrative occupations.

Earlier affirmative action programmes from the early 1950s, which increased after independence and especially from the mid-1960s, had included preferential access to educational opportunities, business licences, as well as employment and promotion, especially in the public sector with the Malayanization and then Malaysianization after independence. Greater Malay political hegemony after the events of May 1969 significantly enhanced such measures. Sanctioned by the NEP, government intervention in the economy grew, and the number of state-owned enterprises increased during the 1970s, ostensibly primarily for redistributive purposes.

The NEP sought to raise the total Bumiputera share of corporate equity to 30 per cent by 1990 from 2.4 per cent in 1970. To this end, the government, especially the Ministry of Trade and Industry (MTI), began to find new ways and means to increase equity held by Bumiputera trust agencies as well as individuals. Educational spending significantly increased to finance Bumiputera secondary and tertiary education, especially with the preferential allocation of scholarships to attend universities in Malaysia and abroad. Bumiputera have also been favoured for employment and promotion opportunities, not only in the government and state-owned enterprises, but also in the private sector, especially enterprises requiring government approval of some kind.

The enlarged role of the post-colonial state, involving greater political and bureaucratic control over planning, was carried further in the 1970s — with greater state intervention and a considerably enlarged public sector, particularly to promote the growth of the Malay capitalist and middle classes. As ethnic Malay demands for increased efforts to economically advance the indigenous Bumiputera community mounted from the mid-1960s, new legislation and institutions were set up for this purpose, often in the form of public enterprises, such as statutory bodies enacted by legal statute. Examples of these include the Urban Development Authority (UDA), Pernas (Perbadanan Nasional Berhad), and the state economic development corporations (SEDCs). The other increasingly widespread form of public enterprise was government-owned (private or public limited) companies (Jomo [ed.], 1995).

Development policy in the 1970s thus saw growing abandonment of *laissez faire* policies in favour of greater state intervention in public resource allocation as well as public sector ownership and control of business enterprises. Though such policies began to adversely affect private investments and encouraged capital flight, especially by the Chinese, this was more than offset by growing public investments as well as privileged foreign direct investment in export-oriented industries.

Export-oriented manufacturing in Malaysia in the 1970s remained limited to relatively low-skill, labour-intensive aspects of production, e.g. electronic component assembly. Though more skilled and complex production processes and training have developed, Malaysia still lags behind neighbours like Singapore. The potential for and likelihood of such progress have been increasingly determined by the interests and preferences of transnational corporations, influenced by their perceptions of the prospects for profits in the host countries. Hence, export-oriented industrialization has significant, but nonetheless limited potential for sustained and integrated industrial development, especially because of the technological and market dependence involved. Despite impressive performance, largely attributable to favourable resource endowments and external conditions, it has become increasingly clear that the sources of export-led growth in the Malaysian economy are not sustainable indefinitely. In fact, the very success of export-led growth in the past has probably discouraged more serious efforts to develop a more balanced and integrated national economy.

In the early 1970s, the Free Trade Zones Act created new customs-free areas with other facilities for the development of export-processing zones. The promotion of more labour-intensive, export-oriented industries seeking cheap labour from the late 1960s and early 1970s succeeded in reducing unemployment, initially at the expense of real wages, until lower unemployment pushed wages up once again from the mid-1970s. After the "tightening" of labour laws in 1980, the industrial relations machinery and labour policies also changed, largely at the expense of labour. Further amendments were introduced to tighten up the already restrictive labour laws, further limiting union rights and increasing government control over them. Such policies were considered necessary for rapid growth and industrialization.

Although there were government attempts to portray itself as a neutral arbiter mediating between capital and labour in the 1960s and 1970s, the state generally favoured the former, as reflected in various amendments to the labour laws. During the state of Emergency after May 1969, labour legislation was amended to limit trade union organization and activity and to allow women to work around the clock, as desired by some of the new industries envisaged. Post-colonial labour legislation was initially enacted to replace the special regulations introduced during the Emergency against the communist-led insurgency, but later reflected changing labour policies of the post-colonial government (Jomo and Todd, 1994).

In the mid-1970s, petroleum production off the East Coast of Peninsular Malaysia began, and the government quickly pushed through the 1974 Petroleum Development Act to ensure that the federal government — instead of the states — would capture the lion's share of oil rents. Petroleum revenue has played a crucial role in the country's development; they were used to salvage government-owned enterprises, e.g. the then largest bank, Bank Bumiputra Malaysia, thrice [first in the mid-1980s, after the Bumiputra Malaysia Finance (BMF) scandal in Hong Kong, and then after the mid-1980s recession, and again, after the 1997–98 regional financial crisis], and prestige projects such as the Daya Bumi project in the mid-1980s and the world's tallest building, the Kuala Lumpur City Centre (KLCC) twin-towers project in the mid-1990s (now known as the Petronas Towers), the new Kuala Lumpur International Airport (KLIA) and the new capital city, Putrajaya.

Relatively high economic growth, coupled with the development of labour-intensive, export-oriented industries and the public sector in the 1970s, led to declining unemployment through the decade. Also, emigration of Malaysian labour to Singapore and other countries increased in the mid and late 1970s. Consequently, real wages rose, and pockets of labour shortages emerged, usually in activities offering low wages, and poor working conditions and future prospects. In order to offset the pressure on wages and overcome labour shortages, the government adopted several measures, most notably by tacitly approving labour immigration, primarily from Indonesia, Southern Thailand (especially to the northern States of Peninsular Malaysia), Southern Philippines (mainly to Sabah) and later, Bangladesh. While the magnitude of this immigration over the last two decades is difficult to measure, current estimates vary from 1.5 to 4 million — i.e. between 15 and 35 per cent — compared to a national population of 25 million and a labour force of over 12 million.

Mahathir's Three Regimes

In mid-1981, Mahathir Mohamad took over as Prime Minister of Malaysia and as president of UMNO. Mahathir's ascension to national leadership coincided with declining primary commodity prices and accelerated foreign borrowings despite much higher market interest rates. The increase in public expenditure in the early 1980s until mid-1982 was counter-cyclical in intent, making up for declining private investment, both domestic and foreign. Under Mahathir's leadership, however, the continued expansion of public sector spending — especially for the financing of non-financial public enterprises (NFPEs), or off-budget agencies (OBAs), in the first half of the 1980s — had an added significance.

More than any previous prime minister of Malaysia, Mahathir wanted to transform Malaysia into a newly industrializing country (NIC) under genuine Bumiputera (indigenous) entrepreneurial leadership. Mahathir's development strategy was not merely imitative. As contradictory and incoherent as his various economic development policies seemed, they initially represented a serious effort, in circumstances not of his own choosing, to transform Malaysia into a NIC. While Mahathir's policies eventually seemed to favour various well-connected business interests, he has to be credited with the major development policy innovations from 1981 until his retirement in late 2003, including the "Look East" policy, his labour policy, the "Malaysia Incorporated" policy, the privatization policy, "Vision 2020", and the policy responses to the 1997–98 crisis, among others. This chapter reviews these key policy initiatives and argues that the three distinguishable economic policy regimes characterized the Mahathir administration which lasted more than two decades from mid-1981.

Mahathir 1: New Roles for the State (1981–85)

After Mahathir took over as Prime Minister, he introduced a second round of import-substitution to promote various heavy industries, similar to the heavy and chemicals industrialization drive in South Korea under General Park Chung

Hee in the 1960s. He also continued to increase public sector employment in the face of the global recession from the early 1980s, induced by the deflationary interventions under US Federal Reserve chairman Paul Volcker. However, as the world economic slowdown dragged on, and commodity prices continued to decline, economic growth in Malaysia became more dependent on public — rather than private — investment. Soon, it was no longer possible to fend off the inevitable, and the economy contracted in 1985.

There had been a rapid increase in domestic debt from the early 1970s, followed by some rise in sovereign foreign borrowings later in the decade. In the early 1980s, serious gaps in the current account balance started to emerge because of declining commodity export prices and weak demand for manufactured exports (especially electronics), as private investments outside of the oil and gas sector dropped sharply (World Bank, 1983). Domestic private investments also declined, largely due to ethnically discriminatory policies against Chinese business interests.

During the 1980–82 international recession, the government adopted counter-cyclical fiscal policies (increased public sector consumption, investment and employment). While the government may have underestimated the causes and gravity of the recession, and presumed it could spend its way out of it, the new Mahathir administration from mid-1981 probably also hoped to secure a strong electoral mandate through such deficit spending. Soon after winning the April 1982 general elections, the government announced an austerity drive (*jimat cermat*), cutting back public spending and reducing earlier job creation commitments.

As they had relatively few significant legal implications, this chapter does not consider the heavy industrialization policy of the early and mid-1980s, the 70 million population policy (targeted to be achieved by the year 2100, ostensibly to create a larger Malaysian market, from 16 million in 1984) and the National Agricultural Policy (first announced in 1984 and then revised in 1993) which Mahathir introduced in the first half of the 1980s (see Jomo, 2003). Briefly, the first policy involved greater state intervention, with public or state-owned enterprises (SOEs) setting up heavy industries as joint ventures with major Japanese manufacturers with the help of (then) cheap official Japanese credit facilities. While the pro-natalist 70 million population policy has serious implications, e.g. for Malaysia's social services, its relationship to legal reform was tangential. And while Mahathir was personally involved in drafting the first (1984) National Agricultural Policy (NAP), which sought to promote more commercially viable smallholder agriculture, careful consideration of the NAP, including the later versions, is a monumental task, with limited legal and regulatory issues of interest here.

In the early and mid-1980s, official attention was given to the promotion of commercial peasant agriculture — involving larger farms using more profitable, productivity-raising and cost-saving modern management methods — for export markets. More public enterprises, such as the land and regional development authorities, were established to clear forested areas for plantation agriculture in Sabah and Sarawak. Such land was often ostensibly under state ownership and could easily be gazetted for such purposes. Meanwhile, agricultural diversification continued, with cocoa promising to be the new hope in the 1980s after oil palm's earlier success.

"Look East" Policy

In mid-1981, Mahathir announced his "Look East" policy. Initially, this policy was widely believed to refer to changing foreign orientation and reference points in a wide variety of economic development matters. "Looking East" seemed to refer not only to efforts to emulate specific aspects of Japanese and South Korean success in terms of economic development such as state intervention to develop heavy industries (Pura, 1985), state encouragement for the establishment of Japanese-style *sogoshosha* trading agencies (Chee and Lee, 1983), efforts to get the government bureaucracy to better serve private sector interests (Shahari, 1985), and even privatization. For a time, "Looking East" was also believed to mean favouring Japanese and South Korean investors and companies bidding for Malaysian government tenders; an estimated six billion ringgit worth of construction projects were given to such companies in the early 1980s (e.g. Chang, 1985).

The industrializing or NIC vision is said to have been reflected by Mahathir's exhortation to "Look East", specifically to Japan and South Korea (Jomo, 1985). Many believed that of the four East Asian NICs, South Korea was explicitly identified from the outset because of its non-Chinese heritage (unlike Taiwan, Hong Kong and Singapore), while Hong Kong and Singapore were disqualified because of the distinct features of their economies. Hence, the only real East Asian choices as models for emulation were Taiwan and South Korea. The choice of Taiwan was, of course, complicated by diplomatic considerations, besides the ethnic factor. Nevertheless, by early 1988, Mahathir and some of his ministers were explicitly touting Taiwan for emulation, and Malaysia successfully attracted Taiwanese investments when its official "southward" policy encouraged investing in Southeast Asia, instead of China.

The Singaporean option of espousing Confucian values — supposedly common to Japanese and Chinese cultures — was obviously not open to Mahathir, given Malaysia's dominant Malay-Muslim culture. Hence, Mahathir was obliged to emphasise that Japanese work ethics were not contradictory, but instead consistent with Islam. This, of course, begged the question of why look if it was all already embedded in Islam.

The impact of the "Look East" policy on the Malaysian economy has been considerable, though often exaggerated or underestimated. Some still insist that it was anti-Western, or even "anti-imperialist". This, of course, ignores the fact that modern imperialism is hardly a Western monopoly. Undoubtedly, the Mahathir administration was more consistent in supporting demands associated with the South, e.g. higher and more stable commodity prices, better aid terms, greater technology transfer and reduced market restrictions in the "North" on manufactured exports from the "South" — though all this was not inconsistent with pro-active integration into the changing pattern of international economic specialization.

"Looking East" involved more than abstract exhortations to work harder. If the "work ethic" were to be considered in the abstract, the industriousness of the Kelantanese or Javanese would have been less controversial and better known, especially to Malays. But their essentially peasant cultures were, of course, quite irrelevant to the official desire to induce greater productivity by wage labour in an industrial capitalist context. The real thrust of the campaign appeared to be the promotion of labour discipline through organizing industrial relations to promote company loyalty (e.g. propaganda campaigns, company welfarism and in-house unions), increase productivity (e.g. work ethics and more "incentive payments") and reduce losses (e.g. quality control circles and "zero defect" groups).

Although Mahathir went to great pains to define the "Look East" policy more narrowly in terms of new work ethics, labour discipline and productivity from the mid-1980s, the "Look East" policy was subsequently seen as a fairly wide-ranging series of initiatives to become an NIC by emulating the Japanese and South Korean "economic miracles". Before the 1986 general elections, many people even thought Mahathir had abandoned the policy, given the little headway actually made, the seemingly diffident official Japanese response and the political liability the policy had become. After the elections, however, Mahathir reiterated his commitment to the policy, even claiming that the ruling coalition's electoral victory had proven popular support for it.

A host of Mahathir policy initiatives perceived to be linked to "Looking East" include heavy industrialization, the preference for "turnkey project" arrangements, the Proton (Malaysian car) project, the encouragement of more co-operative and complementary government-private sector relations under the "Malaysia Incorporated" slogan, and the "privatization" or "denationalization" of potentially profitable economic activities previously undertaken by government. However, most such policy initiatives have had less to do with "Looking

East" than other influences on policymaking. For instance, while the Japanese developed viable SOEs in the nineteenth century only to pass them over to the private sector, the more immediate inspiration for "privatization" in Malaysia was the dismantling of the public sector in the West identified with "Reaganomics" and "Thatcherism" (see Jomo, 1983).

"Malaysia Incorporated": State-Business Corporatism

The role of the Malaysian state in relation to economic development — as defined by the NEP since the 1970s — came under critical scrutiny early in the Mahathir administration. Instead, Mahathir advanced the "Malaysia Incorporated" slogan in an effort to improve relations between the government and the private sector, and to try to get the previously ascendant government to play its ostensibly "traditional" role of serving private business interests in place of the massive public sector growth and sometimes heavy-handed regulation of the 1970s and early 1980s. The term "Malaysia Incorporated" was adapted from the originally pejorative term, "Japan Incorporated", which had emerged in the industrial West in the late 1960s as it began to face what was considered "unfair" competition from more strongly state-backed Japanese business interests (Lee Poh Ping, 1985).

With the Malaysia Incorporated policy, enunciated in 1983, government departments were encouraged to find ways to better serve the private sector, instead of treating it as an adversary. Many government agencies improved counter services, and established high level government-private sector committees to involve the private sector in dialogues to listen to their views. Though very much welcomed by the private sector, these efforts were not sustained, except for the more powerful business interests.

The origins of Malaysia's problems relating to government-private sector relations have been quite different however (Shahari, 1985). While the "Malaysia Incorporated" slogan provided a useful reminder of the role of government desired by much of the private sector, it addressed rather different problems in quite a different context than what the slogan of "Japan Incorporated" or actual Japanese experience suggested. In Malaysia, the slogan referred to efforts to curb and rectify "excesses" associated with overzealous implementation of the NEP — especially by ethnic Malay officials, and resented mainly by ethnic Chinese business interests.

Malaysia's mild economic recession during the mid-1980s was due to a combination of all the above factors: global recession, lower primary commodity prices, reduced demand for manufactured exports, reduced foreign private investment inflows, declining domestic private investments, deflationary fiscal and monetary policies (except for certain spending priorities such as heavy industries), concentration of public investments in import-substituting heavy industries characterized by low capital productivity, tighter international liquidity and higher real interest rates. Immediately, the government responded to the recession with various measures, such as deregulation as well as incentives to further encourage private investment.

Spending was constrained by the sharp drop in oil prices in early 1986 to under US$10 per barrel. The poor outlook for petroleum forced a drastic downward revision of growth and public sector investment targets (which were later revised upwards with higher petroleum and rubber prices in 1987 and increased logging). The major primary commodity price collapses — involving palm oil, tin and petroleum — and the electronics business cycle's low point occurred in 1985. After January 1986, when the petroleum price fell to its lowest level, external demand for Malaysian exports — especially commodity prices — began to recover.

Mahathir 2: Inducing Private Investments (1986–97)

The key turning point for government policy, in terms of economic liberalization, occurred around 1985, following Daim Zainuddin's appointment as Finance Minister in 1984 and after then Finance Minister Tengku Razaleigh Hamzah's failed second challenge for the deputy leadership of the ruling party. The difficulties of introducing potentially unpopular economic measures were eased by Daim's appointment. As he had limited political ambitions, he was quite willing to take responsibility for measures that a politically more ambitious appointee might have preferred to avoid. Without any personal political base in the party, he owed his position to Mahathir, and was hence politically insulated from the party and others critical of or opposed to the economic reform measures.

By the mid-1980s, there was growing dissatisfaction with the government among many, including Bumiputeras, both in the public and private sectors, with some criticizing what they considered unfair government interference in the business world. Large Malay-controlled business groups had emerged on the corporate scene, and were calling for a less regulated economy. Indeed, some of them blamed excessive state intervention for slowing economic growth and undermining private business interests (Khoo, 1992). Partial liberalization of the economy earlier on may have been a boon to the corporate sector, with most businesses benefiting, and hence supportive of further liberalization.

Following Daim Zainuddin's appointment as Finance Minister, the government introduced some economic liberalization measures. This coincided with the contraction of loss-making state-owned enterprises (SOEs), which had grown in the 1960s and expanded rapidly in the 1970s (after the implementation of the NEP), with new ones continuing to grow in the early 1980s as others began contracting. SOE losses wasted precious investment resources, increased the government's financial burden and allegedly slowed economic growth (Kamal and Zainal, 1989). Privatization, which had been officially announced in 1983, gained vigour, and the government actively privatized its assets until there were some 200 privatization projects in the pipeline by the mid-1990s. Privatization was supposed to reduce government expenditures, improve efficiency, encourage private sector involvement in government activities, and provide Bumiputera with opportunities to participate in such activities.

The government sought to attract new, especially foreign investments, e.g. with the 1986 Promotion of Investments Act. The timing was perfect, as manufacturers from Northeast Asia (especially Japan and later, Taiwan) relocated their industries to take advantage of the enhanced incentives, relatively good infrastructure and more lax environmental regulations, as well as comparatively lower production costs due to the lower wages and devalued exchange rates.

On the international scene, the debt crisis from the early 1980s provided the OECD economies, especially the US, with an unprecedented opportunity to impose policy reforms over the largely indebted South after the heady 1970s' attempts to establish a New International Economic Order (NIEO). Fortunately, Malaysia did not experience many of the very painful economic problems that other less fortunate economies of the South experienced in the 1980s. For instance, Malaysia never really suffered from severe capital shortages, and never really borrowed very heavily from abroad until the early 1980s — ironically when liquidity was tighter and real interest rates were higher. And unlike some other late borrowers (e.g. India), its spending, and hence borrowing binge came to an end in the mid-1980s.

As the two Bretton Woods institutions — the International Monetary Fund (IMF) and the World Bank — promoted economic liberalization through stabilization and structural adjustment programmes, the US and its allies worked to build and strengthen an international legal environment more conducive to transnational corporate interests (Dezalay and Garth, 1996). Some of these efforts were unilateral, e.g. then US Secretary of State Schultz's successful efforts in the mid-1980s to force "friendly" governments throughout East Asia to strengthen foreign companies' intellectual property rights, while others were multilateral, e.g. through the Uruguay Round of the General Agreement on Tariffs and Trade (GATT), and its successor, the World Trade Organization (WTO), as well as the Asian Pacific Economic Co-operation (APEC) forum. The creation of an ASEAN Free Trade Area (AFTA) also introduced some convergence in economic regulation at the regional level.

After the second Plaza Hotel meeting in 1985, the US dollar began to depreciate heavily against other major world currencies, particularly the Japanese yen. As the currencies of most industrializing East Asian economies rose in value, raising comparative production costs, the Southeast Asian currencies — including the Malaysian ringgit — declined in worth, even against the falling US dollar. The depreciation of the Malaysian ringgit against the US dollar enhanced Malaysia's attractiveness, especially to East Asian investors.

Labour shortages and the 1988 withdrawal of privileges under the General System of Preferences (GSP) from the first-tier East Asian new industrializing economies (NIE) encouraged relocation of production facilities abroad. Meanwhile, reforms, selective deregulation as well as new rules and incentives made relocation in Southeast Asia as well as China more attractive. For instance, the Malaysian government sought to attract new, especially foreign investments, e.g. with the 1986 Promotion of Investments Act. The Southeast Asian boom from the late 1980s greatly benefited from investments from these first-tier generation new industrialized East Asian economies experiencing rising production costs (due to tighter labour markets), strengthened intellectual property rights as well as stricter environmental regulations. In Malaysia, the massive depreciation of the Malaysian ringgit against the US dollar from late 1985 also contributed to the economic boom. Meanwhile, the Japanese yen and then the Korean won, the new Taiwanese dollar and the Singapore dollar appreciated against the US dollar, and hence, even more against the ringgit, enhancing Malaysia's attractiveness to foreign investors, particularly those from East Asia.

Thus, the policy changes of the mid-1980s appeared successful in reviving growth and industrialization, although there is no evidence that such measures contributed crucially to the boom. Confirmation of the new change in policy direction since the mid-1980s came with the 1991 enunciation of Vision 2020, seen to favour growth, modernization and industrialization. Although foreign direct investment levelled off in the mid-1990s, increased domestic investments — inspired by greater domestic investor confidence — sustained the momentum of rapid economic growth until the 1997–98 regional crisis. The gravity of the crisis and the difficulties of recovery were exacerbated by injudicious policy responses, compromised by cronyism, though there is little persuasive evidence that cronyism in itself precipitated the crisis.

Powerful domestic and foreign interests have influenced the nature of development strategy as well as economic policy-making which the post-colonial Malaysian government has undertaken. Malaysia's experience in the post-colonial period suggests that new economic policy initiatives have generally been accompanied by corresponding legislative and other regulatory reforms to create a legal environment deemed suitable or necessary for pursuing the new policies more effectively. Major economic policy changes have generally come about in response to economic problems or crises attributed to or associated with preceding policies.

However, there is no simple mechanical relationship between economic problems and crises on the one hand and policy and legal reforms on the other. It is often claimed that the Malaysian economic boom from the late 1980s until 1997 was due to the liberalizing reforms introduced from around 1986. These reforms involved some deregulation of economic rules that had discouraged earlier desired investments as well as their replacement with alternatives that were more attractive to potential investors. While the reduction of regulations associated with ethnic redistribution efforts probably encouraged domestic private investments, especially by ethnic Chinese, there are now more — rather than less — trade and investment policy instruments, as suggested by simplistic claims of economic liberalization during this period. Instead, instruments such as the Promotion of Investments Act of 1986, as well as other incentives to encourage high value added/technology investments became part of the new investment environment, arguably contributing to the higher value-added, export-oriented manufacturing-led economic boom of the decade up to 1997.

It is unclear what the effects of these mid-1980s' reforms would have been if they had been introduced earlier, before the depreciation of the ringgit against the greenback and more drastically then, against the yen and other East Asian currencies from 1985, which induced a huge new wave of foreign direct investments from the late 1980s. Tellingly, the significant increase in US high technology investments which US Secretary of State Schultz promised in the wake of the US-imposed strengthened intellectual property legislation of the mid-1980s did not quite materialise, though subsequent Malaysian government incentives to attract such investments from the early 1990s may have been more successful. Similarly, the legislative and other efforts to promote Malaysia's Multimedia Super Corridor (MSC) successfully attracted more than the originally targeted number of investments, though it is not clear to what extent the actual nature of these investments have been misrepresented in order to take advantage of the very generous incentives for MSC-status investments.

Hence, there is no automatic or systematic relationship between legal and economic changes. Furthermore, different parts of Malaysia's legal system have different features, with some parts reasonably harmonized, while others appear less consistent, though rarely are they too dysfunctionally contradictory. These trends have also developed unevenly at various times or episodes. Not surprisingly, there have been some indications of convergence in economic law in the recent period, and this is expected to increase with various regional and global initiatives encouraging greater integration as well as standardization of legal norms, e.g. in connection with various treaties under the auspices of the World Trade Organization (WTO), regional cooperation arrangements as well as bilateral trade and investment agreements. Hence, the scope of standardization has been growing, e.g. in intellectual property law, trade liberalization and regulation, investment regulation, quality control, process requirements, etc.

The Transition from the NEP

In 1990, the 20-year period of the first Outline Perspective Plan (OPP1) for Malaysia's NEP came to an end. The ambitious NEP redistribution targets had been largely achieved by then, with most progress made before the mid-1980s (Jomo, 1990). Despite some controversy over the reliability and comparability of official data, the reduction in official indicators of poverty incidence was impressive, declining from 49 per cent in 1970 to 18 per cent in 1990, close to the 16 per cent target.

Inter-ethnic economic disparities of various types had also declined significantly. Ethnic proportions in economic activities and occupations increasingly reflected demographic shares except in agriculture and government services (which remained predominantly Bumiputera), and in wholesale and retail trade (which remained Chinese-dominated). For eight well-remunerated professions, the Bumiputera share rose from 6 per cent in 1970 to 25 per cent in 1990, with continued ongoing increases in the Bumiputera share. Through government regulation of business opportunities and investments as well as preferential policies for Bumiputera businesses, the Bumiputera share of equity in public listed companies rose from 1.5 per cent in 1969 to 18 per cent in 1983, before hovering around 20 per cent since then. However, various observers advanced persuasive arguments suggesting considerable underestimation of the actual size of the Bumiputera share of corporate wealth in 1990, while the wealth redistribution consequences of the 1997–98 financial crisis are difficult to assess.

Yet, despite the considerable achievement of the OPP1 targets, it is far from clear how much progress had been made in achieving "national unity", the NEP's ostensible purpose (e.g. as reflected in reduced inter-ethnic resentment or improved inter-ethnic relations). For example, relations between Malays and Chinese were, arguably, rather tense in 1987 due to the political machinations of certain political leaders. However, with some cultural and educational deregulation from the mid-1980s and the economic boom of the 1990s, ethnic tensions receded somewhat. Meanwhile, regional grievances — especially in Sabah, Sarawak and Kelantan — became more pronounced, while ethnic minorities — both non-Malay Bumiputeras and non-Chinese non-Bumiputeras — became more alienated than ever before.

Confirmation of the new change in policy direction since the mid-1980s came with the 1991 enunciation of Vision 2020, seen to favour growth, modernization and industrialization over the NEP's emphasis on inter-ethnic redistribution. While foreign investors continued to be courted, the government also reduced restrictions on ethnic Chinese capital, which had also been encouraged by various other reforms, e.g. easier access to listing on the stock market, greater official encouragement of small and medium industries (SMIs) as well as other official efforts mitigating the continued impact of the 1975 Industrial Co-ordination Act, besides greater overall emphasis on the market, rather than regulatory measures. Hence, domestic investments were encouraged by the partial liberalization from the mid-1980s. With such liberalization, many Chinese-owned firms were able to obtain listing, and could thus tap into the domestic capital market for funds for development. With listing, they have had to comply with more stringent reporting requirements and have had to modernise management and operations. However, it remains unclear whether public listing has primarily been intended to raise capital or to enable the beneficial owners to "cash out".

In the early and mid-1990s, official policy encouraged Malaysian firms (especially large corporations) to invest in other developing countries in Southeast Asia, as well as Africa, South Pacific, the former Russian republics, and even Europe and the US (Jomo, 2002). The Malaysian South-South Corporation Berhad (Masscorp) was formed to help large Malaysian firms invest elsewhere in the "South". The government helped such firms by setting up agencies to facilitate trade, export credit and insurance, signing double taxation agreements with various countries, and organizing numerous trade and investment missions led by top government leaders. At the same time, it also organized regional trade talks to liberalise the trading regimes of ASEAN firms. However, this policy was suspended following the 1997–98 crisis in an attempt to revive domestic investments.

Over the years, the government has seen changes to its industrialization strategy. In December 1996, the government announced the Second Industrial Master Plan (IMP2) for 1996–2005 to replace the (first) Industrial Master Plan (IMP) for 1986–95. In September 1996, the government also set up the Multimedia Super Corridor (MSC) intended to promote the information technology industry in the country. The government committed over RM50 billion for the development of infrastructure to support this initiative. At the same time, the government introduced new intellectual property laws to assure investors and provided very generous incentives for new firms in this area.

There were also some interesting developments in the property sector before the 1997–98 crisis. In the aftermath of the 1980s' recession, the government had allowed foreign purchases in the property market. The massive influx of Singaporean buyers — especially in the state of Johor, but also in other parts of Malaysia — sent property prices spiralling in the 1990s. In response, the government imposed a tariff on foreigners buying residential properties, slightly dampening the property and land markets. Meanwhile, state governments continue to pose bureaucratic obstacles to registering land transfers and dealings, thus raising transactions costs.

Unemployment rates fell sharply from the late 1980s, and labour shortages grew, especially in the early and mid-1990s. With the growing sophistication of the economy, shortages emerged in urban, white-collar service occupations as well. Wage rates rose sharply by well over 50 per cent on average during 1990–97. Malaysia has also taken in professionals, e.g. in medicine, engineering and architecture, from other countries, and leading professionals in some sectors are significantly foreign, especially when professional restrictions have been circumvented through various legal loopholes.

Privatization

Public or state-owned enterprises (SOEs) in Malaysia were first set up during the colonial period, and later created for the purpose of ethnic affirmative action from the early 1950s. In the 1960s, and especially in the 1970s, the state established a large number of public enterprises in all sectors, sometimes in collaboration with private capital. Thus, SOEs grew modestly from the mid-1960s and much faster in the 1970s, with the introduction of the NEP in 1971. State intervention grew, with the Government participating directly in the economy through establishment of a large number of public enterprises and agencies. In the early 1980s, new public enterprises spearheaded the economy's diversification into heavy industries.

Poor public enterprise co-ordination and accountability became more evident in the 1980s. The rapid growth of public enterprises generally involved inefficient state intervention almost singularly committed to inter-ethnic wealth redistribution, ostensibly favouring the indigenous Malay community. In effect, however, such intervention primarily favoured politically influential rentiers, rather than genuine entrepreneurs. The growth and proliferation of public enterprises came to an end in the mid-1980s, as the government reduced financial support for most of them, except for those connected with then politically favoured heavy industries.

The growth of public enterprises from the 1970s, especially heavy industries in the early 1980s, was accompanied by declining capital productivity in the economy. The average incremental capital output ratio (ICOR) rose from 2–3 in the 1970s to 5–6 in the early 1980s, while the public sector ICOR rose from 6–7 in the 1970s to 15–16 in the first half of the 1980s. Also, by the mid-1980s, public sector spending — which had been sustained at the high levels of the early 1980s by incurring massive external debt — was constrained by reduced and more expensive resource availability after the profligacy and higher interest rates of the early 1980s and the ringgit and US dollar devaluation from 1985.

Privatization in Malaysia was officially announced in 1983,[1] after Mahathir took over as Prime Minister in 1981 (Mahathir, 1983). Unlike the "Look East" policy which faded in significance by the mid-1980s, privatization achieved new vigour from the late 1980s. The adoption of the Privatization Master Plan (PMP) in 1991 marked a new stage in the private sector moving into activities previously mainly involving the public sector. Privatization gathered momentum with the Master Plan.

As Mahathir consolidated his position in the late 1980s, after fending off political challenges from ruling party colleagues following the economic difficulties of the mid-1980s, privatization became an increasingly important means for sponsoring, supporting and subsidizing the emergence and consolidation of new, politically well-connected, predominantly, but not exclusively, Malay rentiers. While most public sector employees initially felt threatened by privatization (in the sense that job security could no longer be taken for granted), many other Malaysians — fed up with the waste, inefficiency and corruption usually associated with the public sector — were indifferent, if not supportive of this policy. Many Malaysians associated the growth of the public sector with increased state intervention and the ascendance of Malay political and economic hegemony under the NEP, and saw privatization as a desirable policy change that would check, if not reverse these trends.

Privatization exercises in Malaysia often did not even pretend to achieve their supposed efficiency gains, especially when NEP restructuring considerations were invoked, supposedly to increase Bumiputera wealth ownership and business opportunities. With increased Bumiputera competition, where collusion was not easily arranged, political influence and connections became increasingly decisive. In some cases, effective lobbying by private interests determined what was privatized, in what manner, and to whom. Often, privatization in Malaysia did not involve the formalities of an open tender system. Instead, many beneficiaries were chosen on the basis of political and personal connections. This was legitimized by the authorities, who claimed to have a "first come, first serve" policy to favour those who first made "viable" privatization proposals to the government.

The government was only able to privatize profitable or potentially profitable enterprises and activities because the private sector was only interested in these. Thus, privatization did not resolve the fiscal problem in the medium term, as the government gave tax breaks and lost income from profitable public sector activities, and was stuck with financing unprofitable ones. The government rationalized subsidizing private sector beneficiaries of privatization by arguing that the privatized firms would pay taxes on their profits to the government, although this argument obviously could not explain the generous tax breaks and revenue guarantees also provided by the government.

Although privatization was generally well-managed by the government to ensure popular participation and enthusiasm (mainly through discounted share issues), popular outrage against privatization grew with the high charges following the amalgamation of municipal sewerage systems under a "crony" firm, Indah Water Konsortium (IWK) in 1993. The 1997–98 crisis led to suspension of the privatization programme as well as bail-outs, including re-nationalization of some major privatized entities at great public cost. In recent years, Khazanah has emerged as the principal government holding company for previously privatized enterprises.

Privatization — or denationalization — refers to changing the legal status of a business, service or industry from state, government or public to private ownership or control. The term often also refers to the use of private contractors to provide services previously supplied by the public sector. In practice, privatization in Malaysia referred to the following:

1. the sale or divestment of state concerns;
2. public issue of a minority or even a majority of shares in a state-owned public company;
3. placement of shares with institutional investors;
4. sale or lease of physical assets;
5. public-private sector ventures;
6. schemes to draw private financing into construction projects;
7. "contracting out" public services by enabling private contractors to provide services previously provided within the public sector; and
8. allowing private competition where the public sector previously enjoyed a monopoly.

Mahathir 3: Crisis Management, 1997–2003

There is now little serious disagreement that the East Asian economic crises since mid-1997 began as currency crises. It has become increasingly clear that the crises were due to the undermining of previous systems of international and national economic governance due to deregulation and other developments associated with financial liberalization and globalization, i.e. the subversion of effective financial governance at both international and national levels created conditions that led to the crises (Jomo, 1998).

This does not mean that all was well from a macroeconomic perspective. Large current account deficits in Malaysia and some other countries had been financed by short-term capital inflows into the stock market and loans from abroad. Crony capitalism and rent seeking had also been thriving, but, in themselves, did not precipitate and cannot explain the crisis. However, cronyism, nepotism and new crisis-induced political developments influenced official policy responses in Malaysia. More importantly, they exacerbated the crisis and undermined confidence, and thus delayed recovery. Malaysian currency and financial crises became a crisis of the "real economy" mainly due to poor government policy responses.

Despite official claims that the Malaysian ringgit was pegged to a "basket of the currencies of Malaysia's main trading partners", it was virtually pegged to the US dollar for decades from the mid-1970s. This offered certain advantages including the semblance of stability — especially low inflation — desired by the politically influential financial sector, especially since the manufacturing sector has been dominated by foreign multinationals and ethnic Chinese. This state of affairs also reflected the political weakness — in influencing economic policy-making — of exporting manufacturer interests in Malaysia (where much industrial capability outside of resource-based manufacturing is foreign-owned), compared to the financial community.

Meanwhile, equity finance, involving financial dis-intermediation, grew in significance in the 1990s in Malaysia. The establishment of the Labuan International Offshore Financial Centre (IOFC) in Malaysia in 1993 eased access to foreign funds while reducing transparency in related banking practices. These and other reforms — as well as the growth of "private banking" and "relationship banking" in the region and increased competition among "debt-pushing" competitors — weakened the scope and efficacy of national prudential regulation. Other domestic financial sector reforms had also reduced the powers and jurisdiction of Bank Negara Malaysia.

Capital inflows — to the stock market as well as through bank borrowings — helped bridge current account deficits due to the growing proportion of "non-tradables" being produced in Malaysia, much related to construction. These flows were ostensibly "sterilized" to minimize consumer price inflation, as desired by the financial community, but instead fuelled asset price inflation, mainly involving real estate and share prices.

The currency and financial crises suggest that Malaysia's decade-long economic boom until 1997 was built on some shaky and unsustainable foundations. Limited and inappropriate public investments in human resources have held back the development of greater industrial and technological capabilities. Although Malaysia has been reliant on foreign resources, especially immigrant labour, future economic progress cannot be secured by relying on cheap labour, as before.

Malaysia's resource wealth and relatively cheap labour have sustained production enclaves for export of agricultural, forest, mineral and manufactured products. Much of the retained wealth generated has been captured by the business cronies of those in power, who have contributed to growth by re-investing these captured rents, mainly in the "protected" domestic economy, e.g. in import-substituting industries, commerce, services and privatized utilities and infrastructure. Despite various weaknesses, this Malaysian brand of ersatz capitalism — involving changing forms of crony rentierism — sustained rapid growth for four decades. These arrangements came unstuck due to "irrational" herd behaviour greatly exaggerating the impact of "rational" (rent seeking) speculative market behaviour to gain advantage from the region's currency appreciations (Jomo [ed.], 2001).

The over-valued ringgit and other regional currencies emerged from the conjuncture partly due to financial liberalization, which also created the conditions for the asset price inflationary bubble that burst with devastating consequences for the region, exacerbated by injudicious policy responses. Failure to recognize the nature of the processes of accumulation and growth in the region has generally prevented the design and implementation of an adequate pro-active strategy of well-designed and sequenced liberalization. In contrast, Malaysian central bank-guided consolidation of the banking sector has helped ensure its greater robustness and readiness compared to its neighbours, though the new restructuring brought about in the wake of the crisis is less well conceived and less likely to serve its intended ends.

In spite of deregulation measures, government controls on the economy have not disappeared. For instance, in the banking sector, the central bank still sets the pace and parameters for liberalization of the industry, having forced local banks to merge, ostensibly to give them a better chance of survival as the industry opens up to international participation.[2] Meanwhile, the foreign banks already in Malaysia have been repositioning themselves to take advantage of the new opportunities with the changing policy and regulatory environment as the government prepares to open up the country's banking system to other foreign banks. The Securities Commission, set up to regulate the equities market, has put new regulation in place, in the face of market developments and political pressures. Unfortunately, few such reforms have prioritized the governance requirements of new development challenges.

The Politics of Mahathir's Economic Policy

With the benefit of hindsight, it is now clear that many of Mahathir's early policy initiatives failed to garner widespread popular support. The "Look East" policy was ambiguously received, with considerable criticism (not least by those disfavoured by the new preferences) and some costly experiences (e.g. the failed *sogoshoshas*), and eventually faded away. The heavy industrialization policy is generally acknowledged to have been ill conceived and to have contributed to the economic crisis of the mid-1980s. Though the "Malaysia Incorporated" policy was well received by Chinese and foreign business interests, others were largely indifferent. The predominantly Malay bureaucrats correctly perceived it as the beginning of their re-subordination, but failed to organize effectively in their own interests. It should be clear that the mobilizing national vision represented by Vision 2020 was developed through a process of trial and error, of advance and retreat.

When Mahathir took over as Prime Minister, the NEP enjoyed support from the Bumiputera community, especially the Malays, who were expected to be the primary beneficiaries of both the poverty reduction and inter-ethnic redistribution measures associated with it. Non-Bumiputeras reluctantly accepted the NEP as a necessary cost of citizenship, civil peace and personal security, especially in the aftermath of the events of May 1969.

Not surprisingly, therefore, Mahathir could not simply replace the NEP with his own economic agenda for the nation when he first took office. The NEP provided too much of a legitimating ideology for Malay hegemony, on which basis the ruling UMNO had dominated the country since the mid-1950s. Moreover, the expectations generated by the promises of the NEP — especially public sector expansion and increased government intervention — could not be ignored, but instead had to be pandered to if he was to retain political dominance in national and party elections. In any case, for the sake of continued legitimacy, he would need to allow the NEP to run its course until 1990. This also provided a decent interval for a transition that could not be faulted as being illegitimate in so far as the NEP was apparently still in place.

By the time of the announcement of the new post-1990 policies from early 1991, the 1986 economic reforms had been sustained for about five years. Thus, the economic policy changes of the mid-1980s — initially announced as necessary compromises in the face of economic crisis were reiterated and consolidated as part of broader strategy or vision to build a new Malaysia. This strategy was reiterated in Mahathir's Vision 2020 statement and various post-1990 ("post-NEP") policy documents and statements associated with the National Development Policy (NDP) and the Second Outline Perspective

Plan, 1991–2000 (OPP2), as well as the National Vision Policy (NVP) and the Third Outline Perspective Plan, 2001–10 (OPP3). Hence, Vision 2020 came after — rather than before — the major adjustments of the mid-1980s. In the process, what were once portrayed as necessities were recast as virtues, and part of the new national developmental ideology. Although Mahathir's economic policies were initially circumscribed by NEP expectations (even after 1990), and hence subordinated to wealth redistribution considerations, he eventually succeeded in securing broad social and political support for his strategy by the mid-1990s.

While the NEP's success in creating a Bumiputera business community and the privatization policy's success in consolidating executive patronage of politically influential rentiers have undoubtedly undermined simplistic ethnic identification of business interests, the continued popularity of such ethnic stereotypes has been checked by more responsible political leadership. Since the 1990s, the Malaysian political leadership — both in government and in the opposition — has resisted some of the ethno-populist tendencies they have so successfully mobilized and gained from in the past.

It is difficult to say how much of the government policy was captured by private interests. During the NEP period, the existence of political patronage reflected UMNO's influence over government policies. Under Mahathir, there was a growing coincidence of interests between large corporate groups and the government. Captains of the industry built up closer relations with the top political leaders, not only securing lucrative contracts, tenders and other business opportunities, but also influencing government policy formulation to their own advantage. Thus, they managed to secure choice privatization and mega development projects from the government: the Bakun Dam, the Second Link (to Singapore), North-South Highway, power, sewerage, water supply projects, etc. In their defence, Mahathir's regime argued that they were the ones who could deliver.

Rule By Law

In the early 1980s, Mahathir was able to push through his own statist development agenda, emphasizing heavy industrialization and labour discipline. With the deep economic recession of the mid-1980s, he introduced various liberalizing economic policy reforms, which were followed by a sustained economic recovery. Such measures earned corporate support for him, helping him consolidate his position despite the deepening political crisis in the second half of the 1980s. The consolidation of these economic reforms with Vision 2020 later reversed the NEP's redistributive emphasis in favour of more growth-oriented policies (Jomo, 1993b).

Mahathir's commitment to his agenda and his political acumen, as well as the strength of his executive powers enabled him to overcome resistance to his reforms, from within the previously influential bureaucracy, and also from within the dominant party in UMNO. The availability of resource and other rents controlled by the state as well as his own enhanced powers enabled him to reduce resistance to his reforms. Malaysia's adequate resources to finance wastage and excesses have meant that such inefficiencies have been tolerated to some extent, though obviously at the expense of future generations (Jomo, 1990).

The Malaysian experience underscores the importance of the relative autonomy of the executive, as reflected in Mahathir's ability to virtually abandon policies that enjoyed significant support and had generated considerable expectations (which Mahathir discredited by referring to them as having sustained a "subsidy mentality"). Mahathir effectively used and deployed the enhanced autonomy and resources at the disposal of the executive to great political advantage, in the process bringing about the partial and selective economic liberalization so much favoured by big business interests as well as international economic agencies.

During Mahathir's term, resistance to executive-led reform from the bureaucracy was generally weak. During the early NEP period, the bureaucracy was very much in control of conceiving and implementing policies. Given the entrenched bureaucratic interests, one might have expected greater resistance to change. However, as with other situations involving free rider behaviour, those adversely affected generally tried to protect and preserve their own privileges while hoping for others to bear the costs of opposing change. In many cases, incumbent bureaucrats have not experienced a diminution of their formal positions, powers or entitlements, but only of their status and incomes derived from the greater discretionary and other powers they commanded in a more regulated environment with less executive hegemony. Crucially, Mahathir generously rewarded top bureaucrats for their loyalty.

The reduced influence of the bureaucracy on policy may be traced to several factors including:

1. the ascendance of other groups, notably politicians and business executives;

2. the emergence of alternative sources of technical and other competencies, thus depriving the bureaucracy of its previous "monopoly" of knowledge, capacity and ability (the availability of private as well as foreign consultancy services has accelerated this erosion);

3. the inefficiencies of state intervention and public sector expansion, especially in the early 1980s, which undermined the standing of the bureaucracy (outside the politically dominant Malay community, the

official ethnic bias of such intervention meant little support for them outside the Malay community);

4. the attractive opportunities available to bureaucrats leaving the civil service, especially with privatization and other contracting out policies, which encouraged opting out (exit) as well as weakened and compromised potential resistance from the bureaucracy to these developments; and

5. the international anti-statist ideological atmosphere from the 1980s and the academic training of most bureaucrats also favoured economic liberalization.

Clearly, bureaucrats — who were relied upon in the early period of the NEP to develop and implement policies for "restructuring" and poverty eradication — lost influence under Mahathir. While bureaucrats had derived much of their administrative clout under the NEP, under Mahathir, they were required to co-operate with and even serve the private sector interests they once regulated.

Successful politicians favoured by the executive, especially those from the dominant UMNO, were generally patronized with various pecuniary benefits, usually linked with business contracts and appointments to and control of ministries, state agencies and public enterprises. Others were allowed to buy out government-owned enterprises at prices well below market values, thus reducing their opposition to the vast changes taking place in the public sector.

The 1985 economic slowdown was followed by a political crisis, with Prime Minister Mahathir challenged by his erstwhile deputy, Musa Hitam, and the former Finance Minister, Tengku Razaleigh Hamzah. The 1986–88 period also saw various dramatic judicial events, with a series of key High Court and Supreme Court cases decided against the government. Some of these cases hinged on procedural and administrative matters while others were substantive.[3]

As these court decisions came at a time when the Government was besieged by financial scandals, political crises, intra-party factionalism and intra-coalition disputes, they greatly vexed the executive. The straw which probably broke the camel's back probably came when the legality of UMNO's 1987 party elections was raised in the case of *Mohd Noor bin Othman v. Mohd Yusof Jaafar* in 1988. In that case, the 12 plaintiffs who were members of UMNO sought a declaration that the party elections held in 1987 were null and void and for consequential orders to hold fresh elections. There were also other irregularities in the UMNO elections. The defendants contended that only the unapproved branches should be declared unlawful and not UMNO itself. The court dismissed the plaintiff's claim and ruled that not only the unapproved branch so established was an unlawful society, but also UMNO itself. Although the plaintiffs lost their case, they succeeded in obtaining a declaration that the 1987 UMNO elections were null and void and the most appropriate order would be to make no order as to costs.

Subsequently, acting on a letter from Tun Salleh Abbas (then the head of the Supreme Court) addressed to him and after consultation with the Prime Minister, the King ordered Tun Salleh's impeachment for alleged misconduct by a special Tribunal. The Tribunal found against Tun Salleh and he was dismissed from office on 8 August 1988. The UMNO appeal was eventually heard and dismissed. Later, another tribunal was appointed to inquire into allegations of misbehaviour by five Supreme Court Judges who had convened a special sitting to hear an application by Tun Salleh in his abortive attempt to prevent the first Tribunal from sending its final report to the King. This second Tribunal recommended the dismissal of two of the five Supreme Court judges. These episodes brought much acrimony between the Malaysian Bar and the judiciary.

Throughout the legal history of Malaysia, Article 125(3) — which allows the Yang di-Pertuan Agong to appoint a tribunal at the request of the Prime Minister, or the Lord President, after consulting the Prime Minister — has been invoked three times. On 11 June 1988, a Tribunal was appointed to enquire into allegations of misbehaviour by the then Lord President, which eventually led to his dismissal. Among other things, the said Lord President was alleged to have made a speech which had the effect of "imputing that there was interference by the Government with the independence of the Judiciary". Another Tribunal subsequently enquired into allegations of misbehaviour by five Supreme Court judges who had convened a special sitting to hear the application of the said Lord President in his abortive attempt to prevent the Tribunal from sending its final report to the Yang di-Pertuan Agong. This Tribunal recommended the dismissal of two of these Supreme Court judges.

While the Malaysian judiciary was never reputed for its bold assertion of judicial independence — individually, and even more rarely, collectively — it has occasionally expressed dissent from executive decisions. But when the Lord President of the Supreme Court dissented in early 1988, with potentially dangerous implications for the vulnerable prime minister, the executive moved quickly and successfully removed him and some colleagues sympathetic to him from the bench (Lawyers Committee for Human Rights, 1989), reminding the rest of the judiciary of the loyalty expected of them. Not surprisingly, the rest of Mahathir's administration was characterized by judicial compliance, enabling him to move successfully in 1998 against his erstwhile heir apparent and then Deputy Prime Minister and Finance Minister Anwar Ibrahim.

Later, for non-political reasons, a tribunal was appointed in 1992 under the Constitution to enquire into the inability of the then Chief Justice of Malaya to carry out his official duties due to ill health. The Tribunal recommended, to the Yang di-Pertuan Agong, the early retirement of the Chief Justice from office; the recommendation was accepted, and the Chief Justice was duly discharged from office. A few years later, a High Court judge resigned after he was alleged to have pseudonymously authored an article criticizing the government of the day with various judicial and other abuses.

Mahathir also took on the nine royal houses that rule most of the states in Peninsular Malaysia. On the first occasion around 1983, the government organized public campaigns and solicited popular support to further limit the sultans' already limited prerogatives under Malaysia's unique constitutional monarchy system. The outcome, however, was a mutually face-saving compromise, which was rather ambiguous in significance. In the second episode from late 1992 into early 1993, Mahathir's victory was more decisive as he effectively unleashed the compliant mass media to expose royal abuses, thus undermining the legitimacy of the institution.

In real as well as symbolic ways, the ascendance of the executive was confirmed by Mahathir's personal success. The royal houses must surely have been mindful of the uncertainty of their own futures, and consequently, were more restrained in making their own demands of and rent claims against the state — which were generally unpopular and much resented, especially by alternative aspirants to such rents. In so far as some hereditary rulers have occasionally used their offices to exercise some countervailing power against the executive and other branches of the state, this capacity has been undermined.

With its virtually total control of the broadcast and print media, as well as other advantages of political incumbency, the ruling coalition has long been able to successfully portray the opposition as incapable of offering a serious alternative government. Public provision of basic facilities, otherwise considered as legitimate citizenship rights, has been redefined as rewards for support of the ruling coalition. After the elimination of the parliamentary left in the mid-1960s, political contention was primarily along ethnic lines, resulting in the communal polarization of the opposition, leaving the ruling coalition well placed to continue to present itself as representing moderation and inter-ethnic co-operation.

The successful coalescing of the opposition for the 1990 and 1999 general elections was unprecedented in recent Malaysian political history, and though tentative and fragile, the emergence of two rival Malay-led, multi-ethnic political coalitions led to greater consideration of policy alternatives and debates. However, limited public and media access limited the political opposition's capacity to mobilize against the ruling coalition. Through repressive laws such as the Internal Security Act, the Sedition Act, and a host of other legislation, Mahathir's government was able to discredit and even politically eliminate serious political opponents. Most importantly, the advantages of long incumbency, a finely gerrymandered electoral system and other abuses of media control as well as public and private financing have ensured the continued ruling coalition's hegemony after half a century.

Notes

1. The Malaysian government summed up the official arguments for privatization as follows (EPU 1985):

> Privatization has a number of major objectives. First, it is aimed at relieving the financial and administrative burden of the Government in undertaking and maintaining a vast and constantly expanding network of services and investments in infrastructure. Second, privatization is expected to promote competition, improve efficiency and increase the productivity of the services. Third, privatization, by stimulating private entrepreneurship and investment, is expected to accelerate the rate of growth of the economy. Fourth, privatization is expected to assist in reducing the size and presence of the public sector with its monopolistic tendencies and bureaucratic support, in the economy. Fifth, privatization is also expected to contribute towards meeting the objectives of the New Economic Policy (NEP), especially as Bumiputera entrepreneurship and presence have improved greatly since the early days of the NEP and they are therefore capable of taking up their share of the privatized services.

> However, this official rationale for privatization in Malaysia has been refuted on the following grounds. The public sectors need not be badly run (as has been demonstrated by some other public sectors). Also, privatization does not provide a miracle cure for all problems (especially inefficiencies) associated with the public sector, nor can private enterprises guarantee that the public interest is most effectively served by private interests taking over public sector activities.

2. The then Finance Minister's original six bank proposal, widely suspected to give him greater control of the banking sector, was revised, with some concessions to those with access to the Prime Minister, who intervened after some special pleading by those with access to him.

3. Some of these court decisions included the following:

   • Revocation of a foreign correspondent's employment pass on grounds of national security was quashed by the Supreme Court because he had not been given a fair hearing (*J.P. Berthelsen v. Director General of Immigration*, 1987).
   • A federal criminal provision aimed at keeping Muslim radicals in check was struck down by a three to two majority, on the ground that under the

Malaysian constitution, only the state could enact it (*Mamat bin Daud v. Government of Malaysia*, 1988).

- In the case of *Inspector-General of Police, Malaysia v. Tan Sri Raja Khalid bin Raja Harun* (1988), the Supreme Court affirmed a High Court decision that the police had wrongfully detained and charged Raja Khalid under the Internal Security Act.

- A provision allowing the prosecution to withdraw a case from the lower courts and to then send it to the High Court, without a preliminary inquiry, was struck down again by a slim majority because the Supreme Court held that it encroached upon judicial power, vested in the courts under Article 121 of the Constitution (*Public Prosecutor v. Dato' Yap Peng*, 1987).

- The leader of the opposition, Lim Kit Siang, was granted legal standing to obtain an injunction preventing the signing of a government highway contract allegedly tainted because UMNO had a financial interest in the company concerned. On a further application by the government in the same case, a different bench of the Supreme Court later reversed the decision, again by three to two margin (*Government of Malaysia v. Lim Kit Siang*, 1988).

- The refusal of a publishing licence to *Aliran Monthly* was quashed by Harun Hashim J. on grounds of unreasonableness (*Persatuan Aliran Kesedaran Negara v. Minister of Home Affairs*, 1988). He also struck down a statute that prevented junior lawyers from holding office in Bar Council Committees on the ground that it was contrary to the principle of equal protection under the law, but this decision was reversed on appeal (*Government of Malaysia v. Malaysian Bar*, 1986).

- An Internal Security Act detainee, the deputy chairman of the opposition Democratic Action Party and Member of Parliament, Karpal Singh, was released after a successful *habeas corpus* application. Peh Swee Chin J. held that the detention order was made in bad faith. Karpal Singh was, however, rearrested a few hours later, and the government was able to appeal successfully to the Supreme Court (*Minister of Home Affairs v. Karpal Singh*, 1988).

- Sedition charges against the Chairman of the Bar Council, Param Cumaraswamy, were thrown out unceremoniously by the High Court (*Public Prosecutor v. Cumaraswamy*, 1986).

- A post-election political crisis in Sabah was resolved by Tan Chiaw Tong J., who held that Tun Mustapha had been invalidly appointed Chief Minister following the Sabah election (*Tun Datuk Haji Mohd Adnan v. Tun Haji Mustapha bin Dato Harun*, 1987).

CHAPTER 3

Post-colonial Legal Developments

Wong Sau Ngan

After Independence, the legal framework and other colonial institutions were not only maintained, but strengthened and developed. To complete the transition from colonial status to nationhood, new statutes were passed by Parliament to establish new institutions, create new regulatory frameworks for a broad range of economic activities, introduce land tenure reforms and promote uniformity of laws applicable in the different states of the Federation, especially with the formation of Malaysia in 1963. The preceding chapter has provided the political and economic context for the legal developments since.

Post-colonial legal developments were initially characterized by nation-building as well as security priorities. The Government also embarked upon economic development programmes emphasizing economic diversification, rural development and industrialization. Initially, government intervention was limited, but new legislation from the 1970s restricted political freedoms and civil rights besides increasing the economic role of government regulation, intervention and spending. From the mid-1980s, economic deregulation and privatization sought to encourage private investments, while new regulations sought to better regulate the banking sector and achieve technological progress. However, the 1997–98 crisis led to further state interventions and financial sector reforms.

Broad Legal Developments

In the late 1950s and through the 1960s, 110 new laws were approved by Parliament. Of the 110 new laws passed by Parliament, 73 statutes, or 66 per cent, were substantive economic statutes. There was a clear preference for the codification of the law in the form of statutes approved by Parliament. A large number of these statutes were predominantly English-based and, in some cases, virtually reproduced the English models. Where no equivalent English statutes were available, the preference was for Commonwealth statute models, especially from India and Australia such as the Contracts Act, 1950 and the Central Bank of Malaysia Act, 1959.

The body of statutory laws in Malaysia has grown and expanded considerably since the 1970s, and continues to do so. Typically, in order to implement specific economic policies or in response to a specific development, the relevant ministry or authority submits proposals to the cabinet for new laws to be made or for existing laws to be amended. When such proposals involve other relevant ministries or authorities, a process of consultation is put in place to solicit their views or suggestions. Particularly in regard to technical matters, the relevant ministry or authority would prepare the draft legislation, either with the assistance of a legal adviser (posted by the Attorney-General's Chambers to that ministry or authority) or with its own in-house lawyers or personnel.

From the late 1960s onwards, the Government has not set up Law Commissions to make recommendations for law reform, quite unlike the colonial government and in the years soon after independence. Once the Parliamentary Draftsman in the Attorney-General's Chambers has vetted and approved the draft legislation, the proposal, together with the draft legislation, is submitted to the cabinet for approval. The subsequent approval of such legislation by Parliament in both Houses has typically been a matter of course as the ruling coalition has always commanded two-thirds of the votes in Parliament except for a brief period in the early 1970s.

It has not been the normal practice for the government to have extensive consultations with the private sector to solicit its views since the 1970s. If at all done, consultation was on an *ad hoc* basis. It became increasingly common for the government to send teams to visit countries for legal models on the subject matter being considered. Legal models and precedents from other Commonwealth countries have been favoured for obvious reasons.

With effect from 1 January 1978, appeals to the Privy Council from the Federal Court of Malaysia were abolished in criminal and constitutional cases. As for civil cases, appeals to the Privy Council from the Federal Court of Malaysia were abolished with effect from 1 January 1985. Hence, the Federal Court, being the highest court in Malaysia, became the final court of appeal in the country with the new name of "Supreme Court".[1] The abolition of appeals to the Privy Council probably precipitated a mindset among the judges that they were now masters of their own household, and had the duty of determining the future course of legal development in Malaysia. Hitherto, one criticism levied against the judiciary was for their legalistic and "unimaginative" approach in following English precedents and refusing to develop law more appropriate to conditions in Malaysia.

Official data suggests an inverse relationship between the number of commercial cases filed with the Kuala Lumpur High Court and the economic growth rate, probably due to the increase in bankruptcies and loan repayment defaults during and after recessions.[2] A study of the registration and disposal of cases in Malaysian courts for a decade from 1972 was carried out in 1983 by the Judicial Department and the Manpower and Administration Modernization and Planning Unit (MAMPU) of the Prime Minister's Department. At the time of the study, the High Court sitting in Kuala Lumpur was organized into five divisions, pursuant to Practice Direction 1[3] of 1979:

(a)   appellate and special powers division;
(b)   commercial division;
(c)   family and property division;
(d)   personal claims division; and
(e)   criminal division.

Limits to the Rule of Law

States of Emergency

The emergency powers of the Federal Government under Article 150 were amended four times during this period. The 1957 version of Article 150 of the Federal Constitution vests in the State emergency powers modelled on the Emergency Regulations Ordinance 1948, which allowed for parliamentary review of the proclamation of Emergency.

The original Article 150 provided for the Federal Government to have the power to declare a state of emergency throughout the Federation, or in parts of it, under certain circumstances. It also provided for a scheme of government under emergency rule. The provisions to override fundamental rights and the division of powers between federal and state governments were only intended to apply to the extent necessary and only for the duration of the Emergency. This amendment represented a radical departure from the original Article 150, as theoretically, it became possible for the Government to continue a state of emergency indefinitely. This, in fact, is the case; to date, four emergency proclamations subsist in the country.

Article 150 was again amended substantially in 1963. Whereas previously, it was necessary to relate the threat to the security or economic life of the country to war, external aggression or internal disturbance in order for an emergency to be proclaimed, the 1963 amendment widened the circumstances in which an emergency could be declared. Hence, any event threatening the security or economy of the country would now justify the proclamation of an emergency. In addition, the law making power of the Parliament during an emergency was widened and the procedural checks on proclamations of emergency were removed.

During this period, three proclamations of emergencies were made: in 1963, 1966 and 1969 respectively. The 1963 proclamation of emergency was made in response to an ostensible threat of external aggression after Indonesia declared confrontation to oppose the creation of the Malaysian Federation. The 1966 proclamation of emergency is widely viewed to be politically motivated as the events leading to the proclamation of emergency in Sarawak were political moves at the federal level to remove the then Chief Minister of Sarawak.

In 1966, a temporary amendment to Article 150 was made through the Emergency (Federal Constitution and the Constitution for Sarawak) Act, to deal with the so-called constitutional crisis in Sarawak. The Sarawak Constitution prior to 1966 did not authorize the Governor of the state to convene Council Negeri to pass a vote of no confidence on the Chief Minister. By this amendment, this impediment was removed.

The 1969 Emergency came about following racial riots between Malays and non-Malays. Racial tensions, built up during the general elections held on 10 May 1969, were aggravated as the communal frustrations of both Malays and non-Malays were stirred up by candidates and parties openly courting ethnic votes. Non-Malay frustration was largely centred on the government policy of special privileges for Malays in education and public sector employment, whereas the Malays were unhappy with their economic backwardness and perceived government reluctance to advance a Malay cultural agenda.

The 1969 Emergency was unique because of the special administrative apparatus that was set up to administer the Emergency. By the Emergency (Essential Power) No. 1 Ordinance of 1969 made by the Yang di-Pertuan Agong on 15 May 1969, the power to govern by emergency regulations was conferred upon the Government. Another law made the next day, the Emergency (Essential Powers) No. 2 Ordinance of 1969, appointed a special officer called the Director of Operations, who was to be assisted by a newly created National Operations Council to administer the State of Emergency. Section 2(1) of the said Ordinance declared that the executive authority of the Federation was to be delegated by the Yang di-Pertuan Agong to the Director of Operations who was nevertheless to act in accordance with the advice of the Prime Minister. These newly created appointments and bodies were a special feature of the 1969 emergency and have been seen as legitimizing what amounted to a "palace coup" by the then Deputy Prime Minister and his supporters against the incumbent long-serving Prime Minister who eventually "retired" to make way for his successor's *de jure* appointment as Prime Minister.

Another constitutional amendment was made to Article 150 relating to proclamation of emergency. The amendment was occasioned by a decision of the Privy Council striking down emergency legislation signed by the Yang di-Pertuan Agong after Parliament had sat. Basically, the amendment increased the executive power to proclaim a state of emergency and protected the act of proclamation from legal challenge and judicial review.

Independence of the Judiciary

It was envisaged by the Constitution that of the three separate branches of government, the courts are supreme in the sense that:

(a)   they are ostensibly independent of control by the others;

(b)   they can pronounce on the validity, or otherwise, of executive acts of government, both federal and state;

(c)   they can pronounce on the validity, or otherwise, of any law passed by the federal Parliament and state legislatures; and

(d)   they can pronounce on the meaning of any provision of the constitutions, federal or state.

Various mechanisms have been built into the Constitution to try to ensure that courts discharge their responsibilities without fear or favour. For example, though appointed by the Yang di-Pertuan Agong, judges do not hold office at the pleasure of the Yang di-Pertuan Agong. They may only be dismissed by the Yang di-Pertuan Agong on the grounds of misbehaviour or of liability from infirmity of body or mind, or any other cause, and then only on the recommendation of a tribunal consisting of at least five judges and ex-judges. The conduct of a judge may not be discussed in either House of Parliament except on a substantive motion, for which notice must have been given by at least one quarter of the members of that house, and may not be discussed in a State Assembly at all. Judges, once appointed, hold office until the age of 65, or for an extended period, as provided for by the Constitution. Thus, the general presumption is that a judge's appointment is permanent, though several removals and forced resignations since the late 1980s have raised doubts about it.

In 1998, the government initiated a series of constitutional and legislative amendments, which appear to circumscribe the independence of the judiciary. Part IX of the Federal Constitution describes the place and power of the judiciary in Malaysia's constitutional system. Article 121 (in Part IX) was amended in a fundamental way in 1988. The original provision provided that "the judicial power of the Federation shall be vested in two High Courts of co-ordinate jurisdiction and status". Now it reads "there shall be two High Courts of co-ordinate jurisdiction and status … (which) shall have such jurisdiction and powers as, may be conferred by or under federal law". This amendment seems to have had the effect of eliminating the inherent powers and jurisdiction of the Courts. It therefore fundamentally disturbs the concept of the separation of powers and affects the ability of the judiciary to enforce fundamental inherent rights. It tends to make the power of the judiciary subject to the legislature.

A second amendment to Article 145 allows Parliament to enact laws which permit the Attorney-General to determine which Court will hear a particular criminal case, or to transfer a case from one Court to another. According to the amended provision, the legislation may "confer on the Attorney-General power to determine the courts in which, or the venue at which, any proceedings which have power … to institute, shall be instituted, or to such proceedings shall be transferred".[4] This gives rise to concerns when viewed against the political situation in the country.

Executive Power

Various substantial changes were also made to the Federal Constitution in this period, which further entrenched executive powers. For example, in the aftermath of the May 1969 racial riots, an amendment was made to Article 153 of the Constitution, which provides for the special position of the Malays. The amendment made it a crime for a Member of Parliament to address the Parliament in such a manner as to question the privileged position of Malays. The Speaker of the House cannot permit any question on Article 153 to be raised, not even on a substantial motion in the House.

Other significant amendments were made to Articles 66 and 150 of the Constitution, which precipitated a crisis that pitted the rulers against the federal government. The objective of the amendments was to remove ambiguity with regard to the constitutional role of the Yang di-Pertuan Agong in the proclamation of an emergency. The motive for this legislative initiative was believed to be the executive's attempt to check an autocratic, unpredictable or uncontrollable monarch. After an impasse between the rulers and the executive, a compromise was reached in 1984 with the 1983 amendment to Article 150 deleted, and Article 66 substantially amended. The amended Article 66 provides for the obligatory dispensation of the Royal Assent after Parliament has re-debated the Yang di-Pertuan Agong's initial refusal to give assent. Thus, the federal government succeeded in clearly specifying the royal obligation to give assent to bills passed by Parliament.

Administrative Law

Administrative law in Malaysia is rights-based. English common law principles have been accepted and applied. The growth of administrative law in this country has been the direct result of the growth of the administrative apparatus, functions and powers of the state and evolved as an instrument of control over the exercise of bureaucratic powers in ensuring "fair procedure and just decisions by the state".

The early post-colonial period witnessed the development of administrative law affecting the rule making powers of the State and as to when the State would be considered to have acted in excess of its powers.[5] Although there were some court decisions concerning the rules of natural justice during this period, there were no significant judicial pronouncements during this period. This may have been due to the size of the administration in the country, the limited scope of discretionary powers granted to administrative bodies, and the general development of administrative law in other common law countries.

However, the period from the 1970s has witnessed more judicial activism, with landmark decisions that have led to the entrenchment of a number of principles in the administrative law of the country. In checking the exercise of power by a local authority, the Federal Court pronounced in *Pengarah Tanah dan Galian Wilayah Persekutuan Kuala Lumpur v. Sri Lempah Enterprises*: "Every legal power must have legal limits, otherwise there is dictatorship; where it is wrongly exercised, it becomes the duty of the courts to intervene. The courts are the only defence of the liberty of the subject against departmental aggression."

In *Wix Corp SEA Sdn. Bhd. v. Min. of Labour and Manpower* (1980), the old habit of classifying an administrative act as quasi-judicial or "administrative" was abandoned in the face of general acceptance of the concept of fairness. In fact, unreasonable delay in the exercise of a discretion by an administrative authority resulting in injustice and prejudice to the subjects was regarded as abuse of power and unlawful in the case of *Pemungut Hasil Tanah, Daerah Barat Daya v. Ong Gaik Kee* (1983).

In the area of judicial review based on the doctrine of *ultra vires*, the court in the *South East Asia Firebricks* case (1980) maintained that if a wide and elaborate privative clause (exclusion of the jurisdiction of court's power to review) is postulated, then only jurisdictional review is permissible. It should be noted that there was a trend during this period for the greater use of wide and elaborate privative clauses in statutes. The legislative intent of enacting such clauses was undoubtedly to curtail or even exclude judicial review *in toto*. These clauses can be found at Article 150(8) of the Federal Constitution, section 18(c) of the Societies Act, 1966, section 8B(1) of the Internal Security Act, 1960 and section 68A of the Land Acquisition Act, 1960. The degree of court activism in the area of administrative law in this period seemingly corresponded to the greater powers conferred on and exercised by the executive.

In the early 1980s, judicial discussion of matters of legislative or constitutional significance attracted public attention and political controversy, after which they were submitted for judicial consideration and resolution. This suggested a growing role for the law and the judicial process, preferred to blatantly political solutions, especially in areas of contention fraught with ethnic and other such sensitivities. Some of the issues presented to the courts included sedition and parliamentary privileges (*Mark Koding v. Public Prosecutor* [1982]), natural justice and the right to property (*Ong Ah Chuan v. Public Prosecutor* [1981]), the right to pre-acquisition hearing in consonance with the rules of natural justice (*S. Kulasingam A Anor v. Commissioner of Lands, Federal Territory & Ors* [1982]), and language rights (*Merdeka University Bhd v. Government of Malaysia* [1982]).

Nonetheless, Malaysian judges are not "activist" in the way that Indian and American judges are known to be. The judges generally tried to uphold the rule of law as far as they felt able, and their competence and impartiality were rarely questioned. But constitutional law provisions also often exempted executive actions from judicial review, suggesting discretionary, if not arbitrary, executive power, which grew during Mahathir's long administration. The judges' decisions resembled those of the English judiciary more than others, but the judges have also been regarded by many lawyers as somewhat biased to the government, especially the executive branch. This is not surprising because:

(a) the judges were generally trained at the English Bar, and had adopted the values of the English bar and judiciary;

(b) the judges tended to be promoted through the government's judicial and legal services, with a small number elevated from the Malaysian Bar, and so tended to have more sympathy for the executive; and

(c) until 1985, their decisions were subject to appeal to the Privy Council, which was often unwilling to give a "generous interpretation" to the Constitution.

As an indication of the "judicial restraint" exercised, only seven statutory provisions were struck down by the courts in the first 31 years of independence. Of these, three were reinstated on appeal, while one was struck down by the Privy Council. Few cases have been decided since the abolition of appeals to the Privy Council in 1985.

Establishment of Professional Bodies

Another significant development during this period was the setting up of various professional bodies, including professional bodies set up under the Registration of Engineers Act, 1967, the Accountants Act, 1967 and the Architects Act, 1967. Various professions were regulated by legislation that had existed before independence, providing for the registration of engineers, accountants and architects and creating statutory bodies functioning as self-regulatory organizations in the discipline of their members.

With regard to the legal profession, the Malaysian Bar was established pursuant to the Legal Profession Act, 1976. All advocates and solicitors practising in the Peninsular are members of the Bar by operation of law. One of the purposes of the Bar is to represent, protect and discipline its members, and to promote the interests of the legal profession in Malaysia. The body managing the affairs and performing the functions of the Bar is the Bar Council, which consists of elected members of the various State Bar Committees, and other elected members. The Bar Council and the State Bar Committees have existed since 1947, when the Advocates and Solicitors Ordinance, 1947 was passed. This Act was repealed and replaced with the enactment of the Legal Profession Act 1976.

Economic Laws

In relation to the law governing the organization of firms, significant statutes approved by Parliament during this period were the Companies Act, 1965 and the Partnership Act, 1961. The Companies Act, 1965 was promulgated to bring together the company law which prevailed in the component states which formed Malaysia in 1963, and provided a comprehensive legal framework for supervising the operations of companies in the Federation. Under the Companies Act, 1965, a company is required to be registered with the Registrar of Companies by the promoters, by lodging certain prescribed documents, with a small fee. Upon registration, the Registrar issues a certificate of incorporation.

The registration system mandated under the Act constitutes a notice to all at large; a principle adopted from English common law, and provides real protection, for the purposes of company law, to both the public and the name of the owner against later and other registrations of the same or similar company names. There are provisions for disclosure of a company's operations and capital structure, requirements for accounting methods, maintenance of books and records, corporate governance and the winding up and insolvency of a company, all of which are considered to be essential for modern business. Certain provisions were incorporated for the protection of minority shareholders. The Partnership Act, 1961 was also introduced to govern various aspects of a partnership, including the effects of bankruptcy on a partnership.

With the significant growth of the corporate sector in the economy, significant changes were made to the Companies Act, 1965 from the 1970s.[6] The amendments represented the culmination of efforts that started in 1976 by the Registrar of Companies, with assistance from various professional bodies, including the Malaysian Association of Certified Public Accountants, chambers of commerce, financial institutions, banks, major corporations and the Kuala Lumpur Stock Exchange.

Besides seeking to improve administration of the 1965 Act, the major amendments strengthened provisions of the Companies Act, 1965 relating to the protection of investors, e.g. new take-over rules, additional disclosure requirements, and restrictions on the powers of directors. Other amendments sought to liberalize existing restrictions.

The more notable amendments can be summarized as follows:

- requiring mandatory listing of shareholders who have an interest of five per cent or more of a company's voting shares in a register of substantial shareholders;
- excusing companies involved in mergers and intra-group reconstructions from setting up share premium accounts meeting certain criteria;
- widening the range of persons who may be caught under the Act to curb insider trading;
- significantly expanding the information which has to be disclosed in the directors' report;
- restricting directors from issuing shares and disposing of a substantial part of the company's business or assets without prior shareholder approval if this would materially affect company's performance;
- requiring all Malaysian incorporated companies to keep their accounting and other records in Malaysia except for records relating to overseas branch operations;
- revising the auditor's responsibilities and strengthening his position, particularly with respect to group accounts;
- appointing a Panel to supervise and control take-overs and mergers, and provision of a Code for Take-overs and Mergers, thus significantly revising the law relating to take-overs;
- requiring mandatory registration of foreign companies before establishing a place of business in Malaysia;
- allowing exemptions from the requirements for a prospectus in certain circumstances;
- increasing the powers of the Registrar; and
- increasing the penalties for contravention of the Act.

Laws were introduced to further facilitate private economic activity during this period, e.g. bankruptcy, contract, environment, insurance, sale of goods, consumer protection and professional bodies. The Bankruptcy Act, 1967 was introduced to govern bankruptcy proceedings for individuals — as opposed to procedures for the insolvency and winding up of companies. The criteria for determining the financial situation of an individual are far less commercially oriented than those for a company. The legislation provides for the individual's continued existence by prescribing rules concerning property and capacity.

The main development in the law of contract during this period was the application of common law in Malaysia. The 1934 Bill of Exchange Enactment Act had ensured the application of English common law relating to bills of exchange, cheques and promissory notes. The Contracts Act, 1950 made provisions on matters relating to the freedom to contract, legal characteristics of valid contracts, bailment and pledge, agency and guarantees. Though the Contracts Act, 1950 extensively codified the principles of common law on contract, there was still a lacuna in the law. The judicial trend was to apply the law applicable in England wherever the Contracts Act was silent. In the event of a conflict between the Contracts Act, 1950 and English law, the provisions of the Contracts Act, 1950 would prevail. The Specific Relief Act, 1950 provided for the remedy of specific performance and injunctions, while The Bills of Sale Act, 1950 based on the English Bills of Sale Act of 1879 and 1882, governed assignments and transfers of goods as well as the power to take possession of goods as security for a debt. The Moneylenders Ordinance, 1951 regulated all money-lending activities carried out by a person carrying on the business of a money-lender. The Ordinance was modelled on the English Moneylenders Act of 1900 and 1927.

Prior to 1961, the regulation of insurance companies was governed by the Life Assurance Companies Ordinance, 1948 and the Fire Insurance Companies Ordinance, 1948. The inadequacies of these laws led to malpractices by a number of companies, which eventually went into liquidation or defaulted on their claims. Consequently, the Government enacted the Life Assurance Act, 1961. In 1963, a comprehensive review culminated in the enactment of the Insurance Act, 1963. By controlling the insurance industry at the point of entry into the market, the regulatory authority was able to ensure that only financially sound and well-managed companies were allowed to carry out the insurance business. Some degree of control was also extended to insurance intermediaries. The Insurance Act, 1963 was extended to Sabah and Sarawak in 1965.

The Sale of Goods (Malay States) Ordinance, 1957 was enacted at the time of independence, and is more or less a reproduction of the English Sale of Goods Act 1893. The Act has been extended to Penang and Malacca and now applies to all states except Sabah and Sarawak. By reason of section 5(2) of the Civil Law Act, 1956, Sabah and Sarawak are obliged to follow English law, and when there are changes to English law, Sabah and Sarawak are required to apply English law as it stands after the changes.

Consumer protection was provided in the form of the Hire Purchase Act, 1967 modelled on Australian hire purchase legislation. Hirers of goods are entitled to certain statutory rights not found in English common law, such as the right to be supplied with certain documents and information. These features have made hire purchase a popular form of consumer financing. However, the Hire Purchase Act, 1967 only applies to a limited range of consumer goods.

New Economic Policy

Announced in 1970 by the late Tun Abdul Razak, then Deputy Prime Minister and Director of the National Operations Council (NOC), set up during the state of emergency after the events of 13 May 1969, the New Economic Policy (NEP) sought to create the socio-economic conditions for "national unity" through massive economic redistribution programmes to achieve its twin prongs of "poverty eradication" and "the restructuring of society" to reduce inter-ethnic economic disparities. Development policy in the 1970s after the declaration of the NEP saw greater state intervention in public resource allocation as well as more public sector ownership and control of business enterprises.

The Foreign Investment Committee (FIC) was set up as an administrative body in February 1974 to oversee implementation of the restructuring objectives of the NEP with respect to the ownership of assets and wealth in the corporate sector. Together with the establishment of the FIC, the Government formulated a set of guidelines known as "The Guidelines for the Regulation of Acquisitions of Assets, Mergers and Take-overs". The Guidelines provide the framework and procedures for the FIC to regulate and supervise the acquisition of assets, interests, mergers and take-overs. The target set in respect of the corporate sector is for commercial and industrial activities in all categories and scales of operation to have at least 30 per cent Bumiputera participation in terms of ownership and management. The members of the FIC are senior government officials from ministries and departments related to the NEP and the securities industry. Although without the backing of statutory authority, the FIC has been effective in ensuring compliance with its guidelines through its ability to influence various government departments to take appropriate action. The Secretariat to the FIC was established in the Economic Planning Unit of the Prime Minister's Department, which has also acted as the Secretariat for the Panel on Take-overs and Mergers.

In 1974, the Government expressed its intention to regulate the ownership and control of the Malaysian economy by foreign enterprises, and issued broad guidelines to be implemented by the FIC. The Malaysian Courts have held that these guidelines and policies do not have strict legal effect because the FIC is a governmental department and not a statutory authority. Hence, non-compliance with FIC guidelines would not render an instrument illegal.

As a general rule, Malaysian companies were expected to have no more than 30 per cent foreign equity and 70 per cent Malaysian equity, of which 30 per cent had to be held by Bumiputeras, ostensibly consistent with the NEP in the early years. However, this general rule was not always applied and has varied, depending on the industry (e.g. telecommunications, manufacturing, wholesale and retail trade, and multimedia companies) and the specific nature of some companies. In addition, specific projects approved by the Government were exempted from compliance with these guidelines.

There were observations made on the discriminatory nature of the FIC guidelines *vis-à-vis* Article 8 of the Federal Constitution, which recognizes that all persons are equal before the law. There was also fear among some senior government officials that foreign investors, who were generally sensitive to Malaysia's trade policy, would be unnecessarily alarmed if the guidelines were turned into laws. For these reasons, it is believed that the FIC guidelines will remain in its present form. It is also felt that implementation of the guidelines in its present form allows more flexibility than if the guidelines were made into law.

Privatization

From the mid-1980s, legal frameworks and processes were used to effect privatization after a project is selected. The legal framework has been amended to facilitate such transfers. The actual transfer of rights (management responsibility, assets and personnel) may be effected through a negotiated agreement between the parties under existing contract legislation. In some cases, particular legislation may have been introduced to facilitate privatization — for example, by establishing a licensing body and granting licenses. In most cases, whether through contractual means or legislation, legal rights, obligations, powers and duties involve both parties. The government's right to intervene in specific circumstances in the public interest is usually provided for. However, in practice, formal enforcement of such rights is rarely used. Government suasion and directives are often resorted to. Some laws had to be changed to facilitate implementation of the privatization programme. The Pensions Act was amended to allow civil servants to receive their pensions though an entity that has been corporatized. Legislation in specific sectors affected by privatization was also amended to facilitate the privatization programme.

Where a legislative framework exists or has been created or amended as a result of privatization policies instituted by the Government, these legislative frameworks usually provide for the following:

- vesting in the Government all rights and interests in the assets or services of a particular sector;
- the ability to divest or the actual divesting of such rights over assets or services to a corporatized entity;
- the establishment of a separate entity (usually a corporate body or otherwise), which remains accountable to the Minister responsible, with provisions for its functions, powers and duties;
- the regulation of private sector participants by way of licensing;
- the imposition of duties and vesting of powers on licence holders;
- the creation of criminal offences and provision for penalties for various breaches of legislative provisions; and
- safety or minimum standards in operations by such private sector participants in some circumstances.

The changes to infrastructure law facilitated implementation of privatization policies. This is because essential elements of the privatization programme, such as identification of projects to be privatized as well as private sector recipients of privatized projects, have been largely left to the Government's administrative discretion, exercised within the broad legislative or policy framework promulgated. Whether the legal framework will ever be formally implemented has yet to be seen, since implementation of the privatization programme has been partially reversed after the 1997–98 financial crisis. Only Government directives and suasion have been evident to date.

In some sectors, e.g. roads and highways, some terms and conditions are common to all concession agreements. For example, the expected internal rate of return to the project will be at least 12 to 18 per cent. In the event, the company fails to get the guaranteed minimum level of return, the Government reserves the right to take over the project. Other common conditions include requirements imposed on the concessionaire that its equity structure should not be changed for at least the first three years. No information is available as to whether any such agreement has been formally enforced through the courts. In the case of the postal services, the Minister of Energy, Telecommunications & Posts is reported to have said that he would consider taking action under the revised Postal Act against Pos Malaysia Berhad. Similarly, Indah Water Konsortium, the national concession-holder for sewage disposal services, has been given a series of directives by the Government regarding the conduct of its services and activities after numerous complaints by the public.

Taxation

Income tax was first introduced by the British in the Federation of Malaya with the Income Tax Ordinance, 1947 which came into effect on 1 January 1948. Other tax legislation which existed at that time included the Stamp Act, 1949 which imposes a duty on the transfer of instruments, and the Estate Duty Enactment, 1941 which imposed a duty on the value of properties which passes or is deemed to pass on death. The provisions of the Ordinance were based substantially on the Model Colonial Territories Income Tax Ordinance, 1922 designed for the British colonies at that time. The Stamp Act, 1949 was similarly modelled on the United Kingdom Act, 1849.

The Income Tax Act, 1967 repealed and replaced the Income Tax Ordinance, 1947 (together with the Sabah Income Tax Ordinance, 1956 and the Sarawak Inland Revenue Ordinance, 1960). The Income Tax Act, 1967 introduced some significant changes including the following:

- residents were taxed on a world basis;
- commencement and cessation provisions were abolished, and the preceding year basis of taxation became applicable;
- business losses suffered in any year were deductible against income from all sources for that year, and carry forward losses could only be set-off against income from business sources in subsequent years;
- appointment of Special Commissioners for hearing appeals;
- increased penalty for tax evasion and other offences under the Act; and
- wider powers to counter tax avoidance.

The Petroleum (Income Tax) Act, 1967 imposed a special tax on companies engaged in exploration, development and production of oil or natural gas. Because of the special nature of the industry, these companies were taxed at the rate of 45 per cent of their taxable income from mining petroleum in Malaysia; the rate has been 40 per cent from year of assessment 1994. The Supplementary Income Tax Act, 1967 was introduced to impose an additional tax, i.e., a development tax, with effect from year of assessment 1968. Other supplementary taxes introduced later include a tin profits tax and a timber profits tax.

Property Rights

From the late nineteenth century, all the Federated Malay States as well as the Unfederated Malay States and Malacca recognized early Malay customary land tenure where any person who cleared and cultivated land could occupy the land, provided that one-tenth of the produce cultivated was given to the state. Penang, on the other hand, practised the English deed system. The Torrens land registration system was later introduced in the Federated Malay States. These various state laws were eventually repealed by the FMS Land Code of 1926 which consolidated pre-existing laws. Torrens legislation was also introduced in the Unfederated Malay States by way of various state enactments.

Land was, and remains, a State matter. The Federal Constitution, recognizing the importance of land in the colonial economy, provided the basis for more uniform land laws. The late Tun Abdul Razak, a trained lawyer, then Deputy Prime Minister and in charge of the country's rural development programme, was particularly committed to reforming land laws and policies. Under him, the Land Conservation Act, 1960; the Land (Group Settlement Areas) Act, 1960; the National Land Code, 1965 and The National Land Code (Penang and Malacca Titles) Act, 1963 were passed. In East Malaysia, the two laws governing land tenure — namely the Sarawak Land Code (Cap 81) and Sabah Land Ordinance (Cap 68) — were also passed during the same period.

These laws, together with various subsidiary laws passed by the respective states, constitute the Torrens system in Malaysia. As discussed earlier, the Torrens System of land registration served to simplify the registration of titles, to facilitate land dealings, and to secure absolute certainty or "indefeasibility" of title to all registered proprietors, i.e. "real"/or landed property rights. Though the register provides "conclusive proof of ownership" under the Torrens system, in many instances, Malaysian courts have relied on common law principles and rules of equity to interpret the provisions of various land laws in Malaysia. The Torrens system thus better served the needs of colonial capitalism compared to earlier colonial legal arrangements which, in turn, represented departures from English land law than with its feudal encumbrances.

The National Land Code (Penang & Malacca Titles) Act, 1963 was designed to convert all land holdings to Torrens system except those subject to customary tenure in Malacca. Formerly, the deeds system (as is practised in England) applied in these former Straits Settlements states. The Act provides for the establishment of an Interim Register while the conversion process was taking place. When all land and interests have been investigated and enrolled on the Interim Register, the replacement title would represent title under the Torrens system in line with the rest of Peninsular Malaysia.

The National Land Code, 1965 regulates land tenure by providing for land dealings, land use authorization and land planning. Land tenure in Sabah is regulated by the state's Land Ordinance (Cap 68). One feature of this land system is that although it provides for the registration of title, it does not produce an indefeasible title. Rather, registration relates to the validity — or otherwise — of transactions. Some provision has also been made for land held under native customary tenure. Land tenure in Sarawak is regulated by the Land Code (Cap 81), which also provides for the Torrens System. Indefeasibility of title as evidenced by the Register is specifically provided for.

The 1970s also saw changes made to the National Land Code to restrict non-citizens and foreign companies from owning land. Specifically, the 1985 amendments provided that no land subject to the "building" category may be disposed of or dealt with, except by way of a charge or a lien, to a non-citizen or foreign company without prior written approval of state authorities.[7] In the case of land in the "agriculture" category or any condition requiring its use for agricultural purposes, the prohibition was absolute. Here, there are no provisions for any state authority to overrule the restriction.

Any acquisition of land in contravention of the above restriction renders the transaction null and void. Land already owned by non-citizens and foreign companies before the amendments were not affected except that all future transactions of such land would be subject to similar restrictions. However, the restriction on foreign ownership of land as a result of the 1985 amendments did not affect land in the "industry category". This reflected the government's desire to limit foreign land ownership while not hindering efforts to lure foreign investment for the purpose of industrialization.

The Federal Constitution forbids the deprivation of a person of his or her property except in accordance with law. The Land Acquisition Act, 1960 was introduced to allow compulsory acquisition by the state authority of privately-owned land, subject to compliance of procedural safeguards and payment of adequate compensation. The original provisions of the 1960 Act allowed compulsory acquisition by the state of private property only for public purposes, such as the building of schools.[8]

As far as the law of probate and administration is concerned, various statutes existed prior to 1957 or were introduced after independence and had their origin in English common law and English statutes. These statutes are the Probate and Administration Act, 1959; the Small Estates (Distribution) Act, 1955; the Wills Act, 1959 and the Distribution Act, 1958 that only applies to non-Muslims.

Certain principles of English common law, which were incorporated into inheritance laws, were held by Malaysian courts not to be applicable when they conflicted with Islamic law. An example is the common law rule against perpetuities, whereas in Islamic law, a trust or *wakaf* may be created with the custodian or trustee having rights in perpetuity. Another example is in the law of wills. The making of a will is recommended under Islamic law but this duty or right is subject to certain limitations i.e. not more than one-third of the deceased's estate can be disposed of by will and the remaining two-thirds must be disposed of according to principles of Islamic law.

The Control of Rent Act, 1966 was introduced with the intention of curbing skyrocketing rentals as a result of the housing shortage after the Second World War. Generally, rent-controlled premises (or "controlled premises" as described in the Control of Rent Act 1966) refer to those buildings completed before 1 February 1948.[9] This piece of legislation offers some protection to tenants and sub-tenants, especially as regards the chargeable rentals and immunity from eviction without compensation. With effect from 1 September 1997, the Control of Rent Act 1996 was repealed.[10]

Intellectual Property Rights

When Malaya attained independence in 1957, there were two copyright statutes in force, i.e. the Copyright Act, 1911 and the Federated Malay States Copyright Enactment (Cap 73), providing basic protection for intellectual property. When Sarawak and North Borneo (now Sabah) became part of the Federation of Malaysia in 1963, the UK Copyright Act, 1956 became part of the corpus of copyright law in Malaysia, together with the Copyright Act, 1911 and the FMS Copyright Enactment (Cap 73). In the face of a multiplicity of statutes, a single national copyright law was clearly needed. Towards this end, a Copyright Bill, based on the United Kingdom Copyrights Act, 1956 and the New Zealand Copyright Act, was gazetted in 1967. For various reasons, when the bill was tabled in Parliament in 1969, it was principally modelled after the Nigerian Copyright Bill.

The Copyright Act, 1969 came into effect on 1 August 1969, and was applied throughout Malaysia, repealing all copyright laws previously in force. Protection is conferred on subject matter such as literary, artistic and musical works, sound recordings, cinematography films and broadcasts. This copyright protection is accorded to works made by Malaysian citizens or residents. Foreign works were only protected if first published in Malaysia or published in Malaysia within 30 days of first publication elsewhere.

However intellectual property rights protection did not have its current significance. In spite of the introduction of the Copyright Act, 1969, there was little interest in or awareness of copyright law in Malaysia until the mid-1980s, after which intellectual property rights have become more strictly enforced mainly due to pressure from foreign corporate interests, often through governments.

Agriculture

Colonial legislation enacted in the agriculture and commodity sectors mainly affected rice and rubber cultivation as well as tin mining. The Irrigation Areas Act, 1953 established the law relating to the establishment and regulation of irrigation areas in Malaya. In the case of rice, the Padi Cultivators (Control of Rent and Security of Tenure) Act, 1967, which regulates rental rates and the security of tenure of rice cultivators, superseded earlier laws. With respect to rubber, the Rubber Shipping and Packing Control Act, 1949 created a Board to regulate bona fide shipping and packing of rubber for export. The Rubber Industry (Replanting) Fund Ordinance, 1952 provided for the collection of a cess on the export of rubber, the establishment of a Fund into which the money collected was to be paid and the constitution of a Board to administer the Fund and to make financial provisions for approved replanting of existing rubber trees, planting of new rubber and planting of other crops, in the interest of the rubber industry.

Later, after independence in 1957, the Malayan Rubber Research and Development Fund Act, 1958 provided for a cess on rubber grown and administration of a fund for the purpose of financing research, development and promotion to increase or stimulate the production and consumption of natural rubber. In 1962, a corporate body known as the Malaysian Rubber Exchange was established under the Malaysian Rubber Exchange (Incorporation) Act, 1962 for the setting up of a rubber market (including a rubber exchange or settlement house) and for the promotion and regulation of the rubber trade and industry. In 1966, the Rubber Export Registration Act, 1966 was brought into force which precluded any person from exporting rubber without a certificate issued by the Malaysian Rubber Exchange. In that same year, the Rubber Research Institute (RRI) of Malaya was established under the RRI of Malaya Enactment, and later reconstituted under the Rubber Research Institute of Malaya Act, 1966 for the purpose of research and investigation of all problems and matters relating to rubber.

The 1960s also saw the establishment of many authorities and statutory bodies which were empowered with regulatory, developmental and, sometimes, enforcement functions and powers. These include the Federal Agricultural Marketing Authority Act, 1965 (FAMA), the Bank Pertanian Malaysia Act, 1969, and the Malaysian Agricultural Research and Development Institute Act, 1969 (MARDI). During the 1960s and 1970s, various new institutions, often in the form of public or state-owned enterprises, were created to strengthen rural and regional development efforts in the field of agriculture and rural industry. In 1972, the "Board" established under the Malaysian Rubber Exchange (Incorporation) Act, 1962 was amended to mean the Malaysian Rubber

Exchange and Licensing Board under the Malaysian Rubber Exchange and Licensing Board Act, 1972. It was given the responsibility of registering and licensing all persons engaged in the business of packing or shipping rubber for export and the issuing licences to rubber dealers.

In the same year, the Rubber Industry Smallholders Development Authority (RISDA) was established under the Rubber Industry Smallholders Development Authority Act, 1972. RISDA has been responsible for the replanting and new planting of the smallholder sector with modern high-yielding planting materials, and to ensure that the smallholder sector is modernized to improve the economic well being of smallholders. In 1975, the Rubber Price Stabilization Act, 1975 was enacted, which established a national advisory council for rubber price stabilization. The Act merely provides for the council to be able to make regulations to provide for the implementation of any international agreement concluded between Malaysia and any other country or countries for the creation of a scheme for the stabilization of the rubber price in the world market.

The Palm Oil Registration and Licensing Authority (Incorporation) Act, 1976 (PORLA), established PORLA as a corporate body to regulate, co-ordinate and promote all activities relating to the supply, sale, purchase, distribution, movement, storage, export and import of oil palm products and the milling of oil palm fruit and to require the registration and licensing of persons in respect of all activities that fall within the scope of functions of the Authority. In 1979, the Malaysian Palm Oil Research and Development Board was established under the Palm Oil Research and Development Act, 1979 for the establishment and administration of a Fund for the purpose of financing research.

Mining

The Tin Industry (Research and Development) Fund Act, 1953 provided for the collection of a cess on tin exports for a fund, and the constitution of a Board to administer the Fund. The enactment of the Tin Control Act, 1954 provided for the regulation of the production, possession, sale, purchase, movement, delivery and export of tin and tin concentrates, and the implementation of the International Tin Agreement, 1953 in the colony.

The legislative framework for petroleum was first put in place through the Petroleum Mining Act, 1966 to regulate the exploration or mining of petroleum by ensuring that the relevant parties obtained licences or entered into "petroleum agreements" with the relevant authority in the state where they intend to mine or explore. In the mid-1970s, petroleum production — off the East Coast of Peninsular Malaysia — began providentially, just as oil prices soared after 1973. The government quickly pushed through the 1974 Petroleum Development Act to ensure that the federal government — instead of the states — would capture the lion's share of oil rents as would have been the case under the Constitution.

With the Petroleum Development Act, 1974, the entire ownership, and the exclusive rights, powers, liberties and privileges of exploring, exploiting, winning, and obtaining of petroleum whether onshore or offshore in Malaysia, was vested in Petronas, a corporation set up under the Companies Act, and under the direct control of the Prime Minister. In the early 1980s, petroleum gas production — almost exclusively for the Japanese economy — came on-stream, offering yet another primary commodity revenue stream for the Malaysian economy. Oil rents sustained much of the public sector expansion from the mid-1970s until the mid-1980s. In 1984, the Petroleum (Safety Measures) Act, 1984 was enacted to regulate safety in the transportation, storage and utilization of petroleum.

Employment and Labour

Desiring peaceful industrial relations to attract foreign investors to Malaysia, the post-colonial government broke with contemporary English non-interference in industrial relations, and introduced emergency legislation to control trade disputes involving strikes and other forms of industrial action in 1960. At the same time, the Government also introduced compulsory arbitration, a new concept, as arbitration before the Industrial Court was on a voluntary basis before 1967.

The three most important pieces of labour legislation were the following:

(a)   Trade Unions Ordinance 1959;
(b)   Employment Ordinance 1955; and
(c)   Industrial Relations Act 1967.

In the closing stages of the colonial period, political leaders had organized workers into movements to challenge colonial authority, affecting both labour discipline and industrial relations. Until 1940, just before the Japanese Occupation, labour unions were not allowed in colonial Malaya (Jomo and Todd, 1994). Labour unions played an important part in the anti-colonial nationalist movement after the Japanese Occupation. However, most were banned and their leaders detained, with some executed in 1948 as part of the repression against the militant left. With the change in British colonial tactics in the early 1950s, trade union organizations and even a Labour Party were allowed, if not encouraged, by the colonial authorities as part of the late colonial government's efforts to win the "hearts and minds" of the population. Subsequently, the post-colonial government introduced the Trade Unions Ordinance in 1959 to control the growth and development of the trade union movement.

In the field of industrial relations, the most significant development was the introduction of compulsory arbitration, first through the Industrial Arbitration Tribunal in 1965, and later, through the Industrial Court in 1967. Up until that time, there was the Industrial Court, set up in 1941, and later, under the Industrial Court Ordinance, 1948. Essentially, it was a court of voluntary arbitration in the sense that the consent of both parties to the dispute has to be obtained before any reference to the Court. This Court continued to co-exist with the Industrial Arbitration Tribunal up until 1967, when both these Courts were replaced by the present Industrial Court, set up under the provisions of the Industrial Relations Act 1967. Under the present Act, when there is a trade dispute and the matter cannot otherwise be resolved, the Labour (now Human Resources) Minister can refer the matter to the Industrial Court.

Environment

Government response in the form of legislation to environmental problems began as early as the 1920s, with the introduction of the Waters Enactment. This was followed by other legislation, which had relevance — though often only indirectly — to the environment. These included the Forest Enactment, 1934; the Drainage Works Ordinance, 1954; the Road Traffic Ordinance, 1958; the Land Conservation Act, 1960; the Fisheries Act, 1963 and the Factories and Machinery Act, 1967. However, it should be noted that much of this legislation was not specifically designed to address environmental problems, but only to promote "good" housekeeping practices in specific sectors, in line with the government policies of the time.

Legislation for the management of the environment enacted prior to 1974 was largely sectoral in character, focusing on specific areas of activity. Extensive though it may have been, sector-based legislation does not encourage an integrated approach to environmental policy, nor could it cope with increasingly complex environmental problems faced. Consequently, the Environmental Quality Act (EQA) was conceived. Passed by Parliament in 1974, it is the most comprehensive piece of legislation concerning environmental management in Malaysia.

The Act provides for an advisory Environmental Quality Council (EQC) whose functions are generally to advise the Minister in charge of the environment on matters pertaining to the Act and those referred to it by the Minister. In addition, the Act provides for the appointment of a Director-General of Environment whose duties include co-ordination of all activities relating to the discharge of wastes into the environment, prevention and/or control of pollution, and protection and enhancement of the quality of environment through formulation of emission standards, issuing licences for waste discharge and emissions, co-ordination of pollution and environmental research, and dissemination of information and education materials to the public.[11]

The regulations can prescribe standards or criteria, prohibit discharges, emissions or use of any equipment that endangers the environment, and determine the quantum of fines to be imposed. About 60 per cent of the regulations made pursuant to this ministerial power were gazetted in the late 1970s. To assist the Director-General of Environment in administering the EQA, a Division (now Department) of Environment (DOE) was established in 1975. The DOE is the main agency responsible for administering environmental impact assessment (EIA) requirements. EIA reports submitted to the DOE by project proponents are reviewed by a special technical panel, comprising officials from the department and other government agencies, experts from the universities, and representatives from the private sector and environmental non-governmental organizations.

Manufacturing

The absence of colonial laws on manufacturing and industrial development was largely due to the nature of the Malaysian economy then, with few manufacturing activities. The early post-colonial government moderately promoted import-substituting industrialization. Subsequently, legislation such as the Pioneer Industries Ordinance and institutions were created to facilitate this policy emphasis. Thus, the government encouraged firms to manufacture goods previously imported from abroad. Most of these firms were subsidiaries of foreign, mainly, British companies, set up to produce finished products for profitable sale within the protected domestic market.

By the mid-1960s, the problems of import-substituting industrialization had become quite apparent. Foreign experts and consultants encouraged the Malaysian government to switch to export-oriented industrialization. From the second half of the 1960s, the government moved gradually in this direction, setting up the Federal Industrial Development Authority (FIDA).[12] To encourage industrial investment, the Industrial Incentives Act, 1968 was enacted, which offered a different set of incentives more oriented to attracting more labour intensive export-oriented industries. These incentives included tax holidays for pioneer companies, investment tax credits and export allowances.

Infrastructure

Infrastructure is commonly understood as the installations and services essential for the economy of a country, e.g. telecommunications, roads and highways, power/electricity, postal, railway and sewerage services. From a regulatory perspective, much of the infrastructure development in the 1960s was carried out administratively through the various ministries of the federal government. Thus, planning and building roads were undertaken by the Ministry of Works, while railways remained with Keretapi Tanah Melayu (Malayan Railways) under the Ministry of Transport, and postal services with the Postal Department under the Ministry of Energy, Telecommunications and Posts. Sewerage and water services were undertaken by the (national) Water Department of the Ministry of Works.

The Telecommunication Ordinance, 1950 provided for the establishment of a Director General of Telecommunications. This framework was broadly similar to the present Telecommunications Act. However, definitions in the 1960s were narrower, penalties were lower, and there were no provisions then for setting up a telecommunication fund.

The Electricity Act, 1949 provided for the establishment of a statutory body known as the Central Electricity Board (CEB), and for its exercise and performance of functions relating to the supply of electricity and related matters. It also provided for the transfer of all government installations for the supply of energy and the transfer of personnel from the civil service to the CEB. The Act also provided for licensing persons who want to use, work or operate any such installation. In 1965, the name of the CEB was changed to the National Electricity Board (NEB), later known as the Lembaga Letrik Negara (LLN), before being corporatized as Tenaga Nasional Berhad (TNB) in the late 1980s.

Other miscellaneous legislation in the 1950s and 1960s included the Federal Roads Act, 1959, which gave powers to the Minister to declare roads, bridges, ferries or other means of communication in any State under federal jurisdiction. The Drainage Works Act, 1954 was also in force at that time; it established a Drainage Board that could charge rates to cover the cost of construction and maintenance of drains and water course embankments, and designated offences for interference with drainage works.

In some infrastructure sectors (previously the sole purview of the government) liberalized following the government's privatization policy from the mid-1980s, wide powers of discretion remained with the government through licensing provisions introduced in such legislation. Although some administrative procedures have been introduced in the licensing process, the basis on which such licences are issued remain difficult to ascertain, as little public information is available.

Notes

1. The current name of the highest court is the Federal Court.
2. The sharp drop in the number of commercial cases immediately after the mid-1980s may have been due to the increased jurisdiction of sessions courts from RM25,000 to RM100,000 from 1987. A considerable volume of commercial cases might have been diverted to the Sessions Courts instead as a result of the increased jurisdiction. The sessions court jurisdiction was further increased to RM250,000 from 1994.
3. With the exception of the Kuala Lumpur High Court, Practice Direction 1 has never been enforced in other High Courts.
4. For a detailed discussion, see *Report of a Mission on behalf of the International Bar Association*, The ICJ Centre for the Independence of judges and lawyers, The Commonwealth Lawyers' Association and the Union Internationale des Avocats, 2000.
5. Generally, it reflected a rudimentary state of administrative law consisting of court decisions on *ultra vires* issues. For instance, in the case of *Ghazali v. PP* (1964), a licensing condition imposed by the executive not specifically provided for in the statute was considered to be *ultra vires*. The courts were not hesitant to award the remedy of *certiorari* in a clear case of *ultra vires*.
6. The Companies (Amendment) Act 1985 received Royal Assent on 22 May 1985 and was gazetted on 30 May 1985, with amendments becoming operative in January 1986.
7. Limitations on foreign ownership were liberalized in 2006 when the Foreign Investment Committee rules were amended to allow foreigners to purchase property worth over RM250,000 without having to seek prior approval of the FIC.
8. This position has changed with the coming into force of the 1991 Amendment.
9. According to the statistics available (*New Straits Times*, 28 Nov. 1996 and 30 Jan. 1997), the total number of pre-war buildings affected by the Control of Rent Act 1966 were estimated at 38,822, scattered all over Malaysia. Penang has the highest number of rent-controlled premises in Malaysia at 12,609, while Sabah has the lowest number of rent-controlled premises with only 181. Johore had 5,659; Perak 5,531; Malacca 4,135; Federal Territory 2,500; Negeri Sembilan 2,003; Pahang 1,441; Terengganu 1,192; Kelantan 692; Selangor 431; Kedah-Perlis 306 and Sarawak 2,143.
10. The explanatory statement in the relevant Bill of Parliament gives the following reasons:

    > With the passage of time, the Act, which was originally enacted in 1966 to regulate and control the rental of privately-owned buildings built (on

or) before 31 January 1948 owing to the shortage of housing during the post-war period, has since outlived its usefulness.

On the contrary, it has lent itself to abuse with the further sub-letting of the controlled premises by the tenants at the expense of the landlords.

It is now felt that the time has come for the Act to cease to operate, and for the landlords to be able to recover possession of the controlled premises for purposes of development.

However, to alleviate the immediate need for alternative housing consequent upon the repeal and to facilitate adjustments by tenants to payment of rental at market rates, a transitional period is provided for. At the end of the transitional period, landlords are entitled to recover vacant possession of the premises.

11. Section 34A of the EQA (Revised) 1985 requires that a report of the impact on the environment of certain "prescribed and proscribed activities" be submitted to the Director-General of Environment, who would decide whether to accept or reject the report. Section 51 of the EQA allows the minister in charge of the environment to make various regulations in order to protect and enhance the environment after consultation with the EQC.

12. Now known as Malaysian Industrial Development Authority (MIDA).

CHAPTER 4

Financial Sector Legal Developments

Wong Sau Ngan and Shanthi Kandiah

Following the appointment of Daim Zainuddin as Finance Minister in 1984, the Malaysian government adopted a number of financial sector reforms to deepen and broaden financial markets. These developments were in line with international trends consistent with the financial liberalization reforms advocated by the Bretton Woods institutions. The commercial banking crisis in the late 1980s following the mid-1980s' recession and asset market collapses led to strengthened regulation and supervision. The early 1990s saw a stock market bubble following the de-linking of the Kuala Lumpur Stock Exchange (KLSE, now Bursa Saham Malaysia) from the Stock Exchange of Singapore (SES) and massive foreign investment during 1992–93.[1] The end of the bubble in late 1993 led to the introduction of capital controls on inflows in early 1994, which were lifted half a year later, renewing conditions for yet another foreign capital inflow-induced bubble leading to the 1997–98 crisis (Jomo [ed.], 2001). These were followed by various government interventions including capital controls on outflows (Wong, Chin and Jomo, 2005) as well as the new institutional arrangements discussed in Chapter 8.

Financial Regulation

In the post-colonial context, there was a desire for a change in the prevailing currency system to enhance money and credit management, and to foster a favourable climate for further development of domestic enterprise, while the World Bank recommended the establishment of a central bank for the country. A central bank was seen as an instrument of monetary independence, without which political independence would be incomplete. Consequently,

Sir Sydney Caine, the former Vice-Chancellor of the University of Malaya, and Mr. G.M. Watson, an executive of the Bank of England, were appointed to undertake a detailed inquiry into the problems of central banking and to advise on the setting up of a central bank in Malaya, including legislation to bring this about.

Based on the Watson-Caine Report, the central bank of Malaya (later renamed Bank Negara Malaysia with the formation of Malaysia in 1963) was established by the Central Bank of Malaysia Ordinance, 1959.[2] The legislation was primarily modelled on the Reserve Bank of Australia Act. The principal objectives of the central bank were to issue currency in the Federation; to keep reserves safeguarding the value of the currency; to act as banker and financial adviser to the government; to promote monetary stability and a sound financial structure; and to influence the credit situation to the advantage of the Federation. However, the central bank did not assume the currency issue function until 1967 when it replaced the Board of Commissioners of Currency, Malaya and British Borneo, to become the sole currency issuing authority in Malaysia.

The activities of commercial banks operating in the country were brought under the supervision of the central bank with the Banking Ordinance, 1959. The powers conferred on the central bank by the Ordinance placed it at the heart of the financial system. With these powers, including licensing powers, the central bank could influence the activities and operations of banks.

In 1959, the financial structure was comprised of exclusively commercial banks, which were mainly foreign owned. In the absence of a broad range of financial instruments, banks, government trust funds and expatriate enterprises held substantial proportions of their assets in the form of sterling securities. Non-bank financial institutions were non-existent. Hence, an active institution-building programme was initiated by the central bank.

At the end of 1959, there were 26 banks, of which 8 were Malaysian incorporated, which accounted for only 11 per cent of the 111 banking offices in existence at the time, and 6 per cent of aggregate assets in the banking system. Through active encouragement by the central bank, two domestic banks were established in 1960, and another in 1965. The central bank influenced the operations of the banks by directing bank credit to financing priority sectors of the economy such as manufacturing and construction.

In consonance with the objective of developing a diversified financial structure, credit for medium- and long-term industrial projects was made possible through the establishment in 1960 of the country's first development bank, Malaysian Industrial Development Finance Limited, with equity participation by the Federal Government, the Commonwealth Development

Corporation, commercial banks and insurance companies. In 1965, FIDA (now known as the Malaysian Industrial Development Authority) was set up as a statutory body to encourage industrial investment, especially from abroad.

The growing number of finance companies which accept deposits from the public was brought under the supervision of the central bank with the Finance Companies Act, 1969. Finance companies are primarily engaged in instalment credit for retail sales, housing loans, bridging finance, refinancing, factoring, leasing and other commercial lending.[3] They are prohibited from accepting demand deposits. The Agriculture Bank of Malaysia was also established in 1969 (with the passage of the Bank Pertanian of Malaysia Act, 1969) and its main objective has been to promote agricultural development through the co-ordination and provision of credit to modernize agriculture and to mobilize savings in the agriculture sector. Also set up was the Pilgrims Management and Fund Board (through the Lembaga Urusan dan Tabung Haji Act, 1969) to promote and co-ordinate activities, including the mobilization of savings, for Muslim pilgrimage.

The 1970s witnessed major legal developments affecting the financial sector. With the development of the financial system in the 1970s, and after a decade of supervisory experience by the central bank, a comprehensive review of the banking legislation was undertaken. The Banking Act, 1973, which replaced the Banking Ordinance, 1959, provided the central bank with wider scope for manoeuvre in monetary policy and greater flexibility in the use of policy instruments to promote monetary stability, while at the same time tightening controls which the central bank would require to more effectively supervise the operations of the banking system. With this, the central bank embarked on a policy to foster developmental-oriented approach to banking, with the development of new methods and procedures to ensure that credit was readily available to priority sectors or special groups to assist in bringing about a more equitable development. The vast powers of the central bank have been used since 1965 and especially from the 1970s to allocate credit preferentially to Bumiputeras and to sectors of the economy (e.g. manufacturing during the 1970s) that meet the policy goals of the government.

Further amendments were made in 1979 to the Banking Act, 1973 to give effect to the reforms introduced to the structure of liquidity requirements for commercial banks and finance companies, and to bring merchant banks within the ambit of Banking Act, 1973. The establishment of merchant banks is to ensure that merchant banks would fill the need for financial expertise in wholesale banking and corporate financing and would operate on sound management principles.[4] In 1985, comprehensive amendments were made to the Banking Act, 1973, the Finance Companies Act, 1969, and the Central

Bank of Malaya Ordinance, 1959. These amendments substantially consolidated the control of the central bank over financial institutions and involved:

- requiring approval of the Minister of Finance on any acquisition of five per cent of the shareholdings in a financial institution;
- imposing individual shareholding limits in financial institutions;
- prohibiting cross-holdings by commercial banks (including foreign barks operating in Malaysia) in other banks. Similarly, finance companies and merchant banks were prohibited from holding shares in other finance companies and merchant banks respectively;
- requiring approval of the Minister of Finance for changes in control or management of a finance company;
- imposing control of credit limits;
- allowing the central bank, with the concurrence of the Minister of Finance, to grant loans or to purchase shares in a licensed bank or finance company, if the central bank is of the opinion that the financial institution is unable to meet its obligations or is about to suspend payments; and
- introducing general increases in penalties.

This period saw the development of new types of financial intermediaries — the merchant banks and discount houses,[5] that had led to an active money market; the Credit Guarantee Corporation, set up with equity participation from the central bank and commercial banks to provide guarantee cover to banks for loans made to small-scale enterprises; the reorganized National Savings Bank, that mobilized small savings in the enactment of Bank Simpanan Nasional Act, 1974; and two development banks, i.e. the Industrial Bank of Malaysia and the Sabah Development Bank, set up to provide long-term financing for the expansion of productive capacity in capital intensive and high technology industries.

It can be said that despite the substantially enlarged powers of the central bank through amendments made to banking legislation, the preferred enforcement approach of the central bank was through moral suasion, rather than by prosecuting offenders in a court of law. From the time the central bank assumed supervisory control over the banking system up to the mid-1980s, not a single enforcement action was brought to court for non-compliance with the provisions of banking legislation. The central bank preferred to exercise its powers through moral suasion or to "compound" offences for breaches of the law. This may be attributed to the practice of the Bank of England in relying on "winks and nods" to secure desired conduct by financial institutions. The approach adopted by the central bank probably had a lot to do with the belief of senior central bank officials that enforcement through moral suasion would not jeopardize public confidence in the banking system as much as prosecuting a bank in a court of law. It is believed that the litigation-averse banking community also prefers this form of enforcement.

Banking based on Islamic principles was introduced during the 1980s as the government undertook an Islamization campaign. The way was paved for financial intermediation based on Islamic principles with the Islamic Banking Act, 1983 modelled on the Banking Act, 1973 with appropriate modifications, a major one being that banking business is defined to mean business that is in conformity with *Shari'a* principles.[6]

Amendments to various banking laws were introduced in 1986 to further strengthen the financial system and enhance the effectiveness of the Central bank in promoting monetary stability and a sound financial structure. The amendments, covering both policy issues and enabling provisions, were introduced in the form of the Finance (Banking and Financial Institutions) Act, passed by Parliament in October 1986. It mainly provided for the effective implementation of the revamped Export Credit Refinancing Scheme, elimination of errant current account holders, prohibition of loans to the directors and staff of finance companies, and restrictions on the use of the term "finance company" or any of its derivatives in any language.

Apart from amendments to banking legislation, the Essential (Protection of Depositors) Regulations, 1986 were promulgated on 20 July 1986 under section 2 of the Emergency (Essential Powers) Act, 1979. The purpose of the Regulations was to equip the central bank with the necessary powers to investigate promptly and act swiftly to conserve the assets of companies engaged in illegal deposit-taking activities, as well as co-operatives and pawnbrokers, to protect the interests of depositors.

The powers and duties of the central bank under the Essential (Protection of Depositors) Regulations, 1986 are summarized below:

- Investigate the affairs of any deposit-taker;
- Freeze property and restrict departure from Malaysia of persons subject to investigation;
- Act against a deposit-taker, including assuming control of and appointing a receiver for the deposit-taker; and
- Seek and abide by the advice of the Advisory Panel appointed pursuant to section 31A of the Central Bank of Malaya Ordinance, 1958, prior to invoking and exercising its powers under the Regulations.

The Banking and Financial Institutions Act, 1989 (BAFIA) was passed by Parliament in July 1989 after a period of economic recession and stresses in the banking system. The BAFIA received Royal Assent on 23 August 1989 and was gazetted as Act 372 on 24 August 1989. The BAFIA, which provides comprehensive new laws for the licensing and regulation of institutions carrying on the business of banking, finance companies, merchant banks, discount houses and money-broking, and regulation of institutions carrying on certain other financial business, came into force on 1 October 1989, except for provisions in respect of scheduled institutions, which became effective on 1 January 1990. The BAFIA effectively replaced the Banking Act, 1973 and the Finance Companies Act, 1969. However, the Islamic Banking Act, 1983 was not affected.

The introduction of the BAFIA was intended to provide for integrated supervision of the Malaysian financial system, and to modernise and stream-line the laws relating to banking and all other financial institutions. With rapid growth and growing competition in the banking system, the lines blurring among three traditional groups of financial institutions (banks, finance companies and merchant banks) supervised by the Central bank, the methodology for supervision of these institutions increasingly converged, although the legislative basis for supervision had been legally separated under the repealed Banking Act, 1973 and the repealed Finance Companies Act, 1969. The BAFIA provides for all financial institutions to be supervised by the Central bank (including those supervised on an administrative basis), i.e. under one supervisory and regulatory regime.

The BAFIA also provides Bank Negara with a unique power not found in any other banking legislation at that time, i.e. the power to investigate and take corrective actions, including assumption of control over so-called non-scheduled institutions. These comprise statutory bodies (i.e. financial institutions set up by statute and supervised, in most cases, by authorities other than the Ministry of Finance) and any person or corporation neither licensed under the BAFIA nor subject to the provisions of Part III of the BAFIA governing scheduled businesses and representative offices, but nonetheless engaged in the provision of finance. The supervisory and investigative powers of the central bank were significantly strengthened by the BAFIA.

The BAFIA also formalized in law the policy that all branches of foreign banks operating in the country had to be incorporated locally.[7] The branches of foreign banks were given a transitional period of five years (or such longer period as the Minister of Finance may allow) to locally incorporate in order to continue banking in Malaysia. The Government has long encouraged the branches of foreign banks operating in Malaysia to incorporate locally to reflect a more direct and permanent financial commitment by the foreign financial institutions in the country. Upon local incorporation, foreign banks will be allowed to retain 100 per cent foreign ownership. Technically, only their form would change.

Foreign Exchange

Malaysia adopted a structured approach in reviewing the foreign exchange administration policies based on the preparedness of its economy. Over the years, foreign exchange administration policies have been progressively liberalized. In this system, approval requirements for inflows and outflows are mainly prudential in nature in order to ensure financial stability.

On 1 December 1994, the key foreign exchange control rules were liberalized, ostensibly to sustain rapid Malaysian growth. Basically, the liberalization measures were aimed at reducing business operation costs, allowing small and medium-scale industries greater access to credit facilities, increasing the efficiency of cross-border transactions and encouraging multinational corporations to set up their regional operational headquarters in Malaysia. One important change was to allow exporters to retain a portion of their foreign exchange export proceeds in a foreign currency account maintained with any one of the Designated Banks in Malaysia. Exporters were permitted to maintain overnight balances of between US$1 million to US$5 million, depending on the size of their export receipts.

Residents not borrowing domestically could maintain any number of foreign currency accounts with a Designated Bank and overseas branches of Malaysian-owned banks without any restriction on overnight balances. Non-individual residents with domestic borrowings could maintain foreign currency accounts with a Designated Bank or a Licensed Offshore Bank in Labuan to deposit foreign currency receivables other than export proceeds up to an aggregate overnight balance of US$0.5 million, while resident individuals could open foreign currency accounts limited up to US$50,000 with overseas banks, US$100,000 with Licensed Offshore Banks in Labuan and US$100,000 with Designated Banks. In addition, residents could freely obtain — from a licensed bank or licensed merchant bank — any amount of short-term foreign currency trade financing facilities with tenure not exceeding 12 months as well as guarantee facilities in foreign currency.[8]

Following the capital controls introduced in 1998 during the financial crisis, there was a gradual lifting of capital control measures. Liberalization and further simplification of several major foreign exchange administration policies took place in 2004 aimed at enhancing the business environment as well as the efficiency and competitiveness of business operations in Malaysia. With effect from 1 April 2004, the following changes were introduced:

(i)   While maintaining the requirement for exporters to repatriate receipts arising from export of goods when contractually due, which must not exceed six months from the date of export, the rules on reporting of such transactions were abolished or simplified to reduce the reporting burden on businesses;

(ii) Rules on maintaining foreign currency accounts were liberalized further for both individuals and companies. For example, resident companies with domestic borrowings may open a foreign currency account for non-export receivables to retain such receipts with onshore licensed banks with no overnight limits. For resident companies that do not have domestic borrowings, they may also maintain non-export foreign currency accounts with licensed offshore banks in Labuan up to an aggregate overnight limit of US$500,000;

(iii) To enhance access to ringgit funds for business requirements in Malaysia, all permitted ringgit lending limits for various purposes by banking institutions to a non-resident are consolidated into one aggregate limit and raised to RM10 million;

(iv) To provide flexibility for better management of funds, resident individuals employed or staying abroad with their own foreign currency funds may invest in any foreign currency assets, including those offered by onshore licensed banks and licensed offshore banks in Labuan;

(v) For greater diversification and to simplify the approval process, unit trust management companies may invest abroad up to the full amount of net asset value subscribed by non-residents and up to 10 per cent of the net asset value subscribed by residents;

(vi) To deepen the development of the domestic ringgit-denominated bond market, multilateral development banks (MDBs) of which Malaysia is a member and foreign multinational corporations (MNCs) are allowed to issue ringgit bonds in Malaysia; and

(vii) Rules on hedging were also significantly liberalized. For example, MDBs and MNCs that issue ringgit-denominated bonds in Malaysia were allowed to enter into forward foreign exchange contracts with onshore licensed banks to hedge their currency risks. Similarly, non-residents subscribing to these ringgit-denominated bonds are also allowed to enter into forward foreign exchange contracts with onshore licensed banks to hedge their currency risks.[9]

Financial Sector Master Plan

The Financial Sector Master Plan (FMSP), launched in March 2001, sets out the broad strategy for the development of the financial sector (banking sector, insurance sector, Islamic banking and *takaful* [insurance] sector and development financial institutions) over a period of 10 years. The end objective is to develop the financial system to be more competitive, resilient and dynamic. Efforts undertaken during the initial stage of FMSP implementation were mainly directed to enhancing the capacity and capability of domestic financial institutions in order to enhance their level of effectiveness and competitiveness, strengthening the regulatory and supervisory framework, promoting a safe and efficient payments system as well as developing the framework for consumer education and protection.

Hence, one of the key milestones for the FSMP is to improve performance in the banking sector. The industry benchmarking programme, initiated in 2002, has provided banking institutions with a tool to enable more effective strategic focus and business planning, as well as improve the relative ranking of each institution in all areas of performance.[10] The FMSP has also recommended the development of alternative modes of financing in the domestic financial system such as the development of the venture capital industry. Following the phase of strengthening domestic institutions, the next phase envisages gradual liberalization and the development of a more diversified financial services landscape for the entire spectrum of the financial sector.

Financial Institutions	*1998*	*2005*	*2006*
Commercial banks	35	23	22
Finance companies	31	4	0
Investment banks/merchant banks	12	10	14[a]
Discount houses	7	7	0
Islamic banks	1	6	11[b]
Insurance companies	58	42	42
Reinsurance companies	10	7	6[c]
Takaful operators	2	5[d]	8
Development financial institutions	14	13[e]	13[e]

Notes: [a] Includes a merchant bank in the midst of transforming into an investment bank and three universal brokers that transformed into investment banks in January 2007.

[b] Includes a foreign Islamic bank that commences operations in January 2007.

[c] One licence of a foreign reinsure was surrendered following a group rationalization exercise by its parent company abroad.

[d] Includes a *takaful* operator that commenced operations in January 2006.

[e] Of which six development financial institutions are regulated under the Development Financial Institutions Act, 2002 (DFIA) (*The Edge*, 23 April 2002).

Six years into the Financial Sector Master Plan, it would appear that the financial landscape has changed considerably. The table on p. 88 shows the changes and number of financial institutions operating in the banking, insurance, Islamic banking and *takaful*, and development finance sectors.

Financial Sector Profile

The table clearly shows the dramatic change in the ecology of the nation's financial sector following the reforms initiated in the late 1990s.

Regulatory Reforms

Anti-Money Laundering (AML) and Counter Financing of Terrorism (CFT) Measures

In the wake of 11 September 2001, the global community intensified its efforts to enhance measures to detect and deter money laundering and terrorism financing. In Malaysia, the central bank is the secretariat to the National Coordination Committee (NCC) to Counter Money Laundering established in 2000 to formulate anti-money laundering (AML) and to counter financing of terrorism (CFT) measures, to co-ordinate the implementation of these measures and to ensure that the national efforts are aligned with regional and international initiatives.

Five pieces of legislation form the legislative framework for AML and CFT, namely the Penal Code, Criminal Procedure Code, Subordinate Courts Act, 1948, Courts of Judicature Act, 1964, and the Anti-Money Laundering Act, 2001 (AMLA). The money laundering reporting mechanism under the AMLA covers financial institutions and certain categories of non-financial institutions, considered to be high risk in terms of money laundering and terrorist financing activities. In 2003, the number of money laundering predicate offences increased from 122 to 150 serious crimes involving 23 pieces of legislation. The amendments to the Penal Code to criminalize terrorism financing and the amendments to AMLA in 2003 to require the development of appropriate mechanisms to counter financing of terrorism and effective procedures to ensure effective implementation of the UN International Convention for the Suppression of the Financing of Terrorism.

Payments System

The Payments System Act, 2003 was gazetted on 7 August 2003 and came into effect on 1 November 2003. The introduction of the Payments System Act, 2003 was in line with the recommendations in the Financial Sector Master Plan for the adoption of a flexible, proactive and effective regulatory framework for the oversight of the payments system and to increase the efficiency of the payments system.

The objective of the Payments System Act, 2003 is to ensure the safety and efficiency of the payments related infrastructure, and to safeguard the public interest. The Act defines a payments system as "any system or arrangement for the transfer, clearing and settlement of funds or securities". Several arrangements — including the clearing houses recognized under the Securities Industry Act, 1993 or the clearing houses licensed under the Futures Industry Act, 1993 — are excluded from the definition of the payment system as they are subject to the oversight of the Securities Commission under the securities laws. Bank Negara Malaysia is empowered under this Act to require the operator of a payments system or the issuer of a payments instrument to be an incorporated company. To ensure effective supervision and monitoring of a payments system, Bank Negara Malaysia may require the operator of a payments system or the issuer of a payments instrument to submit information on the payments system operated or the payments instrument issued by them.

Deposit Insurance System

Up to 2005, deposits in the banking system enjoyed an implicit guarantee by the government in the event of insolvency of banking institutions. The Financial Sector Master Plan recommended that a deposit insurance system should be adopted for the banking system once the strengthening of the banking institutions had taken place. The features of the deposit insurance system for Malaysia are in place (BNM *Annual Report, 2003*: 150), and incorporate the following features:

(i)   A legislative mandate for the agency responsible for the administration of the deposit insurance system pursuant to the Deposit Insurance Act, 2005.[11] This would ensure clarity of its role and responsibilities within the financial safety net and provide the basis for the statutory powers to be accorded to the agency.

(ii) Compulsory membership for commercial banks (including subsidiaries of foreign banks operating in Malaysia) and other financial institutions accepting deposits. This would avoid the risks associated with adverse selection whereby only small and perceived weaker institutions participate in the system.

(iii) Protection up to the prescribed limit for eligible deposits by all depositors of member institutions. Provisions are made for the agency to approve additional financial instruments as being eligible for deposit insurance to accommodate new types of deposit products that may be introduced in the future.

(iv) Equivalent protection for Islamic and conventional deposits which will be separately insured based on the institution's deposit insurance limit to avoid any competitive distortions between Islamic and conventional banking systems.

(v) Annual premiums to be paid by member institutions to the deposit insurance fund to be based on the institution's total insured deposits. The premiums will be entirely borne by member institutions.

(vi) The implementation of a differential premium system to determine the premiums payable by each member institution.

Corporate Regulation

The Companies Act, 1965 has been amended at various times in the last two decades, i.e. in 1986, 1989, 1991, 1992, 1996, 1998, 2000, 2001, 2002.[12]

Most of the amendments made so far were designed to strengthen the provisions of the Act, particularly relating to the protection of investors and minority shareholders. There were also technical recommendations designed to improve administration of the Act and to remove anomalies. At the same time, the amendments have also increased the public accountability of directors to shareholders and investors by requiring more corporate disclosure. Some notable amendments made were:

• *Providing Additional Protection to Minority Shareholders and Consumers*

(i) Section 84 — This amendment was essentially made to clarify that timeshares and club memberships are in fact "interest" within the meaning of the word in section 84, and that all developers and operators of time-share schemes or golf and recreation clubs, which offer to sell timeshares or club memberships to the public, must comply with the requirements of Division 5 of Part IV of the Companies Act, 1965;

(ii) Section 121 — The new subsection (1A) now requires a company that has changed its name to state the old name for at least 12 months in all documents, letters and whatsoever. The purpose of this new subsection is to avoid confusion among those having dealings with the company. Failure to display the old name, as required, would be an offence under the law;

(iii) Section 122 — New subsection (2) specifically stated that only persons of full age would be eligible for appointments as director of a company. A person is said to be of full age if he has attained the age of majority, i.e. 18 years. The purpose of this amendment was to clear doubts and to prevent persons from using a minor as a director to escape liability;

(iv) Section 132G — The intention behind new section 132G was to prevent the shareholders or directors of a company from making a quick buck for themselves and/or others at the expense of their company and minority shareholders. Under this new section, a company is prohibited from acquiring any shares or assets of another company if a shareholder or director of the company, or a person connected to such shareholder or director, has a substantial shareholding (more than five per cent) in that company. The prohibition is not applicable if the shares of such persons in the other company have been held by them for more than three years, or the assets have been held by that other company for more than three years. Any transaction in contravention of the section entered into or pending completion at the time of the section coming into operation, i.e. 10 September 1992, would be deemed void.

However, after various press reports and objections submitted by various associations representing the corporate sector on its implications, section 132G[13] was further amended to provide for specific flexibility. Transactions that would be exempted from the prohibition include:

(a) subscriptions for new shares for cash consideration;
(b) transactions between a company and a wholly-owned subsidiary, or between wholly-owned subsidiaries of the same holding company;
(c) acquisitions of assets other than shares where the sale is in the ordinary course of business of the selling company;
(d) acquisitions of shares pursuant to a take-over offer which complies with requirements of the law relating to such offers; and
(e) acquisitions of shares of assets pursuant to a scheme of compromise or an arrangement approved by the Court.

The subsequent amendment to section 132G also limits reference to the shareholder of the acquiring company to those who hold substantial shareholdings in the acquiring company. It also limits reference to a member of a shareholder's or director's family to the spouse, child or stepchild of that shareholder or director.

- *Cater to Appeals and Proposals by the Private Corporate Sector*

    (i) Section 67 prohibits a company from granting financial assistance to another party for the purchase of its own shares or shares of its holding company or in connection with the purchase of its own shares or shares of its holding company. This prohibition casts a very wide net, and contravention of this prohibition results in the loan and securities transactions being declared illegal and unenforceable. This section has enabled sophisticated and unscrupulous borrowers to entirely extricate themselves from their contractual obligations by abusing such legal technicalities. Therefore, section 67 was amended to provide an avenue for a third party to recover the financial assistance given in contravention of this section;

(ii) Section 132 — It was felt that the section was too restrictive to the extent that ordinary day-to-day business transactions might be hampered and exemptions should therefore be provided for certain business transactions. The proposed amendments to section 132 take into account certain private sector proposals. It was felt that the upper limit of RM100,000 in respect of the value of the asset acquired from or disposed of to a director, or a person connected to a director, was too low and restrictive. To ensure that the intention of the section was still achieved, the limit was increased to RM250,000;

(iii) Section 132F — This new section provides for specific exemptions from the requirements of section 132F for certain transactions stipulated in the section. The transactions exempted are as follows:

(a) transactions between a company and wholly-owned subsidiaries of the holding company;

(b) transactions entered into by a company being wound up other than because of members' voluntary winding-up;

(c) transactions entered into in the ordinary course of business and on terms not more favourable than those generally available to the public or to employees of the company; and

(d) transactions which do not involve the transfer of cash or property approved by a general meeting of the company.

In 1996, the Companies Act, 1965 was amended again with the amendments coming into effect on 15 August 1996. Some amendments did away with filing documents with the Registrar of Companies, such as lodgement of material contracts for the purpose of prospectus registration, while other amendments removed the requirement for prior approval by a general meeting in issuing shares for certain share-swap deals. One other notable amendment involved streamlining regulation of unit trusts; the regulation of unit trusts now falls under the jurisdiction of the SC.

Reforms Following 1997–98 Financial Crisis

The 1997–98 financial crisis led to reforms to the Companies Act, 1965, e.g. allowing share repurchases by public listed companies.[14] In 1998, the law on share repurchases were amended again to make it more facilitative by the introduction of the concept of treasury stocks.[15] Another post-crisis amendment to the Companies Act, 1965 related to the provisions on the rehabilitation and restructuring of companies that were ongoing concerns.[16] Under these provisions, the High Court can issue summary orders temporarily restraining the creditors from proceeding against the company. During the course of 1998, some 38 public listed companies used the provisions of section 176 of the Companies Act, 1965[17] to seek from the courts temporary relief from creditors for periods of up to nine months on a unilateral basis without the company being required to initiate a process of dialogue with its creditors and without the creditors being given a chance to present their case to the court before the relief is granted.

Given the risk that companies might use this section to pre-empt creditor action and to strip a company of its assets, the Companies Act, 1965 was amended to require that companies secure consent from creditors representing at least half of the value of their debts before an application can be submitted to Court. No less significant is the fact that companies will now be required to submit together with their application a list of their assets and liabilities. This is to prevent the disposal of assets or incurrence of further liabilities during the court protection period.

Amendments to the Securities Commission Act, 1993 and the Companies Act, 1965, which came into effect in July 2000, made some far reaching changes to the regulatory framework governing fund raising activities. Under the amendments, the Securities Commission was mandated as the approving and registering authority for prospectuses in respect of all securities other than shares and debentures issued by unlisted recreational clubs. This has introduced considerable efficiencies as it eliminates the need for issuers to seek approvals from multiple regulators.

The Companies Commission[18] is the principal regulator of corporations. However in terms of its presence on the affairs of public companies and particularly, listed companies, the SC has increasingly encroached on areas traditionally within the domain of the companies regulator. The SC and the KLSE have instituted major changes to both securities laws and listing requirements that have significant impacts on the affairs of corporations. Listed companies are now subject to very detailed disclosure requirements. But quite apart from disclosures, the listing requirements also enter into areas traditionally within the domain of the CA by restricting the voting rights of shareholders, particularly substantial shareholders, in related party transactions.[19]

The critical difference between the provisions of the listing requirements and the CA on related party transactions is that the latter (for example, sections 132E and 132C) does not require the interested shareholders to abstain from voting in a transaction falling within those sections. Thus, there is a divide between the treatment of listed companies where the listing requirements will bridge the gap between the requirements of the CA and the stock exchange regulator's expectations, and non-listed companies which are not subject to the listing requirements of the stock exchange. Amendments have been proposed to the CA, principally through the recommendations of the Finance Committee, to reflect this prohibition on voting by interested persons.[20]

Prohibition against interested shareholders voting in transactions that are required to come before the general meeting is a contentious issue. On the first of these objections, Malaysian law, following English law and the law of Commonwealth jurisdictions, has never prohibited shareholders from acting on the basis of self-interest.[21] Neither have shareholders been visited with the status of fiduciaries.

Consequently, shareholders have been left largely free of restraints on their right to vote, save for the concept of "fraud on a power". This equitable fetter on the freedom to vote arises whenever the right is being used in a way that equity would regard as fraudulent.[22] Yet, as a result of cases of insider abuse, Malaysian policy makers have fashioned listing requirements in ways that constrain the freedom that the common law gives shareholders when it comes to the voting.

Nevertheless, there may be concerns of a legal nature about the manner in which restraints on voting by interested shareholders is being done in Malaysia. The right to vote is a property right. Property rights are guaranteed and protected by the Malaysian Federal Constitution, in particular, Article 13(1), which provides that no person shall be deprived of property save in accordance with written law.

The Finance Committee on Corporate Governance recommended the codification of the prohibition against interested shareholders voting in transactions that they have an interest in.[23]

Companies Commission of Malaysia

Following amendments to the law, the Companies Commission of Malaysia (CCM) was established on 16 April 2002 to succeed the functions of the Registrar of Companies (ROC) and Registrar of Businesses (ROB). The move to corporatize the Registrar of Companies is largely a measure to gain greater autonomy in the management of its financial affairs. This would also enable the CCM to attract new personnel with new and attractive packages. Under the Companies Commission of Malaysia Act, 2001, the Registrar of Companies and Registrar of Businesses specified by the Minister shall be transferred to and vested in the Commission without any conveyance, assignment or transfer. The Companies Commission has the power to regulate corporations and businesses in Malaysia and to administer any law which confers functions and powers on the Commission.

Securities Market

Though the origins of the securities market in Malaysia can be traced to trading in rubber and tin stocks in the post-1910 era, it was not until 1960 that the first stock exchange was set up in Malaysia, which explains the lack of securities legislation before that.

The central bank played an active role in the development of the capital market in that period. The first formal organization of the securities industry was established on 23 June 1930, and was known as the Singapore Stockbrokers' Association. On 18 July 1959, the Association was re-registered as a company under the Companies Ordinance as the Malayan Stockbrokers' Association. At that time, there were only four stockbrokers and there was no stock exchange in Kuala Lumpur. The Malayan Stock Exchange was formally instituted on 21 March 1960 with two trading floors, one in Kuala Lumpur and one in Singapore. Public trading of shares commenced with the four stockbrokers gathering at the clearing-house of the central bank to mark prices. Clerical assistance and telephone facilities were provided by the central bank.

On 6 June 1964, the Malayan Stock Exchange was reconstituted to form a joint exchange under the name of the Stock Exchange of Malaysia, which subsequently became the Stock Exchange of Malaysia and Singapore in 1965. In addition to stocks, shares, debentures and other fixed income securities, the stock exchange also traded in government securities. In 1968, the Government set up the Capital Issues Committee (CIC) under the chairmanship of the Governor of the central bank to oversee the development of the stock market. The Capital Issues Committee operated within a set of administrative guidelines to ensure the orderly development of the capital market and to approve the public offer of securities.

During this period, the market for government securities was thin, with little trading, as most government debt papers were held to maturity by institutions such as the Employees' Provident Fund and the Post Office Savings Bank. In order to provide a range of securities with varying maturities and offering different interest rates and terms of redemption, the government started to issue short term securities of two to five years' maturity in addition to longer term securities of 15 to 20 years with the passage of the Loan (Local) Ordinance, 1959 and the Loan (Local) Act, 1961.

In 1973, there was a major change in the Malaysian securities market when the Stock Exchange of Malaysia and Singapore (SEMS) was formally split into two separate exchanges, i.e. the Kuala Lumpur Stock Exchange (KLSE) and the Stock Exchange of Singapore (SES). This followed termination of currency inter-changeability agreement between Malaysia and Singapore.

With this, the Securities Industry Act, 1973 (SIA) was introduced to provide for regulation of the securities industry and to protect the interests of investors. When the SIA was brought into force in 1976, a new company limited by guarantee, called the Kuala Lumpur Stock Exchange (KLSE), took over the operations of the exchange. Later, a new Securities Industry Act, 1983, replaced the 1973 Act. In addition to ensuring safeguards for proper listing of and dealing in securities, licensing of dealers and maintenance of proper and adequate records, the 1983 Act provided the Registrar of Companies with enforcement and investigative powers.

In the mid-1980s, the adverse global environment took its toll on the economy, which went into recession. Events in 1985 unsettled public confidence with the three-day suspension of the Kuala Lumpur and Singapore stock exchanges. In response to the loss of public confidence with closure of the KLSE in 1985, initiatives were taken to enhance the efficiency and sophistication of the KLSE through legislative and administrative measures.

The following major measures in the regulatory and legal framework for the Malaysian capital market were undertaken in 1986:

- All stock-broking companies were required to be corporatized, thereby doing away with individuals and partnerships;
- The limit on foreign corporate ownership of domestic stock-broking companies was increased from 30 per cent to 49 per cent in July 1985 to upgrade professionalism in the stock-broking industry and to foster stronger links with international markets;
- New guidelines for the "New Issue of Securities and the Valuation of Public Limited Companies" were introduced by the Capital Issues Committee (CIC) in August. Among the major changes were: an increase in the required minimum paid-up capital of a company seeking listing on the Main Board from RM5 million to RM20 million; a wider range of price-earnings multiples for determination of prices of new issues; and additional criteria for rights issues;
- A "Code of Ethics: Guidelines on Share Trading", aimed at preventing grey market and insider trading, was introduced by the central bank for compliance by commercial and merchant banks. It clearly sets out the areas where conflict of interest situations may arise;
- A second board on the KLSE was established to enable small companies to raise additional capital from the public. These companies should have

a paid-up capital of RM5 million to RM20 million, and be viable with strong growth potential; and

- The KLSE committee was revamped to include a full-time executive chairman to be appointed by the Minister of Finance.

Until 1993, Malaysia had no securities commission. Various bodies regulated different aspects of the capital market, including the Capital Issues Committee (CIC), the Registrar of Companies (ROC), the Panel on Take-overs and Mergers (TOP), the Foreign Investment Committee (FIC) and the Kuala Lumpur Stock Exchange (KLSE). The need to establish a single regulatory authority to plan and appraise problems in the capital market from a broad developmental view and to formulate a regulatory system that is practical, efficient and competitive for the capital market was recognized by the Government.

Prior to 1993, some regulatory authorities had been created on an *ad hoc* basis to meet the specific needs or problems faced by the industry. Although the rules and procedures laid down by each agency may not appear to be onerous in isolation, taken together, the requirements of the numerous agencies involved are alleged to have increased transactions costs and time, with a dampening effect on business and corporate activities. To ensure that the Malaysian securities market developed to internationally acceptable, if not attractive, levels to draw foreign investors, the industry has to be continually abreast of international developments to be attractive and competitive. In addition, the development of new instruments to cater for the changing needs of investors and companies, the consequences of technological advances and international trends on the industry, etc. have to be continuously reviewed. Such a role was expected to be best performed by a single regulatory body with a broad overview of the capital market and the power to enforce regulations.

On 1 March 1993, the Securities Commission (SC) was established pursuant to the Securities Commission Act, 1993. At the same time, the Securities Industry Act, 1983 was amended and the Futures Industry Act was promulgated. Any issue or offer of securities in Malaysia requires approval of the Securities Commission (SC). The SC's published policies and guidelines on the issue and offer of securities outline how approval is granted and administered. Legal sanctions exist for any breach of these administrative requirements. The SC has the following functions:

- to advise the Minister of Finance on all matters relating to the securities and futures contracts industries;
- to regulate the issue of securities;
- to regulate the designation of futures contracts;

- to regulate take-overs and mergers of companies;
- to regulate all matters relating to unit trust schemes;
- to be responsible for supervising and monitoring the activities of any exchange, clearing house and central depository;
- to take all reasonable measures to safeguard the interests of persons dealing in securities or trading in futures contracts;
- to promote and encourage proper conduct amongst members of the exchanges and all registered persons;
- to suppress illegal, dishonourable and improper practices in dealing in securities, trading in futures contracts and provision of investment advice or other services relating to securities or futures contracts;
- to consider and suggest reforms of the law relating to securities or futures contracts including changes to the constitution, rules and regulations of any exchange and its clearing house;
- to encourage the development of securities and futures markets in Malaysia; and
- to perform any functions conferred by or under any other Act.

The Commissioners of the SC comprise an executive chairman, four government representatives and four Ministry of Finance (MOF) appointees. The TOP has also been abolished, with the SC taking over the functions of administering the Take-Over and Mergers Code.

In spite of the establishment of the SC in March 1993, the regulatory structure of the securities industry continued to be fragmented. For example, both the ROC and SC share concurrent jurisdiction in respect of regulation of the securities industry. The ROC was given the principal enforcement role in both the Securities Industry Act, 1983 and the Securities Industry (Central Depositories) Act, 1991. The SC was given an investigation role under the Securities Commission Act, 1993 as regards compliance with the Securities Industry Act, 1983 and Securities Industry (Central Depositories) Act, 1991.[24]

Futures Market

With the collapse of commodity prices in the mid-1980s, the Government saw fit to revamp the regulation of commodities trading in the country. The Commodities Trading Commission (CTC) was established under the Commodities Trading Act, 1985 (CTA) as the regulatory authority responsible for the regulation and supervision of the commodity futures industry in Malaysia. The CTA provides that the CTC shall, with the Minister's approval, appoint a Commissioner of Commodities Trading (CCT), who is primarily responsible for enforcing the provisions of the Act and the general administration of the CTC. The jurisdiction of the Act is restricted to futures markets for physical commodities like palm oil, rubber and tin. Futures contracts based on financial instruments, currencies, bonds share indices and other derivative products are outside the purview of the CTA.

Under the Futures Industry Act, 1993, the SC was the single regulatory and enforcement authority for the futures industry, with the exception of the function of licensing market intermediaries, which remained with the ·Licensing Officer under the Ministry of Finance. In his 1996 Budget speech, the Minister of Finance announced the Government's plan to further rationalize the regulatory framework for futures market through amendments to the Securities Commission Act, 1993 and the Futures Industry Act, 1993 to centralize regulation of all futures markets, including the commodities futures market, in the SC. With this, the CTC was abolished.

Extensive amendments were made in 1995 to the Futures Industry Act, 1993. The amendments sought to re-define the concept of futures contracts to clarify its scope. They also facilitated changes in the regulatory structure by transferring the duty to licence intermediaries from the Licensing Officer in the Ministry of Finance to the SC. Changes were also aimed at minimizing legal risks. For example, futures contracts traded on organized exchanges were freed from the threat of illegality under gaming and wagering laws.

Regulatory Reforms

One reason for continuing fragmentation of the regulatory structure might have been the desire to avoid market disruptions by transferring all regulatory functions from the relevant authorities to the SC upon its establishment in 1993.[25] Hence, in 1995, a series of amendments were made to the Securities Commission Act, 1993, the Securities Industry Act, 1983, and the Securities Industry (Central Depositories) Act, 1991 in order to rationalize the regulatory structure. Effective 1 March 1996, the SC became the primary regulatory and enforcement agency over the securities industry.

Areas of regulatory overlap continued. The Registrar of Companies continued to approve prospectuses for any issuance of securities, with the exception of unit trusts (which were transferred to the SC in 1996). The framework for the regulation of private debt securities continues to be shared among the central bank, the SC and the Registrar of Companies.

From its inception, the SC saw itself playing a catalytic role in developing the securities industry. By 1995, it had submitted fundamental and extensive proposals for reform to form the basis of a "modern, flexible yet protective capital market system in the country to enhance its contribution to achieving national economic objectives" (see Securities Commission, *Annual Report 1994*: Chairman's Statement). These reform proposals were intended to:

- provide flexibility in the regulation of capital market activities;
- facilitate a transition from a merit based system to a regulatory system based on timely, accurate and full disclosure of information to investors; increase investor protection and systemic stability; and
- clarify the regulatory framework in terms of the role of the SC, Minister of Finance and market institutions.

By 1996, the move to make Kuala Lumpur a regional capital market centre took shape with official initiatives.[26] Malaysia's political and economic stability, high national savings rate and large domestic investor base were seen as internal strengths to make this a credible objective. The thrust of efforts to meet this objective could be broadly categorized into the following: developing the fund management industry; increasing the liquidity and diversity of Malaysian capital markets, and strengthening the regulatory infrastructure and market microstructures. All these were seen as important pre-requisites to developing a capital market centre.

The mid-1990s' period from 1993 to 1997 saw significant changes in regulation to try to establish the Kuala Lumpur bourse as a regional capital market centre. In meeting this objective, the focus has been on strengthening a number of regulatory foundations — the principles and practices of full disclosure, effective investor protection, greater market efficiency and credible frontline regulation. Key initiatives in this context included the following.

Shift to Disclosure-Based System

The principal thrust of the regulatory framework for the public offering of securities in 1993 was merit-based. Any issue or offer of new securities to the public was subjected to a review of its investment merit by the SC, which might prohibit a public offer of such securities if it was judged not to be fair, just or equitable. Under this regime, the SC was inclined to be more conservative in its judgement and would generally not permit high risk or speculative securities offerings. At the same time, investors took for granted the assessment done by the SC and did not themselves seek to evaluate the risks of investing in the offerings based on information disclosed to them.

A disclosure-based regulatory environment is one in which access to the public securities market for issuers is conditional on providing full and accurate disclosure of all relevant information that would enable an investor to make informed investment decisions. The focus of regulation in this environment lies in ensuring that appropriate standards of disclosure are complied with. It imposes a heavier responsibility on issuers and advisers in respect of the accuracy and completeness of information disclosed by them. Amendments were made to the Securities Commission Act, 1993 in 1995 to reflect this change. A duty to act with "due diligence" was introduced to apply to the issuer, its officers and experts when submitting information to the SC. The SC undertook a phased approach in making this fundamental shift. It envisages achieving a full disclosure-based regulatory environment by the year 2001.

Strengthening Financial Reporting

The focus on enhancing the quality of disclosure was not a narrow technical objective applying only to the offer of securities. The SC also initiated what eventually led to a formal review of the framework for setting accounting standards in Malaysia. Its efforts culminated in the passing of legislation, the Financial Reporting Act, 1997 which came into force on 6 March, establishing the Financial Reporting Foundation and the Malaysian Accounting Standards Board (MASB). Until then, standards had been set by the accounting profession since 1958. The Malaysian Institute of Accountants (MIA) and the Malaysian Association of Certified Public Accountants (MACPA) each issued standards for compliance by its respective members. Through their internal disciplinary procedures, each ensured that members complied with accounting standards.

However, the accounting bodies have no legal authority to ensure compliance and support by persons outside the accounting profession. For instance, they would not be able to ensure that company directors who are non-members comply with these standards. The new framework ensures wider acceptance and compliance with financial reporting standards. It applies to users (banks, investors and shareholders), preparers, auditors and regulatory authorities, and provides for their participation in the development and setting of standards. Under the Act, the Financial Reporting Foundation functions as the organization overseeing standard setting, while the MASB is charged with actually issuing, approving and reviewing the standards.

Front Line Regulator

The other aspect of capital market regulation the SC has embarked upon relies on front line regulators (FLRs) to regulate or police the market. FLRs are market institutions offering quotation and trading, clearing and settlement, and depository facilities. The idea is that given the greater interaction between the FLR and third parties (typically, the public investor), they have a very significant role, not only as market operators, but also in investor protection. Therefore, apart from offering the operating environment, they have to be equally serious about surveillance, audit and examination, and reporting to the statutory authority in the public interest and for investor protection. This expectation of credible frontline regulation is viewed as a critical component of both market development and investor protection. The·KLSE would be the pilot project for this initiative.

Widening Enforcement Options through Civil Enforcement Provisions

A new section 52B was introduced by the Futures Industry Amendment Act to allow an investor, who has suffered loss by relying on a recommendation made by an intermediary that is without reasonable basis, to claim damages from that intermediary. New powers were also introduced to allow an aggrieved person, an exchange, a clearing house or the SC to apply to Court for an order compelling compliance or enforcement of the Act, regulations or business rules of the Exchanges. These provisions would pave the way for the introduction of similar provisions in other securities legislation.

Establishment of Derivative Exchanges

It was felt that the capital market had to develop a greater variety of products to meet the hedging requirements of sophisticated investors, local and foreign. Two financial futures exchanges were approved during this period — the Kuala Lumpur Options and Financial Futures Exchange (KLOFFE), launched in December 1995, and the Malaysian Monetary Exchange (MME), launched in May 1996. The Malaysian Derivatives Clearing House was established to provide clearing-house facilities for KLOFFE and the MME.[27] In this connection, on 13 December 1995, the Guidelines on Securities Lending and Borrowing were introduced to improve settlement efficiency in the securities market and to facilitate development of the financial derivatives market.

Fund Management

Fund management was identified as a critical component in the institutional-ization and professionalization of the market, and successful growth was believed to be dependent on becoming a regional capital market centre. A vibrant fund management industry would boost the capital market by injecting liquidity into the domestic market; introducing higher standards of professionalism in the markets, while ensuring efficient mobilization of domestic savings to fund corporate growth and fuel economic expansion. As Malaysia has a high level of public interest in the stock market, this would increase the liquidity of capital markets through institutional investment vehicles. The SC identified the de-regulation of institutional funds as a key strategy for developing the fund management industry, by having a portion of their funds managed by external fund managers.

On 22 June 1995, the Minister of Finance announced a package of liberalizing measures for the fund management industry. It was announced, in particular, that eligible Employees Provident Fund (EPF) account holders would be allowed to transfer part of their funds in their old age accounts to unit trust funds and external fund managers. The Government also allowed foreign fund management companies (FFMCs), with at least 30 per cent local equity, to manage local institutional funds. This was a policy taken consciously by the Government after balancing the need to liberalize the fund management industry with the obligation to ensure that liberalization is properly managed so as not to adversely affect the development of the nascent local fund management industry.[28]

Market Infrastructure

Many aspects of a market's micro-structure can make a difference in the competition to achieve regional capital market centre status. Clearing, settlement, custodial and registration arrangements have to be more assured and faster than in competing markets. In 1991, the KLSE launched the central depository system (CDS). Basically, the CDS immobilizes scrips by being a super custodian centralizing the holding and handling of securities scrips. The CDS works on a book entry system as a means of representing ownership and movements in securities. In December 1996, the KLSE completed the first phase of conversion from a scrip-based system to a central depository system, when the ordinary shares of all listed companies traded on the Exchange were transferred to the CDS. Phase 2 would see the conversion of non-equity instruments, such as debentures and warrants, to the CDS.

With completion of the immobilization exercise, the SC moved to improve local clearance and settlement practices by shortening the settlement cycle to T+5. The primary objective was to shorten the delay between the trade date and the settlement date, to reduce credit risk, and to minimize exposure for the clearing entity as well as for market participants. It was also the intention to move closer to implementation of the G30 recommendation of T+3 final settlement. This change was to be introduced in phases, starting with closing the mismatch between the time for the buyer to pay and for the seller to transfer his securities to achieve same day funds on T+5. The new T+5 rolling settlement system was successfully launched in August 1997. Soon after, the settlement period was reduced to T+3.

Developments during 1997–2003

1997 saw further developments in the equities market including milestone events like the establishment of the Malaysian Exchange of Securities Dealing and Automated Quotation (MESDAQ), legislative changes to provide for share buy-backs by public listed companies and the release of guidelines to provide for foreign listings on the Exchange. But 1997 will perhaps be better remembered as the year of currency and market turmoil in Asia, which saw steep depreciation of the ringgit, and the market capitalization of the KLSE wiped out by about half from the RM807 billion registered at the beginning of the year, while the KLSE composite index (KLCI) plunged some 60 per cent from about 1200 points. A number of key events compounded the dire situation the market was in.

The "designation" of the KLCI stock at the end of August 1997 resulted in a massive sell-down in the stock market. This effectively restricted dealings in securities to a delivery before sale basis. Additionally, 100 per cent payment was required before a purchase contract was entered into.[29] The move to "designate" stocks gave the perception that it was intended to victimize foreign institutional investors who traded most actively in these counters. The decision to impose designated trading restrictions on stocks was made with the intention to inhibit short selling of composite index stocks. The announcement of designation was made late on 27 August 1997 and was to be effective from the start of the next trading day. There was a strong feeling that the KLSE should have forewarned market players. The decision to designate was subsequently reversed on 5 September 1997.

Another decision was to prohibit regulated short-selling and securities borrowing and lending (SBL). SBL was introduced in 1995 in tandem with regulated short selling (RSS) as part of the efforts to develop the depth and breadth of the capital market. SBL was also considered necessary for market making activity for individual stocks to ensure liquidity on MESDAQ. Several broking companies had been approved to carry out SBL activities. However, after concerns were expressed about RSS and SBL, and their role in facilitating manipulation of the ringgit, both were suspended shortly after the announcement of the designation of the 100 composite index stocks (Wong Sulong, 1997).[30]

In November 1997, UEM Berhad (a public listed company) announced that it had purchased a 32.6 per cent stake in Renong Berhad, an event which rocked confidence in the KLSE as no other single corporate event did in the market crisis of 1997. The acquisition was perceived as a bail-out of a cash-starved company and its major shareholders by a healthy, financially strong company, with scant regard for UEM minority shareholders' interests. UEM and its concert parties had been granted a waiver from having to make a mandatory general offer (MGO) for the remaining shares in Renong by the Foreign Investment Committee (FIC) under Rule 34.2 of the Code on Takeovers and Mergers.

The waiver had ostensibly been granted on grounds of "national interest". This was followed by immense confusion about the conditions of the waiver, and whether it had been withdrawn.[31] After a number of conflicting official statements, as well as much confusion, the Government decided to exempt UEM from making the MGO despite its breach of conditions attached to the waiver. The reinstatement of the waiver gave rise to dissatisfaction that the Government was changing the rules again to accommodate the needs of a particular company and its controlling shareholders, despite the negative implications for UEM minority shareholders' rights This was followed by a massive sell-down of the KLSE, which saw the composite index fall by 16 per cent from 17 to 21 November.

On 31 August 1998, the KLSE announced eight measures to bring offshore trading of Malaysian equities back to the KLSE. Among others, they require all dealings in securities listed on the KLSE to be effected through the KLSE or a stock exchange recognized by the KLSE. A Malaysian brokerage also shall not deal in securities on behalf of a client if it has reason to believe that the transaction is intended to facilitate the dealing in the securities on a bourse not recognized by the KLSE. This effectively brought an end to trading of KLSE-listed Malaysian securities on the Central Limit Order Book (CLOB), the over the counter market operating in Singapore.[32] This meant that investors who had been using CLOB International would have no choice but to use Malaysian stock-broking houses.[33] To add to the woes of CLOB investors, on 14 September 1999, KLSE made a further announcement that from 16 September onwards that "all Malaysian shares held in the CDS accounts of stock-broking companies and custodians acting as agents to facilitate trading on CLOB[34] will no longer be good for all CDS transactions until the migration process of CLOB shares to the KLSE have been formalized and effected."[35]

In other words, all shares registered with the Malaysian Central Depository (MCD) through Singapore's Central Depositary (CDP) (regardless whether they had been bought on CLOB International) were to remain frozen until further notice. This effectively meant that shares held in omnibus or nominee accounts of Malaysian brokers on behalf of their Singapore counterparts could not be transferred or sold until further notice. This move was perceived by the market as a means of ensuring that CLOB investors did not dump the shares and thus drive market prices down. There were suggestions that what should have been a simple process of lodging the names of beneficial owners of CLOB shares in

MCD "had become hostage to a larger issue of Malaysia's efforts to boost its economy by throwing a wall around its currency and stock market".[36]

These actions of the Government in the early stages of the crisis gave rise to concerns about the Government changing rules midstream or changing its policies without adequate notice to investors and the market. Additionally, there existed the perception that majority shareholders with close ties to the Government were shielded from the discipline of the markets, even when their actions were at the expense of minority shareholder rights. The regulatory authorities were subject to severe criticism over lack of transparency and insufficiency in the protection on investor interest. Their autonomy and commitment to enforce laws without interference, fear or favour were questioned.

Progress towards full disclosure-based regulation in the primary markets was also halted. The crisis brought into focus inadequacies in other areas critical to fully establishing such a regime. The most important being a level of corporate governance that would give confidence that a company is professionally and well managed, in the interest of all its shareholders. It was also felt that the ethic of full and timely disclosures — a cornerstone of disclosure-based regulation was not sufficiently established. Additionally, on 5 December 1997, the Minister of Finance announced a package of economic measures which included a constriction on capital raising activities which implied the reintroduction of regulatory merit determination, until the liquidity crunch was over.

Regulatory Reforms

Against this backdrop, efforts were taken to strengthen the regulatory framework. Restoring market confidence was identified as a critical pre-requisite to economic recovery. Key initiatives in this context include corporate governance reforms, amendments to the listing requirements of the stock exchange, laws to require higher standards of disclosure, measures to strengthen the broking industry and stepping up the enforcement capacity of the regulators. The crisis had also highlighted the need for a more rationalized regulatory structure and considerable success was achieved, particularly with respect to the securities issuance process.

Corporate Governance Reforms

After Western conventional wisdom successfully blamed poor corporate governance for the 1997–98 East Asia financial crises, the Malaysian Government sought to regain international credibility despite its early September 1998 policy measures by joining the bandwagon that good corporate governance is necessary to bolster investor confidence and the economy generally. Accordingly, in 1998, the Minister of Finance announced the formation of a high level committee to look into the establishment of a corporate governance framework for Malaysia and to set a series of "best practice" standards for the country. The efforts of that committee, called the High Level Finance Committee, resulted in the February 1999 publication of the Finance Committee *Report on Corporate Governance*. The findings and recommendations of the Finance Committee are being implemented through measures undertaken by the regulatory bodies, principally, the SC, the Companies Commission and the KLSE.

A significant development in Malaysia's corporate governance framework has been the issuance of the Malaysian Code on Corporate Governance (The Code) in 2000. The Code sets out prescriptions on board composition, procedures for recruiting new directors, and remuneration of directors. And while compliance with the Code is not mandated, the listing requirements of the KLSE strengthen the impact of the Code by requiring certain mandatory disclosures. Directors are required to disclose the following:

- Extent of Code compliance and reasons for non-compliance;
- Decision to combine roles of Chairman and CEO
- Results of annual review of the mix of skills and experience on the board;
- Number of board meetings and attendance;
- Directors remuneration in the annual report and membership of the remuneration committee; and
- Activities of the audit committee, number of meetings and attendance.

The 2002 Corporate Governance Survey by the KLSE and Price Waterhouse Coopers showed that over 80 per cent of respondents to the survey found that Malaysia's corporate governance practices had improved since the issuance of the Code.

The KLSE introduced its revamped listing requirements in January 2001. It brought into effect the recommendations of the Finance Committee. New provisions on internal controls, independent directors and financial reporting, to name a few, were introduced. Where investors are most concerned with corporate governance is the extent to which related party transactions have been effected. Thus to safeguard minority shareholders' interests, the KLSE listing requirements were tightened in 1998, now reflected in the revamped listing requirements to:

- Widen the scope of related party transactions to include transactions between listed companies and persons connected to a directors or substantial shareholder;

- Increase the level of information provided in any related party transaction;
- Prohibit a director, substantial shareholder or any person connected to the director or substantial shareholder with any interest in a transaction from voting in any resolution to approve such a transaction; and
- Require a listed company to appoint an independent corporate adviser to advise shareholders on the transaction.

A new Malaysian Code on Takeovers and Mergers, 1998 came into force on 1 January 1999, replacing the 1987 Code. The new Code clearly establishes the SC as its sole authority and regulator. Transparency has been enhanced in the administration of the provisions of the Code and its practice notes, especially in the granting of waivers from the obligation to make a general offer. The Code subjects the exemptive powers conferred on the SC to a clear and transparent criteria as set out in subsection 33A (5) Securities Commission Act, 1993.

Disclosure Framework

There have been significant changes to the financial reporting framework. Quarterly reporting (comprising income statement, balance sheet and explanatory notes including segmental reporting by business activity and geographical location, off balance sheet risks and breakdown of loans by foreign currencies) was made mandatory for all listed companies with financial years ending 1 July 1999. Malaysia is one of the few countries in Asia that enforces quarterly reporting requirements. The period for issue of annual audited accounts has also been reduced. The accounts have to be issued within four months of the financial year's end, instead of six months.

Enhancements to the disclosure framework, have also involved amendment to securities laws. In particular, steps have been taken to achieve transparency of share ownership. Amendments to the Securities Industry Central Depositories Act, 1991 in October 1998 prohibit persons from hiding behind nominee accounts. The amended provisions introduced the concept of an authorized nominee, prohibited global accounts (an authorized nominee may only hold securities for one beneficial owner in respect of each account) and required a beneficial owner of securities to make a declaration that he is the beneficial owner of securities.

The crisis had highlighted weaknesses in the stock broking industry, such as a lack of risk management and compliance with prudential standards. New risk based, capital adequacy requirements were introduced to replace the minimum liquid funds requirements. Additionally, the SC initiated a consolidation policy — i.e. its Policy Framework for the Consolidation of the Stock Broking Industry announced in April 2000 — whereby smaller brokerages would be absorbed by larger ones so as to produce stronger well-capitalized players to withstand the challenges of globalization and liberalization. This policy was adopted by the CMP.

The Securities Commission (Amendment) Act, 2000, which came into effect in July 2000, made far reaching changes in the regulatory framework for fund-raising activities in Malaysia. Very broadly, it positions the SC as the sole regulator of such activities. The amendments mandate the SC as the approving and registering authority for prospectuses in respect of all securities (other than shares and debentures issued by unlisted recreational clubs).[37] This is a critical move in promoting efficiency in the capital raising process.

These reforms also open up significant new opportunities for issuers, in terms of allowing greater variety and innovation in their fund-raising activities. The advertising provisions, for example, seek to provide for a wider range of information that can be contained in post-prospectus advertisements. Preliminary or red herring prospectuses are now allowed thus facilitating the book building process for issuers. Registration and filing fees have also been reduced in order to facilitate the issuers' needs for cost efficient means of raising capital.

In August 1999, the SC was installed as the single regulatory authority for the supervision and regulation of the corporate bond market in Malaysia. Amendments to the SCA introduced a new issuance process for the corporate bond market. The new issuance process is said to be more market driven and efficient. For instance, under the SC's Private Debt Securities (PDS) Guidelines, there is now no mandatory requirement for minimum credit rating, underwriting or minimum shareholders' funds.

With respect to the SC, amendments were made to the Securities Industry Act, 1983 and the Securities Commission Act, 1993 in 1998 and in 2000, to enhance its investigative and enforcement powers, and to increase penalties for greater compliance. The Securities Industry (Compliance with Approved Accounting Standards) Regulations, 1999, empower the SC to enforce compliance with accounting standards by public listed companies. Amendments to the insider trading provisions in the SIA in 1998, give the SC the power to bring a civil action against an offender for disgorgement of up to three times the profit made by the offender, or a civil penalty of not more than RM500,000. Other amendments in 1998 also give the SC greater clout to deal with directors and chief executives of public listed companies. Notably section 99C of the Securities Industry Act, 1983 gives the SC the power to seek the removal of a director from the High Court where the director has been declared bankrupt, has contravened provisions of securities laws or has been convicted of a criminal offence.

Two very senior Deputy Public Prosecutors from the Attorney General's Chambers were seconded to the SC. There is noticeable increase in the number of prosecutions. The prosecutions have more than doubled over the period of 1999–2002 when compared to the six-year period from 1993–98. Section 11 SIA was amended to empower the KLSE to enforce its rules against any person who is under an obligation to comply with the listing requirements of the Exchange. This essentially means that the KLSE is able to enforce its rules not only against the listed companies but also their directors and substantial shareholders. Under section 11, the KLSE may direct the person in default to comply with laws, issue a reprimand or impose a monetary penalty. The maximum penalty that may be imposed by the Exchange was increased in November 1998 from RM250,000 to one million ringgit. The continuing challenge for the regulators is to forcefully address any scepticism about their ability to enforce laws consistently and without interference.

Amendments to securities laws have also sought to ensure effective avenues for investors to enforce their rights. For instance, the Securities Commission (Amendment) Act, 2000 introduced a new civil remedy enabling investors to recover loss or damage arising from false or misleading information contained in a prospectus.[38]

Capital Market Master Plan (CMP)

Concurrently with these efforts, it was felt that what was lacking is a comprehensive yet systematic approach toward the development of the capital market and its components. New information technology, globalization and demographic changes are also giving rise to new opportunities and challenges in the Malaysian capital market. The need to address the lingering effects of the regional financial crisis, particularly the slow recovery of the capital market's regional and competitive position, was also identified. The Capital Market Advisory Council (CMAC) was established in March 2001 to provide independent strategic advice to facilitate the implementation of the CMP.

The principal goal in this area is to enhance the efficiency of the fundraising environment so as to ensure that the Malaysian capital market can be accessed on internationally competitive terms, particularly in terms of cost, capital and regulatory processes. In May 2003, the SC announced the entry into the final phase of its move from a merit-based to a disclosure-based regulatory system. Among others, the processing time for initial public offerings has been reduced from six to eight months to three months. The involvement of multiple approving authorities in the fund raising process has been further rationalized with the Foreign Investment Committee (FIC) aspects of corporate proposals being processed by the SC.

The CMP strongly recommended transforming the Malaysian capital market institutions towards having a single Malaysian exchange. This has led to the consolidation of the various market institutions — the Kuala Lumpur Options and Futures Exchange (KLOFFE), Commodity and Monetary Exchange of Malaysia (COMEX), MESDAQ as well as the Malaysian Derivatives Clearing House (MDCH) within the KLSE Group. Consolidation, the CMP argues, will allow for greater economies of scale and scope, the pooling of resources, greater distribution reach and a more diversified product and revenue base. A single exchange, which is demutualized and listed, would also be in a better position to pursue international strategic alliances as part of the long-term strategy to attract critical mass, market liquidity and relevant expertise to the capital market. With the passing of the Demutualization Act, 2004, by Parliament, the Kuala Lumpur Stock Exchange was converted from a mutual organization to a for profit public company in 2005.

The CMP recommends strengthening the regulatory regime to ensure timely and impartial enforcement of laws, with sufficiently deterrent penalties. Among other things, efforts towards more effective enforcement should ensure that appropriate mechanisms for investor redress and dispute resolution exist that can minimize enforcement cost and delays, and enhance the investigative and enforcement capacity of the SC.

Malaysian Bond Market

The Malaysian domestic bond market experienced significant growth after the 1997–98 financial crisis, partly due to the adoption of various measures to boost issuance activities. Some of the early catalysts involved the very agencies responsible for resolving the worst excesses of the crisis. The funding needs of both Danaharta (the national asset management company) and Danamodal (the bank recapitalization agency) were met by bond issuance. Both Danaharta and Danamodal have wound down their operations.

Coming out of the crisis, Malaysia saw an increase in the disintermediation of investment grade credits from bank lending to domestic currency debt capital markets, as well as a significant shift from non-ringgit funding to domestic currency funding. The large domestic savings pool negated the need to raise foreign exchange funding, so the majority of financially-distressed companies financed their restructuring needs in ringgit.

Although the debt markets remain small relative to the banking system, they have been growing in absolute terms, and efforts are underway to encourage their further development. In just over a decade from 1988 to 1999, the total ringgit bond market grew from RM59.1 billion to RM201.5 billion. Private sector bonds to date recorded the most phenomenal growth with the outstanding amount as at 31 December 2005 of 207 billion ringgit, representing 42 per cent of GDP. Total outstanding bonds, including public sector and private sector bonds, are estimated to be over 80 per cent of GDP for the financial year end 2006. For the future, the Government is intent on developing a more diversified financial system to support a more diversified and industrialized economy. The capital markets are viewed as key to this end.

There are three government agencies regulating the bond market in Malaysia. In July 2000, the Securities Commission (hereafter "SC") was mandated as the single authority in Malaysia entrusted with responsibility for regulating and developing the capital market. The SC's regulatory functions include: approving the issuance of Private Debt Securities (hereafter "PDS") and regulating, licensing and supervising all licensed persons and market institutions including disclosure rules. The Ministry of Finance (hereafter "MOF") has authority over some of the laws related to the securities market (especially on taxation). Bank Negara Malaysia (hereafter "BNM") monitors licensed institutions (commercial banks, finance companies, merchant banks, discount houses and money brokers) to ensure monetary stability and financial structure prudence. In view of the fragmented regulatory structure, close policy coordination is required among the SC, MOF and BNM. To this end, the National Bond Market Committee was established in June 1999 to provide policy direction and to rationalize the regulatory framework for the development of the bond market. Major issues on the bond market are discussed at the National Bond Market Committee, now chaired by the Second Minister of Finance. Membership of the relevant government agencies and authorities facilitated the development of holistic policies and eased implementation of specific action plans. The work of the NBMC paved the way for the formulation of a clear framework and strategy for the long-term direction of the corporate bond market. This was provided in the Capital Market Master Plan (CMP) released in 2001.

An early priority identified during the formulation of the CMP was the need for more streamlined regulation of the corporate bond issuance process. At that point, the time to market for bond issues varied from nine to 12 months. Issuers generally faced the uncertainty of not knowing when their corporate bond issue proposals would be approved or rejected. In view of this, the government accelerated reform of the issuance process by centralizing the regulation of the corporate bond market with the SC on 1 July 2000. Amendments to the SCA established the SC as the sole approving and registering authority for prospectuses in respect of all securities other than shares and debentures issued by unlisted recreational clubs. The centralization of responsibilities with a single authority, the SC, allowed for greater focus on the development of the facilitative regulatory framework needed to address the urgent funding needs of the private sector, as well as to enhance liquidity in the secondary bond market.

An important part of these efforts was the introduction of the *Guidelines on the Offering of Private Debt Securities* ("PDS Guidelines"), which also came into effect on 1 July 2000 and played an important role in significantly streamlining the issuance process. A post-vetting system of approval was introduced, whereby the issuer and the principal adviser needed only to file a declaration of compliance with the PDS Guidelines in order to secure an approval from the SC within 14 working days. The guidelines substantially liberalized private debt securities issuance requirements, and facilitated the speedier approval of proposed bond issues. These provisions included, for example, waivers of the mandatory underwriting requirement and the minimum issuer's shareholders' funds requirement, thus enabling issuers to enjoy greater savings in both cost and time. The PDS Guidelines also introduced waivers of the minimum credit rating requirements to further facilitate issuance activity.

Another key change was in relation to the requirements for commercial paper (CP) and medium-term note (MTN) programme, which had until then been restricted to a maximum tenure of seven years. This restriction was removed, thus giving issuers the flexibility to go up to 10–20 years if they desired standalone MTN programmes. For all debt programmes, irrespective of whether CPs are issued, the SC also allows a two-year period for issuers to implement the programme. This is meant to aid issuers in providing them sufficient flexibility in terms of time-to-market. To enhance the transparency of such programmes, the SC requires disclosure on the terms of the issue prior to each drawdown to aid investors in their investment decisions. Legislative changes were also made to the Securities Commission Act, 1993, facilitating the introduction of a shelf-registration scheme for bonds, whereby eligible corporations could make multiple issues of debt securities within a two-year period with just a once-off approval, subject to certain criteria. Thus, issuers could obtain additional flexibility in determining the timing of their issues.

A key thrust of the developmental agenda was to widen the bond market's product range to suit diverse risk-reward profiles and needs across the spectrum of investors and issuers in the Malaysian capital market. The growing demand for Islamic bond issues in recent years, for instance, encouraged many corporate bodies to raise new funds through the issuance of Islamic bonds using *Shari'a* principles. The inception of the asset-backed securities (ABS) market was also a significant milestone. In April 2001, the SC introduced the *Guidelines on the Offering of Asset-backed Debt Securities* (ABS Guidelines) to facilitate the development of asset securitization in the Malaysian market. Applying a disclosure-based approach, the ABS Guidelines set out clear requirements for offering any asset-backed debt securities. A faster issuance process was also provided for: the maximum approval time taken by the SC for such proposals would be 28 working days. These measures were warmly welcomed by market participants.

Over the period April 2001–June 2003, the SC approved 13 ABS issues valued at around RM7 billion. Improvements in the tax treatment of ABS also helped create a more conducive environment for their issuance. A tax-neutral framework for securitization transactions was announced in Budget 2004, with equal tax treatment given to ABS as to other conventional securities. At the same time, the government proposed that expenses incurred in the issuance of ABS also be granted tax deduction for five years. These proposals would be effective from the year of assessment 2003 onwards.

The search for alternative means of enhancing returns on investments had also seen the growing prominence of derivatives or structured products over the years. Typically more complex than investments in conventional bonds or fixed deposits, a common characteristic of such structured products was the creation of some evidence of indebtedness of an issuer to the investor by means of a contract, note or deposit. In substance, this meant that such products would come under the broad definition of "debenture" under the SCA.18 In consideration of the risk disparity between such structured products and the generic PDS approved under the PDS Guidelines, it was agreed that separate guidelines be formulated to govern the former with a "light touch", while ensuring that investors were made aware that the risks involved in investing in these products could differ substantially from conventional bonds. The SC released the *Guidelines on the Offering of Structured Products* (Structured Products Guidelines) on 10 December 2003. These guidelines effectively facilitated the issuance of structured products, tailored to the needs of sophisticated investors. The Structured Products Guidelines also contained provisions for the SC to give "blanket" approval of completed submissions, in consideration of the fact that some structured products might be less time-sensitive than others. Under this approach, issuers of such products had the flexibility of making an immediate offering or making phased offerings timed to meet the issuers' financing needs.

Tax incentives for issuance of and investment in corporate bonds con-stituted important facets of overall developmental strategy. These included, for instance, the waiver of stamp duty for all instruments relating to the issue and transfer of corporate bonds, and tax exemptions on interest income from corporate bonds (other than convertible loan stocks) received by individuals, unit trusts and listed closed-end funds. There is no capital gains tax, and interest income is exempted in many cases. Withholding tax has been eliminated since September 2004.

Tax Treatment for Bonds	
Process	*Tax Treatment*
Issuance	• No stamp duty for issuance of bonds. • For all bonds approved by BNM or SC, exempt from stamp duty. • For transfer of real estate in the case of ABS issuance, exempt from both real estate taxes and stamp duty. • For selected Islamic bonds and ABS, issuance costs are tax deductible from 2003 to 2007.
Investment	• For individuals, unit trust funds and listed closed-end funds, exempt from income tax for interest income from debentures (excluding convertible loan stocks) approved by the SC.
Trading	• No capital gains tax. Therefore, if recognized as long-term investment, capital gains and losses are exempt from taxes. Gains from trading activities are subject to income tax. • Normal corporate income tax is 28 per cent. Gains from trading activities are subject to corporate income tax.

The volume of PDS issues is growing rapidly. In 2003, new issues of PDS doubled compared to the previous year, partly due to the increase of issuance by the manufacturing sector. There are two types of PDS: KLSE listed bonds and unlisted OTC bonds. There are very few companies who list their bonds on the KLSE as most corporations prefer to issue OTC bonds. In both cases, application to the SC is required. OTC bonds are intended for sophisticated investors and institutions in the securities business such as banks. There are regulations on reselling. Since the rapid growth in 1998, issuance of PDS has become a major source of long-term financing. Major issuers of PDS in recent years belong to industries such as "manufacturing", "Transport, Storage and Communications" and "Finance, Insurance, Real Estate and Business Services". Manufacturing has increasingly become the major issuing sector, while issuances from the Transport, Storage and Communications sector remain stable. Nearly half the corporate bonds issued in 2004 (including Cagamas bonds, Islamic bonds, medium term notes, commercial papers and convertible bonds) have maturity from 6 to 10 years.

As part of the initiatives to broaden and deepen the domestic and regional bond markets in the East Asia Pacific region, the EMEAP group launched the first regional bond fund or Asian Bond Fund 1 (ABF1) in June 2003. Following the success of the US dollar ABF1, the EMEAP Central Banks launched the Asian Bond Fund 2 (ABF2) in December 2005, which is mandated to invest in bonds denominated in local currencies of selected member countries namely PR China, Hong Kong, China, Indonesia, Korea, Malaysia, Philippines, Singapore and Thailand. The ABF2 was launched with the objective of promoting the domestic currency bond market and introducing bonds of multiple currencies in a basket as a new asset class for investors. The launching of the ABF2 also led to the inaugural listing of the ABF Malaysian country sub-fund or ABF Malaysian Bond Index Fund on Bursa Malaysia, which comprised investments in ringgit-denominated Government and quasi Government securities. The listing of the ABF Malaysian Bond Index Fund (the first Exchange Traded Fund in Malaysia) would add more diversity to the listings on Bursa Malaysia and eventually add greater liquidity in the domestic bond market.

On 7 January 2005, several measures were adopted to further enhance liquidity in the bond market and improve the price discovery process. The measures were:

(i)   Repurchase agreements ("repo") were allowed to be actively used as a monetary instrument to manage liquidity in the banking system.
(ii)   Through the Institutional Securities Custodian Programme (ISCAP), Bank Negara Malaysia would borrow securities, mainly Malaysian Government Securities (MGS), from major institutional investors, mainly the Employees' Provident Fund, for its repo operations.
(iii)   Securities lending facility for principal dealers (PDs) were enhanced to facilitate market-making activities.

On 31 March, the ringgit-denominated bonds issued by Multilateral Development Banks (MDBs) and Multilateral Financial Institutions (MFIs) were included as eligible securities to be transacted under repo operations with Bank Negara Malaysia.

Islamic Financial System

Malaysia has a broadly developed Islamic financial system with a diverse range of participants, products and institutions. The enactment of the Islamic Banking Act, 1983,[39] led to the establishment of the first Islamic commercial bank in Malaysia, namely Bank Islam Malaysia Berhad.

In 1993, with the introduction of the Interest-Free Banking Unit ("IFBU") or an Islamic "window" within existing commercial banks, the foundation for a parallel system of conventional and Islamic banking was established within the financial system. Through the IFBU, a commercial bank is able to provide Islamic banking services and facilities without having to set up a separate legal entity or a subsidiary to conduct these activities.

The Islamic inter-bank money market was introduced in 1994 with the issuance of Government Investment Certificates ("GICs").[40] The issuance of GICs was originally based on the Islamic concept of *qardhu hasan* (benevolent loan) which did not permit secondary trading of these instruments. In *qardhu hasan*, the purchase of GICs by any person will be considered as a benevolent loan to the Malaysian government to undertake development projects for the benefit of the nation. The government is obliged to return the principal amount to the providers of funds upon maturity. The *qardhu hasan* contract does not specify any upfront returns; thus, any returns are at the absolute discretion of the government (Saiful, 2005). In June 2001, an alternative concept of GICs, based on *bai'al-'ilnah*, was introduced (Saiful, 2005), which facilitated the trading of GICs in the secondary market. Under the arrangement, the government will sell its identified assets at an agreed cash price to the buyer and subsequently buy back the same assets at an agreed purchase price to be settled at a specified future date. The difference between the selling price and the purchase price represents the profit of the investors (Saiful, 2005).

In 2003, the Central Bank of Malaysia Act, 1958 was amended to facilitate the establishment of a *Shari'a* Advisory Council[41] that advises the Central Bank on all matters relating to *Shari'a*-based financial business regulated by the Central Bank. The Council rulings are given effect by the Central Bank in respect of transactions and business carried on by banks and financial institutions.

In the early stages of the development of the Islamic financial system in Malaysia, the capital market played a relatively minor role as the Islamic banking system had provided the financing needs for Islamic economic activities. In the 1990s, with the impetus given by the corporatization and privatization policy, more companies and enterprises began to raise funds from the capital market to finance their economic activities. At the same time, with the introduction of *Shari'a*-approved securities on the Kuala Lumpur Stock Exchange,[42] investors started to invest in these securities through market intermediaries that operate in accordance with *Shari'a* principles.

In 1982, a Task Force to study the establishment of an Islamic insurance company in Malaysia was established, leading to the enactment of the Takaful Act, 1984, and the setting up of the first *takaful* operator, Syarikat Takaful Malaysia Sdn Bhd in November 1984.[43] In conformity with *Shari'a* principles, the operation of *takaful* in Malaysia was confined within the *tijari* or private sector, based on the Islamic principles of *takaful, mudarabah* and *tabarru'*.[44] The legislation provides that the articles of association of a *takaful* operator must have a provision for the establishment of an internal *Shari'a* supervisory council which should advise the *takaful* operator on its *takaful* operations and ensure that the *takaful* operator is not involved in any elements contrary to the *Shari'a*. The central bank (which is the regulator of the insurance industry) relies on the rulings of the *Shari'a* Advisory Council established under section 16B of the Central Bank of Malaysia Act, 1958 (revised 1994) (Saiful, 2005).

The need to mobilize Islamic banking and *takaful* funds effectively and efficiently in order to enhance liquidity management in these sectors has driven innovation in Islamic capital market products and services and has contributed to the ability of the Islamic financial services industry to operate as a complete system, similar to the conventional system where the capital market provides depth and liquidity to the system. In recognition of the expertise required to adjudicate disputes in respect of Islamic transactions, a dedicated division within the High Court was established in 2004.

Islamic Equity Market

By determining the *Shari'a* compliance status of listed securities, the *Shari'a* compliance framework has become pivotal in influencing the development and growth of Malaysia's Islamic equity market. A *Shari'a* Advisory Council ("SAC") was established in 1996, pursuant to section 18 of the Securities Commission Act 1993,[45] to act as a reference centre at the national level on all matters pertaining to the *Shari'a* compliance of capital market products and services.

The SAC had developed several basic *Shari'a* compliance criteria. The criteria have been determined by reference to the Qur'an and the Sunnah as well as the general principles of *Shari'a*. In this process, the SAC focused on the core activities of companies such as the goods and services offered to their customers. Goods and services which involved the following activities are considered *Shari'a* non-compliant:

- operations based on *riba*;
- operations involving gambling;
- activities involving *haram* (forbidden by Islam) products such as liquor and pork; and
- operations containing an element of *gharar* (uncertainty).

Given the importance of providing guidance to the general public for attaining a better understanding of the Islamic capital market, the SAC's resolutions are published in a book titled *Resolutions of the Securities Commission Shari'a Advisory Council.*

Islamic Unit Trust Funds

Islamic unit trusts are regulated by the *Guidelines on Unit Trust Funds*.[46] For Islamic funds, an additional provision is provided under Chapter 6 of the Guidelines which requires the establishment of an internal *Shari'a* committee to advise the fund, the members of which may be a company or individual who must be registered with the Securities Commission of Malaysia. An Islamic unit trust fund will generally subscribe to the list of *Shari'a*-approved securities endorsed by the SAC to guide the fund in its investments. The number of units in circulation for *Shari'a*-based unit trust funds in Malaysia stood at RM18.62 billion at the end of 2000.[47] Of the 83 approved *Shari'a*-based unit trust funds, 18 were balanced funds, 15 were bond funds, 44 were equity funds,[48] three were fixed income funds and three were money market funds.

Islamic Real Estate Investment Trusts (REITs)

On 21 November 2005, the Securities Commission of Malaysia published the *Guidelines for Islamic Real Estate Investment Trusts* (Guidelines). The Guidelines were introduced to facilitate the development of new Islamic capital market products, making Malaysia the first jurisdiction in the global Islamic financial sector to issue such guidelines and setting a global benchmark for the development of Islamic real estate investment trusts (Islamic REITs). The Guidelines essentially stipulate *Shari'a* compliance criteria to guide management companies in their activities relating to an Islamic REIT, including the types of *Shari'a* permissible and non-permissible rental and investment activities for such a fund.

Islamic Intermediary Services

Islamic stock broking services are carried on under dealer licences issued under section 12 of the Securities Industry Act, 1983. To date, two Islamic stock broking companies[49] offer exclusively Islamic broking services and a few other stock broking companies offering both conventional and Islamic services. In the latter, Islamic broking services are provided through the Islamic "window" structure where Islamic broking services reside within the conventional broking entity.

Another class of Islamic intermediary services are provided by asset management companies that manage funds in accordance with *Shari'a* principles. Although this activity is fairly new in Malaysia compared to Islamic unit trusts, the interest among high net worth Muslim investors to engage professional managers to invest their funds has been increasing gradually. This is evidenced by the existence of at least four licensed asset managers under section 14 of the Securities Industry Act, 1983 that are managing individual funds in accordance with *Shari'a* principles. Typically, the investment activities carried out by these asset managers are based on the SAC list of *Shari'a*-approved securities or an equivalent list provided by the asset manager's own *Shari'a* adviser.

Tax Treatment of Islamic Transactions

Various fiscal measures have been introduced in Malaysia to encourage the use of Islamic financing instruments. These measures were aimed at ensuring that Islamic securities receive similar tax treatment to conventional instruments and addressing issues of tax uncertainties in the treatment of Islamic securities. The tax treatment of certain Islamic financial transactions is different from that for conventional financial transactions. Generally, the former is more likely to be subjected to additional tax burdens due to the different structure of the financial transactions required in the execution of specific *Shari'a* contracts.

Insurance Industry

The year 1988 witnessed a watershed in the regulatory history of the insurance sector, with the industry passing supervision to the central bank of Malaysia with effect from 1 May 1988. To effect this relocation of function, the legislations affecting the industry, namely, the Insurance Act, 1963, the Takaful Act, 1984, and the Central Bank of Malaya Ordinance, 1958 were amended accordingly. With enactment of these legislative amendments, the Governor of the central bank assumed the post of Director General of Insurance/Takaful under the respective Acts.

As a first step, the Insurance Act was also amended to enable the Director General to appoint and authorize central bank officers to inspect, under conditions of secrecy, the books, accounts and transactions of an insurer from time to time, without being required to give prior written notice to the insurer concerned. The main rationale behind the relocation was to streamline and adopt an integrated approach to supervision of the entire financial system in the country, and to realize economies of scale in regulation and supervision. The move had become more urgent with the increasing convergence of cross-holdings and integration of interests between the banks and insurance companies.

Labuan International Offshore Financial Centre

The legislation establishing Labuan as an international offshore financial centre (IOFC) was passed by Parliament in June 1990 and came into force on 1 October 1990. The new laws were:

- The Offshore Banking Act, 1990;
- The Offshore Insurance Act, 1990;

- The Offshore Companies Act, 1990;
- The Labuan Trust Companies Act, 1990;
- The Labuan Offshore Business Activity Tax Act, 1990; and
- The Income Tax (Amendment) Act, 1990.

In general, such offshore legislation is much less extensive and onerous than onshore legislation. The central bank administered the Offshore Banking Act, 1990, the Offshore Insurance Act, 1990, and matters pertaining to exchange control requirements, as stipulated in the new Exchange Control Notice, ECM 16, issued by the Controller of Foreign Exchange. The Offshore Companies Act, 1990 and the Labuan Trust Companies Act, 1990 were both administered by the office of the Registrar of Companies. The Labuan Offshore Business Activity Tax Act, 1990 and the Income Tax (Amendment) Act, 1990 are under the purview of the Inland Revenue Department.

Besides providing an attractive and balanced legislative and tax package to create a conducive regulatory and tax environment and to catalyze Labuan's take off as a viable IOFC, the Government was also committed to upgrading Labuan's infrastructure facilities to attract foreign investors and institutions. A high level committee, headed by the Chief Secretary to the Government, was formed to plan and execute programmes to cater for both the short and long-term needs of offshore investors in Labuan, including transportation, housing, recreation and health. In 1996, the Government set up a single body called the Labuan Offshore Financial Services Authority (LOFSA) with the passage of the Labuan Offshore Financial Services Act, 1996 to take over regulation and administration provided for under the Act. The Prime Minister and the Finance Minister have, on many occasions after the launch of Labuan as an IOFC, gone on international road shows to promote the IOFC.

Competition Law

To date, there is no competitions law in place. However, from time to time, discussions have been officially initiated to consider the following:

- ensuring a framework to enable the Malaysian economy to more effectively compete in the global markets;
- enabling Malaysian companies to more effectively face increasing competition from foreign companies that have come to dominate the Malaysian market;
- providing small and medium-scale industries with the same opportunities as larger industries; and
- ensuring that users are supplied with competitively-priced goods and services.

The absence of a competitions law can be attributed to government policy in wanting to encourage business growth to an optimal size, taking advantage of available economies of scale, given the small size of the Malaysian market.[50]

Notes

1. It has been said that in order to ensure that the Kuala Lumpur Stock Exchange did not "fizzle out" as a result of the split with the Stock Exchange of Singapore, the then Minister of Finance had liberalized the capital account to ensure healthy foreign portfolio flows into the Kuala Lumpur Stock Exchange.
2. The law was revised in 1996 and is now known as the Central Bank of Malaysia Act, 1959.
3. Under the consolidation policy promoted by Bank Negara Malaysia, finance companies within a banking group were required to be merged with the commercial banking entities to provide the full range of banking services. Now, there are no more finance companies in the Malaysian banking system.
4. Now, all merchant banks are required to be transformed into investment banks as a result of the merger between a merchant bank and a stock broking company, or between a stock broking company and a discount house within a financial group.
5. Discount houses were established to act as "liquidity providers" in the money market and were given the unique privilege of accepting call deposits.
6. The first Islamic bank licensed under the Islamic Banking Act, 1983 was Bank Islam Berhad. See below for more discussion of the development of the Islamic financial system.
7. This particular provision met with very strong resistance from the foreign banking community when the bill was tabled in Parliament for debate owing to fears that it was a nationalization policy in disguise. Assurances were given by the government at the highest level that nationalization would not happen, which remains the case today.
8. To stabilize the financial system in 1998, the central bank had introduced capital controls. These controls were incrementally liberalized with the most aggressive liberalization measures introduced in 2005 and 2007.
9. Very aggressive liberalization measures were announced in April 2007; some significant ones include:

    (i)   the net open position limit of licensed onshore banks, previously capped at 20 per cent of the bank's capital base, was abolished;
    (ii) all limits imposed on foreign currency accounts maintained by residents in licensed onshore banks were completely abolished;
    (iii) limits on the number of residential or commercial property loans obtained by non-residents were abolished;
    (iv) non-resident corporations may utilize proceeds from their listing of shares through IPOs abroad;

(v) limits to foreign currency borrowing by resident corporations from licensed onshore banks and non-resident banks were increased to RM100 million equivalent in aggregate;

(vi) residents may hedge their foreign currency loan repayment up to the full amount of the underlying commitment; and

(vii) limits on investment abroad in foreign currency assets by resident institutional investors were significantly increased — unit trust companies were allowed up to 50 per cent of the net asset value from the previous 30 per cent limit.

10. The average total assets and shareholders' funds per domestic commercial bank have more than doubled from RM18.1 billion as at end-1999 to RM44.9 billion as at end-2003, and from RM1.4 billion as at end-1999 to RM3.8 billion as at end-2003 respectively. Return over average assets and return on average equity of domestic banks increased from 0.7 per cent and 8.4 per cent in 2001 to 1.2 per cent and 13.4 per cent in 2003 respectively. The cost to income ratio declined from 41.2 per cent in 2001 to 40.1 per cent in 2003 (BNM *Annual Report 2003*).

11. The statutory authority is called the Malaysian Deposit Insurance Corporation or Perbadanan Insurans Deposit Malaysia.

12. The Finance Committee on Corporate Governance had in 1999 recommended extensive amendments to be made to the Companies Act, 1965 and these were done in 2007.

13. Through the Companies (Amendment) Bill, 2007, the government proposed to repeal section 132G.

14. The Companies (Amendment) Act, 1997 introduced a new section 67A which came into force on 1 September 1997.

15. The treasury stock concept is derived from the United States, where shares repurchased by a company do not have to be cancelled and may be disposed off readily. What a company may or may not do with the Treasury shares and the rights attached thereto are expressly provided by section 67A (3), Companies Act, 1965.

16. Sections 176–81, Companies Act, 1965.

17. During the financial crisis in 1997, there was intense debate on whether the US Chapter 11 bankruptcy provisions should be introduced as a modality to help rehabilitate financially distressed companies. Eventually, it was decided to maintain the existing section 176 "reconstruction model" scheme with the creditor protection provision somewhat strengthened by a 1998 legislative amendment.

18. Previously known as the Registrar of Companies.

19. This was done as a response to stem the loss of market confidence in the governance and integrity of public listed companies and the lack of enforcement initiatives by the companies regulator.

20. The Companies (Amendment) Bill, 2007, finally tabled in Parliament for approval on 8 May 2007, seeks to give effect to these proposed reforms.

21. See, for example, Sir Richard Baggalay — in *North-West Transportation Co v. Beatty* (1877) 12 AC 589 at 593 — said, *inter alia*, "…any shareholder has a perfect right to vote … although he may have a personal interest in the subject matter opposed to, or different from, the general or particular interests of the company". Similarly, Jessel M.R. — in *Pender v. Lushington* (1877) 6 Ch D 70 at 75–6 — said, "There is

if I may say so, no obligation on a shareholder of a company to give his vote merely with a view to what other persons may consider the interests of the company at large. He has a right, if he thinks fit, to give his vote from motives or promptings of what he considers his own individual interest."

22. In the Malaysian context, see Loh (1996: 94, *et seq.*).
23. The Finance Committee identifies several other respects in which there could be improvement to the provisions in the Companies Act 1965.

- In situations where statute provides for shareholder approval, the statute should make it crystal clear that *prior* approval is required. For example, section 132E of the Companies Act 1965 which allows substantial property transactions between directors and persons connected to directors to be ratified by the company at a general meeting. In substantial transactions such as that set out in section 132E, ratification is sometimes the only option for the share-holders due to costs associated with turning back or unwinding a substantial transaction. And certainly in the case of substantial transactions, the need to make speedy decisions must be balanced against protection of shareholders interests generally.

- The provisions on interested or related party transactions in the Companies Act, 1965, save for section 132G do not embrace transactions between a company and a substantial shareholder or persons connected with a substantial shareholder. Section 132E, for example, only embraces transactions between a company and directors and persons connected to the director. This is potentially a very serious omission for not all substantial shareholders sit on boards.

- The laws should be clear as to the circumstances that require shareholder approval. For example, section 132C has given rise to uncertainty as to the scope of meaning of "undertaking", "property" and "substantial value", leading to doubts as to whether in any one transaction, approval of general meeting is needful. Furthermore, it is arguable that only acquisition/disposal which materially and adversely affects the performance or financial position of the company would require the approval of the general meeting. There is ambiguity in construing in any one case whether the transaction is adverse to the company performance or financial position. Section 132E is also ambiguous as to whether it precludes the board from executing a conditional agreement given the wide language of the provision. The KLSE Listing requirements set out better defined criteria for regulation of related party transactions, which sees the introduction of tests such as the assets test, profits test, consideration tests, consideration to market capitalization test and equity or capital outlay tests. The guideline for materiality under the Companies Act 1965 should be formulated in the same manner as laid out in the KLSE rules.

The penalties for breach of the legal provisions in relation to substantial and connected party transactions should be increased. The increase may, for example, be by reference to a multiple of gains made by the offenders (as is now the case for insider trading) or by allowing investors a direct cause of action to seek full compensation for loss from offenders.

24. Altogether, there were five reform packages introduced in 1995–96, 1998, 2000, 2004 and 2007. The 2007 amendments were tabled in Parliament for debate on 9 May 2007. Discussion of some of these reforms is given below.

25. A more plausible reason would be the fact that the agencies vested with the powers would not wish to have their influence or powers taken away from them.

26. It would be fair to say that this aspiration to position Kuala Lumpur as a regional or international financial centre was shelved with the onset of the financial crisis. In 2006, the government has changed its goal to promote Malaysia as an international Islamic finance centre.

27. The derivative exchanges underwent two phases of consolidation — the first involved the merger of KLOFFE and MME as COMEX in 1998; subsequently, COMEX was absorbed into Kuala Lumpur Stock Exchange.

28. In September 2004, the Minister of Finance also announced various liberalization measures in relation to foreign fund managers, essentially allowing for 100 per cent owned foreign fund managers to be licensed in Malaysia and to be able to access domestic funds without having to demonstrate that foreign funds had been brought into Malaysia.

29. The designation of the 100 composite index stocks was made pursuant to Rule 4 of KLSE's trading rules. However it had previously been utilized where there had been inordinate trading activity on particular KLSE counters to curb speculation on the stock.

30. Regulated short selling was reintroduced in Bursa Malaysia in 2006.

31. The SC issued a press release on 4 December 1997. The waivers granted by the FIC were subject to the conditions that any intended increase in shareholdings should only be done through open market purchases, while holdings must be limited to no more than a 50 per cent equity interest in the relevant identified companies. The exemption granted did not extend to any increase in shareholdings by the relevant parties through private treaties or through corporate proposals whether announced or implemented in the future. The press release emphasized that the granting of the exemptions was intended to help improve the depressed share market at that time and to improve investors' confidence in the market. Both were said to be in the national interest. With the announcement that UEM had acquired a 32.6 per cent stake in Renong by 17 November 1997, the holdings of UEM *together with two related parties* who were deemed to be acting in concert under the Code, had in fact increased from 44.3 per cent to 76.9 per cent. There had thus been a breach of the conditions of the waiver as the three parties held more than a 50 per cent stake in Renong.

32. The Stock Exchanges of Singapore and Malaysia became separate in 1973, but Malaysian stocks continued to be listed on the SES, and vice versa, until 1990. CLOB International emerged after the Malaysian authorities withdrew the listing of all Malaysian securities on the Stock Exchange of Singapore in 1990. It was introduced to service Singapore investors wishing to trade regional stocks. There were about 112 Malaysian top quality stocks traded on CLOB out of a total of 129.

33. The Malaysian authorities justified the move on the basis that there was a mutual understanding between the Malaysian and Singaporean governments to close

CLOB. The Singaporean authorities, however, deny ever having made such an undertaking. See *BT Online*, 7 August 1998, "SES denies there is any understanding to close CLOB".

34. Under the CLOB trading system, all shares that are traded in Singapore are actually held in the nominee or omnibus accounts of individual Kuala Lumpur stock-broking companies who have MCD accounts. These Kuala Lumpur brokers are counterparts of Singapore brokers through whom CLOB transactions are being transacted. In Singapore, the transactions and shares were recorded under the individual investors' names under a book entry system with CDP.

35. Excerpt from KLSE announcement, 14 September 1998.

36. See *BT Online*, 15 September 1998, "KLSE freezes all Malaysian shares bought on CLOB", by Ven Sreenivasan.

37. Prospectuses of unlisted recreational clubs fall within the jurisdiction of the Companies Commission of Malaysia (CCM).

38. In 10 May 2007, the Parliament approved an "omnibus" Capital Market & Services Bill, 2007 which consolidates the Securities Industry Act, 1983, the Futures Industry Act, 1993 and Part IV of the Securities Commission Act, 1993.

39. The Islamic Banking Act, 1983, essentially mirrors the provisions of the Banking Act, 1973, which has since been replaced by the Banking and Financial Institutions Act, 1989. Section 2 of the Islamic Banking Act, 1983, defines "Islamic banking business" to mean any business whose aims and operations do not involve any element not approved in Islam.

40. The Government Investment Act, 1983 empowered the Government of Malaysia to issue Government Investment Certificates, an instrument similar to Government Securities (which is a domestic currency denominated sovereign bond), but with returns in the form of dividends, rather than interest. As Government Investment Certificates are regarded as liquid assets, Islamic banks may invest in the Certificates in order to comply with the prescribed liquidity requirements.

41. Section 16B of the Central Bank of Malaysia Act, 1958 (revised 1994), provides that the Central Bank may establish a *Shari'a* Advisory Council which will be the authority for the ascertaining Islamic law for the purposes of Islamic banking, *takaful*, Islamic finance, Islamic development finance, or any other business based on *Shari'a* principles and supervised and regulated by the Central Bank.

42. Now known as Bursa Malaysia Berhad following the demutualization of the Kuala Lumpur Stock Exchange pursuant to the Demutualization Act, 2003.

43. Bank Negara Malaysia, *Annual Report, 2002*.

44. *Takaful* is a pact among a group of people called participants, reciprocally guaranteeing each other against loss or damage that may befall any one of them. *Mudarabah* is a commercial profit sharing contract between the providers of funds (participants) for a business venture and an entrepreneur who agrees or undertakes to pay, thus enabling him to fulfil his obligation of actually conducting the business. *Tabarru'* refers to a sharing and co-operative relationship among policyholders. The concept of *tabarru'* eliminates the element of uncertainty in the *takaful* contract whereby death benefits are taken from a pool of funds consisting of the collective premiums of policyholders and the dividends from their interest-free investments.

45. Sub-section (1) of section 18 of the Securities Commission Act, 1996, provides that the Commission may establish such committee as it considers necessary or expedient to assist it in the performance of its functions under the Act. Under sub-section (1) of section 15 of the Act, the Commission is charged with the mandate to, among other things, "encourage and promote the development of securities and futures markets" in Malaysia.

46. Released by the Securities Commission of Malaysia and available on its website: <www.sc.com.my>.

47. Securities Commission of Malaysia, *Annual Report, 2005*, pp. 2–20.

48. Including 15 *Shari'a* index funds.

49. BIMB Securities Sendirian Berhad was an exclusively Islamic stock broking company established in 1994.

50. Nonetheless, a draft Competitions Act has been circulated to government agencies in 2005 for discussions.

CHAPTER 5

Colonial Land Law and the Transformation of Malay Peasant Agriculture*

Jomo K. S.

British colonial law fundamentally transformed the land tenure conditions associated with pre-colonial Malay peasant agricultural cultivation. This chapter challenges simplistic characterization of pre-colonial Malay society as feudal in the European sense, and shows how land concentration, tenancy and landlordism emerged under the new conditions created by colonial rule. Hence, these new features of Malay peasant society are of relatively recent origin rather than a feature of pre-colonial Malay society which has persisted following colonialism.

Pre-colonial Malaya

Available secondary sources do not yet permit a comprehensive historical overview of class relations in pre-colonial Malaya. Instead, we attempt to provide a (static) view of Malay class relations at the time of British colonial intervention. To provide an outline of pre-colonial Malaya, this chapter reviews the economic, social and political organization of pre-colonial Malay society identified with various agricultural practices and social relations of production, and evaluates the evidence on slavery, debt-bondage, corvée labour, land rent, and commercial tribute.

The commonly cited primary sources on the nature of Malay society immediately prior to "British intervention" are accounts by early colonial officials, which presumably reflect the prejudices, predilections, and vested interests of their authors. This is well-illustrated, for example, by the debate between Maxwell and Swettenham over the nature of pre-colonial Malay land-tenure (see Lim Teck Ghee, 1976; Wong, 1975), with each arguing in support of his own choice of land legislation for the "indirectly colonized" western

Malay States of Perak and Selangor. These very different characterizations of pre-colonial Malay society renders suspect much else that has been written on the subject.[1]

The independent Malayan and then Malaysian nations were undoubtedly products of British colonialism. Prior to the colonial impact, what is now Peninsular Malaysia (previously Malaya) had hosted many different societies. These societies had much in common, but their heterogeneity should not be denied. The uneven advance of colonial control in Malaya also meant that foreign-controlled parts of the peninsula could not but have been affected by their yet un-colonized neighbours, and vice-versa. For example, the earlier colonization of the Straits Settlements from the late eighteenth century must have influenced the social development of the Malayan hinterland which only came under British control about a century later.[2]

Pre-colonial Malay Agricultural Settlement

Pre-colonial Malay society was primarily organized around agrarian production with two main types of cultivation practised. Swidden agriculture or shifting cultivation (*huma* or *ladang*) involved periodic jungle clearing for temporary cultivation, after which the land would be left to revert to secondary jungle. Much of the history of permanent peasant settlement — in the Kedah and Kelantan rice plains, for example — was based on sedentary agriculture mainly involving wet-rice cultivation (*sawah* or *bendang*) (Zahara, 1970). The pressures of population growth have since been most acutely felt in such areas of long-standing permanent cultivation.

The basic production unit was the family, although regular and irregular cooperative activities were organized on a wider — sometimes village (*kampung*) — basis for specific purposes or communal tasks. Land clearance and infrastructural construction, for instance, tended to be communally organized, sometimes involving corvée labour (*kerah*) demanded by the ruling class. Village ties, often involving kin relations, were thus strengthened by communal organization and shared responsibility for various productive and other activities. Social differentiation within Malay village society then did not usually involve class relations. Village unity was the norm, usually supported by shared interests and a common lot, as the ruling class did not usually reside in ordinary villages.

Riverine and maritime waterways as well as land routes served as the primary means of pre-colonial communication and transport. Not surprisingly, the territorial boundaries of several Malay *negeri* (or countries, and referred to as "States" since colonial times) tended to correspond to those of river basins.

Ease of travel and communications provided by the course of a river and its tributaries also facilitated the assertion of political control, backed by military power. The ruler (*sultan*) of the Malay *negeri* usually located himself and his entourage strategically, often at the river mouth or at an important river confluence (*kuala*). Territorial chiefs, with various titles in different *negeri*, e.g. *raja*, *dato*, now often termed an aristocracy (*bangsawan*, *pembesar*) were subject to the sultan, at least nominally. Formal political hierarchies varied in the various Malay *negeri*, as the local chiefs (*penghulu*, *ketua kampung*) prevailed at the village level (see Husin Ali, 1975).

The concept of the state is said to have had its origins in pre-Islamic Hindu influence in Southeast Asia. However, the formal structure of political authority in the Malay *negeri* is generally considered to have been remodelled after the fifteenth-century Islamic Malaccan sultanate. Malacca's domination of the peninsula allowed it to introduce new formal structures of state authority as well as spread Islam. Of course, Malacca's state structure could not be fully replicated in the other *negeri* where local circumstances were different. A political structure erected on a maritime trading empire could not simply be superimposed onto primarily agrarian riverine societies. Hence, Malacca's actual impact may have been limited to its formal political structures as these were superimposed on societies organized on different bases. Thus, for example, similar formal designations came to acquire different meanings in their new contexts.[3]

In most Malay *negeri*, the sultan at least formally dominated a hierarchy of "nobility" and other lesser chiefs who constituted the structure of political authority. But in some *negeri*, "the Sultan had so little real power of government he had no need of an elaborate machine of central government" (Gullick, 1958: 49). In the riverine *negeri*, where shifting cultivation was the norm, the ruling class typically secured its surplus[4] by taxing riverine commerce through strategic location of chiefs on the river's course, thus decentralizing the state structure in such *negeri*, with the sultan not able to fully exercise effective ultimate authority. Thus, although political and economic power remained in the hands of the ruling class as a whole, it was not necessarily led by the sultan.[5]

In the *negeri* where the state provided irrigation, it exercised more effective centralized control over a permanently settled population in the person of the sultan. Sharom (1970: 1) has argued that "a different economic structure in the case of Kedah, compared to the other west coast Malay states, results [*sic*] in a different political situation". Political power in the tin-rich west coast Malay *negeri* was further decentralized by the economic and political impact of expansion of tin production and export for a world market from the mid-nineteenth century. Intra-ruling class rivalry for territorial control thus grew to extract lucrative tributes (resources or mineral rents) from miners.[6]

Thus, pre-colonial Malay society had several types of economic relations existing in various combinations. Different production relations sometimes coexisted in similar technological conditions, though some major differences in the social relations of production were associated with differing technological conditions, e.g. sedentary versus swidden cultivation.

Land Rent

What was the nature of social relations involving agricultural land?[7] The abundance of cultivable land in most of pre-colonial Malaya and the introduction of irrigated rice cultivation in some areas allowed different tenurial systems to emerge. Where shifting cultivation was the general practice, the cultivator's right to the land being worked on was recognized socially. When the land was no longer being worked and the fruits of the cultivator's labour had been exhausted, this right lapsed. The land then reverted to its original status until it was cultivated once again. In these circumstances, then, the proprietary right to a particular area was directly premised on use of that land, an arrangement suitable for shifting agriculture.[8]

A debate on Malay land tenure — particularly over the ruler's claim to eminent domain as the basis for rent exaction — began in the late nineteenth century between the rival colonial officials, Maxwell and Swettenham. In the mid-1970s, David Wong (1975) criticized Maxwell's position while Lim Teck Ghee (1976) sided with Maxwell.

One important issue was whether corvée labour and exaction of a tenth (on agricultural produce) were related to land tenurial relations. If so, it was argued that pre-colonial Malay society involved feudal relations of production with the landed class extracting the producers' surplus in the form of a feudal rent; i.e. if corvée labour and exaction of the tenth are related to land tenure, they may be regarded as a species of feudal rent. A broad definition favours Maxwell's characterization of pre-colonial Malay society as feudal.[9]

David Wong opposed Maxwell's invoking certain juridical categories, implying certain social relations, to make the case for a feudal characterization of pre-colonial Malay society. He specifically disputed Maxwell's interpretation of exaction of the tenth — and therefore, by extension, of corvée labour as well — as part of a feudal land rent incidental to land use. Instead, Wong argued that pre-colonial Malay land tenurial arrangements, in particular, and socio-economic relations in general, were misrepresented by Maxwell's feudal epithet.

Wong also pointed to various kinds of Malay land dealings, "well developed at the time of British intervention".[10] Land dealings presume certain transferable rights to land which, in turn, point to a market in land. Since land was neither scarce nor widely traded, the labour required to clear, prepare and cultivate land created the basis for the pre-colonial market in land. Hence, the value of the land — and presumably the basis for charges (rent) imposed for "letting" out such land — was the labour required to render the land productive. Rental arrangements pre-suppose that the *proprietary right* to land is not limited to the *proprietor's* own use of the land. Similarly, the use of land as loan collateral also reflects the emerging land market in the late pre-colonial period. At least two different land tenure systems had adapted to different agricultural practices in pre-colonial Malaya.[11]

Instead, Maxwell invoked certain controversial juridical categories and distinctions, such as *proprietary, alludial* and *usufructuary* rights, and the notion of the ruler's eminent domain over the land in his realm.[12] The ambiguity in legal interpretation admitted to by Maxwell[13] raises serious doubts about Maxwell's assertions.

Wong insists that Maxwell mistook socially determined limitations on land use as legal limitations on peasant rights to land.[14] The peasant's limited right to land was conditioned by and appropriate to the prevailing agricultural technology and other socio-economic arrangements. In other words, the ecological and technological limitations on land were the basis for Malay social definitions relating to land tenure. However, by itself, this does not negate the juridical structures suggested by Maxwell. After all, such legal categories should have emerged from the socio-economic and ecological circumstances. However, Wong (1975: 18) insists that "the attribution of superior ownership in land to a Malay ruler was, indeed, a total fiction" but there is evidence[15] — admittedly limited — to the contrary. While such legal claims by the ruling class may have had little practical significance in some circumstances, in other situations, they provided the juridical basis — and legitimation — for appropriation of rent or other forms of tribute.

Maxwell claimed that the principle of rent exaction was introduced to the peninsula through Hindu influence and consequently incorporated into Malay custom (*adat*), but went on to argue that customary Malay tenure was also based on Islamic principles (Lim Teck Ghee, 1976: 30). This reference to Islam for legitimation of exaction of the tenth suggest that the ruling class (state's) claim to the tenth had its origins in the Muslim religious tithe, and not in the pre-Islamic (Hindu) era, as claimed by Maxwell. It would have been in the interest of Muslim rulers to make such a religiously sanctioned claim to tithe collection.

There were two related moot issues at the juridical level in this debate. First, did the sultan really have eminent domain? And relatedly, was his claim to the tenth derived from this claim? The evidence suggests that the sultan's superior right to land was legally embodied in several instances, including seventeenth-century Kedah.[16] Predictably, the laws proclaimed by the ruler contain a legal claim to legitimize and enhance his own position. If this was generally the case throughout the Malay *negeri*, as Maxwell claimed, it should come as no great surprise. A ruler's claim to a tenth of the produce could well have been legitimized in terms of his allegedly superior claim over all land in his realm. However, it would be misleading to understand a social relationship — in this case involving the exploitation of one class by another — solely in terms of the juridical legitimacy given to it by the exploiting class.

Evidence of exaction of the tenth appears rather weak, even by Maxwell's own admission.[17] Swettenham, his rival, denied the existence of any evidence of payment of the tenth, as well as of any other recognized system of land tenure.[18] Instead, he argued that exaction of a portion of the peasant cultivator's product was often quite arbitrary, and not usually regular.[19] However, in certain situations where land tenure was more highly developed and property rights to land had been established, regular patterns of rent exaction — by the state as well as by private land-owners — emerged,[20] usually with the emergence of sedentary agriculture. Where shifting cultivation was still the norm, usually in more land-abundant circumstances, such proprietary rights were generally unknown[21] and rent exaction rarely occurred.

The principle of a poll-tax existed in at least some pre-colonial Malay *negeri*. Obviously, a capitation tax would have been easier to collect than a share of the harvest, which would have required more sophisticated collection machinery. Although the evidence of poll-taxes is scattered, it does suggest that there was a gap between doctrine and practice, as with collection of the tenth, and little regularity or uniformity in the incidence of this particular tax[22] between districts, let alone *negeri*. Whether or not a ruler's claims to eminent domain — and hence to the tenth — were embodied in law, the tenth was certainly not consistently exacted throughout pre-colonial Malaya.

And regardless of its existence, whether the ruler's juridical claim to the tenth was actually exercised at all is also doubtful. Maxwell's sole example — of Krian[23] — has been shown to be a possible (complicated) exception, where the tenth exaction may have been a surrogate for some other form of surplus appropriation.[24] Of course, this does not mean that there was no direct appropriation of a portion of the cultivators' produce by the ruling class. This certainly did occur in many places, and was often arbitrary, involving the threatened or actual use of force, i.e. it essentially involved the direct use of coercion, without much recourse to legal legitimation. While such exactions may have been regularized in certain instances, there is little unambiguous evidence of this. The case of fifteenth-century Malacca was perhaps exceptional, not only because of its atypical economy and state structure, but also because demographic conditions then apparently gave rise to a land system which included the right to rent exaction by private land-owners.[25]

Why, then, was the doctrine of the ruler's right to exact the tenth, if and where it existed, not regularized in the rest of the peninsula? For Perak, it has been suggested that: "The sparse population, the low level of productivity, and the importance of mining in the economy explains the general absence of land rent and taxes on subsistence agriculture..." (Sadka, 1968: 385). She might have added that overland transport difficulties, riverine communications, and the nature of pre-colonial commerce favoured other systems of exploitation, such as taxation of riverine commerce. Also, when the sultan's authority was weak (e.g. because of poor coercive capacity), district chiefs had more independence. Then, even if the sultan wanted to exact the tenth, he may not have been able to supervise its actual appropriation on the ground. The exactions could then have varied from the tenth specified by law, and gone to strong territorial chiefs instead.

Regardless of the actual situation prior to colonial intervention, "*the presumption of a Malay ruler's paramount ownership in land was certainly turned into a fait accompli with the establishment of colonial government under the Residential System in the Malay States*" (David Wong, 1975: 20, emphasis added). In the Malay States brought under direct British control from 1874, Wong suggests "that British influence had in the meantime contributed to new development in their land systems", citing Kedah,[26] Pahang and Kelantan. Hence, the characterization of pre-colonial Malay society may actually be of relatively new social conditions due to increasing integration into the world economy as well as British and other influences in the region.

Pre-colonial Malay Society

While it is not possible to make any useful generalizations which transcend time and place, available evidence from recent centuries suggests that taxes on trade were probably the most important income source for the pre-colonial Malay ruling class in most pre-colonial Malay *negeri*. Generally, slavery, peonage and corvée labour did not yield large monetary incomes. Tribute exacted *directly from peasant production* — whether or not legitimized in terms of the ruler's eminent domain — was not generally important, although it became significant in certain exceptional situations, e.g. where the state provided infrastructure for wet rice irrigation rather late in the pre-colonial period in the northern rice bowl areas of Kelantan and Kedah, which were thus able to support significantly higher population densities. Slave labour, corvée labour, trade and other taxes were undoubtedly important for the ruling class, but were rarely directly based on peasant output.

Historical evidence suggests at least two primary modes of surplus appropriation in most of pre-colonial Malay society, i.e. tribute payment and slavery. Tribute-paying affected virtually the entire peasantry including taxes on trade, corvée labour, and even direct tribute from production. Religious injunctions against the enslavement of fellow Muslims resulted in two forms of slavery, i.e. slavery of non-Muslims and peonage or debt-bondage (debt-slavery) of Muslims. Of its various forms, tribute in the form of land rent was only significant in certain circumstances, usually where demographic and other social, ecological, and technological conditions enabled the ruling class to effectively control access to land, e.g. in the older permanently settled wet-rice growing plains of North Malaya.

Colonial Land Policy and Law

Malay land rights prior to colonial intervention were contingent on the condition that it was worked (Jomo, 1986: Chapter 1). Consequently, there was little accumulation of land for purposes other than cultivation. Since land was not rendered scarce by the prevailing system, most farmers could cultivate as much land as they needed or were able to operate. However, ownership under colonial land legislation — in all its variations — bore no relation to the pre-colonial premises based on use of land.

Two aspects of colonial land policy worked in tandem to fundamentally transform land tenure conditions. First, the new land laws introduced by the British juridically defined a new relationship between peasant and land, and hence, to the rest of society. Secondly, colonial land alienation policy controlled the availability of land for peasant cultivation, and also required cultivators to farm under conditions defined by the colonial state. Land law and policy also affected land prices and the use of land as collateral for obtaining credit.

There were many differences between the land laws introduced in the Straits Settlements and those adopted in the Malay States of the hinterland, but neither resembled English land law at that time. Significant variations also existed among the peninsular Malay States, especially between the Federated Malay States (FMS) and the other states, collectively referred to as the Unfederated Malay States (UMS).[27] Lack of uniformity also extends to matters of land administration. The Torrens system of land registration — originally developed in the British settler colony of Australia to facilitate agricultural capitalist expansion — was adopted in the Malay States as contemporary English land law, with its strong feudal heritage, was considered less suitable. Unlike the "less efficacious system of registering deeds" adopted in the Straits Settlements ports for capitalists agriculture the later Torrens system established an "indisputable right of ownership to registered land" through the issue of title certificates in ways far more conducive to agricultural land cultivation. Nevertheless, several crucial elements are common to the land laws of Malaya.[28] Though subsequent post-colonial land codes have managed some degree of standardization, the colonial legal legacy is very much alive.

Under colonial land laws, ownership involved obtaining legal rights to land properly alienated by the authorities. "The practical goals of the land code were to establish a favourable climate for outside investment in land, and to bring Malay smallholdings under Government control" (Kratoska, 1975: 135). As capitalist interests and immigrant peasants from neighbouring islands — attracted by the new conditions established under colonial rule — began to acquire land, the balance available for cultivation diminished in quantity as well as quality. Colonial rule had fundamentally transformed the conditions of land ownership, and therefore, of access to land.[29] Once virtually freely available, land was rendered scarce by a combination of legal, economic and environmental conditions, making acquisition of cultivable land by purchase increasingly necessary. *In the new conditions accompanying colonial rule, land was systematically brought under state or private control, and transformed into a tradeable asset which could be accumulated as a form of investment.* The growing commercialization and monetization of the economy hastened this process, encouraging land transactions and investments.[30]

Colonial land laws also ended shifting cultivation practised by most farmers in the peninsula outside the long-standing permanent agricultural settlements established on artificially irrigated rice plains, especially in northern Malaya. Pre-colonial Malay land systems were compatible with prevailing agricultural practices; for example, (temporary) usufructuary rights while working the land were consistent with the needs of shifting cultivation. British-imposed land legislation, designed to serve the interests of capital, was incompatible with the long-standing practice of swidden agriculture which did not require permanent rights to land ownership.

Colonial land legislation was only one of many blows delivered at swidden cultivation. Colonial rule also brought about a rapid expansion of mining or agricultural land alienated to capitalist interests, diminishing the land available for shifting cultivation. The new land laws meant that cultivation of land without permission from the owners violated property rights. Whatever the validity of the pre-colonial Malay ruler's claim to eminent domain over land, this became a reality under colonial rule with an added significance (David Wong, 1975). Land now ultimately belonged to the state, with some alienated to private interests. Without legally recognized rights to land use, shifting cultivation became illegal. Despite this, however, shifting cultivation practices among Malays took some time to disappear. Legislation prohibiting shifting cultivation by Malays was enacted in Selangor in 1886 and in Perak a decade later (Lim Teck Ghee, 1976: 67); "no effort [was] spared to secure a *settled* population of agriculturalists" (Swettenham, 1948: 261; emphasis added). While administrative and legislative forces put an end to an agricultural practice well adapted to the ecological, economic and demographic environment of the Malay peasantry, little effort was made to create conditions for a viable alternative: the peasants had no choice but to adapt to the new conditions created by the British.

Lim Teck Ghee (1976) has suggested that, whatever their differences on legislative and administrative details, the land policies advocated by early colonial officials were unanimously "liberal" in order to attract immigrants to sedentary agriculture. In contrast to the previous emphasis on trade for the Straits Settlements, economic growth in the Malayan hinterland was to be driven by agricultural expansion. The policies succeeded, and there was a considerable inflow of settlers almost from the outset.

Legislation and other aspects of colonial rule geared to promote this general policy favoured the larger British concerns. For example, agricultural land exceeding 100 acres in size was exempted from reassessment in the 1890 Selangor land code formulated by Maxwell (Lim Teck Ghee, 1976: 19). This liberal colonial land policy was also reflected in the revenue system, e.g. in the form of low quit rent rates. British mining and plantation interests were assured by colonial administrators of easy and cheap access to land, which was often accumulated speculatively, in excess of their anticipated needs. Better land — in terms of mineral potential, soil quality, terrain or access to communications — tended to be allocated to big business interests, especially to those more powerful and influential. The British devised a "system of dual agricultural land taxation, a light one on the affluent European planter and a heavy one on the native cultivator" (Lim Teck Ghee, 1976: 129). There were other discriminatory aspects of colonial agricultural policy and practice,[31] as discrimination against the peasantry in favour of business interests was not confined to land matters.[32]

Land Ownership and Peasant Differentiation

Contemporary landlord-tenant relations in Malay peasant agriculture are some-times said to have originated from allegedly "feudal" pre-colonial relations; according to this view, land tenancy today has its origins in "feudalism".[33] This perspective is not grounded in Malayan history. In fact, the contemporary process of differentiation in relation to land actually developed from conditions created by the peasantry's integration — under colonial auspices — into the world economy (Jomo, 1986).

Emphasis on the colonial origins of contemporary peasant class structure does not, of course, deny pre-colonial influences. The successful establishment of colonial hegemony was partly achieved through cooptation of important sections of the pre-colonial ruling class. Various British concessions to secure this alliance included generous distribution of land property to members of this class. Most of this land is still under peasant agriculture; the rest has either become residential land or been integrated into capitalist enterprises, such as mines and plantations. The significance of these land concessions has yet to be thoroughly surveyed, let alone analyzed, though suggestive glimpses are available. In Mukim Gunung, Kelantan, for example, 271.6 acres, or 32 per cent of the 848.4 acres of agricultural land there was owned by the Sultan of Kelantan, with a further 37.8 acres owned by other members of the Kelantan royal family (Mohd Noor, 1974: 41–7).

Besides large land concessions to members of the pre-colonial ruling class and their heirs, other factors contributed to the unequal distribution of land resources among the peasantry at the beginning of the colonial epoch. The colonial rulers encouraged land development by providing those with money and influence with undeveloped land to be worked, rent-free for some years, by agricultural settlers (T.B. Wilson, 1958: 13). After such land had been developed, rents were introduced. Another procedure was to allow settlers to open and develop land in exchange for land portions for themselves. For example, some of the wealthier early settlers of Kampung Bagan used bonded or indentured labourers (*orang tebusan*) to develop agricultural land (Husin, 1964). Decades later, in the early 1960s, these earlier arrangements were still reflected in the tendency for descendants of the earlier settlers to be landlords, and for descendants of the indentured labourers to be tenants.

Ownership of large tracts of agricultural land allowed the establishment of plantations employing wage labour. However, where agricultural production tended to be organized around the family, as was generally the case for rice cultivation until tractor mechanization from the 1970s, such large pieces of land may instead have been subdivided for operational purposes. Nevertheless, in so far as the subdivided parcels are contiguous and remain under common registered ownership, such large land areas are still represented in cadastral maps as lots, the legal units for payment of quit rent. Such maps suggest that only a small proportion of rice land is owned in large lot titles[34] (Smith and Goethals, 1965: 24; Lim Teck Ghee, *et al.*, 1974: 35). Of course, this does not preclude the existence of many large owners with holdings consisting of several lots of small size, but there is limited evidence of this phenomenon (Scott, 1985).

Demographic pressures on legally — rather than ecologically — limited land resources have resulted in increasing subdivision of holdings which eventually led to "uneconomic" farm sizes and, more recently, the abandonment of such farms, resulting in "idle land". However, the concentration of land-ownership rarely matched subdivision in its effects. Nor did subdivision totally dispossess small land owning peasants (Barnard, 1970: 34). In the absence of alternatives, the importance of land to agriculturalists motivated the impoverished peasant to hold on to his property as long as it could continue to yield some income. Even when sale or forfeiture (due to an unredeemed mortgage) became necessary, land was reluctantly given up in bits and pieces. Hence, the accumulation of land by some in a situation of limited land availability necessarily involved the dispossession of others.

Thus, ironically, the non-substitutability of agriculture land simultaneously emphasized and limited the significance of land-ownership distribution patterns for understanding wealth and income distribution in peasant society. Land has remained essential for agriculture,[35] though with the option of tenancy in commercial farming, ownership has declined in relative significance. Hence, for a long time, the peasant's relationship to land-ownership was the primary criterion for identifying strata among the peasantry (Kessler, 1974; Husin Ali, 1972, 1975).

Generally, there has been an important long-term trend towards some concentration of land-ownership and operation on the one hand, and growing impoverishment and dispossession on the other. The weaker tendency towards concentration is due to complex processes, and cannot merely be attributed to "original" inequalities in land distribution; this is most obvious on the early government-organized agricultural and development schemes where the original settlers started off with equal-sized lots (Swift, 1967: 243; Selvadurai, 1972a: 26).

One consequence of this "land concentration" has been the frequently observed fragmentation of farms, involving the agglomeration of non-contiguous lots under common ownership. Another possible effect of the concentration of land-ownership is tenancy, though this is not a necessary consequence. In the past, concentration of land-ownership, especially in rice areas, has resulted in the exploitation of tenants (including share-croppers), rather than wage labour. Tenancy, and its corollary, landlordism became the main criteria employed to analyze differentiation among the peasantry since the advent of colonial rule. However, large-scale farming, including on rented land, has also led to the reorganization of production involving wage labour, e.g. following recent technological changes in rice production have involved the further transformation of the relations of production.

Joint Ownership and Land Subdivision

It was fashionable to attribute peasant poverty to population growth,[36] by supporting such assertions with superficial evidence. Besides the "uneconomic size" of most peasant farms with subdivision and technological change on limited land, there is considerable evidence of landlessness (e.g. *New Straits Times*, 22 June 1974). Careful examination of the ostensibly demographic pressure on land shifts responsibility for peasant land hunger away from population growth to institutional or legal and economic aspects of the land situation in Malaya (Jomo, 1986: Chapters 3 & 4). Land scarcity emerges as a social condition, the outcome of legal, rather than exclusively ecological and demographic factors.[37]

Illegal farming by "rural squatters" is another manifestation of land hunger in Peninsular Malaysia.[38] Such illegal cultivators testify not only to legal constraints to peasant land access, but also to the actual availability of arable land, underscoring the economic and legal — rather than the ecological and demographic — limits which constrain peasant land use.

The distributive effects of the Islamic inheritance system have also been frequently blamed for joint or co-ownership, subdivision, and fragmentation of Malay peasant land. Customary Malay (*adat*) inheritance systems are considered to have somewhat similar effects, though they are cited less often.[39] Their distributive consequences are, of course, different from other systems of inheritance, such as primogeniture, which privileges the first-born male and does not therefore have similarly divisive effects through the inheritance process. Primogeniture disadvantages those who would have some property rights under the Islamic and *adat* inheritance systems, and hence, is relatively more inegalitarian in principle and consequence.

Although Islamic and adat inheritance practices among the Malay peasantry obviously predate colonialism, the extent of joint ownership, subdivision, and fragmentation of peasant landholdings was not significant in pre-colonial times. Rather, these features only became significant with colonial land legislation and policy, particularly their constraints on land alienation for peasant cultivation. Colonial legal restrictions on increasing cultivated land with demographic increases — by enforcing property rights on alienated land and eminent domain over unalienated land — caused peasant population growth to have such effects. Therefore, it is not the inheritance systems, but the conditions created by colonialism and persisting thereafter, which bear primary responsibility for the subdivisive effects of demographic increase on landholdings. Division of land-ownership is reflected in increased joint or co-ownership as well as the physical subdivision of landholdings. Both tendencies encouraged the sale of affected land, leading to some concentration of land-ownership.[40] Joint ownership is often preferred to subdivision because of the problems identified with ownership of small land holdings (Fisk, 1964: 13). It may also be chosen because of the difficulties and expenses involved in the process of effecting physical subdivision, or the desire of the co-owners to keep the farm holding intact for other reasons. Co-ownership due to Islamic rules of inheritance (*far'aid*) has led to shares of small and awkward sizes.[41] Joint ownership discourages investment and other measures to increase productivity, especially over the long term, while encouraging tenancy.[42]

Reduction of farm size — due to subdivision — made it less feasible to employ certain more productive techniques; certain techniques and equipment — which could yield higher outputs — were more difficult or expensive to employ on smaller holdings, i.e. without certain economies of scale. Certain farming problems — e.g. different operation schedules of neighbouring farms and negligence of neighbours — were exacerbated when there were more smaller-sized farms due to subdivision. Subdivision also tended to lead to farm fragmentation (Aziz, 1958: 24).[43]

To overcome the problems of inadequate land, especially on small sub-divided lots, peasant farmers increased farm sizes by various means, consolidating property through renouncement, gifts, exchange, and sale. Generally, tenancy was the most important means of enlarging farm size. Such actions sought to consolidate various small parcels of land into farms of more viable size. Other factors besides physical subdivision have also contributed to the phenomenon of farm fragmentation.[44] The dispersal of parcels incurs greater time, effort and cost in transporting the farmer, equipment, farm animals, other farming material and, of course, the produce. Travel time can affect production on fragmented rubber smallholdings as productivity in rubber tapping is affected by the time at which incisions are made and latex begins to flow. Parcelling also inhibits utilization of new farm infrastructure, techniques and inputs because of the greater organizational and other difficulties involved (e.g. see Ooi, 1959: 204, 205), though operating a fragmented farm may have certain advantages for multi-cropping and spreading risk.

Concentration of Land-ownership[45]

The accumulation of land property by some — which necessarily involves dispossessing others — or the process of concentration of land-ownership represents — in so far as land is the primary means of production in peasant agriculture — the main, though not the only form of capital accumulation in the peasant sector. Land sales by peasants may be necessitated or motivated by circumstances, or the desire to transform the nature of one's assets. Husin (1975: 82) maintained that small land assets, low incomes, and the seasonal nature of many agricultural pursuits drew peasants into a spiral of chronic indebtedness, sometimes culminating in land sale or forfeiture of property offered as collateral for credit. In such circumstances, extraordinary expenditures often precipitated land sales since the impoverished, and often indebted, peasant usually had no other recourse. A superficial focus on the extraordinary spending episode that culminates in land sale ignores the peasant's context, and leads to the erroneous view that peasants lose their land solely because of such expenditure.[46] Such spending is often characterized as irrational with peasant impoverishment attributed to peasant irrationality.

However, considering the relatively recent origins of peasant differentiation on the basis of land-ownership, there is little reason to expect great concentration of peasant land-ownership or a highly stratified Malay peasant society, though this does not deny trends thus far as well as differentiation along other lines which has taken place.

Land owned is not synonymous with land operated. Past dominance of certain organizational forms of rice production, especially the basic family unit, as well as other factors such as land fragmentation, have limited farm sizes. Through various arrangements, especially tenancy, land is distributed for purposes of cultivation. Sometimes, land-owners rent out their own land and operate land belonging to others (usually to minimize the adverse effects of fragmented ownership), but it is more usual for owners to cultivate their own land. There are many factors, however, which mediate between land-ownership and operation, though ownership does nevertheless have a considerable bearing on land operation. Many a land-hungry farmer can only afford to rent small farm areas,[47] if available, and may also supplement his income with other jobs. The concentration and inequitable distribution of land ownership has a considerable influence on the distribution of farms by size,[48] though the size distribution of farms (e.g. see Selvadurai, 1972a; Eddy Lee, 1976: 22, Table 6) does not quite reflect the distribution of farm-land ownership.

Concentration of land-ownership where the peasant family remains the basic unit of production, has contributed to the development of tenancy among peasant cultivators. The extent of tenancy for land planted with different crops (e.g. Husin, 1972) varies considerably, also varying with average farm size and the concentration of land-ownership (see Jomo 1986: Table 4.16), with many factors contributing to differences in the tenancy rate (see, for example, Huang, 1975a; 1975b). Differences in income due to cultivating different crops and botanical as well as other differences in the production regimes of various crops also influence land-ownership and tenancy. For instance, the annual (and more recently, the twice or even thrice yearly) rice production cycle is certainly more conducive to tenancy arrangements than land planted with perennials.[49] A variety of tenurial arrangements between land-owner and operator can be found in Malay peasant agriculture.[50] Many minor variations exist and the terms used to characterize various tenurial agreements also vary.[51] Fixed rents are payable either in kind (*sewa padi* in the case of rice) or in cash (*sewa tunai*).

Tenancy and Peasant Differentiation

Growing land hunger, concentration of land-ownership, tenancy (and its counterpart, landlordism) and differentiation among the peasantry have emerged as complex processes unfolding with the integration of the Malay peasantry into the British empire. While the colonial impact did not lead directly to capitalist relations of production among the peasantry, the integration of the peasant sector stimulated petty commodity peasant production as well as the emergence of new non-capitalist relations of production (i.e. not involving wage labour). Since peasant social relations of production were transformed by integration — under colonial domination — into the capitalist-dominated market, they were no longer pre-capitalist. Yet, these peasant relations cannot be termed "capitalist" — despite subordination to circulation, especially merchant capital — in so far as they do not involve the direct exploitation of free wage labour by capital invested in agrarian production. In new circumstances created by colonial intervention, the peasantry survived — as peasants, in so far as they continued to have private (direct) access to land while subject to ongoing change. Hence, under colonialism and since, the peasantry has been irreversibly transformed by integration into the world market and subordination to capital. Subordinating the peasantry to capital and the market, new processes of differentiation among the peasantry itself have been set in motion. Unlike the pre-colonial class structure — in which peasants were not significantly stratified at the village level, though subject to extra-local class domination — after colonial integration, peasants became subject to differentiation at the village level as well.[52] The complex dynamics of subdivision and concentration of land-ownership, and the relatively recent colonial origins of peasant differentiation have a bearing on the social relations, forms and consequences of peasant differentiation. "The concentration of ownership in the three areas has not led to a clear-cut class system made up of landlords on the one hand and tenants on the other" (Husin, 1975: 84).

The gravity of the tenancy situation among rice cultivators was highlighted by the 1952 and the 1955 reports of the Rice Production Committee. These resulted in the colonial government's promulgation of the Padi Cultivation Control of Rents and Security of Tenure Ordinance, 1955, legislating a rent ceiling and prohibiting "tea money", among other things. Certain aspects of the ordinance, ostensibly legislation to "protect" tenants, raised serious doubts as to its true purpose; for example, it prohibited tenancy agreements for "less than one season or more than one year" (quoted in Wilson, 1958: 94).[53] In a situation where agreements are not made for less than a season for obvious reasons, this maximum limit actually increased insecurity of tenure by prohibiting leases of longer duration. While rents previously below the newly legislated maxima were raised to the officially tolerated maximum levels, rents exceeding these maxima were rarely lowered (Lim Chong-Yah, 1967: 169). Ambiguities in legislation have tended to be resolved in favour of the stronger party, invariably the land-owners. Perhaps, most significantly, the legislation was not backed by any effective enforcement and the Ordinance has been described as "completely ineffective"[54] (Selvadurai, 1972a: 29).

The gravity of the tenancy situation was exacerbated by the "counter-productive" impact of the 1955 Ordinance. Subsequently, the Padi Cultivators (Control of Rent and Security of Tenure) Act 1967, was duly passed by Parliament. Though legislatively superior (see Selvadurai, 1972a: 29–30), the Act suffered a fate similar to the 1955 Ordinance: responsibility for implementation rests with State governments, which have constitutional authority over land-related matters. Rural landed interests — generally entrenched at the State level rather than the federal level — ensured that the Act largely remained a dead letter. There was considerable resistance from landlords to stipulations of the 1967 Act; economically and politically weak, tenants have not been able to ensure effective implementation (Selvadurai, 1972c: 35) as rents frequently exceeded the stipulated legal maxima (e.g. see Barnard, 1970: 49; Horii, 1972: 59; Lim Teck Ghee, *et al.*, 1974: 60, 61). Legislation which might serve tenant interests is hardly enforced or implemented, while most legislation tends to serve land owners and business interests.

Summary

Land is the primary means of production for peasant farmers. Colonial legislation and policy radically transformed the significance of land in the peasant economy, and hence peasant relations of production. Land law in the colonial order recognized and asserted private property rights in land, rendering it a commodity to be owned, bought, or sold. The new legislation, together with several other measures taken by the colonial government, undermined the practice of swidden agriculture. More importantly, the colonial situation created the conditions for landlordism and its corollary, peasant tenancy. By becoming property which could be traded or used as credit collateral, land could also be subsequently lost through loan default.

Several large tracts of land were provided by the colonial authorities to some members of the pre-colonial ruling class, enabling them to become landlords. However, the origins of peasant differentiation are also to be found in other new tendencies generated by the colonial situation. Unlike during the pre-colonial era, subsequent increases in land cultivated no longer corresponded to demographic growth. Under colonial law, lawful cultivation could only be done on legally alienated land. In the colonial economy, the best available land — in terms of soil conditions, access to communications, etc. — was alienated to British business interests.

With Islamic inheritance law and customary Malay inheritance practices also operating in this context, the outcome has been an increasing ratio of peasants to land, mainly manifested in greater joint ownership and subdivision of landholdings. With other factors differentiating the peasantry, there has been some concentration of land-ownership among peasants. Hence, landlordism, land hunger and landlessness are primarily consequences of colonial law. The integration of the Malay peasantry into the world economy has given rise to new non-capitalist relations of production different from pre-colonial relations. Concentration of land-ownership has led to tenancy (and share-cropping) arrangements. Peasant strata may be differentiated by tenurial status, i.e. location in tenancy arrangements. While the state has wanted to preserve a yeoman peasantry in the interest of political stability, it has not sought to resist tendencies contributing to peasant differentiation and impoverishment as well as abandonment of "uneconomic" land cultivation.

The preceding review of the transformation of Malay peasant production — due to the introduction of colonial land law and other transformations associated with international economic integration, capital accumulation and biased public policies under imperial auspices — underscores some of its mixed consequences, intended or otherwise, for economic development. Peasant agriculture is hardly traditional in the sense of being a vestige of the pre-colonial order, but was instead fundamentally transformed and constrained by the colonial experience and laws. Consolidating colonial land laws have served to undermine an increasingly moribund peasant agriculture in growing contrast to more flexible capitalist plantation agriculture.

Notes

*   This chapter draws heavily on the first four chapters of Jomo (1986), especially Chapters 1 and 4.

1. Since the comments which follow rely largely on such sources of information, they are tentative and subject to subsequent revision as new evidence come to light.

2. No mention is made here of the pre-colonial empires which embraced parts of the Malayan peninsula at one point or another, while the establishment of the Malacca empire in the fifteenth century is generally considered a watershed in pre-colonial Malay history. While the influence of the Malacca sultanate on subsequent Malay society is undeniable, the real significance of its impact remains moot.

3. For example, the titled position of *Laksamana* (Admiral) was formally incorporated into the courts of a number of other Malay sultans, but many of these admirals never went to sea.

4. Class relations and the state presume the existence of a social surplus (henceforth referred to simply as "a surplus"). The existence of a social surplus obviously presupposes an excess over basic and essential consumption requirements. Thus, many "primitive" classless societies did not produce any significant excess in this sense. Consequently, low development of the forces of production may not allow the production of an excess, which is a precondition for the existence of a surplus as defined by the class relations of exploitation. Barring the exceptional situation of famine, most human societies have at least been capable of producing an excess over minimal biological subsistence requirements. Otherwise, they would simply not survive as they cannot even biologically reproduce themselves. While the actual existence of an excess takes a concrete form, the pattern of time allocation between production and other activities may also reflect the existence of a potential surplus.

    The preceding should not be taken to imply that there is a strict and determinate correspondence between the forces and relations of production. Rather, certain relations of production may exist within a range of technological parameters.

5. "The collection of taxes, whether on the tin produced by Chinese miners or on the trade goods destined for Malay and Chinese consumers alike, was correlated with the distribution of political power. In theory the Sultan and other holders of royal offices, such as the Raja Muda, were entitled to collect certain taxes throughout the State. But it was not feasible for them to maintain tax collectors in every district who could neither be supervised nor supported at a distance from the capital. It was inevitable that each district chief should collect all the taxes paid in his district. He was supposed to remit to the Sultan the proceeds of the royal dues. In practice it appears that the Sultan rarely received all that was due to him from outlying districts. He was forced to rely on what he could collect at the royal capital which typically lay at the major confluence or mouth of the main river in the State."

    "The inability of the Sultans to obtain more than a small proportion of the total revenues of the States, especially of the taxes on tin which became so important during the nineteenth century, was the main factor which caused a dispersal of power from the central government of the State to the districts.... The holders of ministerial offices in the Sultan's government had scattered to become district chiefs in order to obtain their share of the revenues" (Gullick, 1958: 127).

6. "The district chiefs whose domains were fortunately endowed with this metal, became the all powerful political figures in the state. One consequence of this was the constant intrigues, and manoeuvering for power among the chiefs not only

among themselves, but also between chiefs and Sultans. The end result was political instability and general chaos in these states" (Sharom Ahmat, 1970: 1).

7. For more elaborate discussions of the nature of the pre-colonial Malay land systems, see Maxwell (1884), David Wong (1975), and Lim Teck Ghee (1976).

8. "At the time when land was abundant, anybody could, as a simple matter of fact, clear forest land for cultivation and occupation…. The basic principle was that if a person abandoned his land leaving it to become *tanah mati* ('dead land'), any other person could then take up such 'dead land' by making use of it. It may be observed that these rules, which seemed to be providing for the 'extinguishment' of a cultivator's right in relation to land, were rather practical rules concerning the reverter of abandoned land to 'forest' land, once again free to be cleared and used by someone else" (David Wong, 1975: 10).

9. This reasoning comes up against the controversy over how feudal relations should be defined. If defined restrictively, it excludes most societal experiences, except for certain European ones, from the feudal category (see Anderson, 1974; Hilton, 1976). Maxwell largely overlooked tribute extracted from trade and viewed pre-colonial Malay society as having been one dominated by feudal relations, with slavery and debt-bondage co-existing.

10. "(a) Out-and-out transfer. It may, in a way, be said to be a transfer of cleared or cultivated land by sale. However, the dealing was not quite a sale of the land but one of a take-over by way of recouping the original cultivator for his labour in clearing the land as well as for any crops he had cultivated or house erected thereon…. (b) 'Letting' (*sewa*). This was an arrangement whereby a cultivator allowed another person to cultivate his land for a return of a share in the produce crops or for a rent in kind or in money. (c) 'security transactions' (generally called *gadai*)…. Presumably, 'security dealings were relatively a late development in a peasant community'" (David Wong, 1975: 11–2).

11. "The customary rules relating to the abandonment of land and their simple customary dealings seemed to be more concerned with actual use of land and the produce crops. Land *simpliciter* was involved as a medium rather than as an object. This is not to deny that some form of 'private ownership' of land (in the wide general sense) was already in the process of evolution in an advanced agricultural settlement such as that of the Malay" (David Wong, 1975: 12).

12. "… a proprietary right is created by the clearing of the land *followed by continuous occupation*…. His right to land is absolute *as long as occupation continued, or as long as the land bears signs of appropriation* … the doctrine that the right to the soil was in the Raja … was not incompatible with the rights of the owners of the proprietary right, for he did not claim an allodial right to the soil, but merely the right to appropriate and keep for himself as much land as he had the power (*usaha*) to clear and keep in cultivation … he did not claim more than a usufruct continuous as long as he chose it to be so, and terminable on abandonment" (Maxwell, 1884: 77–8, 90–1, original emphasis).

13. "The right of the Raja to dispose of waste land *cannot have been seriously exerted* in Malay States in respect of forest land. The old Malay custom which permitted the free selection and appropriation of forest land for the purposes of cultivation

was not interfered with…. That the soil of a Malay State is vested in the Raja is a doctrine not now to be questioned, though it may have *originated in confusion of thought*, the exercise of the rights to collect the tenth and to dispose of abandoned land *being assumed to imply* the existence of a superior right of property in the soil, to which the rights of proprietorship were subordinate…. The Raja's absolute property in the soil, is but a barren right, and as he undoubtedly has, *independently of it*, the right of levying tenths and taxes and of forfeiting lands for non-payment, Malay law does not trouble itself much with speculation about it. Tenant right is the cardinal doctrine of the Malay cultivator, and, as long as that is fully recognized, *it does not matter to him who or what functionary or power may, in theory, be clothed with the original and supreme right to the soil*" (Maxwell, 1884: 90–2, emphasis added).

14. "Clearly, total ownership of land was inconceivable to the Malay cultivators themselves. The limitations of their 'rights' in respect of land were in fact no more than the limitations of the uses of land in the conditions of their social and economic life. Although what a cultivator actually did on his land may be reflected in his relationship with other members of his community in terms of his right to use the land, it is an apparent 'unreality' to transform the historical limitations of land uses known to them into limitations of their rights. Perhaps what is more fictitious in such a western interpretation is not so much its commitment to the concept of absolute total ownership of land as the attribution of such total ownership to the ruler under a native political system…" (David Wong, 1975: 117).

15. For instance, section 16 of the 1667 Kedah Laws of the Dato Seri Paduka Tuan reads: "Land without boundary marks is counted dead and belongs to the Raja" (Winstedt, 1928). This legal tenet clearly indicates the ruler's right to eminent domain. Also, the appendices of Maxwell's 1884 article contain various suggestive extracts from indigenous Malay land codes, though they are far from conclusive in themselves. Various colonial observers before Maxwell also attested to the existence of the ruler's claim to the tenth:

> Fullerton in 1928, was explicit that the Malay lands were liable to the exaction of the tenth of the produce. Newbold confirmed that the population in the Peninsula was subject to the imposition of a tenth of the produce wherever it happened to settle. Maxwell's father … had written that although it was well-known by the old Malay law that the sovereign was the owner of the soil, every man had the right to clear and occupy all forest and waste land subject to the payment to the ruler of one tenth of the produce of the land; he had concluded that the rights thus acquired were not prescriptive but customary. More recently, Sir Frederick Weld, in 1880, had said that "the Malay custom, which always appear to have been recognized as a basis for our procedure admitted the right of the cultivator to occupy the land permanently so long as he paid to Government tenths of the produce and continued to cultivate it" (Lim Teck Ghee, 1976: 31).

16. It can, of course, be argued that Kedah was exceptional in so far as it was subject to Siamese influence.

17. Maxwell, advocate of the doctrine of the Sultan's eminent domain and of his related right to collection of the tenth, admitted: "The only purely Malay province in which I have personally seen the tenth of the grain collected by a native Government is the Krian province in Perak" (Maxwell, 1884: 97–8).

18. In 1890, Swettenham maintained:

> ... there was not in the pre-Residential period any system of payment by tenths, or, indeed, any recognized system of native tenure of any kind. The people occupied and cultivated such lands as they chose, and paid nothing for them, but the authorities, Sultan, State Officer, local headman, or anak Raja, whoever had the power or might, dispossessed the occupants at pleasure, or helped themselves to any produce that they thought worth having whenever they felt able and inclined (Swettenham, as quoted in David Wong, 1975: 18).

Three years later, in 1893, Swettenham provided yet another picture:

> The Malay cultivator was not the owner of the land he occupied, that he was a tenant at will ... that the Malays possessed no proprietary rights over the land, that no land can be said to have descended to them from their forefather, and that, while the rulers never admitted any claim to the land on the part of the people, these last never advanced any such claim, but frankly stated, as they do now, that the land belonged to the Ka-raja-an (Swettenham, quoted in Lim Teck Ghee, 1976: 28).

One cannot but suspect that the characterizations these colonial officials made of pre-colonial Malay society were adjusted to fit the specific political positions they were advancing at particular times.

19. Sharom Ahmat (1970: 2) also mentions that "there was always the fear that a large harvest might merely mean that the successful cultivator had to part with the excess on the demand of some chief, petty or otherwise". Sharom is writing on Kedah, a *negeri* where agricultural settlement was of a relatively more settled and permanent character and where one would expect land rent exactions to be comparatively more regularized.

20. Fifteenth-century Malacca provides an example, according to Newbold (1971: 255). There, land was privately owned and landlords exacted a rent of a third of the produce. Evidence of what appears to be private ownership of land may be imputed from some of the laws regarding land dealings, to which mention was made earlier. Also, an examination of the Kedah Laws (Winstedt, 1928) indicates the existence of private land-ownership.

21. Quoting Marsden's *Sumatra*, Newbold suggests that, outside Malacca, "Land is so abundant in proportion to the population that they scarcely consider it as a subject of right, any more than the elements of air and water, excepting in so far as in speculation the prince lays claim on the whole" (Newbold, 1971: 224–5).

22. In Pahang, it was called the *hasil banchi*, whereby every male Malay and Chinese was required to pay $1.33 each upon demand (Jang Aisjah Muttalib, 1972: 49). The reference to the Chinese presence may suggest that this practice began after

the Chinese were in Pahang. If it was of recent origin, it may have arisen under the influence of changing conditions in the region, and may well not have been an old Malay practice. In Perak, Wilkinson (1971: 136, 138) writes that the *Bendahara*, the premier-chief of Perak, was entitled "to collect a capitation-tax of 50 cents from every household. This revenue was known as the *beman kalur*". The *Sadika Raja*, one of the eight Perak chiefs, enjoyed among other things, "a capitation-tax of 70 *gantangs* of rice from every household". Writing of the same *negeri* for the same period, Emily Sadka noted that:

> The poll tax was not commonly levied, though there are references to a poll tax of fifty cents on every male in Perak, levied by the Bendahara, a poll tax of $2 on every married man in this district, levied by the Maharaja Lela, and a tax of $2.25 levied by the Sultan on every household in Krian, which was the royal district (Sadka, 1968: 385).

23. See note 17.
24. Of course, this may also be looked at inversely. Then, the practices elsewhere would all become exceptional with Krian being the sole exemplar of the norm.
25. See note 20.
26. "… Kedah … saw in 1883 the promulgation of two proclamations by its Sultan which purported, *inter alia*, to impose land-tax (*hasil tanah*) on all land-holdings; to require the obtaining of a permit for clearing forest land, and to provide for the issue of documents of title for occupied land…. All these were clearly indicative of a process of transformation of a Malay ruler's political authority into his superior ownership of land in the new conditions of the nineteenth-century Malay peninsula under direct or indirect colonial influences" (David Wong, 1975: 20).
27. David Wong has comprehensively discussed the emergence and legal significance of such legislation in the Malay States. Lim Teck Ghee (1976) has provided a detailed historical account of the development of the prototype land legislation in Perak. Jacoby has also discussed the significance of the law affecting land tenure for peasant cultivation (IBRD, 1955). See also Das (1963).
28. "The system of land-tenure as it evolved in the Federated Malay States of Perak, Selangor, Negri Sembilan and Pahang served as a model for successive British Agents and Advisers in the Unfederated Malay States of Kelantan, Kedah, Perlis, Terengganu and Johore…. In this it reflected the tendency of British policy towards uniformity, but the application of similar legislation to a number of disparate communities, differing in density and composition of population, methods of cultivation, the extent of the intrusion of alien economic forces, and the degree to which customary inheritance practices have been modified by Islam, resulted in a land tenure situation displaying considerable local variation" (H. Wilson, 1975: 120).
29. "Under the terms of the new legislation, all land which had not been alienated, nor reserved for a public purpose, nor reserved forest, was considered to be State Land, the ownership of which rested in the ruler of the State in which it was located" (H. Wilson, 1975: 130).
30. "… in Krian, in 1874, it was difficult to get ten dollars an *orlong* for excellent rice land by *pulang belanja* [return of expenses], but when security of tenure and the

full right of alienation of the soil were introduced in the district by the British Government, it became possible to sell the same land for $60 or $70 an *orlong*" (Maxwell, 1884).

31. "... the easier acquisition of state-sponsored credit by planters, the greater participation by Government and heavier investment of state revenue in plantation agricultural schemes and the lack of interest shown by Government experimental gardens in native crops" (Lim Teck Ghee, 1976: 130). Administrative actions adopted to improve peasant agriculture were few and even these "proved to be more in the way of half-hearted, disjointed and niggardly measures rather than a concerted programme" (Lim Teck Ghee, 1976: 141).

32. In the last quarter of the nineteenth century, colonial expenditure in the Malay States was mainly oriented to the promotion of the tin industry, which British capitalists were anxious to wrest control of, and which was the most important export of the region, as far as British industry was concerned. Thus, for example, the first railways were built to connect tin-mining centres with coastal ports. Later, as rubber took the place of tin, colonial expenditure shifted accordingly. Even on the rare occasions when colonial expenditure was ostensibly to serve peasant interests, e.g. in the development of the Krian Irrigation Scheme to promote rice production, the ultimate interests served were still the capitalist employers of rice-eating workers and the colonial state which had to pay for rice imports with foreign exchange. For further discussion, see (Jomo 1986: Chapter 3).

33. For example, "Fixed rents originated as feudal dues, which were continued after the disintegration of the Raja feudalism" (T.B. Wilson, 1958: 10).

34. "There are only one hundred and twenty titles of over thirty-five acres each (10 Kedah relong) in the whole of the west coast padi plain from the southern district boundary of Krian in Perak to the northern Siamese border of Perlis."

    "These few large titles are outstanding in size, and range up to 210 acres each with an average of 91 acres, whilst throughout this area, all rice land titles averaged only five acres. Consequently this handful of titles accounts for over 11,000 acres, or about three per cent of the main rice land area in which they are found."

    "Each title often has more than one owner, usually the result of subdivision or inheritance. But fragmentation is less common and less advanced than on holdings of normal size, and it tends to be outweighed by plural ownership, i.e. the possession by the same owner of whole or part shares in other holdings. In one instance in Krian, six persons are named as co-owners on each of four large titles, which together total over 900 acres of rice land."

    "Over all the rice lands of north-west Malaya, approximately three owners existed for each of these large titles, i.e. about 350 owners owned about three per cent of the main rice land area in the form of large holdings. Thus only a small proportion of the main rice land is shown, by the *prima facie* evidence of the cadastral sheets, to be concentrated in the hands of a few proprietors, although some of these possess some very large properties" (T.B. Wilson, 1958: 63–4).

35. Rent has been identified as the largest cost item in rice production, e.g. see T.B. Wilson (1958: 22); and Lim Chong-Yah (1967: 168). Selvadurai (1972c: 16) estimated, from a survey of rice production in Krian, Perak, that land accounts for

at least 82 per cent of total "farm capital". This should be viewed in the context of the extent of tenancy in rice production, since for the average farm size of 3.1 acres, only 1.6 acres is owned while the rest is rented. However, such estimates may now have to be revised downward in recognition of recent technological changes in rice and other agricultural production requiring heavy investments in machinery, chemicals, etc. Nevertheless, it is hardly likely that such increases in fixed capital investments detract from the centrality of land to peasant production.

36. "The root cause of poverty boils down to a race between population growth on the one hand and technological progress and opening up of new lands on the other" (Lim Chong-Yah, 1967: 173).

37. "... overpopulation is likewise a historically determined relation, in no way determined by abstract numbers or by the absolute limit of productivity of the necessaries of life, but by limits posited rather by *specific conditions of production.*"

38. Current studies have only touched on them tangentially (e.g. see Guyot, 1971; Noor, 1974; Husin, 1975).

39. Kuchiba and Tsubouchi (1967: 470) mention that inheritance according to Islamic law and Malay custom (*adat*) were about equal in number in the Kedah village they studied.

40. "... the increase in the number of joint owners, and the diminution in the size of the interests of individual owners, was a strong incentive to sell the land to someone in a position to purchase it as a composite unit. The new owners were naturally not the impoverished and landless in the reservation, but persons who already owned substantial income-producing holdings or who had other substantial sources of income" (Fisk, 1961: 21).

41. "Thus we find co-owners with 1/127-th shares and others with 9/64-th shares and so forth" (Aziz, 1958: 23).

The Payne Land Administration Commission in Malaya stated in 1958:

Without attempting to find fantastic cases, but merely looking through records at random, we came across nine persons having shares in a small-holding in the following proportions:

$$\frac{12522}{57024}, \frac{12522}{57024}, \frac{6276}{57024}, \frac{3080}{57024}, \frac{1540}{57024}, \frac{1464}{57024}, \frac{732}{57024}, \frac{1569}{57024}, \frac{10893}{57024}$$

In another two acres, one rood, the shares held by eight people respectively were:

$$\frac{1}{2}, \frac{1}{14}, \frac{1}{14}, \frac{1}{14}, \frac{1}{14}, \frac{331737}{2286144}, \frac{27909}{2286144}, \frac{130242}{2286144}$$

Numerous similar illustrations could be given. In one instance we were informed that the share of rural land inherited by one beneficiary amounted to three square feet, and he insisted on having it (quoted in Lim Chong-Yah, 1967: 171).

42. "Co-ownership tends to result in neglect of land or use of poor techniques, lack of conservation measures and unwillingness to make long-term improvements to the land. It also tends towards landlordism because it is simpler *for* the co-owners

to share the value of the rent rather than any other economic arrangement" (Aziz, 1958: 24).

43. "A consequence of subdivision is that farmers find a single piece of land too small. In order to make better use of their time and energy they try to operate several pieces of land. Generally the pieces they inherit, buy or rent will not be contiguous. This process where the pieces of land on particular farms are scattered about the village is called fragmentation" (Aziz, 1958: 23).

44. "... under the combined effects of scarcity of land, the question of the peasant's place of residence after marriage, the laws of inheritance, etc., the land owned by the peasants is geographically dispersed, and the result is a strong tendency to fragment the cultivated land holdings" (Kuchiba and Tsubouchi, 1967: 472).

45. Concentration of land-ownership refers to the process whereby land parcels, previously owned separately, are brought under common ownership. In so far as such land is not contiguous, it gives rise to fragmentation of land owned. Concentration, as discussed in relation to land-ownership, cannot therefore be viewed as analogous to the concentration of capital.

46. For example, Swift (1967: 251) has argued that maintenance of a certain level of "normal" consumption is not a major cause of land sales. Instead, he suggests, land transfers are usually caused by the incurrence of extraordinary expenditure.

47. For example, pre-season rent payments economically limit the amount of land a poor peasant — who might otherwise be willing and prepared to cultivate a larger area of land — can rent.

48. Barnard has suggested that most rice farmers who are able to cultivate more than the "economic minimum" have at least two parcels. "This suggests that the process of accumulation of land by a minority has, in the long run, possibly as great an effect on patterns of landholding as the opposite process of the fragmentation [sic] or division of holdings into increasingly smaller units among the majority" (Barnard, 1970: 34).

49. For example, slaughter tapping of rubber trees by tenants can affect the long-term productivity of the trees, whereas similar possibilities with tenant rice farmers are more difficult to come by.

50. Tenurial arrangements between individuals differ fundamentally from those between individuals and the state, such as freehold, leasehold, and temporary occupation licences. The latter do not come into consideration here though they are not without significance for peasants. Whether or not the ground rent claim based on ownership of land property is exploitative will not be debated here. In the view presumed here, rent is a claim to surplus labour, and is therefore necessarily exploitative. An alternative neo-classical economic perspective would deny this, e.g.: "The existence of tenancy ... cannot be automatically construed as detrimental or indicative of 'exploitation'. Tenancy may be an efficient means of farming by dividing labour between those who are more efficient in cultivation and those who are more efficient in management" (Y. Huang, 1971: 706).

51. The five basic types of agreements defined in terms of form of rent payment, and ownership and trust arrangements are listed here together with the most common equivalent Malay terms (T.B. Wilson, 1958: 11):

fixed rent	*sewa*
crop-sharing	*pawah*
lease	*pajak*
loan	*gadai*
mortgage	*jual janji* (literally "promissory sale")
ownership	*sendiri*
trust	*pelaka*

52. "Subdivision and fragmentation interact as causal factors with indebtedness, tenancy, and other features of rural poverty in a cumulative process of circular causation, not only to bring about increasing inequalities in the distribution of rural income, land and capital, but also to expedite the disintegration of the very *kampong* socio-economic structure itself" (Aziz, 1958: 24).

53. "The Ordinance specifies the duties of tenants to practise good husbandry, but does not specify the duties of landlords to keep a clean title, make-up-to-date registration of ownership details, pay land dues and rates, and maintain survey boundary marks. The Agreement Form prescribed by the Ordinance requires tenants 'to defray all expenses and perform all work necessary for the construction, and putting and keeping in order of any dams, etc.' which is landlord's responsibility as a capital improvement and, if executed by the tenant, should be subject to compensation" (T.B. Wilson, 1958: 95).

54. The exception which proved the rule took place in parts of Kedah for one season: "Police prosecution of eight landlords for extortionate rents in four *mukim* of Kedah in 1956 and 1957, did ensure almost 100 per cent registration of tenancy agreements in the 1956/57 season compared with an overall 15 per cent registration for the rest of Kedah and Perlis" (T.B. Wilson, 1958: 96).

CHAPTER 6

Labour Laws and Industrial Relations

Jomo K. S. and Vijayakumari Kanapathy

Large-scale production under colonialism was initially organized with un-free labour under indenture or otherwise not able to make employment choices associated with labour freedom elsewhere in modern capitalist economies. Free labour in the modern sense began to emerge in the 1930s following earlier colonial efforts to "free" Chinese labour from Chinese employers and the protests of Indian nationalist activists protesting the exploitation and abuse of Indian labourers in colonial Malaya. Communist-led "political unionism" right after the Japanese Occupation was suppressed from 1948, with "economic unionism" encouraged as part of the colonial counter-insurgency strategy "to win hearts and minds".

As this chapter will show, post-colonial labour legislation complemented industrialization strategies and responded to changed economic conditions. Post-colonial union activity was initially often associated with social-democratic activism. Repression against the non-insurgent left from the mid-1960s also affected labour activism. The post-1969 effort to develop a new social contract initially involved an effort to promote tripartism involving organized labour, employers and their government. In the 1980s, Mahathir sought to promote Japanese-style industrial relations without significant improvements in employee welfare, in-house or company unions instead of trades unions and various state-sponsored attempts to divide the major labour centres.

The general attitude of the colonial government towards labour relations was one of "denial". In the closing years of the colonial period, politicized leaders had organized workers into movements to challenge colonial authority, affecting both work discipline and industrial relations. Before the Japanese Occupation, labour unions were not allowed in colonial Malaya and there was no trade union law in existence until 1940 (Jomo and Todd, 1994). After the war, laws were passed to govern wages (e.g. the Wages Councils Ordinance, 1947), compensation payable to employees who sustained injuries in the course of work, and the general welfare of employees. Labour unions played an important part in the anti-colonial nationalist movement after the Japanese Occupation. However, most were banned and their leaders detained, with some executed in 1948 as part of the repression against the militant left. Union membership dropped by two-thirds due to the repression of 1948. The Trade Disputes Ordinance (1949) severely curbed the right of workers to strike, especially those in "essential services", which is loosely defined.

With the change in British colonial tactics in the early 1950s, trade union organizations and even a Labour Party were allowed, if not encouraged, by the colonial authorities as part of the late colonial government's efforts to win the "hearts and minds" of the population. These laws included the Worker Compensations Ordinance, 1952 and Employment Ordinance, 1955. When first enacted, the Employment Ordinance was only intended to apply to employees earning a monthly salary of no more than RM700.[1] Statutory minimum non-wage benefits were set under the Employment Ordinance, 1955. However, the Ordinance only clearly covers non-casual workers earning less than RM1,250 a month; industrial relations laws are unclear on the status of sub-contract, temporary and probationary workers if a prior written employment contract does not exist. In addition, the Employment Ordinance, 1955, provides for summary dismissal of workers on potentially spurious grounds such as misconduct.

Post-colonial Industrial Relations

Subsequently, the post-colonial government introduced the Trade Unions Ordinance, 1959 to control the growth and development of the trade union movement. The Trade Unions Act, 1959 governs the formation of unions, their form of organization and financial controls. Realising the importance of peaceful industrial relations as one of the factors attracting foreign investors to Malaysia, the post-colonial government broke with the English preference for abstention from industrial relations, and introduced, in 1960, emergency legislation to control trade disputes involving strikes and other forms of industrial action.

In the field of industrial relations, the most significant development was the introduction of compulsory arbitration, first through the Industrial Arbitration Tribunal in 1965, and later, through the Industrial Court in 1967 under the Industrial Relations Act, 1967. Until that time, there was the Industrial Court, set up in 1941, and later, under the Industrial Court Ordinance, 1948. Essentially, it was a court of voluntary arbitration in the sense that the consent of both parties to the dispute had to be obtained before any reference to the Court. This Court continued to co-exist with the Industrial Arbitration Tribunal up until 1967, when both these Courts were replaced by the present Industrial Court, set up under the provisions of the Industrial Relations Act, 1967. Under the present Act, when there is a trade dispute and the matter cannot otherwise be resolved, the Labour (now Human Resources) Minister can refer the matter to the Industrial Court at the joint request of the trade union, representing the workers, and the employer, or a trade union representing the employer. The Minister may also refer any trade dispute to the Court if he is satisfied that it is expedient to do so.

In 1971, amendments to the Industrial Relations Act of 1967 limited the right to strike by designating various issues non-strikeable, strengthened the power of management by no longer requiring employers to state reasons for dismissal, bolstered "responsible" unions and fragmented labour unity. Under provisions of the Employment Ordinance, officers of the Department of Labour are empowered to decide on matters relating to conditions of employment and wage advances; their decisions can only be reversed by the High Court. This exposes workers to the whims and fancies of officials.

To ensure greater flexibility in wage determination and to foster the growth of a responsible workforce, amendments were made in 1988 to three major pieces of labour legislation, namely the Industrial Relations Act, 1967, the Trade Unions Act, 1959 and the Employment Act, 1955. Among other objectives, the amendments sought to promote industrial harmony, reduce wage rigidities and raise labour productivity to improve Malaysia's international competitiveness. Some of these reforms were revised following the 1997–98 crisis.

Union leaders have also been detained under and intimidated by the Internal Security Act under which a person can be jailed indefinitely without trial. In addition, "management functions" pertaining to promotions, transfers and redundancies are legally considered prerogatives not subject to collective bargaining, and a federation of unions can only be formed if it consists of unions whose membership is confined to a particular trade or industry. Malaysian labour laws also allow the formation of in-house unions even when a national union already exists in the industry.

In general, the growth and development of trade unions in the country have reflected government interventions to control trade union activities. Trade union membership dropped in the early 1970s in response to repressive legislation, but picked up around the mid-1970s, when union activities grew again. This has been attributed to the increase of Malays in wage employment, especially in the public sector, and the desire of the government to project a new social contract.

Rapid structural transformation in the economy and changes in the sectoral distribution of labour has altered the role, representativeness and functions of trade unions. While about one-third of union members were employed in agriculture in 1969, their representation dropped to less than ten per cent by the turn of the century. Over the same period, the proportion of union members in manufacturing increased to 22 per cent, while union membership in services expanded marginally by 3 per cent.

The degree of unionization in the public sector has been greater than in the private sector, though industrial actions have been more frequent in the private sector. Public sector unions have fewer rights than private sector unions. In terms of union size, the previous trend towards large memberships in a relatively small number of unions has been partly reversed by government efforts to promote in-house unions. Though less bureaucratic and better able to handle problems of individual members in particular work places, small unions lack the necessary clout and resources to bring about significant change.

While several concessions were granted to trade unions in the 1970s, this period also saw the introduction of stringent laws and regulations in 1971, 1976 and 1980, and the use of the Internal Security Act (ISA) — which provides for arbitrary arrest and indefinite detention without trial — against labour. Trade unions capable of agitating effectively for higher wages have been shut out as far as possible. The 1980s witnessed the introduction of more policies to suppress the labour movement. In 1980, the government introduced amendments to further tighten the already restrictive labour laws, further limit union rights and increase constraints on unions, while improving overtime payments and retrenchment benefits.

Government interventions alone did not suppress trade union development. Internal disputes, partly caused by differences in opinions on labour issues and partly due to intense personal rivalry and power struggles, led to serious splits in trade union organizations, preventing them from representing labour more effectively. The lack of consensus among leaders, particularly between public and private sector unionists, and frequent public bickering has seriously affected their credibility and strength, and made it easier for the government to undermine the labour movement in the country.

Though many trade union leaders have had experience, they have largely failed to run the labour centres effectively. The inability of the unions to organize widespread industrial action enabled the government to take restrictive measures against unions and labour without fear of any retaliatory response from labour. Unions could not oppose labour laws as these do not come within the definition of a "trade dispute", and therefore, no dissenting industrial action could be legally organized.

Labour Legislation

Labour standards, employee welfare and industrial relations in Malaysia are governed by a series of laws that have evolved over the past six decades. Of these, the Employment Act, 1955 (Akta Kerja, 1955), the Trade Unions Act, 1959 (Akta Kesatuan Sekerja, 1959), and the Industrial Relations Act, 1967 (Akta Perhubungan Perusahaan, 1967) are the principal pieces of legislation that affect labour, and have undergone substantive amendments aimed at regulating and controlling wage labour in the country.

— The Employment Act, 1955 sets out the terms and conditions of service, and the minimum benefits that have to be accorded.

— The Trade Union Act, 1959 allows most Malaysian workers to engage in trade union activities with some exceptions.

— The Industrial Relations Act, 1967 (IRA) defines the legal framework for employer-employee relations.

— The Employees' Social Security Act, 1969 is essentially an insurance scheme to protect workers against contingencies. The Social Security Organization (SOCSO) was set up to implement, administer and enforce the Act which offers two protection schemes, i.e. the Employment Injury Scheme and the Invalidity Pension Scheme.

— All employees, irrespective of their occupation, are covered by the Employees' Provident Fund Act, 1951. Both employers and employees make mandatory contributions to the Fund, which can be withdrawn upon retirement, death, disability or emigration. Partial withdrawals are allowed for specific purposes.

— Malaysia does not have a national minimum wage, but the Wages Councils Act, 1947 provides for minimum wages in those sectors or regions of the country where a need arises.

— The Workers' Minimum Standards of Housing and Amenities Act, 1990 regulates the type of housing and basic utilities to be provided to employees on plantations.

The Employment Act, 1955 is the most important piece of legislation governing employment matters. It stipulates minimum standards with respect to wages, working hours, leave, termination and lay-off benefits. However, the Act covers only those earning RM1,500 or less and those engaged in manual labour irrespective of their wages. The terms and conditions of employment of others are regulated by common law usage or by their employment contract. The Industrial Relations Act and the Trade Union Act deal specifically with industrial relations in the country. The rest of the legislation provides for the welfare of workers, mostly in accordance with ILO Conventions and Recommendations.

The major acts and their respective administrative and enforcement agencies are as follows:

(i)   Employees' Social Security Act, 1969 — Social Security Organization (SOCSO)
      [Akta Keselamatan Sosial Pekerja, 1969 — Pertubuhan Keselamatan Sosial (PERKESO)]
(ii) Workmen's Compensation Act, 1952 — Labour Department
      (Akta Pampasan Pekerja, 1952 — Jabatan Buruh)
(iii) Employees' Provident Fund Act, 1951 — Employees' Provident Fund
      (Akta Kumpulan Wang Simpanan Pekerja, 1951 — Kumpulan Wang Simpanan Pekerja)
(iv) Occupational Safety and Health Act, 1994 — Occupational Safety and Health Department
      (Akta Keselamatan dan Kesihatan Pekerjaan, 1994 — Jabatan Keselamatan dan Kesihatan Pekerjaan)
(v)   Wages Council Act, 1947 — Labour Department
      (Akta Majlis Penetapan Gaji, 1947 — Jabatan Buruh)
(vi) Workers' Minimum Standards of Housing and Amenities Act, 1990 — Labour Department
      (Akta Standard-Standard Minimum Perumahan dan Kemudahan Pekerja, 1990 — Jabatan Buruh)

Collective Bargaining

As elsewhere, the principal function of trade unions in Malaysia has been the negotiated improvement of members' wages and working conditions. Unions and employers negotiate wages and conditions, and since 1975, it has been mandatory to register collective agreements reached with the Industrial Court. Since then, the number of collective agreements recognized has risen from 155 in 1975 to 324 in 2004. However, the coverage of workers by collective agreements is very uneven, with some industries having well-established collective agreement procedures and others having none.

The Industrial Relations Act, 1967 defines the legal framework for collective bargaining. Unions and employers negotiate wages and working conditions, and since 1975, it is mandatory to register all collective agreements reached with the Industrial Court. Since then, the number of collective agreements recognized has risen significantly from 155 in 1975 to 324 in 2004. All collective agreements are binding for a period of three years.

Amendments to the Industrial Relations Act as well as changes in the attitude and role of the Labour (later Human Resources) Ministry have also increasingly restricted the role of unions in collective bargaining. The government succeeded in reducing strikes drastically compared to earlier decades through legislative restrictions imposed in 1971 and again in 1980. Though some unions are still legally allowed to organize strikes, government actions since 1980 have forced trade unions to resort to less effective forms of industrial action, such as picketing.

The scope for collective bargaining, in terms of the subjects open to negotiations, has been increasingly restricted over time. Bargaining management decisions in respect to recruitment, promotions, transfers, job assignments or termination of employment by dismissals or retrenchment is not permitted. The Industrial Relations Act, 1967 also prohibits collective agreements in pioneer industries from providing better terms and conditions of service or employment than those provided for under the Employment Act, 1955 during the first five years of operation.

Strikes are allowed, but are subject to various restrictions: prior notice has to be given, a strike ballot has to be taken, the secret ballot registered within seven days with the Director-General (previously Registrar), who has 90 days to check its validity. In addition, strikes are prohibited once a dispute has been referred to arbitration by the Minister of Labour. The definition of strikes has been expanded to include unauthorized reductions in work such as go-slows. With these restrictive measures, the government has succeeded in reducing strikes drastically from a peak of 64 strikes with 45,749 workdays lost in 1975 to only 9 strikes in 1988, including 5,784 workdays lost. Union activity and industrial actions generally rose as the labour market tightened, and the number of strikes increased to 23 in 1991. More recently, the number of strikes fell to three in 2004. Union activity is closely linked to labour market conditions and strengthens the bargaining position of trade unions as the labour market tightens, as in the early and mid-1990s until the 1998 downturn and the slower economic growth since.

The Employment Act, 1955 provides for an adjudicating machinery, i.e. the Labour Court, where an employee may seek redress on disputes arising out of any provisions of the Act or contract terms which involve payment of wages or other cash benefits. Besides the Labour Court, the Industrial Court — established under the Industrial Relations Act, 1967 — provides one other avenue for redress, irrespective of the amount earned. The Industrial Court deals with cases where employees have been terminated without just cause or excuse, and seek to be reinstated in their former employment.

To cope with economic uncertainty and increasing international competitiveness, firms everywhere are moving towards greater employment and wage flexibility. Malaysian employers responded to economic recovery and deregulation in the mid-1980s by hiring more temporary and contract workers. By doing so, they were able to hire and fire more easily as and when the need arose, and thus held down labour costs. Employers were able to circumvent employment protection regulations and non-wage costs by avoiding social security contributions and other institutional rigidities such as collective agreements.

Since the mid-1980s, increasing casualization has occurred in selected sectors through the use of more contract workers, either through direct contract for service or through subcontractors, part-time work and home-based work. Casualization is more prevalent in sectors hiring more migrant workers such as plantation fieldwork, construction activities, sales (promotion of consumer products), the transport industry and components production, such as for garments, electronics, metal fabrication and wood-based industries.

Employment flexibility may enhance efficiency, but unless accompanied by labour laws and regulations to accord adequate protection for those affected by the changing terms of employment, it would lead to greater labour insecurity as well as worse terms and conditions of employment. The trend seems to be towards partial deregulation to enhance labour flexibility generally, especially in the more regulated formal sector. There seem to be few efforts to regularize employment conditions in the informal sector, which remains largely beyond the scope of most labour laws and regulations.

Only about 9 per cent of the labour force and less than 15 per cent of all wage labour is organized, due to stringent legislation, official and employer discouragement as well as weak trade union organization. Growing use of cheaper immigrant labour, increasing labour flexibility and government encouragement of in-house unions and rival labour centres have effectively weakened trade union power. In the face of other repressive legislation, Malaysian unions have generally failed to develop sufficient bargaining power to obtain substantial improvements for their members or to counter government restrictions on the labour movement.

Nonetheless, the last three decades have witnessed the international development of several new labour standards, which have raised existing standards and established new ones in Malaysia in many employment related fields including wages, other employment benefits, safety and security. Malaysia has also developed a fairly well-developed machinery to enforce some minimum labour standards, including regulations to safeguard the safety and security of workers.

Pressure to improve labour standards has mainly come about as a result of rapid socioeconomic development and rising public awareness, which has increased social consciousness in the labour force, as well as external pressures by international trade union organizations and other activist groups. More recent labour market reforms, such as improvements in worker training and education, have been primarily motivated by employer concerns and government interventions in the face of rapid technological development and greater international competitiveness, some of which have improved incomes and the standard of living of workers.

Industrial Disputes

The Industrial Relations Department is responsible for the prevention and settlement of industrial disputes through its conciliatory services. Conciliation is invariably the first option available to both parties. However, in the event of failure to settle, the dispute could be referred for binding arbitration to the Industrial Court (Mahkamah Perusahaan) by the Minister of Labour, either on the basis of a joint application by both parties or at the Minister's initiative. The Industrial Court, established under the Industrial Relations Act, 1967 is an integral part of the industrial relations system in the country, and is the ultimate arbiter of industrial disputes in the country. The government assumes a fairly active role in dispute settlements. The Minister not only refers disputes for binding arbitration to the Industrial Court but also uses his power and influence to convince both parties to modify their demands to maintain industrial peace and stability.

The success rate of collective bargaining is roughly 50 per cent at the stage of direct bilateral negotiations, 25 per cent at the stage of conciliation (assisted negotiation) with the remaining 25 per cent referred to arbitration. Of the deadlocked negotiations, 50 per cent are referred to arbitration voluntarily at the joint request of both labour and management. As noted above, strike activity is minimal, with about three per cent of the total disputes in 1991 resulting in strikes.

The Court, in making an award, is required to "have regard for the public interest, the financial implications, and the effect of the award on the country, the industry concerned and also to the probable effect on similar industries" (Section (4) Industrial Relations Act 1967). As noted earlier, all collective agreements have to be recognized by the Industrial Court, implying that the Court has the power to refuse to register a collective agreement if it is not deemed to be in the national interest. The Industrial Court is under the Ministry of Human Resources and is headed by a President. The President is assisted by eight other chairpersons from the legal profession with at least ten years experience. All administrative matters are handled by the Registrar. Each of the cases referred to are presided by either the President or one of the Chairpersons and two other panel members. The panel members for each case are chosen from a gazetted list of about 100 members appointed from employers' associations and trade unions for terms of two years.

Other Labour Market Institutions

National Authorities

The Ministry of Human Resources (Kementerian Sumber Manusia) is the principal agency responsible for most matters affecting the labour market.[2] It is organized into the following departments, each with its own functions:

(i)   Labour Department (Jabatan Buruh)
(ii) Industrial Relations Department (IRD) (Jabatan Perhubungan Perusahaan)
(iii) Department of Trade Unions Affairs (Jabatan Hal Ehwal Kesatuan Sekerja)
(iv) Occupational Health and Safety Department (Jabatan Keselamatan dan Kesihatan Pekerjaan)
(v)   Manpower Department (MD) (Jabatan Tenaga Rakyat)
(vi) National Vocational Training Council (NVTC) (Majlis Latihan Vokasional Kebangsaan)
(vii) Human Resources Development Council (HRDC) (Majlis Pembangunan Sumber Manusia)

The Labour Department administers and enforces labour standards and protection measures laid down under the labour laws. It provides technical advice to industries and potential investors on matters related to labour laws, and decides on disputes between employees and employers regarding terms and conditions of employment through the Labour Courts (Mahkamah Buruh).

The Industrial Relations Department monitors and fosters harmonious relations between employers and employees. It provides conciliatory services to assist in the prevention and settlement of trade disputes and industrial actions, as well as disputes pertaining to unfair dismissal. Processing of claims for recognition by trade unions to enable them to pursue collective bargaining is also handled by the IRD.

The Department of Trade Union Affairs is in charge of supervising, directing and controlling all matters related to trade union activities as provided for under the Trade Unions Act, 1959 (Akta Kesatuan Sekerja, 1959).

All industrial training activities come under the purview of the MD, NVTC and the HRDC. The MD carries out training through its various technical training institutes established throughout the country, while the NVTC promotes, coordinates and reviews vocational and industrial training in the country. The HRDC stimulates training in the private sector through a mandatory levy-grant scheme.

Employers' Associations

The Malaysian Employers' Federation (MEF) (Persekutuan Majikan-Majikan Malaysia) is the most representative employers' organization in the country. It is not involved in collective bargaining, but offers advice to its members and influences government policy by submitting memoranda to the government on a range of subjects pertaining to the labour market. Being the most representative organization of employers, it is also invited to sit on the boards of several government statutory bodies involved in employee affairs and the National Labour Advisory Council (Majlis Penasihat Buruh Kebangsaan), the tripartite forum set up to discuss matters pertaining to labour. The Council was set up in the mid-1970s and then revived in the late 1980s with representatives from relevant government agencies, employers' associations and the trade unions.[3] It is supposed to be a consultative mechanism for discussing labour relations as well as ways and means to overcome problems by arriving at a consensus, although it does not have much of a track record to inspire much confidence. It usually convenes about four times in a year, and is chaired by the Minister.

Trade Unions

Although in principle, any seven persons could form a union, the Director-General (formerly Registrar) of Trade Unions (RTU) has wide discretionary powers in recognizing unions, including the ability to accord registration, to cancel registration (e.g. if there are more than two unions catering to the same workers), and to determine the nature of the bargaining unit.

Most unions are small, with about half having less than 200 members. The growth of smaller unions is largely due to the government's policy of encouraging Japanese-style in-house unions. As of 1995, there were 366 in-house unions, accounting for about 43 per cent of total union membership, and about half of them were in the private sector. With rapid structural change in the economy and the sectoral redistribution of labour, the membership in agriculture fell from about a third in 1969 to 9 per cent in 2005, whereas union membership in manufacturing increased more than three-fold from 7 to 24 per cent during this period, less than the share of manufacturing workers in the wage labour force. Union membership grew at a slower pace in the 1980s (by 2.3 per cent per annum) and since, compared to the 1970s (by 5.9 per cent per annum). This has been largely attributed to the restrictive legislative and non-legislative actions by the government to weaken the trade union movement (Jomo and Todd, 1994).

The Malaysian Trade Union Congress (MTUC) (Kongres Kesatuan Sekerja Malaysia) is the major association of unions, mainly from the private sector, while the Congress of Union of Employees in the Public and Civil Services

(CUEPACS) (Kongres Kesatuan Pekerja-Pekerja di Dalam Perkhidmatan Awam) is the most representative organization of public sector unions. In 2004, there were 611 unions, with a total membership of 783,108 members, which was about 8 per cent of the total employed in the country.

Public/Independent Employment Services

The Manpower Department provides employment services through its labour departments located at the state and district levels throughout the country. Job-seekers can register with the local labour departments, which then places them in vacancies reported by employers. An Electronic Labour Exchange was launched in 2001 to facilitate job search and job placements. The Labour Department also provides career guidance to job-seekers. In general, the services of the Labour Department are in greater demand during periods of high unemployment, such as in the mid-1980s or late 1990s.

The Manpower Department also administers and enforces the Private Employment Agencies Act, 1981. All private agencies are required to obtain licenses from the Manpower Department, and there are currently about 760 registered private employment agencies in the country, with the majority located in the Klang Valley. A small fee is usually charged for their services, and in most cases, the employer absorbs the fee.

The tight labour market in the mid-1990s reduced the dependence of job-seekers on employment agencies and the intake of large numbers of foreign workers encouraged private employment agencies to be more actively engaged in the recruitment and placement of foreign workers.

Minimum Pay

Malaysia does not have a statutory national minimum wage, but the Wage Councils Act, 1947 provides for minimum wages in those sectors or regions of the country where the need arises. Under the law, workers in an industry who believe that they need the protection of a minimum wage may request that a wage council be established. Representatives from labour, management and government sit on the council. At present, minimum wages apply only to employees in hotel and catering services, shop assistants, cinema workers, as well as stevedores and cargo handlers in Penang. There are an estimated 140,000 workers, or 2 per cent of the workforce, covered by the minimum wages set by the various wage councils.

Working Time

The law permits a 48-hour working week. In other words, the working hours per day should not exceed eight hours. These eight hours of work must be performed within a span of ten continuous hours from the time work begins for the day. If work is performed after the end of the ten-hour period, then it is deemed as overtime work even though a worker may not have actually done eight hours in the day. Time given for rest is generally not included in the calculation of working hours. In practice, however, the average number of hours worked varies between industries, ranging from 39 hours in the banking industry to about 46 hours in manufacturing.

The limit of eight hours per day can be varied subject to certain conditions, but under no circumstances, can a worker be required to work for more than 12 hours in any day inclusive of overtime work. Any one day in each week should be set aside as a rest day. The current hourly rates of overtime pay for working on days of rest is twice the hourly pay, and for working on holidays 3.5 times the hourly pay.

Females are prohibited from working in industrial or agricultural undertakings between 10 p.m. and 5 a.m. and from commencing work for the next day without having had 11 consecutive hours of rest. The Director General of Labour can, however, grant exemptions with respect to the former in special cases, provided the female worker consents to such arrangements, and the employer provides free transport. In addition, the employer has to pay a night shift allowance.

The Child and Young Persons Employment Act, 1966 (Akta [Pekerjaan] Kanak-Kanak dan Orang Muda, 1966), prohibits the employment of children (below 14 years) and young persons (14 to 16 years), except under certain conditions. One of the main conditions imposed concerns the number of hours worked and the time during which they are allowed to work. The details are summarized in Table 1.

With regard to annual leave, an employee is entitled to paid annual leave at the ordinary rate of pay after having completed 12 months of continuous service with an employer. The number of days of annual leave increases with the duration of employment:

- 8 days if employed for less than two years.
- 12 days if employed for two or more, but less than five years.
- 16 days if employed for five years or more.

Maternity Benefits

Malaysia provides generous maternity benefits compared to most other developing countries. Female workers in the private sector are entitled to 60 consecutive days of maternity leave with pay, while those in the public sector

Table 1. Regulations Pertaining to the Employment of Children

Employment of a Child *(below 14 years)*	*Employment of a Young Person* *(14 to 16 years)*
i. Engaged only in employment involving "light work suitable to his capacity" in any undertaking carried on by his family. ii. Only permitted to work between 7 a.m. to 8 p.m. iii. Not permitted to work for more than 3 consecutive hours without a period of rest of at least 30 minutes. iv. Cannot work for more than 6 hours a day, but if attending school, the total time spent at work and at school cannot exceed 7 hours in a day. v. Cannot commence work on any day without having had a period of not less than 14 consecutive hours free from work.	i. May be engaged in any undertaking (whether or not the undertaking is carried on by his family) where the employment is suitable to his capacity. (However, a female young person may not be employed in hotels, bars, restaurants and boarding houses or clubs unless such establishments are operated by her parents.) ii. Permitted to work only between 6 a.m. to 8 p.m. iii. Cannot work for more than 7 hours a day, but if attending school, the total period spent in school and at work cannot exceed 8 hours in a day. iv. Cannot work for more than 4 consecutive hours without a period of rest of at least 30 minutes. v. Cannot commence work on any day without having a period of rest of not less than 12 consecutive hours free from work.

are also given 60 days with pay for up to five surviving children as of May 1998 (42 days previously). In both cases, the employer bears the cost of maternity pay. Employers are prohibited from terminating the services of a female employee during this period, or during the 90 days following her maternity leave if she has been certified unfit to work due to illness related to her pregnancy. Paternal leave is not provided for under the law, but it has become a common practice for the private sector to grant leave, ranging from a minimum of one to a maximum of four days. The norm is usually one day, but increasingly, more companies are granting two days. Paternity leave in the public sector was raised from three to seven days in 2003.

Part-time and Temporary Employment

Malaysian labour laws are silent on temporary workers. In practice, however, most temporary workers have verbal understandings that can be modified from day to day or from week to week. Others have a written contract for some short-term period such as one to three months. In other words, temporary workers lack both income and employment security (Standing, 1989). In 1992, about 1.2 per cent of those employed in manufacturing were part-timers. This represented a slight drop from 1.4 per cent in 1985, when the incidence of part-time workers increased as employers began to hire more part-timers to cope with economic uncertainties during the recession. The incidence of part-time employment has been gradually declining to 0.7 per cent in 2003. The Employment Act, 1955 was amended to explicitly specify the terms and conditions of part-time and temporary work. This was done with a view to encourage housewives, students and retirees to enter the job market, to ease the tight labour market, by reducing the financial burden on employees.

Worker Participation

Malaysia does not have any legal provisions for worker participation. However, a few manufacturers, especially the electronic firms that have moved away from labour-intensive assembly operations to high-technology-based production, now operate more flexible work practices that encourage worker participation. These new production processes use techniques such as Total Quality Control (TQM), Just-in-Time (JIT) and Materials Requisition Planning (MRP) which require worker inputs into decisions on the shop floor.

Discrimination

Presently, there is no anti-discrimination legislation to guarantee equal opportunities in recruitment, career development, social security and working conditions, regardless of race, religion or gender. Nonetheless, Malaysia ratified the United Nations Convention on the elimination of all forms of discrimination against women (CEDAW) in 1995. The Federal Constitution, however, provides for equality of persons under Article 8, Clause 1, which states "All persons are equal before the law and entitled to equal protection of the law." However, Clause 2 states:

> Except as expressly authorized by this Constitution, there shall be no discrimination against citizens on the ground of religion, race, descent or place of birth in any law or in the appointment to any office or employment under a public authority or in the administration of any law relating to the acquisition, holding, or disposition of any property or the establishing or carrying on of any trade, business, profession, vocation or employment.

Thus, discrimination is allowed in accordance with the special provisions of the Constitution, which also allows for Malay "special privileges", ostensibly to compensate for the economic backwardness of this "indigenous community". Since the Independence of Malaya in 1957, it has been "understood" that such privileges also extend to the aboriginal communities (Orang Asli) of the peninsula. Since the formation of Malaysia in 1963, such privileges have also been extended to the "indigenous" (Bumiputera) communities of Sabah and Sarawak. It is sometimes alleged that, in practice, Malays and other Muslims have gained disproportionately from these privileges.

These privileges have been especially important for differential access to educational opportunities and financing, especially at the tertiary and secondary levels, as well as public sector employment and promotion opportunities. Non-Bumiputeras (mainly ethnic Chinese and Indians) as well as non-Muslim Bumiputeras (who constitute the largest single cultural grouping in Sarawak and perhaps in Sabah as well) are therefore ethnic/cultural groups who experience official discrimination by the state. On the other hand, many Bumiputeras and ethnic Indians allege discrimination by ethnic Chinese and sometimes by foreign employers.

There is also unsystematic evidence of gender discrimination, but the patterns seem to vary with location, industry, and even managements. The female labour force participation rate is lower than for males, but there is also considerable variation in this matter, much of it unrelated to discrimination.

The growth in the employment of legal as well as illegal (both documented and undocumented) foreign workers in the Malaysian economy in the last two decades has contributed to the casualization of employment relations as well as a new labour market segmentation, resulting in poorer wages and working conditions for foreign workers generally, especially those illegal and undocumented.

Disability

Disability provisions for those in employment were originally provided for under the Workmen's Compensation Act, 1952. However, the implementation of the Employees' Social Security Act, 1969 has superseded the former, and most of the workers who were formerly covered under the Workmen's Compensation Act are now protected by the provisions of the Employees' Social Security Act.

Currently, the Workmen's Compensation Act is only applicable to establishments with less than five employees, while those with five or more employees and those earning RM2,000 and more are covered by the Employees' Social Security Act. The Workmen's Compensation Act pays compensation to workers for injuries arising out of, and in the course of their employment. All medical fees have to be paid for by the employee. In addition, if the disability lasts for 14 days or more, compensation will be paid every half-month for all the days the workman was not able to work, equivalent to one-third of his wage or RM135, whichever is lower, up to the period the disability ceases or up to a maximum of five years. In the event of total disability, a lump sum compensation is made out, depending on the age of the employee, and in the event of death, a lump sum equal to 45 months earnings, or RM14,000, whichever is less.

The Employees' Social Security Scheme is essentially an insurance scheme to protect workers against contingencies related to work. It includes two types of protection schemes, i.e. the Employment Injury Scheme and the Invalidity Pension Scheme, and is administered by the Social Security Organization (SOCSO). The former provides an employee with protection for industrial accidents that occur at work and while travelling from residence to work place, where he takes his meals during an authorized break or during a journey which is directly related to his job. This Scheme also provides coverage for occupational diseases. The Invalidity Pension Scheme provides the employee with 24-hour coverage in the event of invalidity or death resulting from whatever cause.

All employees earning RM2,000 or less monthly are required to contribute to SOCSO, while those earning more than RM2,000 and who have never registered or contributed to SOCSO are given the option to join subject to agreement by both employer and employee. However, once such an employee is covered under this Act, he will continue to enjoy coverage irrespective of his monthly salary. The Scheme is funded by contributions from employers and employees. An employee is required to contribute 0.5 per cent of his wage for the Invalidity Pension, while the contribution for the Injury Scheme is borne entirely by the employer.

Health and Safety

Health and safety at workplaces were once the responsibility of the Factories and Machinery Department (Jabatan Kilang dan Mesin), which enforced the Factories and Machinery Act, 1967 (Akta Kilang dan Mesin, 1967) and 12 other subsidiary regulations. These legislative provisions stipulate the minimum safety requirements in factories. However, in 1994, the Occupational Safety and Health Act (OSHA) was introduced, with wider scope and coverage to include all work places. The aim is to emphasize the importance of health and safety in the industrial sector, which was increasingly being compromised. There have been over a hundred thousand reported industrial accidents yearly from 1991 to 1995, and over 50 per cent of the accidents reported in the country are in manufacturing.

The Occupational Health and Safety Department was established in 1994 in place of the Factories and Machinery Department to enforce both the laws. Since then, the number of accidents at work gradually declined to 72,666 in 2004. This department is supposed to ensure the safety, health and welfare of persons exposed to safety and health risks arising from activities at the workplace or from operation of high risk machinery. Its principal functions include monitoring, inspecting and auditing safety and health hazard control measures at workplaces. It formulates regulations and guidelines and undertakes promotional and advisory work pertaining to occupational safety and health. Finally, it conducts investigations on work-related accidents and diseases.

A National Occupational Safety and Health Council (Majlis Keselamatan dan Kesihatan Nasional) was also established in accordance with the Act. The Council is a tripartite forum for discussing, studying and investigating matters regarding the safety, health and welfare of workers at the workplace. There is also the National Institute of Occupational Safety and Health which provides consultancy and advisory services to industries, develops and conducts training programmes, and carries out research on occupational health and safety.

Enforcement of Individual Worker Rights

Employee rights with respect to the terms and conditions of service are granted by the Employment Act, 1955. The rights of those not covered by the Employment Act, i.e. those earning more than RM1,500, are regulated by common law usage or by the terms and conditions of their employment contract. According to the Employment Act, an employer has the right to terminate an employee after giving notice for a minimum period, which varies according to the number of years of service: four weeks for less than two years; six weeks for two to five years; eight weeks for five years and more. Termination without notice by either party is possible in the event of wilful breach of any of the conditions in the contract of service.

The Termination and Lay-off Benefits Regulation, 1980 provides benefits to a worker whose employment is terminated or laid-off after he has been in employment for a continuous period of not less than 12 months. Before an employee is laid-off, he/she must be given prior notice as provided for in the terms and conditions of service. The employer must also pay for the balance of annual leave due and other minimum benefits. The minimum benefit that the employee is entitled to increases with the number of years in service:

- 10 days' wages for every year of continuous service with the employer if he has been employed for a period of less than two years.
- 15 days' wages for every year of continuous service with the employer for a period of two years or more but less than five years.

- 20 days' wages for every year of continuous service with the employer if he has been employed for five years or more.

The Employment Act, 1955 provides for adjudicating machinery, i.e. the Labour Court, where an employee may seek redress on disputes arising out of any of the provisions of the Act. The Labour Court is presided over by a gazetted Labour Officer. The procedure for the hearing of cases is informal and parties may or may not be represented by counsel. In 2005, 2,209 cases were adjudicated in the Labour Court, with 3,652 cases still pending. The Labour Courts provide speedy relief at less cost to aggrieved employees who would otherwise have to go through protracted litigation at considerable cost in civil courts.

In the case of unfair dismissal, all employees, irrespective of the amount they earn, can lodge a complaint with the Industrial Relations Department within sixty days. The Industrial Court has the right to grant reinstatement or compensation. Compensation is usually awarded, instead of reinstatement, in cases where both parties have lost confidence in each other and/or where hostility between the two parties has become irreparable. For all other infringements of employee rights, employees not covered by the Employment Act have to seek redress through civil courts.

Concluding Remarks

Labour laws in post-colonial Malaysia have sought to regulate industrial relations in order to ensure national economic competitiveness. To ensure social order, the government has sought to reduce unemployment. These efforts were successful enough to ensure full employment by the early 1990s, despite the tolerance of mass labour immigration from the 1980s. More than anything else, the resulting labour conditions have served to improve wage and working conditions. Although only a very small proportion of wage earners are unionized, and a disproportionately high share of them are from the public sector, where the option of industrial action is more severely restricted, they have had some limited successes in improving industrial relations and labour conditions. The incremental emergence of a fairly comprehensive legal and administrative framework has thus served to improve wages and working conditions. More recently, labour market reforms have included moves to encourage greater efficiency in labour utilization through enhanced employment and wage flexibility as well as enterprise-based training.

Changes in the labour market and the role of the state have also meant changes in the role of unions. The requirements of international competitiveness and the need to attract foreign investment have been invoked to justify even stricter limitations on trade unions. In Malaysia, the National Labour Advisory

Council (NLAC) was revived in the early 1990s as a forum for tripartite consultation, but has failed to gain traction. The failure to ensure genuine labour representation has undermined efforts to develop tripartism which would significantly enhance the state's legitimacy and support, and its capacity for successful planning, coordination and implementation of public policies affecting the workers.

Though there apparently is a harmonious industrial relations climate in the country, labour-management relations have hardly been equitable. Harmonious relations between labour and management cannot become sustainable if the government is seen to be weakening the collective strength of wage labour. Employers and the government must be willing to allow an increase in unionization rates and to allow trade unions to thrive independently so that they can participate as more equal partners in development.

Allowing the formation of national labour centres and industrial federations could facilitate constructive collective action and strengthen corporatist institutions to enhance both labour flexibility as well as security. Legal impediments to organize and negotiate effectively on wages as well as terms and conditions of employment need to be reviewed in line with changes in the domestic and international environments to ensure that the gains from development are equitably shared between employees and employers. Successful corporatism could encourage trade unions to enter into centralized collective bargaining which could enhance the efficiency of other public policies as well, most importantly overall economic development policies, especially investment, human resource and technology policies.

Education and training enhance firm flexibility and ensure that firms are able to cope with changing skill requirements. Further, successful upgrading of industries — to achieve higher value added and greater technology and skill intensity — will lead to displacement of workers with obsolete skills. Such older workers need to be retrained in order to remain gainfully employed, and appropriate institutions to facilitate such transitions need to be designed and put into place.

Rapid technological changes also require the workforce to be increasingly flexible, and to be able and willing to receive training on an on-going basis. These dynamic changes imply a different facilitating role for the government and an increasing role for the private sector in education and training because the private sector is expected to be more responsive to technological changes and market trends, while the state may not have adequate financial resources. Quality technical education is expensive, and the government can assist by granting fiscal and financial assistance, as it has begun to do. Current policies encourage a greater role for the private sector in education and training compared to before.

Trade unions should facilitate the development of a more skilled workforce by adopting a more pro-active role in promoting the training and retraining of their members.

Wage flexibility, through the promotion of a performance-related wage mechanism that links wages to productivity, is officially being encouraged to cope with the increasingly competitive and volatile environment. Existing legislation allows a satisfactory degree of wage flexibility through the use of incentive-based and collectively bargained bonuses, overtime wages and other discretionary allowances. While wage flexibility keeps unit labour costs down and safeguards employment stability, provisions within a flexi-wage system must ensure minimum living standards and hence wages. The implementation of a successful flexi-wage system also requires sound industrial relations and a broad consensus on how productivity gains are to be shared.

Malaysian labour laws remain silent on temporary workers, and hence, the terms and conditions of employment of these workers, including employment security, are at risk. Temporary and casual workers need income protection as well as contractual security, and the regulatory framework to protect such vulnerable workers is long overdue. Meanwhile, the increasingly widespread use of contract labour has served to undermine the ability of such contract employees to ensure labour security. It is increasingly recognized that the neglect and poor welfare of such workers adversely affects the interests of all workers.

Increasing liberalization and globalization will probably continue to reduce the power of the state and increase the power of market forces, including the labour market, as well as the prerogatives of employers. In such circumstances, the role of the government should be to strengthen institutions and mechanisms that can contribute towards striking a fair balance between pressures for enhancing competitiveness and for ensuring wages and working conditions are improved. The failure to develop appropriate institutions to ensure that the interests of employees will be enhanced together with overall economic development has contributed to the failure of human resources to lead the process of economic development by accelerating structural change and technological progress.

Notes

1. There were several amendments made subsequently, which resulted in its application to employees earning a monthly salary of not more than RM1,500 since the early 1990s.
2. In the case of Sabah and Sarawak, the respective State Labour Departments are in charge of most labour market matters.
3. Members from the employers' associations and trade unions are appointed by the Minister of Human Resources for a term of two years at a time.

CHAPTER 7

Investment and Technology Policy: Government Intervention, Regulation and Incentives

Jomo K. S.

The industrialization of East Asia is often portrayed as a success story of *laissez-faire* economic development. The World Bank (1993) depicted the late development of Southeast Asia — especially Malaysia, Indonesia and Thailand — as principally due to economic liberalization from the mid-1980s (for a critique, see Jomo, *et al.*, 1997). While there are obviously some elements of truth in this caricature, it is fundamentally misleading.

This chapter will show the crucial significance of government policy interventions in advancing the industrial development of post-colonial Malaysia. In particular, it will underscore the central role of economic regulation as well as incentives in the selective promotion of certain investments, industries and technologies. The previous chapter reviewed how labour laws also complemented such efforts in order to support various industrial policy priorities as they changed over time.

Historical Context

Most industries which emerged during the colonial era were set up to avoid the otherwise high transport costs of certain exported or imported goods, such as factories for refining tin-ore and bottling drinks, besides engineering workshops to maintain transport and other equipment such as tin dredges. The initial impetus for other industries often came when economic relations with the colonial powers were weak, e.g. during the Great Depression and the Japanese Occupation.

The British were reluctant to encourage domestically-produced manufactured goods for two reasons. The substitution of imported manufactures by protected domestic production would reduce import duty revenue for the government. It would also raise the prices of such goods, putting upward pressure on wages, thus reducing profits for employers (see Edwards 1975: 288, 315). Thus, manufacturing was not very significant in the Malaysian economy during the colonial era, while plantation rubber agriculture and tin-mining dominated. With emphasis given to export-oriented raw material production and British manufactured imports, local industry was largely confined to processing raw materials for export and producing certain items for local consumption, especially if "naturally" protected, e.g. by transport cost considerations.

After independence in 1957, and especially during the 1960s, the Malaysian economy began to diversify from the twin pillars of the colonial economy, i.e. rubber and tin. Nevertheless, primary commodity production continued to dominate the economy in the early decades after independence. Malaysia extended its colonial pre-eminence in rubber, tin and pepper, to palm oil and tropical hardwoods. Petroleum exports grew from the mid-1970s, and petroleum gas as well as cocoa became increasingly significant from the early 1980s. The export orientation of the Malaysian economy has also been sustained by Malaysia's largely export-oriented industrialization since the 1970s.

Import-Substituting Industrialization

In contrast to colonial policy, the post-colonial Malayan and Malaysian governments have actively sought to promote industrialization. While early industrialization efforts seemed erratic and haphazard, government policies from the late 1950s favoured import-substitution industrialization, with government intervention largely limited to the provision of tariff protection, infrastructure facilities, tax exemptions and other incentives. The strategy sought to encourage foreign investors to set up production, assembly and packaging plants in the country to supply finished goods previously imported from abroad.

The Government first encouraged foreign-led import-substituting industrialization (ISI) after Malayan independence with the promotion of private investments and public investments in infrastructure. Legislation and institutions were created to facilitate this policy emphasis. Industrial estates, power and communication facilities were developed under the Pioneer Industries Act (1958). Tariff protection was generally *ad hoc*, increasing with the level of processing. Until the mid-1960s, tariff protection was low for fear of increasing input and consumption costs as well as the newly-elected government's fear of being perceived as unduly favouring the predominantly Chinese domestic business community (Alavi, 1996).

To promote import-substituting industries, the government directly and indirectly subsidized the establishment of new factories in industrial zones with new industrial credit facilities provided by the government-created Malayan Industrial Estates Limited (MIEL) and Malayan Industrial Development Finance (MIDF) respectively. Most import-substituting industries were set up as subsidiaries of foreign, mainly British companies to finish goods produced with imported materials for more profitable sale within the protected domestic market. Many of these industries only replaced imports of finished goods with imports of semi-finished goods (e.g. motor car assembly). The technology used, often more suited to foreign conditions, was typically imported from the parent company abroad, usually generating little employment in the process due to minimal vertical and horizontal linkages. Policies to attract such industries often involved government tax breaks. Since most of these industries were generally capital-intensive and did not require much labour, unemployment as well as wage rates in these industries rose during this phase.

Industrial investments were quite responsive to these government efforts. During the 1960s, manufacturing output grew from 9 per cent of total GDP in 1960 to 13 per cent in 1970. Tax incentives were offered to industries which qualified for pioneer status from 1958, and from the beginning of the 1960s, import-substituting industries were also encouraged by providing protection through import duties and quotas with the establishment of the Tariff Advisory Board (see Edwards 1975: 288). Even with the generous tax holidays, the greatest incentive to the growth of the manufacturing sector then was provided by protection. Without such protection, the tax holidays and other tax concessions would have had little appeal on their own (for more details, see Edwards 1975: 289, 298).

Although protective tariffs were a major instrument of import-substituting industrial development from 1958, the nominal rates of protection in Malaysia were not very high in the period 1959–68. As many of the industries established were merely packaging and assembling imported components for sale in the protected domestic market, the low domestic value added ratio to sales value meant that a low nominal rate of protection actually observed a high effective rate of protection.

Given the potential for lucrative profits with such protection, it is hardly surprising that the investing companies lobbied influential Malaysians assiduously, e.g. by offering them directorships on the boards of subsidiary companies in Malaysia. Private profitability did not reflect "social efficiency" as measured by the domestic resource costs of foreign exchange earnings. The high profits mainly accrued to foreign-owned companies, which tended to remit their profits as they had little interest or incentive to invest further in the Malaysian economy.

The real output growth rate of industries qualifying for pioneer status tax incentives from the government quickly peaked, and then dropped quite dramatically, reflecting the inherent limitations of import-substituting industrialization in a small economy open to international trade and investment. The small domestic market not only reflected the country's relatively small population and its relatively low income levels. Perhaps more importantly, its skewed distribution of income, and hence expenditure, also shaped the structure of effective demand, i.e. the nature of the domestic market for particular goods.

Without more equitable distribution, which might transform the pattern of effective demand, domestic industrial production for mass consumption could not expand very much. In addition, import-substituting manufacturing's employment generating capacity was limited, due to its relatively capital-intensive nature as well as weak linkages to the rest of the Malaysian economy. With the growth of big industry out-pacing small-scale enterprise, and with capital-intensive industries expanding much faster than labour-intensive ones, employment creation lagged considerably behind investment growth during the period of import substitution.

By 1969, consumer goods enjoyed an average effective protection rate (EPR) of 72 per cent, and intermediate goods 33 per cent. However, without achieving economics of scale, industries accorded protection were often inefficient, except for some light processing and assembly industries (garments, wood and furniture). There was no effective appraisal or monitoring programme to ensure that these industries became internationally competitive (Rasiah, 1995). Although manufacturing had the highest growth rate by sector (Table 4), it did not generate much employment with its small economic base, capital intensity of foreign direct investments and limited linkages to the rest of the domestic economy (World Bank, 1980). In 1970, it generated 13.9 per cent of GDP, but only 8.7 per cent of employment.

Following the switch to export-orientation in the late 1960s, import-substitution gradually lost significance in terms of output growth and employment generation, though it continued to coexist with the former. While foreign firms dominated most industries in the 1960s, import-substituting industries became increasingly locally owned. Even today, Malaysian-owned industries are generally more likely to be import substituting or resource-processing for export, rather than export-processing with imported intermediate inputs.

Export-Oriented Industrialization

By the mid-1960s, the inherent limitations of the Malaysian import-substitution strategy were becoming clear. In 1965, the Federal Industrial Development Authority, or FIDA (later known as MIDA, the Malaysian Industrial Development Authority), was set up to encourage industrial investment, and began operations in 1967. By this time, many transnational corporations were planning to relocate their more labour-intensive production processes abroad, especially to East Asia, to reduce production costs. The 1968 Investment Incentives Act reflected this strategic switch in emphasis from import-substitution to export-oriented industrialization.

Foreign experts and international consultants were encouraging the Malaysian government to switch to export-oriented industrialization from the second half of the 1960s. The government moved in this direction with the enactment of the Industrial Incentives Act of 1968, which offered a different set of incentives oriented to attracting more labour-intensive export-oriented industries, compared to the import-substituting oriented Pioneer Industries Ordinance of the previous decade. To promote foreign direct investment in labour-intensive export-oriented industries, the 1968 Act offers a wide range of new incentives including tax holidays for pioneer companies, investment tax credits and export allowances.

Malaysia pursued export-oriented industrialization (EOI) in the 1970s, with its promise of many jobs producing for a large international market compared to the few jobs producing for the limited domestic market of import-substituting industrialization (ISI). Tax concessions (e.g. investment tax credits, accelerated depreciation allowances, tariff exemptions on imported raw material) and infrastructure were provided under the Investment Incentives Act, 1968, and Free Trade Zones Act, 1971. Incentives to encourage employment and industrial spatial dispersal included labour utilization and location incentives.

Many observers associate the switch to export-oriented industrialization with the NEP as the policy gained traction in the 1970s. The introduction of the NEP coincided with the switch from ISI, which had exhausted its first "easy stage" by the mid-1960s. Efforts to promote export-oriented industries were launched from the late 1960s, but only picked up from the early 1970s. The new emphasis was supported by the government's commitment to industrializing Malaysia's economy as the switch to export-oriented industrialization gave fresh impetus to industrial growth. Government efforts to attract and encourage export-oriented industries were in full swing by the early 1970s. New measures were introduced to facilitate and encourage manufacturing in Malaysia for export, mainly using imported equipment and materials. A favourable investment climate, generous fiscal incentives, and a literate and English language comprehending labour force helped Malaysia on its export-oriented growth path.

With its 1972 Free Trade Zones Act, the government opened free trade zones (FTZs) to offer investors an environment suited to internationally linked export processing, with controlled labour, subsidized infrastructure, expedited customs administration, and freedom from import duties and export taxes.[1]

To date, there are 12 such zones all over the country. Companies located in the zones are subjected to very minimal customs control formalities for their imports of raw materials, parts, machinery and equipment as well as for exports of their finished products.

Licensed Manufacturing Warehouses (LMWs) have also been established where it is neither practical nor desirable to establish a free trade zone. In 1975, the Licensed Manufacturing Warehouse (LMW) programme extended similar treatment to individual factories set up outside the zones. This facility is offered to companies that export at least 80 per cent of their products and import almost all their raw materials.

With the government fixed on employment generation, MIDA focused on investment promotion and employment generation, and made little attempt to screen foreign investment proposals, target particular sectors (electronics dominated FTZ production and general exports), or impose performance requirements for technology transfer or local content.[2]

In FTZs, imports are automatically exempt from duty, and minimal customs formalities are imposed on the importation of raw materials and parts, as well as on the export of final goods. Companies can enjoy these benefits by manufacturing their products in FTZs or in Licensed Manufacturing Warehouses (LMWs), where no FTZ is available. A company has to export at least 80 per cent of its output and import most of its components and parts to be eligible to set up production in an FTZ or as an LMW.

Tax incentives shifted from IS to EO firms. Lucrative incentives — such as pioneer status and investment tax credit of between five to ten years — were offered to attract such EO firms. When pioneer status expired, firms were often given investment tax credits for additional periods while many firms also enjoyed accelerated depreciation allowances. When these expired, some firms opened new plants or introduced new products to qualify for new incentives (see Rasiah, 1993). Meanwhile, foreign firms producing for export have been allowed to retain full ownership. Although IS industries continued to enjoy high, albeit declining tariffs, new incentives were mainly for EO firms.

Labour laws were also amended in late 1969, during the state of Emergency in the aftermath of the post-election May racial riots to favour the new, mainly labour-intensive export-oriented industries, by strengthening the Registrar of Trade Unions' discretionary powers (e.g. to prevent electronic factory workers from unionization), by allowing previously prohibited night shift work for women, by further restricting the right to strike, and by otherwise limiting trade union activities and rights (Jomo and Todd, 1994).

Export-oriented industries are of two main types. Resource-based industries have involved increased processing of older (e.g. rubber, tin) and newer (e.g. palm oil, timber) primary commodities for export. Although rubber, palm oil and wood processing has continued to expand, non-resource based export industries have grown faster and generated more employment since the 1970s. Many have relocated certain labour-intensive manufacturing processes to Malaysian FTZs and licensed manufacturing warehouses (LMWs). Electrical and electronic components have accounted for slightly more than half of total manufactured exports since the mid-1980s (Jomo, 2007: Table 2).

As will be elaborated below, EO industries generally involved higher levels of investment, employment and growth than inward-oriented industries and have enjoyed various government subsidies. Double deduction on corporate income tax is given to all exporting firms. EO firms utilized the double deduction benefits given for training as well as for research and development (R&D). Apart from resource-based industries (e.g. wood and rubber) and government car, steel and cement production, foreign firms were the major beneficiaries of training and R&D incentives. Apart from a few government-dominated heavy industries, EO firms have become more subsidized than IS firms.

Heavy Industrialization

Before the 1980s, there was little deepening of the IS sector into second stage import-substitution for several reasons: the domestic market was relatively small, the level of local technological capabilities was low, levels of protection were moderate by developing country standards and there was little encouragement from the government to deepen industrial linkages or to become internationally competitive. Protracted tensions between the ethnic Malay-dominated government and ethnic Chinese business limited and biased official efforts to promote the Malaysian private sector, with most government efforts mainly encouraging Malay business. A substantial EO sector had developed in Malaysia by the beginning of the 1980s, superimposed on the ISI sector, promoted in the 1960s. This was the context for the new Mahathir government to launch a heavy industrialization programme in the early 1980s.

The heavy industrialization programme was to be carried out through a new public sector agency, HICOM, set up in 1980. The government set up HICOM to diversify manufacturing activity, develop more local linkages (which both IS and EO failed to do), promote small and medium Malay enterprises and advance technological development by collaborating with foreign firms and investing in local R&D. "Heavy industrialization" in Malaysia has meant setting up a hot briquetted iron and steel billets plant, two more cement plants, the Proton national car project, three motorcycle engine plants, a petroleum refining and petrochemical project, and a pulp and paper mill.

Although requiring long gestation periods, the performances of heavy industries are now generally acknowledged to have been disappointing. Unfortunately, most Malaysian government's heavy industries faced stiff international competition from the outset (though in some cases, only temporarily, due to excessive global production capacity) and major gluts on the world market and required heavy protection, with apparently little likelihood of viability otherwise, e.g. in the case of steel, cement, petrochemicals, shipbuilding and repairs (see Pura, 1985; Jomo [ed.], 1994; Jomo, 2004). Costs of production and management were high by international standards, with the situation exacerbated by low capacity utilization (see also Ariff and Semudram, 1987: 46, 47). The heavy industries drive resulted in several costly failures, as when the Perwaja steel plant's prototype technology failed to operate successfully. The automotive project has been expanded by government subsidies and import protection. Imminent import liberalization, threatens to further undermine its failure to become internationally competitive.

Ethnic Redistribution

Undoubtedly, the Malaysian Government has long been interventionist in development policy, especially *vis-à-vis* the industrial sector. It has used tariff protection to develop the ISI sector, and has offered tax concessions and FTZ/LMW status privileges to promote the EOI sector. However, its industrial policy can be much more effective and efficient, as government intervention in Malaysia has long been subject to NEP-style inter-ethnic redistribution considerations.

The investment policy regime became more regulated with the NEP as the government promulgated a comprehensive industrial licensing system under the Industrial Co-ordination Act (ICA) of 1975. The ICA's primary purpose was to regulate the expansion of ethnic-Chinese business to ensure inter-ethnic corporate wealth redistribution in favour of the indigenous Bumiputera (primarily ethnic Malay) communities. The Act also established ethnic guidelines for employing (and promoting) workers.

According to the Industrial Co-ordination Act, 1975, the NEP target of 30 per cent foreign ownership by 1990 only affected firms selling to the domestic market, and not fully export-oriented firms located in the country or fully foreign-owned firms registered abroad. Malaysia attracted FDI in manufacturing, involving the relocation of certain aspects of the production processes of global firms enjoying technological and market leadership (Rasiah, 1996). Foreign ownership of fixed assets in manufacturing industries averaged 52 per cent in 1975, with the highest for electrical/electronic (82 per cent), beverages and tobacco (79 per cent), petroleum and coal (79 per cent), textiles (63 per cent) as well as furniture and fixtures (59 per cent).

The ICA enables the Malaysian government — through MITI and MIDA, which is under MITI's authority — to decide which manufacturing activities and investments should be permitted, and to revoke a license at any time.[3] The ICA also authorizes the licensing officer to impose *any* condition to obtain the license. Thus, the government wields great power in deciding which manufacturers can invest. By imposing conditions on the license, it can determine how manufacturers conduct their business.

The ICA's ostensible purpose was to "secure orderly development and growth in the country's manufacturing sector" (MIDA, 2002), with the licensing requirement used to advance Bumiputera equity and participation requirements. Manufacturing companies have generally been required to reserve at least 30 per cent of their equity for Bumiputera interests since 1975 (MIDA, 1986: 5–8). Firms above a minimum equity threshold level were required to share equity, usually 30 per cent, with Bumiputera partners. The 30 per cent target was not explicitly mentioned in the ICA itself. Rather, it was the overall target for Bumiputera ownership of listed corporate wealth by 1990. However, equity requirements were temporarily relaxed following the East Asian crisis.

Thus, the ICA was probably responsible for the decline in domestic private investments, especially in the decade 1976–85, when capital flight was estimated at US$12 billion (Jomo, 1990). Although the ICA could have served as an instrument of industrial policy, it has associated regulatory intervention in Malaysia with redistribution. Not surprisingly then, most ethnic Chinese domestic private manufacturing enterprises have been wary, if not resentful of government intervention generally, and industrial policy in particular.

Since 1986, the amended 1975 ICA, which is still in effect, requires all firms engaged in manufacturing with shareholder equity exceeding RM2.5 million, or with more than 75 full-time employees, to obtain a manufacturing license from the Secretary General of MITI (MIDA, 1986: 1). A license also has to be sought if an already licensed firm wishes to expand its production capacity or product range. There have been no significant changes to these regulations since 1986.

Multinational exporters operating in the FTZs were largely unaffected by changes in domestic investment policy during the 1970s and 1980s as they were exempt from the new equity-sharing guidelines, and found little difficulty in complying with government directives to employ a large percentage of Bumiputera workers, who were mostly young unskilled female school-leavers.

Mahathir's promotion of heavy industries from the early 1980s temporarily generated some well-paid, high skilled jobs, mainly for Bumiputeras. Some of these industries, especially Proton, have been supplied by Bumiputera suppliers, mostly joint-ventures with Japanese automotive parts suppliers. However, the chequered record of these heavy industries has meant that some of these jobs have been short-lived while others remain vulnerable in the post-Mahathir era.

New Manufacturing Investment Incentives from 1986

Mahathir's more interventionist approach in the early 1980s combined with global recession, to slow FDI inflows before a turnaround after the mid-1980s. Following the recession of the mid-1980s, Malaysia re-emphasized EOI with the first Industrial Master Plan (1986–95). Tax incentives (e.g. double deduction on export credit refinancing, further export promotion incentives) as well as greater access to credit — by raising financing limits — and subsidized interest rates prior to or upon shipment of products were provided. Thus, the problems of heavy industrialization were followed by the promulgation of a ten-year Industrial Master Plan (IMP) for 1986–95, which laid out a programme for detailed sectoral interventions. The IMP urged more stringent screening of foreign investment (including an expanded negative list of sectors closed to foreign ownership), mandatory export requirements for all new FDI, and detailed technology transfer and local content targets.

The government sought to influence investment quality with an array of positive incentives. The mid-decade recession caused the government to shelve the IMP's proposals for more rigorous FDI screening. Instead, it overhauled its investment regime to attract greater FDI inflows. Foreign investors were permitted to set up wholly owned subsidiaries in all enterprises exporting at least 80 per cent and majority foreign-ownership in projects exporting at least half of output.

The IMP selectively targeted activities for strengthening comparative advantages by providing critical inputs for industrial development (skills and training, technical support, finance, quality improvement) and more focused import protection (Lall, 1995a). Trade was to be gradually liberalized, but infant industry protection would continue to be used. The public sector would remain in the automotive, petrochemical, iron and steel and cement industries where investments required are large and gestation periods long. Government's policies to attract export-oriented MNCs have also become more selective. New MIDA incentives should attract FDI into higher value-added and more technology-intensive processes. Regional cooperation would serve industrial policy ends.

Malaysia also introduced additional incentives to increase local content before these were phased out by the new GATT/WTO rules. Industrial policy instruments became more consolidated and focused with the IMP. The corporate tax structure now allows for more effective use of selective incentives. Trade policy, including protection, is now more in line with overall industrial promotion efforts. Meanwhile, some heavy industries started to export, while technological and managerial capabilities seemed to be developing in the protected industries (Lall, 1995a).

In 1985, the manufacturing sector had experienced a three per cent contraction in output compared with 1984. With this depressed performance of the manufacturing sector and the overall economy, the government undertook deliberate efforts to introduce structural adjustments for liberalization and deregulation, hoping to encourage private sector investment in the manufacturing sector and to enhance the competitiveness of existing industries.

Among the measures undertaken was relaxation of the requirements governing the licensing of manufacturing companies under the Industrial Co-ordination Act, 1975. Effective from 12 December 1985, the level to qualify for exemption from licensing to undertake manufacturing activities was raised from RM250,000 shareholder funds and 25 full-time employees to RM1.0 million shareholder funds and 50 full-time employees. Subsequently, on 24 October 1986, the exemption limits were further raised to RM2.5 million shareholder funds and 75 full-time employees.

Since 1986, and especially from 1988, efforts to deepen domestic participation and localization have taken new dimensions. New incentives for exports, training, as well as research and development have been offered (see also Malaysia, 1992). Pioneer status and investment tax allowances have been given to "strategic firms", including firms with at least 30 per cent domestic sourcing of inputs since 1991.

While the government merely offered incentives to investors meeting export, employment, capital investment and locational targets until the mid-1980s, it assumed a more pro-active role from the second half of the 1980s. Incentives have been increasingly tied to technological deepening and exports, and to greater domestic sourcing of inputs for a decade from 1991. This strategy encouraged EO transnationals, especially Japanese firms, to relocate to Malaysia (Rasiah, 1993). The policy shift also strengthened backward linkages. The 1990s also saw some changes in financial incentives, e.g. the government reduced tax benefits for export-oriented firms other than strategic industries from 100 to 70 per cent.

These and other changes were codified in the 1986 Promotion of Investments Act, which offered a new round of Pioneer Status tax holidays and increased investment tax allowances for capacity expansion. Indirect exporters, including suppliers to FTZ firms were exempted from the ICA's equity-sharing guidelines and given export tax incentives. These changes extended access to the incentives in FTZs to the wider investment regime, and to forcefully commit Malaysia to an FDI-led industrialization strategy. Although the government rejected the IMP recommendation of an expanded negative list of sectors closed to foreign investment, it retained existing regulations requiring 70 per cent Malaysian equity ownership in seven supporting industries, including plastics parts, coils, transformers, wire harnesses, power cord sets, and telephone cords and connectors. This timely embrace of foreign investment met with tremendous success over the following decade. FDI flooded into Malaysia from Japan, East Asia, U.S., Europe and Singapore.

The 1985 revision to the 1968 Industrial Incentives Act liberalized the guidelines on FDI to allow foreigners greater equity participation in companies, rising with the degree of export orientation. The 1968 Act was later replaced with the Promotion of Investment Act, 1986. Full foreign ownership was permitted for projects that exported at least 80 per cent of their output. Projects that export less than 80 per cent were allowed less foreign equity participation, with the maximum permissible level rising with the degree of export-orientation, the level of technological sophistication, as well as the greater the positive spin-off effects, the capital outlay and the value-added.

In line with the relaxation of the requirements governing the licensing of manufacturing companies under the Industrial Co-ordination Act, 1975, intended to attract greater foreign investment, the guidelines on foreign equity participation were revised on 30 September 1986 to permit foreign investors to hold up to 100 per cent foreign equity, provided the company's manufactured output does not compete in the domestic market and the company exports at least 50 per cent of its production. This was followed by further liberalization in 1988, when foreign investors were allowed to hold 100 per cent equity in projects catering for the domestic market if they were unable to find suitable Malaysian partners for their projects. They would be allowed to hold this equity level for five years from the date of beginning operation, subject to the condition that the company export at least 20 per cent of its output.

At the same time, in line with the measures undertaken by the government in 1986 to relax the guidelines on foreign equity participation, the NEP ruling on local equity participation was also liberalized to promote non-Bumiputera initiatives to establish manufacturing projects. Hence, for projects initiated by non-Bumiputeras on a joint-venture basis with foreigners, if 70 per cent or more of the equity is taken up by foreigners, the balance of the equity can be retained by the non-Bumiputeras concerned. If foreigners take less than 70 per cent of the equity, non-Bumiputeras can hold 30 per cent, with the balance reserved for Bumiputeras. However, in special circumstances, non-Bumiputeras may be permitted to take up the entire balance of the equity, if agreed to by the

Ministry of International and Trade and Industry (MITI). For projects initiated by Bumiputeras on a joint-venture basis with foreigners, if less than 70 per cent of the equity is held by foreigners, the balance will be reserved for Bumiputeras. However, if Bumiputeras are unable to take up the entire balance, MITI could allow part of the balance to be held by non-Bumiputeras.

Apart from the approvals required under the ICA, manufacturing companies in Malaysia have to obtain various other licenses, permits and approvals before they can start production. Some of the approvals required are for formation of a locally incorporated company; purchase of industrial land, building plans, supply of utilities, certificate of fitness for used machinery, trade/business licenses, certificate of fitness for buildings, sales tax license, etc. The licensing officers have total discretion in deciding whether or not to issue licenses. However, it is generally acknowledged that such discretion has been increasingly liberally exercised.

The Government also introduced a new Promotion of Investment Act, 1986 (PIA) to replace the administratively cumbersome and increasingly dysfunctional Investment Incentives Act, 1968. The new Act provided attractive tax incentives for the manufacturing, agriculture and tourism sectors, including:

- a five-year tax holiday for "Pioneer Status" industries, irrespective of the level of investment;
- an investment tax allowance (as an alternative to the pioneer status incentive) of 100 per cent of qualifying capital expenditure incurred within five years from the date of approval of the project;
- an income tax abatement of ten per cent of value added in exports and five per cent of the value of local raw materials used in exports;
- a three-year extension, to 1988, of the accelerated depreciation allowance and the reinvestment allowance; and
- double tax deduction for the export credit insurance premium incurred and export promotion expenses.

In 1988, the PIA was further amended to provide for:

- an abatement of adjusted income of up to 50 per cent based on the company's export performance in relation to total sales;
- an export allowance of five per cent based on the f.o.b. (free on board) value of exports for trading companies which export the products of manufacturing companies;
- a five per cent abatement of adjusted income for all manufacturing companies which comply with the NEP guidelines; and
- extension, on a selective basis, of pioneer status from five to ten years for new companies.

Besides the Promotion of Investments Act, the government offered a new round of Pioneer Status tax holidays, and widened the scope of investment tax allowances for expansion projects for existing investors. Indirect exporters, including suppliers selling to firms in the FTZs, were exempted from the Industrial Co-ordination Act's equity-sharing requirements, and granted access to export tax incentives. The broad impact of these changes was to generalize many of the liberal rules obtaining in the FTZs to the wider investment regime, and to commit Malaysia to an FDI-led industrialization strategy.[4]

After the government introduced new liberalizing economic policy reforms, business sentiment improved. In addition, new investments poured in from more developed countries in East Asia, notably Japan, Singapore and later, Taiwan. As the government policy reform efforts not only benefited foreign investors, but were also seen as helping non-Malay entrepreneurs, domestic firms became more supportive of the policy reforms. Politically influential corporate groups developed various means to better advance their interests, while appreciating the greater freedom and flexibility, as well as reduced tax burdens and regulations.

From 1 October 1988, the Malaysian Industrial Development Authority (MIDA) was designated the Centre on Investment (COI) at the federal level, while the state economic development corporations (SEDCs) performed similar functions at the state level. This means that investors need only approach MIDA to obtain all the necessary approvals/permits required at the federal level. An Advisory Services Centre was created within MIDA, with representatives from various ministries/agencies such as the Immigration Department, Customs and Excise Department, Department of Environment, Ministry of Human Resources, Telekom Malaysia, Tenaga Nasional for electricity security services, and the Health Department to provide relevant services to investors.

MIDA also took over the processing of various applications previously undertaken by different ministries/agencies. Traditionally, MIDA/MITI receives, evaluates and conveys decisions in respect of applications for manufacturing licenses; applications for investment incentives under the Promotion of Investments Act; expatriate posts initially required; exemptions from import duties and sales taxes on raw materials, parts and components; and applications for tariff protection. After setting up the COI and streamlining measures, MIDA also deals with applications for customs duty exemptions on machinery and equipment used in manufacturing projects (previously Department of Customs in the Treasury); applications for approval of technical agreements (previously MITI); applications for training incentives (previously Ministry of Human Resources); and R&D applications (previously Treasury); applications for immigration approvals related to manufacturing investments such as extension of Business Visit Passes (previously Immigration Department); approval for extension of overtime work (previously Ministry of Human Resources) and request for verification of tariff codes (previously Customs). All these measures have expedited administrative decision-making of applications by foreign investors and enabled them to implement their projects smoothly.

Recognizing the critical need for technology transfer for industrialization, the transfer of industrial technology has been regulated. All agreements to be signed between licensed Malaysian companies and foreign parties pertaining to technology transfer arrangements are screened to ensure effective transfer of technology and protection of local interests. The screening and approval of agreements were first carried out by the MITI from 1968 when the Investment Incentives Act was promulgated to attract labour-intensive, export-oriented investments in the manufacturing sector.

When MIDA was designated the COI in October 1988, the task of screening all agreements was transferred to MIDA. Subsequently, on 30 April 1990, this condition in the manufacturing license was relaxed to only cover technology transfer agreements signed with foreigners pertaining to agreements such as joint-ventures, technical assistance and know-how, licensing, trademarks and patents, turnkey and management contracts. In view of recent global trends regulating technology transfer, the government liberalized regulatory policies pertaining to the approval of technical agreements while strengthening enforcement of intellectual property rights more generally.

The ICA guidelines were again further liberalized in 1992, resulting in more attractive equity guidelines for foreign participation: more equity condition is imposed on manufacturing projects that export 80 per cent or more of their production. For projects exporting between 20 to 79 per cent of their production, foreign equity ownership of up to 79 per cent may be allowed, depending on factors such as the level of technology, spin-off effects, size of investment, location, value-added and utilization of raw materials and components. For projects exporting less than 20 per cent of their output, foreign equity ownership up to a maximum of 30 per cent is allowed. However, for projects producing "high technology" or priority products for the domestic market, as determined by the government from time to time, foreign equity ownership of up to 100 per cent may be allowed. For projects that involve the extraction, mining and processing of mineral ores, foreign equity participation of up to 100 per cent is permitted.

The US dollar depreciated heavily against other major world currencies, particularly the Japanese yen, after the Plaza accord of September 1985. As the currencies of most East Asian newly-industrialized economies rose, the Malaysian ringgit declined, even against the US dollar. The ringgit depreciation lowered Malaysian production costs. Real wage costs also declined over the mid-1980s with the rise in unemployment as well as new labour policies and laws weakening organized labour and enhancing labour flexibility. In fact, the Southeast Asian boom from the late 1980s benefited greatly from investments from the Northeast Asian economies experiencing rising production costs, tightening labour markets as well as stricter environmental restrictions. The end of Generalized System of Preferences (GSP) privileges for the East Asian NIEs in February 1988 also encouraged industrial relocation to countries that still qualified including Malaysia.

Tax exemptions and provision of infrastructure successfully attracted FDI. The repatriation of FDI profits (investment income) overseas increased by some threefold from 1980 to 1990. Leakages through such net transfers of profits overseas as well as imported capital and intermediate goods reduced domestic ownership of value-added. The mid-1980s' change in policy direction was confirmed by the 1991 announcement of Vision 2020, seen to favour growth, modernization and industrialization over the NEP's emphasis on inter-ethnic redistribution. While foreign investors continued to be courted, the government also encouraged ethnic Chinese capital with various other reforms, e.g. easier access to listing on the stock market, greater official encouragement of small and medium industries (SMIs) as well as other governmental efforts to mitigate the ICA. The overall emphasis on the private sector and market forces, rather than regulatory measures, was also favourably received by the private sector. The official policy in the early and mid-1990s, of encouraging local firms (especially large corporations) to invest overseas (Jomo [ed.], 2002), where the scope for Malaysian government influence has been limited, has been perceived as another indication of government support for the private sector.

Tax Incentives

The Malaysian government promotes manufacturing development with selective protection by offering incentive schemes to investing firms. While the Malaysian government does not directly subsidize industrial production, as it does certain agricultural activities (e.g. rice production), it offers various incentives, including indirect subsidies, to manufacturing firms. Tax incentives have been quite important for investment decisions. Most tax incentives currently available are to be found in the Promotion of Investments Act, 1986, various amendments since, as well as other legislation. These provide both direct (i.e. income tax exemption) as well as indirect tax incentives (e.g. exemption from import duty) (MIDA, 2002).

These incentives have been available since 1986. Some of the more important incentives during this period include: pioneer status, investment tax allowance, industrial adjustment allowance, infrastructure allowance, industrial building allowance, various single and double deduction incentives, various import and excise duty as well as sales tax exemptions and drawbacks (MIDA 1986; 2002).

The Pioneer Status (PS) and the Investment Tax Allowance (ITA) schemes have been the two most important incentives. A firm granted pioneer status (PS) is exempted from income tax for five years; in many cases, the exemption may be extended for ten years. A company granted PS normally enjoys a tax exemption on 70 per cent of its statutory income, but in many cases, the exemption may cover up to 100 per cent of income. The tax exemption rate depends on the activity or product that makes a firm eligible for PS. Thus, PS consists of sub-programmes designed to promote industrial linkages, investments in certain locations as well as high-tech production and R&D. The most generous and important tax incentive, by far, during the period since 1986 has been the PS (Gustafsson, 2007; Rasiah, 1995).

The Investment Tax Allowance (ITA) functions as an alternative to PS, especially to promote large capital investments requiring long gestation periods. A company that avails itself of an ITA receives a tax allowance on capital investments, instead of being exempted from income tax. In all other respects, the ITA works like PS: it promotes certain products and activities, with the level of the allowance depending on the product or activity. Like PS sub-programmes, ITA sub-programmes also seek to promote industrial linkages, regional development and R&D.

One PS and ITA sub-programme provides incentives for "high technology companies". A firm can apply for PS and enjoy 100 per cent tax exemption for five years, or for a five-year ITA equivalent to the 60 per cent tax exemption provided MIDA considers the output a "high technology product", the company has R&D expenditures of at least one per cent of gross sales, and it has a trained and experienced scientific and technical staff exceeding seven per cent of its total workforce.

Strategic projects involving "products or activities of national importance" may enjoy either PS, with 100 per cent tax exemption for ten years, or a five-year ITA equivalent to 100 per cent to promote national firms active in R&D. They generally involve heavy capital investments with long gestation periods, high levels of technology, extensive linkages, and "have significant impact on the economy" (MIDA, 2002: 13).

PS and ITA programmes also directly promote R&D. PS — with 100 per cent tax exemption for five years — is offered to "contract R&D companies", while 100 per cent ITA for ten years is available for "R&D companies" (MIDA, 2002: 28). Furthermore, all companies undertaking in-house research are eligible for a 50 per cent ITA for ten years, and can enjoy a "double deduction on revenue (non-capital) expenditure for research" (MIDA, 2002: 29).

Another scheme of "incentives for a knowledge-based economy" helps national firms create knowledge-based assets. Firms with "strategic knowledge-based status" can access these incentives. To be eligible, companies must have the potential to generate knowledge content; high value-added operations; high technology; a large number of skilled workers; and a knowledge-based corporate master plan (MIDA, 2002: 34–5). Strategic knowledge-based status gives PS with 100 per cent tax exemption for five years, or a 60 per cent ITA for five years.

Only limited incentives were offered to R&D companies in 1986. In 1992, Malaysia had R&D expenditure of 0.8 per cent of GDP, compared to two per cent in South Korea (Jomo and Felker, 1999). Malaysia increased the incentives for R&D and targeted firms in strategic sectors. The government realized that tax incentives alone might not be enough to raise R&D expenditures. The Industry R&D Grant Scheme (IGS), created in 1997, funds private research undertaken in collaboration with public universities or other public R&D organizations, among other things.

The Reinvestment Allowance (RA) is for manufacturing companies that spend to expand production capacity, modernize and upgrade production facilities, diversify into related products, and automate production facilities (MIDA, 2002). The allowance is equivalent to 60 per cent of the firm's expenditure for 15 consecutive years.

Under the Income Tax Act of 1967, the Industrial Building Allowance (IBA) can be granted to companies constructing or purchasing a building for "special purposes" (Ministry of Finance homepage). Eligible companies are given an annual allowance for 30 years equivalent to a one-time 10 per cent income tax exemption, but the allowance is now equivalent to three per cent annually.

Since the late 1980s, incentives for exporting firms have been extended in the form of export abatement allowances and double deduction exemptions. Foreign investment from East Asia since the mid-1980s has resulted in some technological deepening and greater linkages. In 1988, the double deduction for training incentive (DDTI) was introduced. Since 1993, firms with more than 50 employees have been required to participate in the official Human Resource Development Fund (HRDF). Since 1991, a local sourcing condition has also been included for firms applying for pioneer status and investment tax allowances although local content requirements have since been prohibited by the WTO.

The statutory corporate income tax rate in Malaysia was 40 per cent until it was reduced to 35 per cent in 1994, 30 per cent in 1995 and 28 per cent in

1998. The reductions in the statutory corporate income tax rate were intended to encourage investment. The effective tax rate has actually been lower in view of generous investment incentives, including the accelerated depreciation allowances introduced in 1977, as well as the generosity of depreciation allowances from 1980 and of re-investment allowances from 1988. The marginal effective tax rate (METR) for investments — the difference between pre-tax and post-tax rates of return to investments, i.e. the tax due — payable on equity in Malaysia has been lower than in all other ASEAN countries except Singapore and Thailand (Table 1). The World Bank (Pellechio, Sirat and Dunn, 1989, cited in Wee, 1997) estimated that the METR would be zero if the statutory tax rate is less than 30 per cent due to these investment incentives. There have also been increasing tax exemptions for spending on insurance, education and computers, which encourage investment as well as human resource development.

Table 1. East Asia: Marginal Effective Tax Rate, 1989 (%)

	Statutory Rate	*Marginal Effective Tax Rate (%)**	
		All Equity	*50% Debt*
Hong Kong	18.5	17.3	9.6
Indonesia	35.0	41.6	34.1
Japan	33.3	39.2	29.4
Korea	30.0	33.1	24.6
Malaysia	40.0	32.0	20.5
Philippines	35.0	40.4	31.9
Singapore	40.0	28.4	15.2
Taiwan	25.0	31.0	28.0
Thailand	35.0	24.9	18.6

Note: * Difference in rates of return before and after tax.
Source: Pellechio, Sirat and Dunn (1989), cited in Wee (1997: Table 4.16).

The Malaysian government has extended its export promotion measures since the mid-1980s. From 1986 to 2000, no company in Malaysia had to pay import duties on raw materials or components used for manufacturing export under the programme called "Exemption from Customs Duty on Direct Raw Materials/Components". Since there are no export level requirements, the importation of machinery and equipment is duty-free. Some tariffs are still imposed on machinery and equipment used in production processes. But under the "Exemption from Import Duty and Sales Tax on Spares and Consumables" programme, a firm can avoid paying the tariff by exporting at least 80 per cent of its products (MIDA, 2002: 40).

The Drawback of Import Duty, Sales Tax and Excise Duty uses exemptions from import duties to promote exports. Under the Customs Act of 1967, the Sales Tax Act of 1972 and the Excise Act of 1976, manufacturing companies can get a drawback on import duties, sales tax and excise duty if they have paid such duties on parts, raw materials or packaging materials used to manufacture an export product (MIDA, 2002: 40).

Direct tax incentives for exports not tied to import tariff exemptions also exist. The IBA allowance, which subsidizes the construction and purchase of buildings used for "special purposes" with a tax allowance, also promotes exports. The ECR and export credit insurance schemes also promote exports. Only companies and banks that produce goods for export, or are indirectly engaged in export activities, can avail themselves of these schemes.

Clearly, Malaysia has not reduced the number of tax incentives since 1986. The actual effects of tax incentives on the economy have increased during the period. The most generous and important tax incentive, by far, during the period since 1986 has been the PS (Gustafsson, 2007). Several researchers (e.g. Rasiah, 1995) suggest that tax incentives have been quite important for investment decisions.[5]

Enhancing Technology[6]

The Malaysian government has long used discretionary investment incentives to improve the composition and nature of investment inflows. Since 1986, the main goals have been to attract investments in higher-technology activities and to deepen industrial structure by encouraging more integrated industrial clusters. The Ministry of Trade and Industry first began screening and approving technology transfer agreements under the Investment Incentives Act, 1968. With the Industrial Coordination Act, 1975, the authorities could attach conditions to the manufacturing license. Malaysian companies have been required to secure approval from the Ministry's Technology Transfer Unit before entering into agreements with foreigners involving joint-ventures, turnkey contracts, technical know-how and assistance, management, services (including employment of expatriate personnel), purchasing, marketing, royalty payments, and the use of patents and trademarks.

Since MIDA was designated the national investment centre (one-stop agency) in 1988, screening has been conducted by MIDA. This requirement was relaxed in 1990, to only cover agreements involving joint-ventures, technical assistance and know-how, licensing, trade marks and patents, turnkey contracts and management. Further liberalization of regulatory policies for the approval of technical agreements has followed (Jegathesan, 1995: 17–8).

Government assistance as well as incentive schemes to encourage techno-logical capacity building include the Double Deduction Incentive scheme for Approved Training (DDIT) initiated in 1987, the Intensification of Research in Priority Area (IRPA) Fund established in 1988, the Industrial Technical Assistance Fund (ITAF) set up in 1990, and the Human Resources Development Fund (HRDF) begun in 1992. New initiatives to promote technology development have included the Malaysian Technology Park set up in Cheras, Selangor, in 1988. The Malaysian Technology Development Corporation (MTDC) was set up as a public-private joint venture in 1992 to commercialize Malaysian research findings, encourage technology-based companies and catalyse venture capital development. The Malaysian Industry Government Group for High Technology (MIGHT) was set up in 1993 as a joint initiative between the government and the private sector to exploit new business opportunities involving research and technology, while the Kulim High-Technology Industrial Park was set up in the early 1990s as a science city of the future.

Tax deductions were offered for approved firm expenditures on training as well as research and development (R&D) in the mid-1980s (Felker with Jomo, 2007b). These had relatively little impact since many large companies already enjoyed tax relief. Difficult application and post-expenditure reimbursement procedures have also deterred many small companies from applying. Tax incentives were extended in 1990 to MNCs that set up regional Operational Headquarters (OHQs) to provide management services, logistics and co-ordination for subsidiaries in Malaysia. The OHQ scheme has since met with modest, but respectable results (Felker with Jomo, 2007b).

After a broad review of MIDA's investment policy regime, more changes were initiated in 1991. These reforms made the incentive regime more neutral by phasing out tax incentives for exports and reducing the scope of Pioneer Status tax holidays. The government could thus use full tax exemptions to induce investments in specific high technology sectors. MIDA began screening pioneer status applications more rigorously using four criteria: value-added, local content, "technology depth", and linkages. Investors could still apply for Pioneer Status or Investment Tax Allowance on other grounds, including decentralization (investment in East Malaysia) or, for qualifying as a "strategic" or "high-tech" project.

In 1995, MITI elaborated the shift in investment policy by announcing new criteria for general investment promotion as well as special incentive programmes for "high-technology" and "strategic" investment projects. Proposals involving less than RM55,000 capital investment per employee (CIPE) would henceforth be turned down unless they met other criteria: value-added of 30 per cent or more; 15 per cent of workforce in managerial, technical, or supervisory (MTS) positions; location in marginalized states; or activities deemed strategically beneficial to Malaysia's industrial progress.

Special incentive programmes were launched for high-technology projects, including computers and computer peripherals, liquid crystal displays (LCDs), medical equipment, biotechnology, automation equipment, advanced materials, opto-electronics, software, alternative energy, and aerospace. High-technology projects would receive ten-year tax holidays for 100 per cent of corporate income, and enjoy greater freedom to employ expatriate researchers or scientists as well as to hold unrestricted foreign exchange accounts in local banks. Finally, a catchall category of "strategic" investment projects gave the government considerable discretion in granting full ten-year tax holidays for specific projects.

Recognizing that the shortage of skilled labour had constrained techno-logical upgrading, the government also reformed incentives for human resource development. In 1993, the government replaced an existing tax incentive for corporate training expenses with the Human Resources Development Fund (HRDF), a payroll levy and training subsidy scheme. Firms employing more than 50 workers are required to contribute one per cent of their payroll to the Fund, and can apply for reimbursement of a percentage of expenses on approved training programmes, including their annual in-house training programmes. Over the next decade, the Fund collected some RM1.03 billion in payroll levies from employers. The government extended the scheme to small and medium sized industries (SMIs) in 1996, but with limited success.[7] Besides revamping its investment incentives, the government created a series of direct funding mechanisms for high-technology industries during the early and mid-1990s. In 1993, the Ministry of Finance established Khazanah Holdings as a special-purpose vehicle to invest in strategic and high technology projects.

MITI issued a Second Industrial Master Plan (IMP2) for 1996–2005 em-phasizing more locally integrated industrial clusters. IMP2 sought to stimulate backward integration by encouraging investments in component production, design and R&D, indigenous infant industries in a few sectors, as well as forward integration into trading, marketing, and local brand development.

With the 1997–98 crisis, the government further liberalized conditions for manufacturing FDI. The mid-1998 National Economic Recovery Plan lifted all restrictions on foreign equity in new manufacturing projects, for two years, regardless of degree of export orientation. Existing joint-ventures selling to the domestic market were allowed to increase their foreign shareholdings, while wholly foreign-owned firms, previously required to export 80 per cent of output, were permitted to sell up to half their output locally. Blanket exemptions from import duties were given to all machinery, equipment and imported inputs for export production. The recovery plan also exempted existing foreign investors from complying with the terms of their investment licenses. With the late 1980s' FDI influx during the early 1990s, the government revised the investment regime to emphasize investment quality in terms of technology content and value added.

Since 1972, the inter-ministerial Foreign Investment Committee (FIC) enforced equity ownership rules for domestic and Bumiputera investors when approving most large-scale foreign and domestic non-manufacturing investment projects. The FIC also allocated shareholdings reserved for domestic and Bumiputera investors. The business community had long voiced concern about the discretionary authority wielded by the inter-ministerial Foreign Investment Committee, which, despite its name, held approval authority over most large-scale foreign as well as domestic non-manufacturing investment projects.

After the crisis, Malaysia considerably expanded the scope for foreign ownership, and suspended many pro-Bumiputera affirmative-action regulations impinging on foreign investors. Meanwhile, the government maintained its efforts to encourage foreign participation in key sectors, while maintaining major stakes in the financial, automotive, telecommunications, energy, and transport sectors. In 2002, the SC allowed unlisted foreign companies to take over the assets of listed firms without complying with guidelines requiring minimum Bumiputera ownership. In 2003 though, the power to approve mergers and acquisitions was taken from the FIC and given to the Securities Commission (SC).

Concluding Remarks

The 1959 Pioneer Investment Ordinance sought to attract import-substituting industrial investments while the 1968 Investment Incentives Act shifted the focus to export-oriented industrial investments. A number of other export incentives appeal to both foreign and domestic investors. They include export credit refinancing; double tax deduction for expenses incurred for export promotion and export credit insurance; industrial building allowance for warehousing export goods; import duty exemption and drawback of excise and sales taxes paid for imported intermediate goods; sales tax exemption for imports of machinery and equipment; and other tax incentives for R&D, training and industrial upgrading to promote efficiency.

Private manufacturing investment in Malaysia has been encouraged by tax and other incentives, rather than by adjusting interest rates. The government has also influenced investments by signalling its desire to see more investments in favoured sectors and industries with special incentives. Besides the provision of incentives, other methods of influencing private investment have included directing bank loans and other credit facilities to favoured sectors and activities and amending policy measures for the approval of foreign investment, including the privatization of government projects. The procedures for influencing investments have been modified to benefit favoured sectors and to discourage investments in others. In this way, investment priorities and levels have been influenced.

Beyond its broad commitment to reducing unemployment, the Malaysian authorities are not considered particularly labour or union friendly. There is no general minimum wage policy, formal unemployment insurance or unemployment relief scheme. The enforcement of regulations designed for labour protection leaves much to be desired. The Employment Act (1955) provides for various allowances, leave and retrenchment benefits for private sector workers with wage incomes of no more than RM1,500 per month in Peninsular Malaysia, while the Labour Ordinance (Sabah Cap. 67) and Sarawak Labour Ordinance (Cap 76) (SLO, 1959) provide corresponding regulations for the respective Borneo states. The authorities have discouraged trade unionism in order to attract investments, particularly in labour-intensive export-oriented industries. Trade unions were not allowed in electronic industries until 1989, and even then, only in-house (company) unions have been allowed. In recent years, outsourcing as well as the trend towards greater labour flexibility has further weakened the influence of trade unions.

Despite its high savings rate, Malaysia has long encouraged foreign direct investment (FDI) to provide additional financial resources for growth and employment creation, and to secure access to international management expertise, new technology and foreign markets in order to accelerate structural change. Until September 1998, Malaysia implemented liberal exchange controls to maintain investor confidence. It concluded investment guarantee agreements providing for protection against nationalization and expropriation, compensation in the event of nationalization, capital and fees payment as well as settlements in accordance with the Convention on Settlement of Investment Disputes. It also grants generous tax holidays, investment tax allowances, reinvestment allowances and export allowances to encourage them to establish operations in Malaysia.

These investment regulations have been further liberalized since the 1998 recession. FDI — rather than portfolio investment — has long been a very important source of net capital inflows from abroad. Although FDI was supposed to fill the savings-investment gap the in OPP1 (1986–95) and

OPP2 (1996–2005) periods, the huge savings rates over the years suggest that the financing gap has not been major. The encouragement of FDI has instead sought to gain access to external markets, international management expertise as well as cutting edge technologies controlled by transnational corporations. Thus, investment and technology policies, or industrial policy, in Malaysia have sought to ensure that investment contributes to national industrial development priorities, including employment objectives.

As the economic crisis swept Southeast Asia in 1997 and 1998, the Malaysian government took additional steps to liberalize conditions for manufacturing FDI. The National Economic Recovery Plan issued in mid-1998 lifted all restrictions on foreign equity in new manufacturing projects, regardless of export orientation, for a period of two years. Pre-existing joint ventures serving the domestic market were permitted to increase their foreign shareholdings, while wholly foreign-owned firms, previously required to export 80 per cent of output, were now permitted to sell up to half their output locally. By April 1999, some 49 joint-venture companies had increased their foreign ownership ratio with capital injections totalling RM3.45 billion.[8] The government granted blanket exemptions from import duties to all machinery and equipment imports, as well as to all inputs used in export production. Beyond all these adjustments to the rules, the recovery plan explicitly declared a "hands off" attitude towards existing foreign investors' compliance with the terms of their investment licenses.

As Malaysia recovered from the 1997–98 financial crisis, Khazanah became the main holding company for the *de facto* re-nationalization and restructuring of financially distressed financial, infrastructural, and industrial conglomerates, including toll-way operator PLUS, Malaysia Airlines, Proton, Bumiputera-Commerce Bank, United Engineers Malaysia, and others.

Malaysia has maintained a relatively free trade regime, with the exceptional rise of tariff protection during the import substitution industrialization efforts of the early 1960s and heavy industrialization of the 1980s. Tariff rates have been low by international standards. The un-weighted average import tariffs decreased from 14.1 per cent in 1960 to 9.0 per cent in 1980, 4.9 per cent in 1990, 1.2 per cent in 2000 and 0.8 per cent in 2005. Export duties have also been reduced from 9.2 per cent in 1980 to 2.5 per cent in 1990, 0.3 per cent in 2000 and 0.4 per cent in 2005 (calculated with data from Bank Negara Malaysia). Tariffs have been reduced and abolished with trade liberalization commitments, e.g. with participation in the General Agreement on Tariffs and Trade (GATT) and its successor, the World Trade Organization (WTO). They have also been reduced for imports from partners in regional free trade agreements such as the ASEAN (Association of Southeast Asian Nations) Free Trade Agreement (AFTA).

Notes

1. The development of export processing industries in Malaysia was rapid in the 1970s. "The importance of EPZs in Malaysia is unique among the developing countries establishing these zones. Nowhere else is their role as significant, either in absolute terms or as a proportion of overall manufacturing activity" (Warr 1987: 30).

2. A Technology Transfer Unit established in 1975 within the Ministry of Trade and Industry screens technology transfer agreements to prevent inflated royalty fees or clauses that restricted exports, but in practice, the regulations have not been stringently applied or monitored (Anuwar, 1992: 87–94). The automotive sector was subject to a separate local-content programme managed by an inter-agency committee also housed in the Ministry of Trade and Industry.

3. Manufacturers with grievances can appeal decisions to MITI.

4. Though the government set aside the IMP's recommendation of an expanded negative list of sectors closed to foreign investment, it did maintain existing regulations that required 70 per cent Malaysian equity ownership in seven supporting industries, including plastics parts, coils, transformers, wire harnesses, power cord sets, as well as telephone cords and connectors.

5. See, for instance, Rasiah (1995).

6. This section draws heavily on Felker with Jomo (2007b).

7. Figures reported in *New Straits Times*, 20 March 2002. A World Bank (1997: 61) study concluded, "HRDF has had a significant role in increasing training among medium and large firms ... but not small firms.... Among purely domestic firms, HRDF has only been effective in increasing the training of large firms with over 250 employees."

8. *The Star*, 6 April 1999.

CHAPTER 8

Institutional Initiatives for Crisis Management, 1998

Wong Sook Ching and Jomo K. S.

This chapter reviews the major institutional initiatives by the Malaysian authorities from mid-1998 to address the economic meltdown precipitated by the Asian financial crisis of 1997–98. Although these initiatives have not received as much attention as the more controversial capital control measures introduced later on 1–2 September 1998, they were far more crucial to the official effort to restore and try to increase low cost credit facilities as well as liquidity in the economy. The initiatives sought to refinance the banking system, take over large non-performing loans and restructure major corporate debt of firms closely associated with the regime.

The official Malaysian initial response to the Asian financial crisis from July 1997 radically changed course in early December 1997 when then Finance Minister Anwar Ibrahim promulgated a series of conventional macroeconomic policy measures after five months of declining confidence in response to the regime's early counter-cyclical, but quixotic policy responses. Several weeks later, then Prime Minister Mahathir Mohamad created the National Economic Action Council (NEAC), led by himself, to address the crisis. Former Finance Minister Daim Zainuddin was soon put in charge of the NEAC although his earlier policy advice — e.g. favouring an even larger fiscal contraction in late 1997 — was even more pro-market and pro-IMF compared to Anwar's pro-cyclical turn in early December 1997.

By the second quarter of 1998, the NEAC had come out with an Action Plan and Anwar reversed his December 1997 policies by trying to reflate the economy with counter-cyclical public spending measures, particularly favouring small businesses and farmers, perhaps in anticipation of the party's annual convention in late June, when he came under strong attack from his enemies. Later, Mahathir accused him of being homosexual and for having favoured family members and political allies. By this time, he had announced the creation of several special purpose vehicles to save and recapitalize the banking system, and to restructure large corporations considered deserving of special governmental support. These three new creations — Danaharta, Danamodal and the CDRC — are described below and were far more important in facilitating bank, corporate and consequently, economic recovery than the far more controversial and better known capital controls introduced in early September 1998 (Jomo, 2003).

Danaharta[1]

Danaharta, or Syarikat Pengurusan Danaharta Nasional Bhd, the national asset management company[2] was set up on 20 June 1998, under the Ministry of Finance to acquire non-performing loans from banks, or to put it differently, to carve out bad debts from local banks.[3] Unlike the asset management companies in South Korea and Thailand, Danaharta is neither a rapid disposition agency nor a warehousing agency. Rather, it was granted a wider range of restructuring options, with the only stipulation being maximizing recovery value.[4] Furthermore, Danaharta could not only take legal action[5] to recover security through the bankruptcy process and sell the loans to a third party, but could also take a more active role in rehabilitating companies since Danaharta's powers include the power to force management and ownership changes within the companies.

Nonetheless, given the risks associated with such a strategy (Wong, Jomo and Chin, 2005: Box 4.1), Danaharta outlined strict loan restructuring guidelines to avoid many problems of moral hazard.[6]

Danamodal[7]

Danamodal, or Danamodal Nasional Bhd, the bank recapitalization agency, was incorporated on 10 August 1998 with an anticipated life span of 5 to 7 years.[8] The rationale for establishing Danamodal was threefold:

(1) to ensure that the banking sector recapitalization process was commercially driven and that investment decisions were made according to market-based principles;

(2) to avoid delays in addressing recapitalization and non-performing loans issues which would have a drag effect on the financial system and economic recovery; and

(3) to avoid direct capital injection by the government into banking institutions as this was deemed undesirable and could lead to conflicts of interest in the future.

To address problems of moral hazard inherent in such an exercise, Danamodal operated on the first-loss principle, under which losses arising from past credit decisions are born by shareholders. See the BNM website[9] for an overview of Danamodal's vision and mission statement, guiding principles, and operating guidelines, as well as the stabilization measures undertaken by Danamodal and the financial system.

Corporate Debt Restructuring Committee (CDRC)[10]

The government also addressed the problems of the corporate sector (i.e. to restructure corporate debt over RM50 million) through the formation of a Corporate Debt Restructuring Committee (CDRC), a non-statutory body, in October 1998, under Bank Negara Malaysia (BNM). The CDRC was formed to provide a platform for both borrowers and creditors to work out feasible corporate debt restructuring schemes[11] without having to resort to legal proceedings, especially for large debtors. Put differently, the objective of the committee, like its counterparts in Indonesia, South Korea, and Thailand, was to minimize losses to creditors, shareholders, and other stakeholders through co-ordinated voluntary workouts that sidestep the formal bankruptcy procedure.[12]

Existing insolvency legislation in Malaysia was clearly more institutional-ized than in either Indonesia or Thailand. Nonetheless, it was unpopular with creditors and did not provide the range of solutions to preserve value for other stakeholders in complex corporate groups with multiple creditors.[13] The purpose of the committee was thus to persuade financial institutions not to precipitate insolvency.[14]

In August 2001, the CDRC, under new leadership, announced three new measures to spur corporate restructuring which included: (1) a revamp of CDRC membership to include representatives from Pengurusan Danaharta Nasional Bhd and the Federation of Public Listed Companies; (2) changes to the framework and approach of the CDRC to accelerate restructuring efforts;[15] and (3) an increase in the frequency of financial disclosure, i.e. regular disclosure and quarterly reporting to keep the market abreast of the progress of restructuring (*The Star*, 10 August 2001).

The CDRC now had the authority to implement management changes. Furthermore, the agency could then appoint liquidators to settle non-performing loans (NPLs). Previously, the CDRC had merely acted as a mediator with limited authority between creditors and borrowers (*The Star*, 13 August 2001). For a detailed look at the principles of the CDRC framework, its objectives, terms of reference, key principles governing the corporate workout process, processes and guidelines, revised debt restructuring guidelines, and revised framework, refer to the CDRC website.[16]

Bank Restructuring

Cleaning Up the NPLs

Following the prolonged crisis and worsening economic conditions, banks became increasingly reluctant to provide new lending. Rising NPL levels encouraged them to be more cautious and to avoid incurring more bad loans. To relieve banks of their NPLs prior to merger, Danaharta was set up in June 1998 to purchase and manage NPLs from banking institutions with a gross value of at least RM5 million (NEAC, 1999: 34).[17] In other words, Danaharta sought to carve out bad debts from Malaysian banks. This was to enable them "to refocus on lending to viable business and economic activities which could support economic recovery, without being burdened by the task of managing non-performing assets" (NEAC, 1999: 34).

By the end of 1999, Danaharta had acquired RM45.5 billion of NPLs from the financial system, of which RM35.7 billion were loan rights acquired (LRA)[18] from the banking system (BNM, 2000). This constituted 42 per cent of the NPLs in the banking system then, and reduced the residual NPL level from its peak of 9 per cent in November 1998 to 6.6 per cent in December 1999 (based on the old 6-month arrears classification). Danaharta accumulated the NPLs in two ways (Danaharta, 2002: 3):

(1) Acquiring NPLs from almost 70 financial institutions at an average discount rate of 54.4 per cent, with payment made either by issuing zero-coupon Danaharta bonds to the selling financial institution or in cash (especially when purchasing Islamic loans or loans from development financial institutions). The total cost involved using this mode of acquisition was RM9.03 billion.

(2) Being assigned to manage the NPLs of Sime Bank and Bank Bumiputra Malaysia on behalf of the government which had decided to have these now defunct banks acquired by other banks.

Having completed this loan acquisition phase by 2000, Danaharta then focused on the management and resolution of loans and assets under its administration in 2001. Vested with the legal powers to facilitate and expedite this enormous task, Danaharta adopted various asset management techniques to maximize recovery values, including active restructuring and rescheduling, and schemes of arrangement[19] for viable loans, foreclosure[20] and appointment of special administrators for non-viable loans. The Pengurusan Danaharta Nasional Berhad Act of 1998 confers on Danaharta the power to appoint special administrators to manage the affairs of distressed companies. A special administrator is a company auditor or person who has the requisite experience to revive a distressed company and come up with a workout proposal aimed at maximizing the recovery value on the business.

Danaharta acquired and managed RM47.7 billion of total loan rights in its portfolio. Of these loans, Danaharta expected a recovery rate of 57 per cent (50 per cent for acquired loans and 63 per cent for managed ones) from the outstanding value of the loan rights acquired (inclusive of accrued interest). Before winding up its operations in 2005, Danaharta expected total recovery of RM30.19 billion. It had already collected and received RM18.93 billion in cash and non-cash assets by the end of 2002.

Danaharta was fully funded by the government (see Wong, Jomo and Chin, 2005: Table 6.7). As at the end of 2002, it had total capital and outstanding liabilities of RM14.54 billion. With most of its government-guaranteed bonds maturing in 2004,[21] Danaharta needed to generate enough cash to redeem all its bonds when they became due. As changes in the value of non-cash assets (securities and properties) due to market uncertainties affected recovery receipts, the ability to quickly realise non-cash assets during the lifespan of Danaharta would have an important bearing on its success. Danaharta had two options that could cause taxpayers to bear the burden if it failed to redeem the bonds as scheduled. It could roll over the bonds for up to five years, by turning the zero-coupon bonds into interest-bearing bonds, or the government guarantee could be invoked to bear any shortfall in the bond redemption exercise.

Banking on immunity from legal challenges to its sale of property, stock and other assets, Danaharta has been recovering value from the bad debts it bought from Malaysian financial institutions after the 1997 Asian financial crisis. However, its legal immunity was threatened in late November 2002 after the Malaysian Court of Appeal ruled that the provision in the law (Section 72 of the Danaharta Act) giving Danaharta immunity from injunctions was "unconstitutional and void" (Jayasankaran, 2003: 45). Several outstanding legal suits involving applications for injunctions not only slowed down its operations, but also threatened its credibility. Two years later, the Federal Court set aside an injunction granted by the Court of Appeal to a private firm to stop Danaharta from selling its land — charged to Danaharta for a non-performing loan — to a third party even though it was now willing to pay a higher price than the third party for recovery of the charged land (*The Star*, 16 January 2004).

Recapitalizing Malaysian Banking Institutions

Danamodal was established in recognition of the constraints facing banking institutions trying to raise capital on their own in adverse financial circumstances. To address problems of moral hazard, Danamodal operated on the first-loss principle, under which losses arising from past credit decisions were born by shareholders. The capital injections have been in the form of equity or hybrid instruments. Incorporated on August 1998 as a wholly-owned subsidiary of the central bank, Bank Negara Malaysia (BNM), it received RM3 billion as initial seed capital. Anticipating a worst case scenario, BNM had estimated that RM16 billion would be required to bring the risk weighted capital ratio of all domestic banking institutions to at least 9 per cent (NEAC, 1999: Appendix 3).

To minimize the use of public funds, and hence the taxpayers' burden, Danamodal's operations have been based on commercial or market principles. In identifying the banks needing recapitalization, Danamodal used objective guidelines developed by BNM. The steps to be followed included, but were not limited to:

- in-depth analysis of the competitive position and financial standing of each banking institution;
- quantification of potential synergies to be realized through consolidation;
- CAMEL (capital, assets, management, earnings, liquidity) analysis.

Danamodal only recapitalized viable banking institutions based on assessments and due diligence reviews conducted by reputable, international financial advisors. After the capital injections, Danamodal instituted reforms through its nominees appointed to the boards of these banking institutions.

Besides expediting the consolidation of more capitalized domestic banking institutions, as a strategic shareholder in recapitalized banking institutions, Danamodal was in a better position to facilitate the rationalization of banking institutions in conjunction with their consolidation. Thus, Danamodal complemented Danaharta and other financial restructuring and economic recovery measures. Although there is no obligation for any banking institution to enter into an agreement with Danaharta, banking institutions that receive capital assistance from Danamodal have been required to sell their eligible NPLs to Danaharta to reduce their NPL ratio below 10 per cent.

No capital injections have been made into financial institutions since December 1999 as the capital position of banking institutions had continued to improve (BNM, 2002: 134). Total capital injections into ten banking institutions declined from RM7.5 billion to RM2.1 billion on 22 December 2001 following repayments by three of the banking institutions (see Wong, Jomo and Chin, 2005: Table 6.8). With recapitalization completed, Danamodal focused on managing its surplus funds and ensuring sustainable returns to its assets before ceasing operations in 2003. With net tangible assets of RM2.3 billion, Danamodal was able to redeem its RM11 billion bonds in October 2003.

Bank Mergers

The Bank Negara Malaysia (BNM) had been attempting to consolidate the fragmented banking industry for some time. However, past calls since the late 1980s for banks to merge voluntarily have largely been ignored. Only one merger between two ailing banks — i.e. Bank of Commerce and United Asian Bank — took place in mid-1991. Lucrative oligopolistic bank profits, largely assured by banking regulation, have meant that the desire to maintain banking licences remains strong.

A new two-tier regulatory system (TTRS) was introduced in December 1994 to provide incentives for smaller banks to merge. To qualify for privileged first tier status, banks must have equity of at least RM500 million.[22] These privileged first-tier banking institutions were subject to less regulation, engaging in a wider range of activities previously denied to all institutions such as opening foreign currency accounts. Rather than resorting to bank mergers, shareholders often preferred heavy short-term borrowings to inject more capital into the banking institutions in their zeal to meet the TTRS requirements. This exerted undue pressure on bank managements to generate the requisite returns to the newly injected capital in order to service their loans (see BNM, 1999: 210). Consequently, this new regulatory system led to a sharp increase in aggressive and imprudent lending activities, which eventually resulted in poor asset quality, which increased the risk of the banking system as a whole. Given these adverse developments, the TTRS was subsequently abandoned in April 1999.

The financial crisis had given the BNM greater powers to implement its merger programme for domestic banking institutions. In response to the earlier failures to achieve mergers voluntarily, in July 1999, the government unveiled a tough plan to have only six "anchor banks" after the proposed mergers (see Wong, Jomo and Chin, 2005: Table 6.11). All banking institutions were given two months to sign a Memorandum of Understanding (MOU) and eight months to complete the exercise.

Few dispute the rationale for bank mergers in Malaysia. There have been too many bank branches (see Wong, Jomo and Chin, 2005: Table 6.12) competing for depositors with the extensive branch networks of other savings institutions (including the National Savings Bank and credit cooperatives including Bank Rakyat), resulting in socially wasteful duplication of services, which also undermines achieving economies of scale in the provision of banking services. Although there were 39 finance companies in 1997, more than 70 per cent of the business was concentrated in five or six of the larger finance companies.[23]

Although the cost of banking services should decrease following some rationalization of branches and staff relocation, it is far from clear that the

Malaysian approach to bank consolidation would bring about a much more efficient banking sector. Concerns have been raised about the speed and scale of the mergers and the somewhat biased selection of anchor banks. Of the six anchor banks selected, the choice of Maybank and Public Bank was uncontroversial as they are not only the country's largest but they are also reasonably well run. The selection of Southern Bank, despite its relatively smaller size, was uncontroversial as it was well managed and did not need any government bail out (see Wong, Jomo and Chin, 2005: Table 6.13).

Most controversial was the inclusion of two smaller banks — Multipurpose Bank and Perwira Affin Bank — apparently due to political influence (see Jayasankaran, 1999). Multipurpose Bank is controlled by businessmen viewed as close to former Finance Minister Daim, while Perwira Affin Bank is controlled by the Armed Forces Fund Board (LTAT). Ironically, some efficient, but smaller banks — owned by ethnic Chinese interests[24] — were not selected, particularly Hong Leong Bank which has never lost money or needed any government bail out. It has been well managed with no NPLs purchased by Danaharta. It made profits, even during the financial crisis. Bank mergers may thus produce bigger banks without significantly enhancing their efficiency and competitiveness.

It is not clear why efficient mid-sized banks should be taken over by bigger, but weaker banks. More than half the RM39 billion in bad loans absorbed by the government came from two big domestic banks, i.e. the now defunct Sime Bank and Bank Bumiputra, rescued by RHB Bank and Bank of Commerce respectively via mergers (Jayasankaran, 1999). As pointed out by *The Economist* (1999):

> … bigger banks are not necessarily any safer than smaller ones…. Bank for International Settlements (BIS) worries that the current restructuring of the banking industry could cause strains, as "competitive pressures interact with stubborn cost structures and heighten incentives for risk-taking". That is especially dangerous since bigger banks are more likely to be considered "too big to fail", and hence to carry a greater implicit government guarantee.

Due to the strong objections to the number and composition of the proposed banking groups, short time frame for consolidation, ensuing negative market reaction and appeals by affected parties, Prime Minister Mahathir decided to allow ten — instead of six — banks to remain in a revised merger plan announced in October 1999. To speed up the merger process, various tax incentives[25] were granted to domestic banking institutions that signed sale and purchase (S&P) agreements or conditional S&P agreements on or before the end of August 2000.

The revised merger policy did not, however, address the fear of likely concentration of banks in the hands of a few closely connected to the government. For example, the merger plan between Arab-Malaysian Banking Group, one of the selected anchor banks, and Utama Bank Group (UBG), a small bank with disproportionate political influence based in Sarawak, "encapsulates the pitfalls of merger politics" (Jayasankaran, 2000). The deal was opposed by UBG's controlling shareholder, Cahya Mata Sarawak Bhd (CMS), linked to the state's powerful, long-serving Chief Minister. Sarawak remains politically vital to the ruling National Front coalition; e.g. in the 1999 general election, the Chief Minister led the ruling National Front to a clean sweep of the state's 28 parliamentary seats, representing almost 15 per cent of the total number of parliamentary seats. In late December 2000, the merger exercise failed, apparently due to differences over management control and pricing. UBG's second attempt to merge with EON Bank also met with a similar fate in early February 2001. UBG then made no secret of its intention to become an anchor bank (Jayasankaran, 2001) and eventually took over the RHB financial group and bank, apparently after its founder, and principal shareholder Rashid Hussain, fell foul of then Finance Minister, Daim Zainuddin.

On 2 February 2001, then Finance Minister Daim rejected RHB Capital's proposal to buy back RHB Bank's irredeemable non-cumulative preference shares from Danamodal, even though Rashid offered to pay Danamodal a 38 per cent premium over the one billion ringgit outstanding balance (Jayasankaran, 2001). After helping banks get back on a sound financial footing, Danamodal was supposed to eventually dispose of its stakes in the banks into which it had injected funds. As Rashid's offer would clearly benefit Danamodal, the move to block the deal that would have re-established Rashid's control over RHB Bank sparked off speculation that the Finance Minister wanted to oust Rashid from control of the bank.

Bank Utama was given approval in a letter dated 19 April 2001 from the then Finance Minister to the Utama Banking Group Bhd (UBG) and Rashid Hussain Bhd to begin merger talks. The merger between RHB Bank and Bank Utama was finally signed on 20 March 2002. The plan was for UBG to buy over Malaysian Resources Corporation Bhd (MRCB)'s 22.7 per cent stake as well as Rashid Hussain's 23.9 per cent stake in RHB, which held a 55.4 per cent stake in RHB Capital Bhd (the immediate holding company of the group).

Financial restructuring efforts to deal with the banking crisis helped strengthen the banking system. The removal of NPLs by Danaharta and bank recapitalization by Danamodal significantly strengthened the banking sector. While Danamodal and Danaharta made significant progress in strengthening the banking system, government-imposed bank restructuring measures in Malaysia did not effectively address some weaknesses, especially in poor and biased regulatory enforcement and interference by powerful interest groups in decision-making. The bank consolidation programme from 1999 did not resolve the fundamental problems of the Malaysian banking system. There is little evidence that banking sector reforms significantly enhanced economic recovery, let alone created the financial basis for sustained economic growth and structural transformation. With much cherry-picking, and (often more efficient) foreign banks waiting at the gates with international financial liberalization, it is not clear that the banking reforms successfully prepared the sector for such foreign competition.

Corporate Debt Restructuring

Bank recapitalization and restructuring exercises alone were considered insufficient to ensure a strong and sustained economic recovery. A more comprehensive solution to Malaysia's banking and corporate woes required corporate debt restructuring. The various flaws and abuses in the Malaysian bank and corporate restructuring programmes do not imply rejection of the need for government-led bank and corporate restructuring exercises to address some consequences of the 1997–98 Asian financial crises.

The key lesson to be drawn is that such government-led and publicly financed exercises need to be fair, transparent, accountable and judiciously executed, e.g. by ensuring objectivity in the acquisition and recovery criteria used in restructuring exercises. More market-based approaches utilized elsewhere proved to be relatively "sluggish" and ineffectual, and hence, more deleterious for the economies concerned in the long run.

Since the health of the corporate and banking sectors was inter-related, bank restructuring may not be complete without the restructuring of corporate debt, which impinges on the level of NPLs in the banking sector. With the global economic slowdown, especially in the US in 2001, Malaysia could no longer count on fast growth to allow its corporations to recover and to pay off their debts. Meanwhile, the lacklustre performance of capital markets also hampered implementation of some debt restructuring schemes. Thus, Malaysian corporate debt restructuring needed greater private sector involvement, but that was unlikely to be forthcoming until there was stronger evidence that the government was serious about debt restructuring and greater transparency (Ranawana, 2001).

Recognizing the need to toughen its approach, on 9 August 2001, CDRC unveiled three new initiatives aimed at expediting the resolution of debt restructuring under its purview. The initiatives were:

(1) Expanding the CDRC to include representatives from Danaharta and the Federation of Public Listed Companies to ensure that the relevant sectors

were better represented. The CDRC began to utilize the legal powers of Danaharta to hasten the restructuring process (Gabriel, 2001). The CDRC passed some cases to Danaharta, with borrowers losing control with the appointment of special administrators or with liquidation.

(2) Changing the framework and approach of the CDRC to accelerate restructuring efforts. Hence, for example, restructuring could take place with the approval of 75 per cent — rather than 100 per cent — of the creditors.

(3) Establishing a schedule — with clearly identified deadlines — for resolution of each case handled by the CDRC.

During its four years of operations, the CDRC resolved 48 cases with total debts amounting to RM52.6 billion, representing approximately 65 per cent of the total cases under its auspices (see Wong, Jomo and Chin, 2005: Table 6.10). Of the resolved cases, 32 have been fully implemented. The recovery profile of the resolved cases shows that 83 per cent of recovery proceeds were in the form of cash, redeemable instruments and rescheduled debt. The closure of the CDRC on 15 August 2002 marked the conclusion of the debt restructuring efforts undertaken, after which resolution of the remaining 16 cases — involving debt of RM16.6 billion — would be monitored by their respective Creditors Steering Committees and Danaharta.

From Privatization to Re-nationalization

The Asian financial crisis exposed weaknesses especially those entrenched in poorly privatized corporations previously operating in a relatively comfortable business and financial environment. Financially prudent and economically sound corporations were tested, with some "exiting". Nonetheless, a few privatized entities embarked on ambitious expansion programmes that left them over-extended and over-leveraged, thus increasing vulnerability to abrupt credit crunch and adverse business conditions.

The privatization[26] of Malaysia's national sewerage system, airline, car project, and light rail transit (LRT) system was part of the government's attempts to improve efficiency and increase investment through owner-managed enterprises. This was achieved through some form of subsidy, given the high capital costs, low margins (at least in the medium term), and large externalities. State support was also required because the owners could not charge high tariffs or fares to cover their costs. In the case of Perusahaan Otomobil Nasional Bhd (Proton), the national car project, protection was desperately needed, ostensibly to provide "earning rents"; "high" import tariffs raised the relative prices of imported vehicles, thereby helping Proton's growth.

Ironically, the gains from privatization, i.e. improved efficiency and competitiveness, and meeting of long-term targets by privatized entities were generally "patchy". This was partly due to weak regulatory framework — which was imperative to ensure that incentives were in place to induce the owners to improve efficiency and invest — and *ad hoc* intervention by the government through various ministries. Moreover, these failures can be attributed to institutional failure that led to incorrect privatization choices, poor screening and selection, and weak regulation.

An example of an incorrect privatization choice was the privatization of the sewerage system that proceeded without sufficient information on the performance, assets and condition, and customer base of the existing system, or an adequate legal framework. This led to the operator having to take over and maintain more assets than originally agreed, three tariff revisions following consumer opposition, and bill collection problems, which raised operating costs and reduced revenue and cash flow. The government's privatization of public transit systems was also unfeasible to begin with without some form of state support given the cost of infrastructure and general inability of such systems to cover operating costs. For instance, fares only covered 30 to 40 per cent of operating costs in the US and 55 per cent in the UK (Hakim, *et al.*, 1996). In the case of the two operational LRT systems, this figure was 44 per cent (STAR) and 22 per cent (PUTRA) in 1999 (Halcrow Consultants, 1999).

While most countries underwrite the costs of construction and subsidize such public transportation operations, the Malaysian government chose to leave the financing of the LRT system largely to the private sector. According to the former head of the government's Corporate Debt Restructuring Committee (CDRC), infrastructure projects required state funding as only the state, and not banks, could provide long-term funds given the long gestation period (FinanceAsia.com, 24 July 2000). The government provided long-term, low interest loans directly (in the form of government and infrastructure support loans) and through state institutions (e.g. the Employees Provident Fund and the Development and Infrastructure Bank). Moreover, in order for the company to even have a chance to breakeven or generate profits without adversely affecting consumer demand and welfare, huge fare subsidizations were required.

In the case of Malaysian Airline System Bhd (MAS), the poor purchase structure and industry problems would have made it difficult for private ownership to address the airline's long-term capital investment requirements. The purchase was financed entirely through loans, but low profit margins, large externalities, and regular bankruptcies inherent to the industry meant that revenues could not be guaranteed to generate sufficient profits to repay the loan, let alone increase investment.

Proton, on the other hand, was probably not viable to begin with. An ambitious project to spearhead Malaysia's industrialization process, it was closely modelled after the Korean car industry's success but failed to take into account the different global market conditions, necessary scale economies (which were beyond the domestic market), high capital costs, and excess global capacity due to intense competition. Despite the government postponing the lowering of tariffs — as part of the Common Effective Preferential Tariff programme under the ASEAN Free Trade Agreement (AFTA) — from 2003 to 2005 (*The Sun*, 21 June 2000), Proton's alternative (Japanese) director has suggested that Proton might still not be competitive by 2005 (*The Sun*, 25 July 2000). It was therefore unlikely that privatization would have made a difference. Apparently, cross subsidization — relatively higher domestic price compared to export price with better quality for export markets — helped Proton penetrate the overseas market, though their market share is miniscule.

High import tariffs were used to protect the domestic carmaker and ensure the viability of the cross-subsidization strategy. Since Proton and Perodua are ostensibly "national car-makers", both have enjoyed a 50 per cent discount on excise duties. Proton's vehement stalling to include automobiles in the ASEAN Free Trade Area (AFTA) has raised doubts about their ability to compete successfully without such advantages. Anticipation of lower prices for non-national car models, especially from Japanese and South Korean carmakers, since 2003 has apparently discouraged consumers from buying the "national cars". As a result, Proton's market share shrank to 49 per cent in 2003 from 59 per cent in 2002 as its car sales fell by 27.5 per cent to 155,420 units in 2003. Proton's declining market share — and sales revenue — resulted in a net loss of RM42 million in the third quarter of the financial year ending 31 March 2004, compared with a profit of RM197 million in the corresponding quarter the previous year (*The Star*, 24 April 2004). However, for the financial year ending 31 March 2004, the group reported a net profit of RM510.1 million, down significantly from the RM1.1 billion recorded in 2003. The significant drop in pre-tax profit — from RM1.36 billion for the financial year ending 31 March 2003 to RM592 million for the subsequent financial period — reflected the sharp decrease in sales from RM9.27 billion in 2003 to RM6.47 billion in 2004, also reflected in Proton's share price (*The Star*, 29 May 2004).

The absence of open bidding in all four cases can be said to have compromised the quality of awardees. With the exception of one LRT operator and Proton's owner, none of the major awardees had much relevant experience. STAR was a consortium formed and headed by Taylor Woodrow (a UK housing, property development, construction and engineering company) and Adtranz (a train manufacturer owned by DaimlerChrysler, which was later sold to Canada's Bombardier Transportation in 2000). Although Taylor Woodrow and Adtranz had a majority 30 per cent share in the consortium, state institutions had a combined share ownership of 50 per cent. Berjaya Group, the company that headed Indah Water Konsortium (IWK — the consortium awarded the sewerage treatment concession), had no experience in public works aside from some small road-building projects (Gomez and Jomo, 1999). The owner of MAS had never run an airline or been associated with similar business, having made his fortune from a cellular (mobile) telephone monopoly. The remaining two LRT operators[27] did not have experience building or operating public transport systems. Proton's owner was an automotive engineer with some relevant experience, but the government chose to bypass the rest of the existing car assembly industry.

Poor choice of awardees exacerbated by political patronage may be a major explanation for the failures of privatization in Malaysia that greatly increased the cost of government-led "bail outs" which reversed mostly the one-time gains from the privatization programme. The owners of IWK, MAS, Proton and the LRT system were all closely linked to the United Malays National Organization (UMNO) leadership at the highest level, and patronage can be said to have influenced the poor choice of awardees, weakening incentives to increase efficiency and investment. The choice of awardees was important given the national significance of many of these projects, and the government was aware of the risks percentage and need for careful assessment of track records, credit ratings, and intentions: "They must not be the kind of people who would sell their shares for quick gains" (Mahathir, 1998a: 29). The prime minister defended this by arguing that successful awardees "had already proven their ability to run big operations" (*New Straits Times*, 27 November 1995) and were already rich and successful businessmen (Mahathir, 1998b).

The poor choice of awardees was not only reflected by the financial difficulties of these companies (with the exception of Proton, which remained protected and profitable), but also in the performance of the owners' other businesses, all of which were debt-ridden. This reduced the ability of the owners to continue financing the privatized projects, and the government was forced to re-nationalise them when the owners clearly could not break even, even in the medium term. According to the new head of the CDRC in 2001, the subsequent replacement of these owners with professional managers was to separate the powers between chairman and chief executive officer in order to "alleviate the problems of owner-managers who have their own debt problems" (*Far Eastern Economic Review*, 18 October 2001).

Regulatory failure, on the other hand, is perhaps best exemplified by the government's "arbitrary administrative action" when it revised tariffs, not once, but three times, in the case of IWK. The privatization of the sewerage and LRT systems sought to facilitate capital accumulation through the allocation of short-term (construction) and long-term (concession) rents. The concessionaire can thus earn profits at the end or at the beginning, by overstating construction costs.[28] The 60-year concession period for the LRT privatization can be seen as providing long-term monopoly rents, while the decision to privatize infrastructure construction, instead of underwriting capital costs and privatizing operations, as elsewhere, offered further rents. This was also consistent with growing investments in the country involving construction.

Similarly, by creating a monopoly from an essentially decentralized sewerage system run by 144 local authorities, potential efficiency gains from privatizing to several different operators were ignored to ensure monopoly rents. For example, the government could have privatized sewage treatment to more than one operator along the lines of the 19 urban centres outlined in the national sewerage development programme (see Pillay, 1994). According to Ridzuan Halim, there is "no advantage organizing sewerage works on a national basis since there is little sense centralizing or collecting sewerage on a national basis" (*The Edge*, 1 June 1998).

Hence, while regulation is normally needed to limit monopoly rents, this may not be the case where the state seeks to create such rents to promote capital accumulation. The government also effectively failed to regulate the LRT system by not accounting for the large externalities that necessitated some form of state support. The unlikelihood of repaying the capital costs meant that the operators had lost the incentive to be efficient (Halcrow Consultants, 1999). Moreover, the owners of both operating LRT companies had little incentive to improve efficiency given their debt burdens and government guaranteed incomes, which made the prospect of breaking even unlikely.

In the case of MAS, this was partly due to the externalities inherent in the airline industry. In addition, previous management decisions on fleet expansion added to the new owner's debt burden and the government continued to limit domestic airfares and require MAS to fly to unprofitable destinations that impinged on the airline's revenue stream. The picture that emerges then is one of entrepreneurial failure, compounded by poor investment decisions and inappropriate regulation, which eventually led to re-nationalization in some cases. Persistent policy failure was partly due to a combination of a highly centralized, insulated, non-transparent and unaccountable political executive, and the country's rich natural resource endowment (e.g. see Bowie, 1988; Jesudason, 1989) that diluted imperatives for economic efficiency.

Lessons

In the last quarter of 1998, the regional turmoil came to an end as East Asian currencies strengthened and stabilized after the US Federal Reserve Bank lowered interest rates enough to reverse capital "flight to safety" in the US. In the first quarter of 1999, Thailand, Indonesia and South Korea posted positive growth rates, while Malaysia's recession went into its fifth quarter. By the end of 1999, of the four, Malaysia's recovery was second only to South Korea's, with their stronger recoveries continuing into 2000.

Capital controls did not cause the recovery in Malaysia to be slower than in the other crisis countries (Wong, Jomo and Chin, 2005). The 1998 collapse was less deep in Malaysia than in Thailand and Indonesia, while the recovery in Malaysia was faster after early 1999. Malaysia's pre-crisis problems were less serious to begin with owing to strengthened prudential regulations after the late 1980s' banking crisis (when non-performing loans went up to 30 per cent of total loans). There were strict controls on Malaysian private borrowing from abroad, with borrowers generally required to demonstrate likely foreign exchange earnings from investments to be financed with foreign credit. Hence, although Malaysia seemingly has the most open economy in the East Asian region after Hong Kong and Singapore, with the total value of its international trade around double national income, its foreign borrowings and share of short-term loans in total credit were far less than the more closed economies of South Korea, Indonesia and Thailand before the regional crisis.

The control measures were only part of a package of measures to revive the Malaysian economy. Focusing solely on the control measures ignores the significance of the other measures. It is possible for the effects of successful controls to have been wiped out by the failure of accompanying programmes, or vice versa. Very importantly, the conceptualization, financing, governance and actual operations of national asset management corporations involved in bank and corporate debt restructuring were especially crucial in shaping the nature, speed and strength of national economic recovery as well as subsequent corporate capacities and capabilities.

Credit facilities for share as well as property purchases were actually increased as part of the package. The government even encouraged its employees to take second mortgages for additional property purchases at its heavily discounted interest rate. Although otherwise appreciative of Malaysian measures, including the role of the central bank, Rajaraman (2003) noted that the property sector "continues to account for 40 per cent of NPLs", and that the controls introduced "in 1999 to prohibit lending for construction of high-end properties came five years too late to avert the financial sector softening that was a contributory, if not the precipitating, factor in the 1997 crisis. Controls on connected lending, now in place, came five years too late". Ringgit credit facilities by residents to non-residents are also allowed for up to RM200,000, well below the earlier pre-1998 limit of RM5 million, though not to purchase immovable property in Malaysia.

However, the forced bank mergers in the wake of the crisis were poorly conceived, if not downright biased to suit certain political interests, and hence less likely to achieve their ostensible ends. The authorities' push for the rapid merger of banks and financial companies were not well designed to enhance synergies, efficiency and competitiveness beyond achieving certain economies of scale and reducing some wasteful duplication and redundancy. The consolidation of the financial sector may be desirable to achieve economies of scale and other advantages in anticipation of further financial liberalization. But its acceleration in response to the crisis seemed less well conceived except to take advantage of the financial institutions' weakness and vulnerability during the crisis.

The window of opportunity offered by the mid-1998 government initiatives was also abused by certain powerfully-connected business interests, not only to secure government funded bailouts at public expense, but also to consolidate and extend their corporate domination, especially in the crucial financial sector. Capital controls were part of a package used to save friends of the regime, at public expense. For example, while ostensibly not involving public funds, the government-sponsored restructuring of the ruling party-linked Renong conglomerate actually cost the public, billions of ringgit in foregone toll and tax revenue. Also, non-performing loans (NPLs) of the thrice-bankrupted Bank Bumiputra — taken over by politically well-connected banking interests with its huge debt cleared — were not heavily discounted like other banks' NPLs, although it had long abandoned its ostensible "social agenda" of helping the politically dominant Bumiputera community for all practical purposes.

Notes

1. Sources for this appendix are Haggard (2000) and Danaharta's website: <http://www.danaharta.com.my/>.
2. A definition of an asset management company as provided by Danaharta can be obtained from its website. "Assets" here refer to both loans and tangible assets, with the preferred source of repayment being realization of gain through reconstruction and rehabilitation of the asset while other forms of repayment include identified cash flows from acquired assets, existing business operations and disposal of collateral.
3. With paid-up capital of RM250 million [approximately US$65 million (US$1 = RM3.8)], Danaharta raised RM25 billion in working capital in zero-coupon government-guaranteed bonds.

4. Refer to Danaharta's website for its asset acquisition guidelines, framework for acquisition methodology, background to and summary of Pengurusan Danaharta Nasional Berhad Act 1998 and other information.

5. Danaharta has the legal authority to conduct liquidation procedures.

6. These included the ability to displace management and appoint "special adminis-trators" to manage distressed companies, the requirement that shareholders take appropriate "haircuts" in any loan rescheduling, and the provision that borrowers are provided only one opportunity to implement a restructuring plan (Thillainathan, 2000).

7. This appendix draws from Haggard (2000) and the Danamodal website: <http://www.bnm.gov.my/danamodal/ff_vital.htm>.

8. Danamodal fell under the central bank (Bank Negara Malaysia, BNM), and was to be funded by capital raised in the form of equity and hybrid instruments, or debt, in both domestic and international markets, to minimize the use of public funds. The central bank provided the initial seed capital of RM3 billion, and another RM2 billion on a standby basis.

9. See <http://www.bnm.gov.my/danamodal/ff_vital.htm>.

10. This section draws from Haggard (2000) and the CDRC website: <http://www.bnm.gov.my/CDRC/>, *The New Straits Times*, 9 Aug. 2001, *The Star*, 10 Aug. 2001, and *The Star*, 13 Aug. 2001.

11. The CDRC thus acts as an advisor and mediator between creditors and debtors in debt restructuring.

12. With the formation of the CDRC, companies have opted for this friendlier arrangement to resolve their debt problems, instead of going to court to defend themselves against the creditors.

13. For the most part, the usual receivership and liquidation administrations do not discriminate between viable and non-viable businesses, resulting in the inevitable closure of affected companies (in most cases). Section 176 has proven to be very unpopular with the financial institutions.

14. A CDRC workout includes initial meetings between debtors and creditors, appointment of independent consultants to design a restructuring programme for the debtor, an initial review of business viability, a formal standstill among creditors if the restructuring exercise proceeds, and oversight of restructuring plans. Even then, the arrangement is informal, has no legal status and can be called off by either side at any time. In the beginning, before certain changes were made and the power of the CDRC increased, it did not have Danaharta's power to force management and ownership changes within companies (*The New Straits Times*, 9 Aug. 2001).

15. Under the revised restructuring guidelines, a borrower must have a minimum aggregate debt of RM100 million (compared with RM50 million previously), exposure to at least five creditor banks, an on-going, viable concern, and sufficient cash generation to cover operating expenditure, to be eligible for CDRC assistance. Furthermore, companies can be referred to the CDRC by corporate borrowers or bank creditors accounting for at least 25 per cent of total debt. To speed up the restructuring process, deadlines would be set for each of the debt restructuring processes and each case should be completed within six to nine months, with debt

reorganization agreements to be signed within the first three months. In the first month, the CDRC would evaluate the case, form a creditors' steering committee and prepare an interim standstill agreement. In the subsequent three months, scheme advisors and solicitors would be appointed, and the workout proposal would be implemented after creditor approval had been secured (*The Star*, 10 August 2001).

16. See <http://www.bnm.gov.my/CDRC/>.
17. With paid-up capital of RM250 million (approximately US$59 million), Danaharta raised RM25 billion in working capital through zero-coupon government-guaranteed bonds.
18. Loans outstanding from financial institutions at the point of acquisition. It comprises both principal outstanding as well as interest.
19. This refers to schemes, voluntarily negotiated by borrowers and creditors, to restructure the loans.
20. This refers to the sale of property and securities.
21. The first tranche of bonds were due on 31 December 2003.
22. The minimum shareholder funds for commercial banks were subsequently increased to RM1,000 million in December 1998.
23. See <http://www.bnm.gov.my/pa/1998/0102.htm>.
24. The number of banks under ethnic Chinese control will shrink from 11 to 2.
25. These tax incentives — which comprised exemptions from stamp duty and real property gains tax, as well as tax credit for 50 per cent of the accumulated losses of banking institutions acquired — were intended to reduce acquisition costs and enhance the value of the merged entities <http://www.bnm.gov.my/pa/2000/0731. htm>.
26. The definition of "privatization" in Malaysia is so broad that it includes cases where private enterprises are awarded licenses to participate in activities previously the exclusive preserve of the public sector, as in the case of television broadcasting from 1984. Contracting out of services, especially by municipal authorities (e.g. involving garbage disposal and parking), and private ownership or even contracted leasing of public properties — e.g. enabling the imposition of tolls on roads previously built by the Public Works Ministry or the Malaysian Highway Authority (Lembaga Lebuhraya Malaysia, LLM) — are also frequently considered to be cases of privatization. In Malaysia, when a state-owned enterprise (SOE), legally formed as a government department or statutory authority, is privatized, it necessarily entails corporatization, or the formation of a limited company incorporated under the Companies Act, 1965. On the other hand, the privatization of an SOE that has been constituted as a limited company would merely entail a transfer of share ownership from the public to the private sector without any change in the legal form of the enterprise.
27. PUTRA and KL Monorail (formerly Rapid People Mover).
28. See interview with Chellappah Rajandram, the former head of the CDRC (FinanceAsia.com, 26 July 2000).

CHAPTER 9

Corporate Governance Reform for East Asia

Jomo K. S.

After the East Asian crises began in mid-1997, it was widely presumed, especially by those in the West that the debacle was due to the current account problems typical of several preceding Latin American crises. Soon, however, it became clear that the East Asian crises could not be explained by conventional old and new currency crisis theories. In early 1998, three influential and powerful economic commentators — then US Federal Reserve chairman Alan Greenspan,[1] then US Deputy Treasury Secretary Lawrence Summers and IMF Managing Director Michel Camdessus[2] — blamed the crises on East Asian corporate governance malpractices. For example, Larry Summers (2000) argued that the East Asian crisis was "profoundly different because it has roots not in improvidence but in economic structures. The *problems that must be fixed are much more microeconomic than macroeconomic*, and involve the private sector more and the public sector less" (Baker, 1998). A new conventional wisdom quickly emerged as reformers sought to promote greater transparency in economic relations, further reduce the role of government in the economy, erode "cosy" government-business relations, and insist on arm's length relations between businesses and their banks, ostensibly to address these alleged flaws. But as Paul Krugman (1999) has asked, "if the system was so flawed, why did it work so well for so long, then fail so suddenly?"

This chapter critically reviews the recent corporate governance discourse, especially the principles and rationale for favouring Anglo-American or Anglo-Saxon style corporate governance. In particular, the corporate governance principles and reforms advocated by the World Bank and the Organization for Economic Cooperation and Development (OECD) are critically reviewed. We first ask whether corporate governance reforms are really as necessary as they are often made out to be. The characteristics of corporate governance, finance and competition in emerging markets are then compared to the World Bank-OECD reform agenda as well as the criteria of corporate arrangements most conducive to "catching up" development.

Are Corporate Governance Reforms Necessary?

The G-7 assigned the task of reforming corporate governance to the OECD and the World Bank. The guidelines and principles proposed by the OECD have been widely presumed to epitomize "good" corporate governance. As such, adherence to these principles and guidelines is supposed to improve and increase (both foreign and domestic) investor confidence, which would lead to greater foreign[3] and domestic investment, and better access to capital in global markets at lower cost, thereby spurring economic growth.[4]

The central issue in corporate governance for them is how the suppliers of finance control the managers of corporate investments. From their perspective, "Corporate governance deals with the ways in which suppliers of finance to corporations assure themselves of getting a return on their investment" (Shleifer and Vishny, 1997). The five basic principles of corporate governance promoted by the OECD and the World Bank have been summarized in the main World Bank document on corporate governance (Iskander and Chamlou, 2000), which claims that the principles are based on tenets of "fairness, transparency, accountability and responsibility" (see Box 9.1).

The World Bank report acknowledges that "there is no one-size-fits-all blueprint for corporate governance". However, as Singh, Singh and Weisse (2003) note, the report only claims that it does not seeks to impose the Anglo-Saxon model of corporate governance in a footnote that can only be found by careful reading:

> (The report) does not advocate one form of ownership structure over another and certainly not the Anglo-US models. These markets have developed over time in response to investor needs, institutional capacity and the investing preferences of the population. They cannot be easily copied in other environments (Iskander and Chamlou, 2000: 53, footnote 1).

It also states that a country's corporate governance model should be prepared according to these principles and should be "nationally owned". As Singh, Singh and Weisse (2003) observe,

> However, the entire thrust of the report's arguments and its definition of "best practice" structure detailed in the appendices to the report, belies any assertion that it treats the different models of corporate governance equally. It is indeed hard to find much daylight between the report's conception of "best practice" and the Anglo-Saxon model of corporate governance,

---

Box 9.1. Principles of Corporate Governance

- *Protection of shareholder rights* to share in company profits, receive information about the company, and influence the firm through shareholder meetings and voting.
- *Equitable treatment of shareholders*, especially of minority and foreign shareholders, with full disclosure of material information and prohibition of self-dealing and insider trading.
- *Protection of stakeholder rights*, as spelled out in contracts and in labour and insolvency laws, in a framework that allows stakeholder participation in performance-enhancing mechanisms, giving stakeholders access to relevant company information, and allowing effective redress for violations of stakeholder rights.
- *Timely and accurate disclosure and transparency* on all matters material to company performance, essential for market monitoring of companies, and shareholder ability to exercise voting rights, with accounting according to quality standards of disclosure and audit, and with objective auditing by independent assessors.
- *Diligent exercise of directors' responsibilities* to guide corporate strategy, manage the firms' executive functions (such as compensation, business plans, and executive employment), monitor managerial performance and achieve an adequate return for investors, implement systems for compliance with relevant laws (tax, labour, competition, environment), prevent conflicts of interest and balance competing demands on the company, and, with some independence from managers, consider the interests of all stakeholders in the company, treat them fairly, and give them access to information.

---

which leaves little doubt that it is the preferred system ... the genesis of the corporate governance project was a questionable analysis of the Asian crisis on which far-reaching policy proposals have been based.

Maher and Andersson (2000: 1) found that the "corporate governance framework can impinge upon the development of equity markets, R&D and innovative activity, entrepreneurship, and the development of active small and medium size enterprises (SMEs) sector, and thus impinge upon economic growth". But, there is little real evidence that adherence to these principles of corporate governance necessarily leads to the optimal outcomes desired, as claimed by OECD and World Bank documents. Also, as Unger (1998: 24–5) notes, "there are always alternative sets of arrangements capable of meeting the same practical tests". Rodrik (1999: 14) observes: "We need to maintain a healthy scepticism towards the idea that a specific type of institution — a particular mode of corporate governance, social security system, or labour market legislation, for example — is the only type that is compatible with a well-functioning market economy."

Also, it is not clear what constitutes "good" corporate governance and which mechanisms will induce good corporate governance. For example, there is still an ongoing debate as to whether chief executive officer (CEO) "duality" (i.e. the CEO is also chair of the board of directors) will contribute to better corporate performance. "Agency theory argues that shareholder interests require protection by separation of incumbent roles of board chair and CEO (whereas) stewardship theory argues (that) shareholder interests are maximized by shared incumbency of these roles" (Donaldson and Davis, 1991: 49). After all, agency theory assumes that the agent (in this case, the CEO) tends to act in his or her own self-interest, which will probably not completely coincide with the interests of the corporation. Therefore, giving the authority and power of both CEO and board chairman to an individual could result in abuse of power at the expense of other shareholders.

On the other hand, stewardship theory presumes that the CEO stewards the corporation to maximize shareholders' interests and will do everything possible to enhance the interests of the corporation. Hence, when an individual is both CEO and board chair, strategic decisions can be speedily implemented since there is less likelihood of "disagreement" and greater likelihood that both the CEO and the board are of the same mind. Clearly, agency theory and stewardship theory offer very different views of how a CEO's role and powers will affect corporate performance.

According to Maher and Andersson (2000: 35), "the search for good corporate governance practices should be based on an identification of what works in defined countries, and to examine the conditions for transferability of these practices to other countries. There is a need, therefore, for continued research that identifies what are the crucial improvements needed in different systems and in different situations." Furthermore, changes in corporate governance systems entail risks, uncertainty and costs, at least in the short term. Hence, careful consideration of a country's corporate governance institutions, taking into account its corporate history and culture, is necessary to bring about the most appropriate reform. The corollary, of course, is that no "one size fits all" and so-called best practices or benchmarks may often be inappropriate or even have unintended perverse consequences.

Instead, numerous considerations and questions, which cannot possibly be discussed in detail here, need to be addressed. One is how to develop corporate governance frameworks and mechanisms that elicit socially desirable outcomes, including desirable levels of investment, for all major stakeholders. This is often difficult to achieve in practice, in light of the various, often contradictory, if not opposing, motives and objectives of stakeholders. For example, shareholders are primarily concerned with returns to their investments; creditors want to be repaid (sometimes requiring borrowing firms to minimize risk, although riskier projects generally entail higher returns); managers want to maximize their (personal) benefits (often at the expense of others, including shareholders); and large shareholders with control of the firm ("insiders") want to maximize their own interests, often at the expense of smaller minority shareholders ("outsiders"). Corporate governance mechanisms and systems also vary by industry, sector, type of activity, and over time. The effectiveness of any particular system will be influenced by differences in legal and regulatory frameworks, historical and cultural factors, and the nature of product and factor markets. Corporate governance in this context is broadly concerned with finding mechanisms that elicit firm-specific investments by various stakeholders (including employees and suppliers), and encourages active cooperation among stakeholders in creating wealth and jobs, and sustaining financially sound enterprises.

A good corporate governance framework is also expected to reward (controlling) shareholders directly monitoring corporate performance, while ensuring that they do not appropriate excessive rents at the expense of other stakeholders. While some degree of ownership concentration is considered necessary to address the moral hazard problem between managers and shareholders,[5] such ownership concentration should be subject to strict rules of disclosure and transparency to protect minority shareholders and creditors.

The emphases in self-assessment exercises promoted by the international financial institutions — such as the Asian Development Bank (ADB) — focus on five corporate governance problems: lack of effective oversight by directors; poor disclosure; poor compliance with regulatory and statutory requirements; tight insider control; and shareholder and creditor passivity.

Recent efforts to identify and promote corporate governance international best practices have often been based on erroneous premises, analyses and policy recommendations. Corporate governance reforms invariably involve and promote ostensible "best practices", codes and standards which often become yardsticks or even conditionalities for a country seeking preferential or emergency credit. However, there is little evidence that such corporate governance reforms will enhance economic growth or private sector performance in most emerging market economies. Some reform advocates in developing countries propose stock market governance reforms that are even more extreme than those recommended by the international financial institutions (Singh, Singh and Weisse, 2003).

Corporate Governance in Emerging Markets

Share Ownership and Control

World Bank evidence on corporate governance structures, including the structure of share ownership and relevant laws, suggest that the widely-held corporation is mainly an Anglo-American phenomenon. In developing countries, the share of family controlled firms among the top 20 publicly-traded companies is much higher than in the United Kingdom and the United States, while the situation in other developed countries varies considerably. State ownership and control of large firms is significant in Italy, Israel, Singapore and Austria, with state control of nearly half of the top twenty publicly-listed firms. Ironically, Russia and most Eastern European transition economies now have more private ownership than many Western European countries, while Italy, Israel and Singapore have the largest state-owned sectors in the world.

In the World Bank sample of nearly 3,000 publicly-traded firms in nine Asian countries (Claessens, Djankov and Lang, 2000), Japan is the only country with Berle and Means-type dispersed or widely-held share ownership when ten per cent equity ownership is defined as providing control. Most other Asian countries sampled had firms dominated by families, with the share of family-controlled firms rising with lower definitions of control. And apparently, concentration of economic power among a few families is not necessarily antithetical to efficient functioning, transparency and profitability, as in Sweden.

Crony Capitalism

In the wake of the Asian crisis, after the irrelevance of traditional currency crisis theories became painfully obvious, powerful Western interests argued that "crony capitalism" — close relations between large capitalists and their government allies — had caused the economic collapse. Crony capitalism allegedly involves collusion between business and political elites, and can arise despite widely dispersed ownership. In any case, crony capitalism does not really pose a corporate governance problem since the owners are likely to have the right incentives to act in the company's interest as they do not face typical agency problems (Berglof and von Thadden, 1999). As mentioned earlier, there is no evidence of a clear and direct link between the share of GDP controlled by such firms and economic performance (Claessens, Djankov and Lang, 2000). The role and influence of such family-controlled groups cannot explain the crisis or its timing. Instead, Singh, Singh and Weisse (2003) suggest that family-controlled firms in developing countries have contributed to late development and industrialization.

The OECD/World Bank Corporate Governance Proposals

A series of papers by Rafael La Porta, Florencio Lopez-de-Silanes and Andrei Schleifer (La Porta, *et al.*) (1999) on corporate governance, finance and law has provided much of the theoretical and empirical bases for the World Bank and the OECD's advocacy of particular reforms. Their central proposition is that there is a systematic causal relationship between the legal framework, corporate behaviour, corporate financing, corporate performance and economic growth. The greater the protection for minority shareholders and creditors, the more external financing firms can obtain. In turn, access to external finance modifies corporate behaviour and improves corporate performance, enhancing economic growth.

La Porta, *et al.* also argue that lack of protection for minority shareholders leads to share ownership concentration, and that corporations in Anglo-American common law countries pay out more dividends and have higher share prices than firms in civil law countries. Their evidence suggests faster development of stock markets under common law legal systems than under civil law systems. They argue that the legal system better classifies economies than the distinction between "bank-based" and "stock market-based" financial systems. La Porta, *et al.* also claim that civil law countries have lower accounting standards, more corruption, less efficient judicial systems and poorer protection for creditors and shareholders, leading to poorer corporate governance and lower economic growth. The clear policy implication is that economies should adopt the more efficient common law system based on transparency and arm's length relations. This will not be easy in the face of vested interests related to concentrated share ownership and crony capitalism.

Berglof and von Thadden (1999) reject the La Porta, *et al.* theoretical framework as too limited for examining corporate governance issues in developing countries. They argue that the La Porta, *et al.* characterization of corporate governance in emerging markets is too limited. La Porta, *et al.* focus on the protection of the providers of external finance, ignoring labour relations, supplier relations, local community relations and the government, while Berglof and von Thadden do not consider external finance as the only, or even the main constraint on firm growth.

Berglof and von Thadden also dispute the La Porta, *et al.* studies' Anglo-American benchmark, namely the Berle and Means-type corporation. They argue that the La Porta, *et al.* approach may only be relevant for transitional economies, where the previously state-owned enterprises have been taken over by the previous managers through management buy-out privatizations. In such circumstances, Berglof and von Thadden acknowledge that improved investor protection may help attract outside capital and thus require restructuring. In other emerging markets in developing countries however, the typical firm is likely to be family-controlled or have concentrated share ownership of some other type. The major corporate governance challenges for such firms are family succession and maintaining control while raising funds from outside.

Berglof and von Thadden also note that causality between legal system and financial structure can run in either direction. The legal system may lead to a certain financial structure, as La Porta, *et al.* claim, but financial structure may equally plausibly lead to certain legal norms, i.e. the law adjusts to economic and political changes. Hence, while the presumed legal determinism of La Porta, *et al.* is plausible, it is nonetheless hypothetical and presumed. Maximizing investor protection reduces the efficiency gains from lower agency costs due to concentrated ownership. Greater investor protection may also lead to short-termism, characteristic of firms in Anglo-American stock market-based economies, resulting in lower levels of investment and more financial speculation (Singh, 2000).

Glen, Lee and Singh (2001) offer other criticisms of La Porta, *et al.*, pointing to major changes in corporate financing and stock market developments in emerging markets over the last two and a half decades. Such large variations cannot simply be attributed to changes in corporate law or legal system origins. For example, enormous changes occurred in Indian stock market development and financing over a relatively brief period of time without any major changes in India's corporate legal framework (see Singh, 1998).

Many emerging markets experienced major increases in stock market activity after some financial liberalization from the 1980s. Singh (1997) and Singh and Weisse (1998) argue that this was not due to switching from civil to common law, but rather to economic policy changes. Without altering their basic civil or common law framework, the laws and their consequences changed in line with such changes in economic policy. Of course, changes in the legal framework can lead to changes in economic institutions and performance.

Also, the relationship between law and economic policy is mutually interactive or dialectical, rather than one-way, as suggested by La Porta, *et al.* Hence, the La Porta, *et al.* legal origin approach cannot adequately account for the recent changes in corporate financing and stock market developments in emerging markets. While legal origin may explain some of the variation, it cannot explain the basic policy changes. As Maddison (1991) shows, Anglo-American corporate governance may only have been more conducive to growth in certain historical circumstances.

Also, La Porta, *et al.* assume that economies with a civil law tradition — and, consequently, less protection for outside investors — have been either willing to accept or are ignorant of the economic costs or fundamental flaws of their legal system. By their logic, Germany and France were either ignorant or irrational for not importing a common law system over the last century. They also fail to explain why economic growth in both Japan and Germany was, on average, faster than in the UK and the US over the twentieth century.

Corporate Governance and Finance in Emerging Markets

Operating in under-developed and more imperfect capital markets, firms in developing countries generally have little choice but to finance most of their investments and growth from internal sources, i.e. retained profits, as they have less recourse to the stock market to finance their investment projects. Information and regulatory weaknesses of emerging stock markets as well as the compromised market reputations of most firms in these markets imply that pricing is more likely to be noisy and arbitrary, resulting in greater share price volatility, discouraging firms from trying to raise funds through new market issues. Greater share price volatility reduces the efficiency of market signals and discourages risk-averse investors from raising funds through stock market listings. Since most large corporations in emerging markets are mainly family controlled (Claessens, Djankov and Lang, 2000; Iskander and Chamlou, 2000), they may be reluctant to issue equity to avoid losing control.

Mainstream corporate finance theory therefore suggests that such firms will follow the typical "pecking-order" of preferences hierarchy for financial sources, i.e. first, internal sources, next, long-term bank borrowings, and last, the stock market. As many takeover risk-averse firms may avoid the stock market, stock market listings would be low. Singh and Hamid (1992) and Singh (1995) found that the hundred biggest listed manufacturing firms in ten emerging market economies relied much more on external — rather than internal — finance and new share issues than suggested by the "pecking-order" hypothesis, resulting in the rapid growth of stock market listings in many emerging market economies in the 1980s and 1990s. Such firms were largely self-financing, relying on unexpectedly high proportions of equity financing. Large firms in developing countries were expected to depend heavily on external — rather than internal — finance due to the limited development and imperfections of capital markets in developing countries. For Singh (1995), this greater reliance on external financing in developing countries was due to the faster growth of such firms and the consequently greater need for external capital. Such finance was often made available by emerging market governments, while smaller firms faced credit rationing.

Singh (1995) also attributes the great use of equity finance to the government's encouragement of stock market development to facilitate privatization as well as external and domestic financial liberalization, leading to stock market booms. The resulting lower cost of equity capital and higher real interest rates increased the relative costs of debt finance. For Singh, once these temporary factors become less relevant, the situation would revert to the normally low levels of equity financing, with corporations avoiding new share issues. The desire of families to retain control over large firms and the greater share price volatility of stock markets in developing countries thus conspire to discourage the greater use of equity finance.

Corporate Finance and Corporate Governance

Corporate governance is widely acknowledged to be closely associated with corporate finance. Corporate governance is defined by Shleifer and Vishny (1997) in terms of regulations and procedures which guarantee that investors and creditors in a company can get their money back and will not be expropriated by those who manage the company. Apparently, corporate governance does not effect long-term growth, or other factors may more than compensate for poor corporate governance in doing so. Alternatively, other systems of corporate governance may also be conducive to economic growth.

With such heavy reliance on equity financing by firms in large developing countries, stock markets should significantly affect corporate governance behaviour through movements in share prices or the market for corporate control. For stock market proponents, liquid secondary equity markets lead to better fund allocation, resulting in more efficient and successful firms obtaining capital at lower cost, while less efficient or profitable firms face higher equity capital costs. This should result in more efficient and profitable firms, bringing about greater technological progress and economic growth.

However, for Keynes, the pricing process may be compromised by speculation, and hence, less than efficient. Tobin distinguishes between two concepts of share price efficiency: *information* efficiency, when all currently available information is incorporated into share prices, and *fundamental valuation* efficiency, when share prices accurately reflect future discounted corporate earnings. Actual stock market prices are more likely to reflect the former, rather than the latter, owing to the behavioural psychology characterizing the stock market. In Keynes' beauty contest analogy, the successful investor is the one who correctly anticipates the likely movements of other stocks in the market rather than the one who really appreciates the fundamental values of corporations. Thus, fads, manias, panics herd behaviour, contagion and so forth cause stock market values to diverge significantly from underlying values. Such volatility further undermines the ability of share prices to efficiently transmit signals to market participants.

The stock market also encourages managers to pursue short-term profits — at the expense of long-term investments — in order for firms to achieve earnings targets to meet market expectations. Any serious shortfall will quickly lower share prices, making the firm vulnerable to takeover. Various analysts have ascribed poorer UK and US economic performance *vis-à-vis* Japan and Germany — with their bank-based financial systems — to the short-termist demands of finance, resulting in lower investments in technological upgrading and additional capacity. More generally, stock market development has often accelerated the ascendance of finance over productive enterprise. In the Anglo-American framework, companies are more likely to rise or fall due to financial engineering, rather than due to innovative products or more efficient processes. Within the firms themselves, managers trained in accounting and finance prevail over the engineers, even in manufacturing companies.

Corporate Governance and Takeovers

The market for corporate control — i.e. the ability of outside investors to take over a corporation, including through hostile bids — is often hailed as the greatest achievement of the stock market on the Anglo-American financial system. This market supposedly improves corporate efficiency by enabling those who can manage corporate assets more productively to gain control of them. Thus, better managers who can raise firm profitability and their share prices take over less well run firms. An active market for corporate control — posing a credible threat that inefficient managers will be replaced — is thus expected to ensure that incumbent managers will seek to improve corporate performance and maximize shareholder value. Even if quoted firms are not directly susceptible to changes in share prices because they almost exclusively use internal finance, the market for corporate control supposedly still serves to discipline managers. And even if all firms are managed efficiently, the amalgamation of some — through mergers or takeovers — can still improve resource allocation.

Singh and others have challenged such orthodox claims about the market for corporate control. In reality, it is much easier for a large firm to take over a small one — rather than the converse (Singh, 1992) — even in advanced economies. While theoretically, a small, efficient firm may take over a less efficient larger company, this rarely happens in practice (Hughes, 1991). Rather, predatory large groups (Singh, 1995) may take over more efficient, smaller firms, thus reducing competition and efficiency. In takeovers, relative size usually counts more than relative efficiency. An active market for corporate control may encourage managers to "build empires", not only to increase oligopolistic market power, but also to avert hostile takeovers by becoming larger.

An efficient takeover mechanism presumes perfect information. Market participants need accurate information on corporate profitability under existing managers and likely profitability under alternative management. But such information is rarely available, and this problem is likely to be worse in developing countries.

Also, takeovers are a very expensive way of changing management, usually involving considerable transactions costs, which undermine the ostensible efficiency gains from such processes. Economies without active markets for corporate control have avoided such costs, while developing other systems for disciplining managers. There is actually little evidence that corporate governance necessarily improves after takeovers since not all takeovers have disciplinary consequences, as many acquisitions are motivated by pre-emptive empire-building or asset-stripping considerations.

Furthermore, even if managers seek to maximize shareholder wealth, they could be better off being myopic in the face of takeover threats and signal-jamming. Thus, takeovers could actually worsen short-termism. Also, while takeovers can be used to avoid honouring implicit contracts between workers and managers (Shleifer and Summers, 1988), revoking such implicit contracts can undermine the accumulation of firm-specific worker capabilities.

These criticisms of the ostensible virtues of markets for corporate control are especially relevant to developing countries, as shareholdings are not usually widely dispersed and disclosure levels are worse. Not surprisingly then, hostile takeovers are rarer in developing countries, but have increased with large foreign transnational corporations (TNCs) engaging in takeovers, e.g., in the wake of the 1997–98 East Asian crises. With limited funds and poorer access to international capital markets, usually in times of distress, domestic firms are generally less able to compete with or resist such "fire-sale FDI". Such large TNC takeovers undermine market competition in such smaller economies.

Financial liberalization and stock markets can negatively affect corporate governance in other ways. Financial liberalization also strengthens interactions between two volatile markets — the stock market and the foreign exchange market. During the 1997–98 East Asian crises, there was negative feedback or a vicious circle between the stock and currency markets. As stock markets declined, investors pulled out, moving their funds into foreign currencies, depreciating the currency, further lowering stock market returns in foreign currencies. A stock market bubble can cause an overvalued real exchange rate, which adversely affects the competitiveness of tradables. Conversely, a collapse in currency and equity values will encourage "fire-sale" takeovers as the expected rates of return in foreign currencies increase significantly due to the sharp declines in currency values and domestic share prices.

High Gearing of Developing Country Corporations

Companies in developing countries seem to be highly geared by international standards if the ratio of total debt to total equity — not long-term debt to equity — is confident. The gearing of corporations in developing countries is generally high (see Singh, Singh and Weisse, 2003: Table 10), reflecting the extensive use of more easily available short-term debt to finance their often rapid growth. After the East Asian crises, the IMF, affected governments and market commentators all urged reducing gearing ratios.

High gearing ratios allow families reluctant to raise money by issuing new equity to retain control of companies by borrowing instead. High ratios can reduce agency problems by forcing managers to improve productivity and profitability. Bank of International Settlements (BIS) regulations served to encourage short-term over long-term lending while regulatory changes facilitated borrowing from foreign banks which generally offered lower interest rates. Before the East Asian crises, high gearing ratios were not onerous since short-term debt was continuously rolled over, i.e. it virtually became long-term debt. However, during the East Asian crises, these high debt levels became the major source of vulnerability and short-term creditors were no longer willing to roll over their debt. Meanwhile, the stock market collapses encouraged the flight of portfolio capital investments. With much of the debt denominated in US dollars, the collapse of the stock market and real economy fed the currency collapse, as described above.

Conglomerates and Efficiency

In the absence of appropriate supporting institutions and markets, which generally take a long time to develop, Singh, Singh and Weisse (2003) argue that the Anglo-American strategies emphasizing "core competence" and "focus" are generally unsuitable for business groups in emerging markets. Large family-owned conglomerates have been blamed for the Asian crisis because of their lack of transparency, poor corporate governance, deficient accounting and lack of focus. The owners are said to have been more interested in empire building than in raising shareholder value. Moral hazard is attributed to the size of such business groups, becoming "too big to fail" for governments. High gearing ratios are also said to be symptomatic of cronyism among corporations, banks and the government. Family business groups often have in-house banks, ostensibly used to finance risky projects or excessive investments, leading to over-capacity. Such business groups have, in fact, led growth and industrialization in developing countries. Leff (1978, 1979) and Amsden (1989, 2000) have highlighted the crucial role of such conglomerates, which have grown and diversified organically, rather than emerged from takeovers; many are engaged in a wide variety of activities, with few apparent synergies among them.

Corporations in developing countries are often at a serious disadvantage *vis-à-vis* those from advanced countries that have well-established brand names and large advertising budgets that create significant entry barriers to firms in developing countries. The Korean *chaebol* has been an institutional means to reduce this handicap, e.g. often by building a reputation for the *chaebol* as a whole, rather than for particular product lines. By 1990, 11 Korean firms were in *Fortune* magazine's top 500 corporations, compared to none 20 years before (Amsden and Hikino, 1994; Singh, 1995). Amsden and Hikino (1994) suggest that the existence and efficiency of privately owned business groups in late industrializing countries have been due to their managers becoming adept at choosing, obtaining and adapting suitable foreign technologies for many different industries.

The popular view is to restructure the *chaebol* along Anglo-American lines, as recommended by the Bretton Woods institutions in order to maximize shareholder value as well as to strengthen minority shareholders and the representation of non-executive directors on company boards. Singh (1998, 1999) and Chang and Park (1999) have argued that this is not the most desirable reform. Instead, Singh (1999) proposes building on — rather than undermining — the close relations between government, business and finance. He recommends a new "social corporatism", extending government-business relationship to labour and civil society, and notes that Anglo-American-style arm's length relations between government, business and labour tend to degenerate into adversarial relations during crisis, that make desired changes even more difficult to achieve.

Corporate Governance and Competition

Alchian (1950) and Friedman (1953) suggested a close relationship between competition, selection and corporate governance. They suggested that regardless of the separation between ownership and control (Berle and Means, 1933), competitive selection in product markets ensures that managers maximize profits. Hence, only optimal ownership patterns and corporate governance structures survive such "natural selection" in the limiting conditions of perfect competition and unfettered entry (Winters, 1964). For Winters (1964), imperfect competition, barriers to entry and/or economies of scale, and different corporate governance systems can co-exist, while managers would not need to maximize profits to survive.

Such findings shift the argument to the capital market and the market for corporate control. Alchian and Kessel (1962) and Manne (1965) suggest that notwithstanding the degree of competition in product markets, perfect competition in the capital market and the market for corporate control would resolve the agency problem by forcing managers to maximize shareholder wealth. Even if product markets were wholly monopolized, firms that did not maximize monopoly profits would become takeover targets for those wanting to do so. Profit maximization would maximize share prices on the stock market, providing an incentive for a takeover. Thus, selection through the capital market would ensure optimum corporate governance.

But asymmetric information, transactions costs, the free rider problem and capital market imperfections may prevent the capital market takeover mechanism from adequately addressing corporate agency problems. Considerable evidence suggests that selection through the market for corporate control is not necessarily on the bases of efficiency, profitability or stock market valuation. While profitability may matter, size seems to matter more. Large, relatively less profitable companies have much better chances of survival than small profitable ones, while large firms ,almost invariably take over small ones with some notable exceptions, e.g. the US junk bond market of the 1980s and 1990s. Indeed, acquisitions may enable a large unprofitable company to protect itself against takeovers by becoming larger through acquiring smaller firms.

Most emerging markets have yet to develop active markets for corporate control of the Anglo-American type. Even if such markets emerge, they are likely to be far from perfect, e.g. in terms of information. Hence, such markets are unlikely to satisfactorily resolve their corporate governance problems (Singh, 1998). With such difficulties with the market for corporate control, it is increasingly agreed that corporate governance problems are rife because of the many imperfections in product markets and the market for corporate control.[6]

Concluding Remarks

Developing countries need independent analyses to properly assess the proposed corporate governance reforms from their own interests and perspectives, in order to consider and adopt alternatives more appropriate to their conditions and priorities. The claim by powerful US and IMF officials that the principal cause of the East Asian crises was poor corporate governance has no empirical basis. Instead, the fundamental cause of the crisis was inappropriate financial liberalization prior to the crisis.

The Anglo-American model is grounded in common law jurisprudence and corporate law, perhaps suited for the dispersed share ownership of large corporations in these countries. Such corporations face specific governance problems, principally agency problems, due to the separation of control from ownership. But this ownership pattern is rare in developing countries or even in continental Europe, where family control is more prevalent. Corporate governance issues for such firms are thus quite different.

As such, there is no *a priori* reason to believe that family-based corporate governance and associated "relationship banking" are necessarily inferior to the Anglo-American arm's length stock-market model (Singh, Singh and Weisse, 2003).[7] In so far as the Anglo-American system seems less able to resolve agency problems, is more short-termist and also prone to speculative stock market bubbles, it is probably less conducive to technological catch-up and other requirements of sustained long-term economic development.

Since the East Asian financial crises, family-based conglomerates have been identified in the financial media with crony capitalism, and said to have caused moral hazard and economic instability. Alternatively, such relations and arrangements may be seen as an institutional feature conducive to resolving co-ordination and collective action problems. Furthermore, there is no evidence of any causal relationship between crony capitalism and the East Asian crises.

The La Porta, *et al.* approach's basic proposition has been that the legal protection afforded to minority shareholders and creditors determines the availability — ease and "affordability" — of external finance. However, Singh, Singh and Weisse (2003) argue that stock market changes are principally due to economic policy, not legal system changes, while Glen, Lee and Singh contend that large variations in corporate finance patterns cannot simply be attributed to the legal system. Singh, Singh and Weisse (2003) also argue that this approach to the determinants of investment and growth is too narrow, and that the La Porta, *et al.* conclusions are overstated and ignore important realities of corporate finance in developing countries. Nor does it allow for the interaction between legal structure and corporate finance, while the legal determinism they presume is moot. The La Porta, *et al.* privileging of minority shareholders and creditors over other stakeholders is also neither analytically justified nor best for policy.

Contrary to the conventional view ("pecking order" theory, whereby large firms finance their growth from retained profits, rather than by issuing new equity on stock markets), large firms in developing countries have relied overwhelmingly on external sources, facilitated by greater financial liberalization, to finance asset growth in the last two decades (Singh, Singh and Weisse, 2003). Hence, stock markets have helped large firms to raise considerable external finance. But pricing is often dominated by speculation, herd behaviour and fads that undermine efficient resource allocation (Singh, Singh and Weisse, 2003) and involve other risks. Ostensible market-based solutions to corporate governance problems through takeover mechanisms are flawed and involve high costs, especially in developing countries.

Following the East Asian crises, conglomerates in the region were alleged to be poorly run, too large, unfocussed, heavily indebted and a source of moral hazard because they were "too big to fail". An alternative view is that conglomerates represent an efficient response to labour, capital and product markets in developing countries, helping overcome market imperfections and advance industrialization (Singh, Singh and Weisse, 2003). The conglomerates' debt difficulties during the East Asian crises arose from their exposure to short-term foreign credit (encouraged by financial liberalization), rather than just high debt-equity ratios although some imbalances and over-extensions may have occurred. Financial liberalization thus helped increase borrowing, especially during the economic boom.

All things considered, developing countries should not be quick to blindly adopt corporate governance reforms based on the Anglo-American arm's-length model clearly favoured by the OECD, the World Bank and most influential reform advocates. The specific reforms advocated, e.g., best practice codes, reflect this orientation. These are presented as the best available, if not the only option, and such thinking has determined loan conditionalities, policy advice and performance benchmarks set by these institutions and others under their influence.

Also, it may not be feasible and may even be counter-productive to adopt the Anglo-American model. In any case, it is not easily transplanted and adopted into a different business, legal, social and cultural environment. Pistor (2000) suggests that the formal adoption of international standards and legal frameworks may well have different, even perverse outcomes and consequences.

Lastly, to improve our diagnosis of corporate governance problems and policy responses, it would be beneficial to consider potential interrelations among finance, economics, management and law for a more holistic and comprehensive (but also more complex) analysis, and to not assume *a priori* that "orthodox" principles or "mainstream" corporate governance guidelines are the best available, and can be universally applied to and adopted by developing countries (even if they have proved successful in developed countries, which can no longer be assumed after recent US corporate governance scandals). Improving corporate governance should therefore be viewed as an evolutionary process that must necessarily change with changing economic, business, and political environments.

Notes

1. "(In the last decade or so, the world has observed) a consensus towards, for want of a better term, the western form of free-market capitalism as the model which should govern how each individual country should run its economy.... We saw the breakdown of the Berlin wall in 1989 and the massive shift away from central

planning towards free market capitalist types of structures. Concurrent to that was the really quite dramatic, very strong growth in what appeared to be a competing capitalist-type system in Asia. And as a consequence of that, you had developments of types of structures, which I believe at the end of the day were faulty, but you could not demonstrate that so long as growth was going at 10 per cent a year" (Greenspan, 1998).

2. "In Korea, for example, opacity has become systemic. The lack of transparency about government, corporate and financial sector operations concealed the extent of Korea's problems — so much so that corrective action came too late and ultimately could not prevent the collapse of market confidence, with the IMF finally being authorized to intervene just days before potential bankruptcy" (Camdessus, 1998).

3. However, there is a need to distinguish between different types of foreign direct investment (FDI) — i.e. "green-field" investment, reinvestment of FDI profits, and mergers and acquisitions — and (short-term) portfolio investments, since investments impact the country in different ways. Since "green-field" investment involves new capacity, presumably financed with foreign exchange brought into the host country by foreign corporations, it is usually the preferred type of FDI.

4. See Claessens, *et al.* (1998) for a survey and assessment of corporate governance in Malaysia.

5. Ownership arrangements involving concentration, institutional shareholding, and interlocking relations between banks and non-financial corporations could enable owners to effectively monitor management, and ensure a significant degree of control. But too much concentration poses problems as well. Hence, incentive mechanisms as well as corporate laws and regulations (primarily embodied in other laws such as company laws, competition laws and securities laws) are needed to address potential "distortions" of any corporate governance system while realizing the benefits of that system.

6. The separation of ownership from control imposes agency costs on shareholders which are assumed to vary inversely with the intensity of competition in product markets and the efficiency of selection in capital markets.

7. The apparent weaknesses of a bank-based financial system do not imply that a market-based financial system is necessarily superior. Market-based financial systems are also flawed and imperfect. Levine (2000: 28) notes that "distinguishing between bank-based and market-based financial systems is not particularly useful for understanding long-run growth, output volatility, or financial fragility". Rather, his study strongly suggests that countries with greater degrees of (overall) financial development (both banks and markets) enjoy substantially greater economic growth rates. Also, financial development — the legal rights of outside investors and the efficiency of the legal system in enforcing those rights — is strongly and positively linked with long-run growth (Levine, 2000: 33). Clearly, East Asian countries need not replace their relatively more bank-based systems with a capital market-based financial system. Instead, better design and implementation of disciplining mechanisms and (dis)incentive systems to develop a more "balanced" and development-oriented financial system are needed.

Glossary

1MP	First Malaysia Plan, 1966–70
2MP	Second Malaysia Plan, 1971–75
3MP	Third Malaysia Plan, 1976–80
4MP	Fourth Malaysia Plan, 1981–85
5MP	Fifth Malaysia Plan, 1986–90
6MP	Sixth Malaysia Plan, 1991–95
7MP	Seventh Malaysia Plan, 1996–2000
8MP	Eighth Malaysia Plan, 2001–05
ADB	Asian Development Bank
AFTA	ASEAN Free Trade Area
APEC	Asian Pacific Economic Co-operation
BAFIA	Banking and Financial Institutions Act 1989
BMF	Bumiputra Malaysia Finance
BN	Barisan Nasional
BOT	build-operate-transfer
CCM	Companies Commission of Malaysia
CDP	Central Depository (Singapore)
CDS	Central Depository System (Singapore)
CEB	Central Electricity Board
CEO	chief executive officer
CIC	Capital Issues Committee
CLOB	Central Limit Order Book
CMAC	Capital Market Advisory Council
CMP	Capital Market Masterplan
COI	centre on investment
COMEX	Commodity and Monetary Exchange of Malaysia
CTA	Commodities Trading Act 1985
CTC	Commodities Trading Commission
DDP	Draft Development Plan
DOE	Division (then Department) of Environment
EIA	environmental impact assessment

EPF	Employees Provident Fund
EQA	Environmental Quality Act
EQC	Environmental Quality Council
FAMA	Federal Agricultural Marketing Authority
FDI	foreign direct investment
FELDA	Federal Land Development Authority
FFMC	foreign fund management company
FFYP	First Five Year Plan
FIC	Foreign Investment Committee
FIDA	Federal Industrial Development Authority
FLR	front line regulator
FMS	Federated Malay States
GATT	General Agreement on Tariffs and Trade
GSP	General System of Preferences
ICA	Industrial Co-ordination Act 1975
ICOR	incremental capital output ratio
ICP	Inter-Departmental Committee on Privatization
IMF	International Monetary Fund
IMP1	(First) Industrial Master Plan, 1986–95
IMP2	Second Industrial Master Plan, 1996–2005
IOFC	international offshore financial centre
IWK	Indah Water Konsortium
KLCI	KLSE composite index
KLIA	Kuala Lumpur International Airport
KLOFFE	Kuala Lumpur Options and Financial Futures Exchange
KLSE	Kuala Lumpur Stock Exchange
LLN	Lembaga Letrik Negara
LOFSA	Labuan Offshore Financial Services Authority
MACPA	Malaysian Association of Certified Public Accountants
MAMPU	Manpower and Administration Modernization and Planning Unit
MARDI	Malaysian Agricultural Research and Development Institute
MASB	Malaysian Accounting Standards Board
Masscorp	Malaysian South-South Corporation Berhad
MCD	Malaysian Central Depository
MDCH	Malaysian Derivatives Clearing House
MESDAQ	Malaysian Exchange of Securities Dealing and Automated Quotation
MGO	mandatory general offer
MIA	Malaysian Institute of Accountants

MIDA	Malaysian Industrial Development Authority
MITI	Ministry of International Trade and Industry
MLO	Malaysian Labour Organization
MME	Malaysian Monetary Exchange
MOF	Ministry of Finance
MSC	Multimedia Super Corridor
MTUC	Malaysian Trades Union Congress
NAP	National Agricultural Policy
NDP	National Development Policy
NDP	National Development Policy, 1991–2000
NEB	National Electricity Board
NEP	New Economic Policy
NFPE	non-financial public enterprise
NIC	newly industrializing country
NIEO	New International Economic Order
NOC	National Operations Council
NVP	National Vision Policy, 2001–10
OBA	off-budget agency
OECD	Organization for Economic Cooperation and Development
OPP1	(First) Outline Perspective Plan, 1971–90
OPP2	Second Outline Perspective Plan, 1991–2000
OPP3	Third Outline Perspective Plan, 2001–10
PAP	Privatization Action Plan
PERNAS	Perbadanan Nasional Berhad
PIA	Promotion of Investments Act, 1986
PMP	Privatization Master Plan
PORLA	Palm Oil Registration and Licensing Authority
RISDA	Rubber Industry Smallholders Development Authority
RM	Ringgit Malaysia (Malaysian currency)
ROB	Registrar of Businesses
ROC	Registrar of Companies
RRI	Rubber Research Institute
RSS	regulated short selling
SAC	Shari'a Advisory Council
SBL	stock borrowing and lending
SC	Securities Commission
SCANS	Securities Clearing Automated Network Services
SCORE	System on Computerized Order and Routing Execution
SEDC	state economic development corporation
SEMS	Stock Exchange of Malaysia and Singapore

SES	Stock Exchange of Singapore
SIA	Securities Industry Act 1983
SME	small and medium (size) enterprise
SMI	small and medium industry
SOE	state owned enterprise
TNB	Tenaga Nasional Berhad
TNC	transnational corporations
TOP	Panel on Take-overs and Mergers
UDA	Urban Development Authority
UMS	Unfederated Malay States
WTO	World Trade Organization

Bibliography

Adam, C.S. and W. Cavendish (1995). "Early Privatizations". In Jomo K.S. (ed.). *Privatizing Malaysia*. Westview, Boulder, pp. 98–137.

Ahmad Ibrahim (1971). "The Civil Law Ordinance in Malaysia". *Malayan Law Journal*, December: lviii.

Alavi, Rokiah (1987). "The Three Phases of Industrialisation in Malaysia: 1957–1980s". MA thesis, School of Development Studies, University of East Anglia, Norwich.

———— (1996). *Industrialisation in Malaysia: Import Substitution and Infant Industry Performance*. Routledge, London.

Alchian, A.A. (1950). "Uncertainty, Evolution and Economic Theory". *Journal of Political Economy* 58(3): 211–22.

Alchian, A.A. and R.A. Kessel (1962). "Competition, Monopoly and the Pursuit of Pecuniary Gain". *Aspects of Labour Economics*. National Bureau of Economic Research, Princeton.

Amsden, Alice (1989). *Asia's Next Giant: South Korea and Late Industrialization*. Oxford University Press, New York.

———— (2000). *The Rise of "the Rest": Challenges to the West from Late-Industrializing Economies*. Oxford University Press, Oxford.

Amsden, Alice and T. Hikino (1994). "Project Executive Capability, Organisational Know-How and Conglomerate Corporate Growth in Late-Industrialisation". *Industry and Corporate Change* 3(1): 111–47.

Amsden, Alice and Ajit Singh (1994). "The Optimal Degree of Competition and Dynamic Efficiency in Japan and Korea". *European Economic Review*, April: 941–51.

Anderson, Charles (1974). *The Political Economy of Social Class*. Prentice-Hall, Englewood Cliffs.

Anderson, Perry (1974). *Lineages of the Absolutist State*. New Left Books, London.

Anyam v. Intan (1948). 1, *Legal Network Services*: 111.

Anuwar, Ali (1992). *Malaysia's Industrialization: The Quest for Technology*. Oxford University Press, Singapore.

Ariff, Mohammed (1991). *The Malaysian Economy: Pacific Connections*. Oxford University Press, Kuala Lumpur.

Ariff, Mohamed and Murthi Semudram (1987). "Trade and Financing Strategies: A Case Studies of Malaysia". Working Paper No. 21, Overseas Development Institute, London.

Arrow, Kenneth (1962). "The Economic Implications of Learning by Doing". *Review of Economic Studies* 29: 155–73.

Arthur, Neal, Gerald Garvey, Peter Swan, and Stephen Taylor (1993). "Agency theory and 'Management Research': A Comment". *Australian Journal of Management* 18(1), June: 93–102.

Aziz, Ungku Abdul (1958). "Land Disintegration and Land Policy in Malaya". *Malayan Economic Review* 3(1): 22–9.

Baker, G. (1998). "US Looks to G7 Backing on Asia Crisis". *Financial Times*, 19 February.

Bank Negara Malaysia (various issues). *Annual Report*. BNM, Kuala Lumpur.

_____ (1988). *Annual Report, 1987*. Bank Negara Malaysia, Kuala Lumpur.

_____ (1995). *Annual Report, 1994*. Bank Negara Malaysia, Kuala Lumpur.

_____ (various editions). *Money and Banking in Malaysia*. BNM, Kuala Lumpur.

_____ (various issues). *Quarterly Economic Bulletin*.

Barnard, Rosemary (1970). "Organization of Production in a Kedah Rice Farming Village". Ph.D. thesis, Australian National University, Canberra.

Berglof, Eric and Ernst-Ludwig von Thadden (1999). "The Changing Corporate Governance Paradigm: Implications for Transition and Developing Countries". SITE working paper, Stockholm Institute of Transition Economics, Stockholm School of Economics, Stockholm.

Berle, A. and G. Means (1933). *The Modern Corporation and Private Capital*. Macmillan, New York.

Blair, Margaret M. (1995). *Ownership and Control: Rethinking Corporate Governance for the Twenty-First Century*. The Brookings Institution, Washington, DC.

Bowie, Alasdair (1988). "Industrial Aspirations in a Divided Society: Malaysian Heavy Industries, 1980–1988". Paper for Association for Asian Studies annual meeting, San Francisco, 25–27 March.

_____ (1991). *Crossing the Industrial Divide: State, Society, and the Politics of Economic Transformation in Malaysia*. Columbia University Press, New York.

BT Online (1998a). "SES Denies there is any Understanding to Close CLOB". 7 August.

_____ (1998b). "KLSE Freezes all Malaysian Shares Bought on CLOB" by Ven Sreenivasan. 15 September.

Camdessus, Michel (1998). "Speech to Transparency International". 9 February. Reported in *IMF Survey*.

CARPA (1988). *Tangled Web: Dissent, Deterrence and the 27th October 1987 Crackdown in Malaysia*. Committee Against Repression in the Pacific and Asia (CARPA), Sydney.

Caves, R. (1998). "Industrial Organization and New Findings on the Turnover and Mobility of Firms". *Journal of Economic Literature*, December: 1947–82.

Chang, Ha-Joon and Hong-Jae Park (1999). "An Alternative Perspective on Post-1997 Corporate Reform". Processed, December, Faculty of Economics, University of Cambridge, Cambridge, UK. <http://econ.cam.ac.uk/facult... chaebolpdf.pdf>

Chang Yii Tan (1985). "Tilting East". In Jomo K.S. (ed.). *The Sun Also Sets: Lessons in 'Looking East'*. 2nd ed. INSAN, Kuala Lumpur.

Chang, H.-J. (2000). "The Hazard of Moral Hazard — Untangling the Asian Crisis". *World Development*, April: 775–88.

Che Omar bin Che Soh v. Public Prosecutor (1988). 2, *Malayan Law Journal*: 55.

Chee Peng Lim (1994). "Heavy Industrialisation: A Second Round of Import Substitution". In Jomo, K.S. (ed.). *Japan and Malaysian Development: In the Shadow of the Rising Sun*. Routledge, New York.

Chee Peng Lim and Lee Poh Ping (1983). "Japanese Joint-Ventures in Malaysia". In Jomo K.S. (ed.). *The Sun Also Sets: Lessons in 'Looking East'*. INSAN, Kuala Lumpur, pp. 242–49.

Claessens, Stijn, S. Djankov, J. Fan, and L.H.P. Lang (1998). "Ownership Structure and Corporate Ownership in East Asia". World Bank, Economic Policy Unit, Finance, Private Sector and Infrastructure Network, Washington, DC.

Claessens, Stijn, S. Djankov, and L. Lang (2000). "The Separation of Ownership and Control in East Asian Corporations". *Journal of Financial Economics*, October–November: 81–112.

Corbett, J. and T. Jenkinson (1994). "The Financing of Industry, 1970–89: An International Comparison". Discussion Paper No. 948, Centre for Economic Policy Research, London.

Crouch, Harold (1992). "Authoritarian Trends, the UMNO Split and the Limits to State Power". In Joel S. Kahn and Loh Kok Wah (eds). *Fragmented Vision: Culture and Politics in Contemporary Malaysia*. Asian Studies Association of Australia in association with Allen & Unwin, Sydney.

Das, S.K. (1963). "The Torrens Systems in Malaya". *Malayan Law Journal*, Singapore.

de Soto, Hernando (ed.) (2000). *The Mystery of Capital: Why Capitalism Triumphs in the West and Fails Everywhere Else.* Basic Books, New York.

Demirguc-Kunt, A. and E. Detragiache (1998). "Financial Liberalisation and Financial Fragility". *Proceedings of Annual Bank Conference on Development Economics.* The World Bank, Washington, D.C.: 303–31.

Dezalay, Yves and Bryant G. Garth (1996). *Dealing in Virtue: International Commercial Arbitration and the Construction of a Transnational Legal Order.* University of Chicago Press, Chicago.

_____ (2002). *The Internationalization of Palace Wars: Lawyers, Economists, and the Contest to Transform Latin American States.* University of Chicago Press, Chicago.

Domowitz, L., J. Glen, and A. Madhavan (2001). "International Evidence on Aggregate Corporate Financing Decisions". In A. Demirguc Kunt and R. Levine (eds). *Financial Structure and Economic Growth.* MIT Press, Cambridge, MA.

Donaldson, G. (1961). *Corporate Debt Capacity.* Division of Research, Graduate School of Business Administration, Harvard University, Boston.

Donaldson, Lex and J.H. Davis (1991). "Stewardship Theory or Agency Theory: CEO Governance and Shareholder Returns". *Australian Journal of Management* 16(1), June: 49–64.

Dooley, Michael and J. A. Frankel (eds) (2002). *Managing Currency Crisis in Emerging Markets.* University of Chicago Press, Chicago.

Drabble, John N. (2000). *An Economic History of Malaysia, 1800–1990.* St. Martin's Press, New York.

Edwards, Chris (1975). "Protection, Profits and Policy: An Analysis of Industrialisation in Malaysia". Ph.D. thesis, University of East Anglia, Norwich, U.K.

Edwards, Sebastian and J.A. Frankel (eds) (2002). *Preventing Currency Crisis in Emerging Markets.* University of Chicago Press, Chicago.

Economic Planning Unit (EPU) (1985). *Guidelines on Privatization.* Economic Planning Unit, Prime Minister's Department of Malaysia, Kuala Lumpur.

Fan Yew Teng (1989). *The UMNO Drama: Power Struggles in Malaysia.* Egret Publications, Kuala Lumpur.

Far Eastern Economic Review, 18 October 2001.

Feldstein, Martin (ed.) (2002). *Economic and Financial Crises in Emerging Market Countries.* University of Chicago Press, Chicago.

Felker, Greg, with Jomo K.S. (2007a). "Investment Policy in Malaysia". In Jomo K.S. (ed.). *Malaysian Industrial Policy.* NUS Press, Singapore.

_____ (2007b). "Technology Policy in Malaysia". In Jomo K.S. (ed.). *Malaysian Industrial Policy.* NUS Press, Singapore.

Fisk, E.K. (1961). "Productivity and Income from Rubber in an Established Malay Reservation". *Malayan Economic Review* 6(1). April: 13–21.

_____ (1964). *Studies in the Rural Economy of South East Asia.* Eastern Universities Press, Singapore.

Foong, James (2002). *Malaysian Judiciary — A Record.* Sweet & Maxwell, London.

Friedman, Milton (1953). *Essays in Positive Economics.* The University of Chicago Press, Chicago, IL.

Ghazali v. Public Prosecutor (1999). 7, *Current Law Journal*: 110.

Glen, Jack, K. Lee, and Ajit Singh (2001). "Persistence of Profitability and Competition in Emerging Markets". *Economics Letters*, August: 247–53.

_____ (2003). "Corporate Profitability and the Dynamics of Competition in Emerging Markets: A Time Series Analysis". University of Cambridge, ESRC Centre for Business Research, Working Paper No. 248, 2002. Subsequently published in a revised version in *Economic Journal*, November: F465–F484.

_____ (2003). "Capital Structure, Rates of Return and Financing Corporate Growth: Comparing Developed and Emerging Markets, 1994–2000". In R. Litan, M. Pomerleano, and V. Sundararajan (eds). *The Future of Domestic Capital Markets in Developing Countries.* Brookings Institution Press, Washington, DC.

_____ (2005). "Corporate Governance, Competition, and Finance: Rethinking Lessons from the Asian Crisis". *Eastern Economic Journal* 31(2) Spring: 219–43.

Goddard, J.A. and J.O.S. Wilson (1999). "The Persistence of Profit: A New Empirical Interpretation". *International Journal of Industrial Organization*, July: 663–87.

Gomez, E.T. (1990). *Politics in Business: UMNO's Corporate Investments.* Forum, Kuala Lumpur.

_____ (1991a). *Money Politics in the Barisan Nasional.* Forum, Kuala Lumpur.

_____ (1991b). "Malaysia's Phantom Privatization". *Asian Wall Street Journal*, 8 May.

_____ (1994). *Political Business: Corporate Involvement of Malaysian Political Parties.* Centre for East and South East Asian Studies, James Cook University, Townsville.

Gomez, E.T. and Jomo K.S. (1999). Malaysia's Political Economy: Politics, Patronage and Profits. Cambridge University Press, Cambridge.

Government of Malaysia v. Lim Kit Siang (1988). 2, *Malayan Law Journal*: 12.

Greenspan, Alan (1998). "Testimony before the Committee on Banking and

Financial Services, US House of Representatives". 30 January, US Federal Reserve, Washington, DC.

Grossman, S.J. and O.D. Hart (1980). "Take-Over Bids, the Free Rider Problem and the Theory of the Corporation". *Bell Journal of Economics* 11: 42–64.

Guggler, K., D.C. Mueller, and B. Yortoglu (2003). "The Impact of Corporate Governance on Investment Returns in Developed and Developing Countries". *Economic Journal*, November: F486–F510.

Gullick, J.M. (1958). *Indigenous Political Systems of Western Malaya*. Athlone Press, London.

Gustafsson, Fredrik (2007). "Malaysian Industrial Policy, 1986–2002". In Jomo K. S. (ed.). *Malaysian Industrial Policy*. NUS Press, Singapore.

Guyot, Dorothy (1971). "The Politics of Land: Comparative Development in Two States of Malaysia". *Pacific Affairs* 44(3), Fall: 368–89.

Guyton, Lynne (1996). "Japanese Manufacturing Investment and Technology Transfer to Malaysia". In John Borrego, Alejandro Alvarez Bejar, and Jomo K.S. (eds). *Capital, the State and Late Industrialisation: Comparative Perspective on the Pacific Rim*. Westview, Boulder.

Haggard, Stephan (2000). *The Political Economy of the Asian Financial Crisis*. Institute of International Economics, Washington, DC.

Haji Laungan Tarki bin Mohd Noor v. Mahkamah Anak Negeri Penampang (1988). 2, *Malayan Law Journal*: 85.

Halcrow Consultants (1999). "Kuala Lumpur Public Transport Restructuring Final Report". Corporate Debt Restructuring Committee, Kuala Lumpur.

Hilton, Rodney (ed.) (1976). *The Transition from Feudalism to Capitalism*. New Left Books, London.

Hoekman, B.M. and M. Kostecki (2001). *The Political Economy of the World Trading System*. Oxford University Press, Oxford.

Hoffman, Lutz and Tan, S.E. (1980). *Industrial Growth, Employment and Foreign Investment in Peninsular Malaysia*. Oxford University Press, Kuala Lumpur.

Horii Kenzo (1972). "The Land Tenure System of Malay Padi Farmers: A Case Study of Kampong Sungei Bujor in the State of Kedah". *The Developing Economies* 10(1), March: 45–73.

Huang, Yukon (1971). "The Economics of Padi Production in Malaysia". Ph.D. thesis, Princeton University, Princeton, New Jersey.

_____ (1975a). "Some Reflections on Padi Double-Cropping in West Malaysia". In David Lim (ed.). *Readings in Malaysian Economic Development*. Oxford University Press, Kuala Lumpur.

_____ (1975b). "Tenancy Patterns, Productivity and Rentals in Malaysia". *Economic Development and Cultural Change* 23(4), July: 703–18.

Hughes, Alan (1991). "Mergers and Economic Performance in the UK: A Survey of the Empirical Evidence, 1950–1990". In J. Fairburn and J.A. Kay (eds). *Mergers and Merger Policy.* 2nd ed. Clarendon Press, Oxford.

Husin Ali, Syed (1964). *Social Stratification in Kampong Bagan.* Malayan Branch of the Royal Asiatic Society, Singapore.

_____ (1972). "Land Concentration and Poverty among Rural Malays". *Nusantara*: 1.

_____ (1975). *Malay Peasant Society and Leadership.* Oxford University Press, Kuala Lumpur.

Inspector-General of Police, Malaysia v. Tan Sri Raja Khalid bin Raja Harun (1988). 1, *Malayan Law Journal*: 182.

International Bank for Reconstruction and Development (IBRD) (1955). *The Economic Development of Malaya.* Johns Hopkins University Press, Baltimore.

International Monetary Fund (IMF) (1997). "World Economic Outlook: Crisis in Asia, Regional and Global Implication". Interim Assessment, December. International Monetary Fund, Washington, DC.

_____ (1998a). *World Economic Outlook.* International Monetary Fund, Washington, DC.

_____ (1998b). "Mr. M. Camdessus' Address to Transparency International, 'Good Governance has become Essential in Promoting Growth and Stability', 9 February". *IMF Survey* 27(3).

Iskander, M.R., and N. Chamlou (2000). *Corporate Governance: A Framework for Implementation.* The World Bank Group, Washington, DC.

Jayasankaran, S. (1999a). "Merger by Decree". *Far Eastern Economic Review*, 9 September.

_____ (1999b). "Changing Fortunes". *Far Eastern Economic Review*, 23 December.

_____ (2000). "Merger Muddle". *Far Eastern Economic Review*, 10 August.

_____ (2001). "Bank Restructuring: A Political Conundrum". *Far Eastern Economic Review*, 22 February.

Jayasuriya, Kanishka (1999). "Introduction: 'A Framework for the Analysis of Legal Institutions in East Asia'". In K. Jayasuriya (ed.). *Law, Capitalism and Power in Asia: the Rule of Law and Legal Institutions.* Routledge, pp. 1–27.

J.P. Berthelsen v. Director General of Immigration (1987). 1, *Malayan Law Journal*: 134.

Jang Aisjah Muttalib (1972). *Pemberontakan Pahang, 1891–1895.* Dian, Kota Baru.

Jegathesan, J. (1995). "Key Deregulation and Regulatory Issues in Industry and Technology Malaysia". Paper presented at the World Bank Regional Workshop on "Managing Regulatory Policies and Reforms in East Asia: The Changed Role and Rules of the State", Kuala Lumpur, 3–7 July.

Jenkins, Glen (1987). "Sultans as Symbols". *Far Eastern Economic Review*, 30 June: 29.

Jesudason, James V. (1989). *Ethnicity and the Economy: The State, Chinese Business and Multinationals in Malaysia*. Oxford University Press, Singapore.

Joh, S.W. (2003). "Corporate Governance and Firm Profitability: Evidence from Korea before the Economic Crisis". *Journal of Financial Economics*, May: 287–322.

Johnson, S., P. Boone, A. Breach, and E. Friedman (2000). "Corporate Governance in the Asian Financial Crisis". *Journal of Financial Economics*, October–November: 141–86.

Jomo K.S. (1986). *A Question of Class: Capital, the State, and Uneven Development in Malaya*. Oxford University Press, Singapore.

_____ (1989). *Beyond 1990: Considerations for a New National Development Strategy*. Institute of Advanced Studies, University of Malaya, Kuala Lumpur.

_____ (1990). *Growth and Structural Change in the Malaysian Economy*. Macmillan, London.

_____ (1993a). *Industrialising Malaysia: Policy, Performance, Prospects*. Routledge, London.

_____ (1993b). "The Way Forward?: The Political Economy of Development Policy Reform in Malaysia". Inaugural lecture, University of Malaya, Kuala Lumpur, 20 July.

_____ (1994a). *U-Turn? Malaysian Economic Development Policies After 1990*. Centre for East and South East Asian Studies, James Cook University, Townsville, Queensland.

_____ (1994b). "Introduction". In Jomo, K.S. (ed.). *Japan and Malaysian Development: In the Shadow of the Rising Sun*. Routledge, London.

_____ (1994c). "The Proton Saga". In Jomo, K.S. (ed.). *Japan and Malaysian Development: In the Shadow of the Rising Sun*. Routledge, London.

_____ (1996). "Public Enterprise Policy". In Jomo K.S. and Ng Seuw Kiat (eds). *Malaysia's Economic Development: Policy & Reform*. Pelanduk Publications, Petaling Jaya for Malaysian Institute of Economic Research (MIER), Kuala Lumpur.

_____ (2001). "Growth after the Asian Crisis: What Remains of the East Asian Model?" G-24 Discussion Paper Series, No. 10, March, United Nations Conference on Trade and Development, Geneva, and Center for International Development, Harvard University, New York.

_____ (2003). *Southeast Asia's Paper Tigers: From Miracle To Debacle And Beyond.* Routledge, London.

_____ (2004). *M Way: Mahathir's Economic Legacy.* Forum, Kuala Lumpur.

_____ (2007). "Industrialisation and Industrial Policy in Malaysia". In Jomo K.S. (ed.). *Malaysian Industrial Policy.* NUS Press, Singapore.

_____ (ed.) (1985). *The Sun Also Sets: Lessons in 'Looking East'.* INSAN, Kuala Lumpur, 2nd ed. (1st ed., 1983).

_____ (ed.) (1994). *Japan and Malaysian Development: In the Shadow of the Rising Sun.* Routledge, London.

_____ (ed.) (1995). *Privatizing Malaysia: Rents, Rhetoric, Realities.* Westview, Boulder.

_____ (ed.) (1998). *Tigers in Trouble: Financial Governance, Liberalisation and Crises in East Asia.* Zed Books, London.

_____ (ed.) (2001). *Malaysian Eclipse: Economic Crisis and Recovery.* Zed Books, London.

_____ (ed.) (2002). *Ugly Malaysians? South-South Investments Abused.* Institute for Black Studies, Durban.

Jomo K.S. and Ishak Shari (1986). *Development Policies and Income Inequality in Peninsular Malaysia.* Institute for Advanced Studies, University of Malaya, Kuala Lumpur.

Jomo K.S., Khong How Ling, and Shamsulbahriah Ku Ahmad (eds) (1987). *Crisis and Response in the Malaysian Economy.* Malaysian Economic Association, Kuala Lumpur.

Jomo K.S. and C.B. Edwards (1993). "Policy Options for Malaysian Industrialisation". In Jomo K.S. (ed.). *Industrialising Malaysia: Policy, Performance, Prospects. Routledge,* London: 316–34.

Jomo K.S. and Patricia Todd (1994). *Trade Unions and the State in Peninsular Malaysia.* Oxford University Press, Kuala Lumpur.

Jomo K.S. and Peter Wad (1994). "In-House Unions: 'Looking East' for Industrial Relations". In Jomo, K.S. (ed.). *Japan and Malaysian Development: In the Shadow of the Rising Sun.* Routledge, London.

Jomo K.S. with Yun-Chung Chen, Brian C. Folk, Irfan ul-Haque, Pasuk Phongpaichit, Batara Simatupang, and Mayuri Tateishi (1997). *Southeast Asia's Misunderstood Miracle.* Westview, Boulder.

Jomo K.S. with Greg Felker (eds) (1999). *Technology, Competitiveness and the State: Malaysia's Industrial Technology Policies.* Routledge, London.

Jomo K.S., Chang Y.T., Khoo K.J., *et al.* (2004). *Deforesting Malaysia: The Political Economy and Social Ecology of Agricultural Expansion and Commercial Logging.* Zed Books, London.

Journal of Economic Perspectives (JEP) (1990). Special Issue, Spring.

Kahn, Joel S. and Loh Kok Wah (eds) (1992). *Fragmented Vision: Culture and Politics in Contemporary Malaysia*. Allen & Unwin, Sydney, for Asian Studies Association of Australia.

Kamal Salih and Zainal Aznam Yusof (1989). "Overview of the New Economic Policy and Framework for the Post-1990 Economic Policy". Processed, Malaysian Institute of Economic Research, Kuala Lumpur.

———— (1989). "Overview of the NEP and Framework for 1990 National Economic Policy: Options". *Malaysian Management Review* 24(2): 13–61.

Kaminsky, G.L. and C.L. Reinhart (1999). "The Twin Crises: The Causes of Banking and Balance-of Payments Problems". *American Economic Review*, June: 473–500.

Keasey, K., S. Thompson, and M. Wright (eds) (1999). *Corporate Governance*. Edward Elgar, Cheltenham.

Kessler, Clive (1978). *Islam and Politics in Malay State: Kelantan, 1838–1969*. Cornell University Press, Ithaca, NY.

Khalid Ibrahim (1987). "Monitoring Government Companies: Central Information Collection Unit (CICU) Findings". *Ilmu Masyarakat* 13 (October–December): 49–58.

Khan, Mushtaq H. (2006). "Capitalist Transformation". In Jomo K.S. and Erik Reinert (eds). *The Origins of Development Economics*. Tulika, New Delhi.

Khanna, T. and K. Palepu (2000). "Is Group Affiliation Profitable in Emerging Markets? An Analysis of Diversified Indian Business Groups". *Journal of Finance*, April: 867–91.

Khanna, T. and Y. Yafeh (2001). "Business Groups and Risk Sharing around the World". Social Science Research Network (SSRN) Working Paper Series. Available at <http://papers.ssrn.com>, 25 January.

Khoo Boo Teik (1995). *Paradoxes of Mahathirism*. Oxford University Press, Kuala Lumpur.

Khoo Khay Jin (1992). "The Grand Vision: Mahathir and Modernisation". In Joel S. Kahn and Loh Kok Wah (eds). *Fragmented Vision: Culture and Politics in Contemporary Malaysia*. Allen & Unwin, Sydney, for Asian Studies Association of Australia.

Khor Kok Peng (1983). *The Malaysian Economy: Structure and Dependence*. Maricans, Kuala Lumpur.

———— (1987). *Malaysia's Economy in Decline*. Consumers' Association of Penang, Penang.

Kratoska, Paul H. (1975). "Peasants, Yeomen and Rice Farmers. Cultural Categories in British Malaya". Ph.D. thesis, University of Chicago.

Krugman, Paul (1999). *The Return of Depression Economics*. Penguin, Harmondsworth.

Kuala Lumpur Stock Exchange (KLSE) (1998). "Announcement, 14 September, 1998". Kuala Lumpur Stock Exchange, Kuala Lumpur.

Kuchiba, M. and Y. Tsubouchi (1967). "Paddy Farming and Social Structure in a Malay Village". *The Developing Economies* 5(3): 463–85.

La Porta, Rafael, Florencio Lopez-de-Silanes, and Andrei Shleifer (1999). "Corporate Ownership around the World". *Journal of Finance*, April: 471–517.

Laffont, J. (1999). "Competition, Information, and Development". Annual World Bank Conference on Development Economics, The World Bank, Washington, D.C.: 237–57.

Lall, Sanjaya (1992). "Technological Capabilities and Industrialisation". *World Development* 20(2), February.

———— (1994). "Malaysia's Export Performance and Its Sustainability". January, unpublished study.

———— (1995a). "Malaysia: Industrial Success and the Role of the Government". *Journal of International Development* 7(5), September–October: 759–73.

———— (1995b). "Introduction". In World Bank. "Made in Malaysia". World Bank/UNDP, Kuala Lumpur, mimeo.

Lawyers Committee for Human Rights (1989). *Malaysia: Assault on the Judiciary*. Lawyers Committee for Human Rights, New York.

Lee, Eddy (1976). "Rural Poverty in West Malaysia, 1957–70". World Employment Programme Working Paper, International Labour Office, Geneva.

Lee Poh Ping (1985). "Malaysia Incorporated". In Jomo (ed.). *The Sun Also Sets: Lessons in 'Looking East'*. 2nd ed. INSAN, Kuala Lumpur.

Leff, N. (1978). "Industrial Organization and Entrepreneurship in Developing Countries: The Economic Groups". *Economic Development and Cultural Change* 4: 661–75.

———— (1979). "Entrepreneurship and Economic Development: The Problem Revisited". *Journal of Economic Literature* 17: 46–64.

Lemmon, M. and K. Lins (2003). "Ownership Structure, Corporate Governance, and Firm Value: Evidence from the East Asian Financial Crisis". *Journal of Finance*, August: 1445–68.

Levine, Ross (2000). "Bank-based or Market-based Financial System: Which is Better?". Working paper no. 00-05, Carlson School of Management, University of Minnesota, Minneapolis.

Lim Chan Seng v. Pengarah Jabatan Ugama Islam Pulau Pinang (1996). 3, *Current Law Journal*: 231.

Lim Chong-Yah (1967). *Economic Development of Modern Malaya*. Oxford University Press, Kuala Lumpur.

Lim Pao Li and Anna Ong Cheng Imm (2007). "Performance Requirements in Malaysia". In Jomo K.S. (ed.). *Malaysian Industrial Policy*. NUS Press, Singapore.

Lim Teck Ghee (1976). *Origins of a Colonial Economy: Land and Agriculture in Perak 1874–1897*. Penerbit Universiti Sains Malaysia, Penang.

_____ (1977). *Peasants and Their Agricultural Economy in Colonial Malaya, 1874–1941*. Oxford University Press, Kuala Lumpur.

Lim Teck Ghee, George Elliston, and David Gibbons (1974). *Land Tenure Survey, Farm Locality DII Muda Irrigation Scheme*. Centre for Policy Research, Universiti Sains Malaysia, Penang.

Lim, Linda (1998). "Liberalization has served Southeast Asia well". In Isabelle Grunberg (ed.). *Perspectives on International Financial Liberalization — Responses to Discussion Paper 12: International Financial Liberalization by John Eatwell*. Discussion Paper No. 15, Office of Development Studies, UNDP, New York, pp. 45–54.

Lo Sum Yee (1972). *The Development Performance of West Malaysia*. Heinemann Educational Books, Kuala Lumpur.

Loh Siew Cheang (1996). "Corporate Powers: Controls, Remedies and Decision-Making". *Malayan Law Journal*, Kuala Lumpur.

Maddison, Angus (1991). *Dynamic Forces in Capital Development: A Long-Run Perspective*. Oxford University Press, Oxford.

Mahathir Mohamad (1983). "New Government Policies". In Jomo K.S. (ed.). *The Sun also Sets: Lessons in 'Looking East'*. INSAN, Kuala Lumpur, pp. 276–78.

_____ (1998a). *The Way Forward*. Weidenfeld & Nicolson, London.

_____ (1998b). *The Challenges of Turmoil*. Pelanduk, Petaling Jaya.

_____ (1991). "Malaysia: The Way Forward". Speech delivered at the inauguration of the Malaysian Business Council. Institute of Strategic and International Studies (ISIS), Kuala Lumpur.

Maher, Maria E. and Thomas Andersson (2000). "Corporate Governance: Effects on Firm Performance and Economic Growth". February. Available at SSRN: <http://ssrn.com/abstract=218490> or DOI: <10.2139/ssrn.218490>.

Malaysia (various years). *Official Year Book*. Government Printer, Kuala Lumpur.

Malaysia (1971). *The Second Malaysia Plan, 1971–1975*. Economic Planning Unit, Prime Minister's Department, Kuala Lumpur.

_____ (1972). *Organization of the Government of Malaysia*. Economic Planning Unit, Kuala Lumpur.

_____ (1973). *The Mid-Term Review of the Second Malaysia Plan, 1971–1975*. Economic Planning Unit, Prime Minister's Department, Kuala Lumpur.

_____ (1976). *The Third Malaysia Plan, 1976–1980*. Economic Planning Unit, Prime Minister's Department, Kuala Lumpur.

_____ (1979). *The Mid-Term Review of the Third Malaysia Plan, 1976–1980*. Economic Planning Unit, Prime Minister's Department, Kuala Lumpur.

_____ (1981). *Fourth Malaysia Plan, 1981–1985*. Economic Planning Unit, Prime Minister's Department, Kuala Lumpur.

_____ (1984). *The Mid-Term Review of the Fourth Malaysia Plan, 1981–1985*. Economic Planning Unit, Prime Minister's Department, Kuala Lumpur.

_____ (1986). *The Fifth Malaysia Plan, 1986–1990*. Economic Planning Unit, Prime Minister's Department, Kuala Lumpur.

_____ (1989). *The Mid-Term Review of the Fifth Malaysia Plan, 1986–1990*. Economic Planning Unit, Prime Minister's Department, Kuala Lumpur.

_____ (1991a). *The Second Outline Perspective Plan, 1991–2000*. Economic Planning Unit, Kuala Lumpur.

_____ (1991b). *The Sixth Malaysia Plan, 1991–1995*. Economic Planning Unit, Kuala Lumpur.

_____ (1993). *The Mid-Term Review of the Sixth Malaysia Plan, 1991–1995*. Economic Planning Unit, Prime Minister's Department, Kuala Lumpur.

_____ (1995). *The Seventh Malaysia Plan, 1996–2000*. Economic Planning Unit, Prime Minister's Department, Kuala Lumpur.

_____ (1996). *Second Industrial Master Plan, 1996–2005*. Ministry of International Trade and Industry, Kuala Lumpur.

_____ (1999). *The Mid-Term Review of the Seventh Malaysia Plan, 1996–2000*. Economic Planning Unit, Prime Minister's Department, Kuala Lumpur.

_____ (2001a). *The Eighth Malaysia Plan, 2001–2005*. Economic Planning Unit, Prime Minister's Department, Kuala Lumpur.

_____ (2001b). *The Third Outline Perspective Plan, 2001–2010*. Economic Planning Unit, Prime Minister's Department, Kuala Lumpur.

_____ (2004). *National Accounts Statistics*. Department of Statistics, Kuala Lumpur.

_____ (2006). *The Ninth Malaysia Plan, 2006–2010*. Economic Planning Unit, Prime Minister's Department, Kuala Lumpur.

Malaysian Bar & Anor. v. Government of Malaysia (1986). 2, *Malayan Law Journal*: 225.

Malaysia, Ministry of Finance, High Level Finance Committee (1999). "Report on Corporate Governance". February, Ministry of Finance, Kuala Lumpur.

Malaysian Industrial Development Authority (MIDA) (1987). *MIDA Report, 1987*. Malaysian Industrial Development Authority, Kuala Lumpur.

Mamat bin Daud v. Government of Malaysia (1988). 2, *Malayan Law Journal*: 119.

Manne, H.G. (1965). "Mergers and the Market for Corporate Control". *Journal of Political Economy* 73: 693–706.

Mark Koding v. Public Prosecutor (1982). 2, *Malayan Law Journal*: 120.

Maxwell, William E. (1884). "Law and Customs of the Malays with Reference to the Tenure of Land". *Journal of the Straits Branch*, Royal Asiatic Society 13: 75–220.

Mayer, C. (1988). "New Issues in Corporate Finance". *European Economic Review*, June: 1167–88.

Merdeka University Berhad v. Government of Malaysia (1982). 2, *Malayan Law Journal*: 356; 2, *Malayan Law Journal*: 243.

MIDA (1991). *Malaysia: Investment in the Manufacturing Sector*. Malaysian Industrial Development Authority, Kuala Lumpur.

_____ (2002). "Investment in the Manufacturing Sector: Policies, Incentives and Procedures". Malaysian Industrial Development Authority, Kuala Lumpur.

MIDA-UNIDO (1986). *The Industrial Master Plan, 1986–1995*. Malaysian Industrial Development Authority, Kuala Lumpur.

Ministry of Finance, Malaysia (various issues). *Economic Report*. Government Printers, Kuala Lumpur.

Minister of Home Affairs v. Karpal Singh (1988). 3, *Malayan Law Journal*: 29.

Mohd Noor bin Othman v. Mohd Yusof Jaafar (1988). 3, *Malayan Law Journal*: 82.

Mohd Noor Mohd (1974). "Masalah pemilikan tanah di Mukim Gunung". *Jernal Antropoloji dan Sosioloji* 3: 41–47.

Montes, Manuel (1998). *The Currency Crisis in South East Asia*. Institute of Southeast Asian Studies, Singapore.

MoSTE (1990). *Industrial Technology Development: A National Plan for Action*. Ministry of Science, Technology and Environment, Kuala Lumpur.

Mueller, D. (1997). "Merger policy in the United States: A Reconsideration". *Review of Industrial Organization*, December: 655–85.

Myers, S. and N. Majluf (1984). "Corporate Financing and Investment Decisions when Firms have Information that Investors do not have". *Journal of Financial Economics* 13(2): 187–221.

New Straits Times, 22 June 1974.

New Straits Times, 27 November 1995.

New Straits Times, 18 October 1996.

New Straits Times, 9 August 2001.

Newbold, T. J. (1971). *Political and Statistical Account of the British Settlements in the Straits of Malacca, with a History of the Malayan States* (2 vols.). Oxford University Press, Kuala Lumpur; 1st published in 1839.

Nor Kursiah bte Baharuddin v. Shahril bin Lamin & Anor (1997). 1, *Malayan Law Journal*: 537.

North, Douglass (1990). *Institutional Change and Economic Performance.* Cambridge University Press, New York.

North-West Transportation Co v. Beatty (1877). 12, *Appeal Cases*: 593

Odagiri, H. (1992). *Growth through Competition, Competition through Growth: Strategic Management and the Economy in Japan.* Clarendon Press, Oxford.

Ong Ah Chuan v. Public Prosecutor (1981). 1, *Malayan Law Journal*: 64.

Ooi Jin Bee (1959). "Rural Development in Tropical Areas with Special Reference to Malaya". *Malayan Journal of Tropical Geography*: 12.

Pack, Howard and Larry Westphal (1986). "Industrial Strategy and Technological Change: Theory vs. Reality". *Journal of Development Economics* 22: 87–128.

Peacock, A. and G. Bannock (1991). *Corporate Take-Overs and the Public Interest.* Aberdeen University Press for the David Hume Institute, Aberdeen.

Pemungut Hasil Tanah, Daerah Barat Daya v. Ong Gaik Kee (1983). 1, *Legal Network Services*: 14.

Pender v. Lushington (1877). 6, *Chancery Division*: 75–6.

Pengarah Tanah dan Galian Wilayah Persekutuan Kuala Lumpur v Sri Lempah Enterprises (1979). 1, *Malayan Law Journal*: 135.

Persatuan Aliran Kesedaran Negara v. Minister of Home Affairs (1988). 1, *Malayan Law Journal*: 440.

Phelps, E.S. (1999). "The Global Crisis of Corporatism". *Wall Street Journal*, 25 March.

Pillay, M.S. (1994). "Privatization of sewerage services in Malaysia". Paper presented at the 20th Water, Engineering and Development Centre Conference, Colombo. Available from: <http://www.lboro.ac.uk/departments/cv/wedc/papers/20/plenary/pillay.pdf>.

Pistor, Katrina (2000). "The Standardization of Law and its Effect on Developing Economies". G-24 Discussion Paper No. 4, June, UNCTAD, Geneva, UNCTAD/GDS/MDPB/G24/4.

Pistor, Katrina, P.A. Wellons and others. *The Role of Law and Legal Institutions in Asian Economic Development, 1960–1995.* Asian Development Bank, Manila.

Porter, Michael (1990). *The Competitive Advantage of Nations.* Macmillan Press, London.

Prasad, Eshwar, Kenneth Rogoff, S. Wei, and M.A. Kose (2003). "Effects of financial globalisation on developing countries: Some empirical evidence". IMF, March.

Public Prosecutor v. Cumaraswamy, Param (1986). 1, *Malayan Law Journal*: 518.

Public Prosecutor v. Dato' Yap Peng (1987). 1, *Current Law Journal*: 550.

Pura, Raphael (1985). "Doubts over Heavy Industrialisation Strategy". In Jomo K.S. (ed.). *The Sun Also Sets*. INSAN, Petaling Jaya (reprinted from *Asian Wall Street Journal*, 10–11 June 1983).

_____ (1985). "Heavy Industrialization". In Jomo K.S. (ed.). *The Sun Also Sets: Lessons in 'Looking East'*. 2nd ed. INSAN, Kuala Lumpur.

Rajaraman, Indira (2003). "Management of the Capital Account: A Study of India and Malaysia". In UNCTAD (ed.). *Management of Capital Flows: Comparative Experiences and Implications for Africa*. United Nations, Geneva, pp. 109–83.

Ramstetter, Eric D. (1991). *Direct Foreign Investment in Asia's Developing Economies and Structural Change in the Asia-Pacific Region*. Westview, Boulder.

_____ (ed.) (1991). *Direct Foreign Investment and Structural Change in the Asian-Pacific Region*. Westview, Boulder.

Ranawana, Arjuna (2001a). "Al at last — Malaysia focuses on debt restructuring". *Asiaweek*, 10 August.

_____ (2001b). "Failure is not an option". *Asiaweek*, 7 September.

Rao, V.V. Bhanoji (1976). *Malaysia Development Pattern and Policy, 1947–1971*. Heinemann Educational Books, Singapore.

_____ (1976). *National Accounts of West Malaysia, 1947–1971*. Heinemann Educational Books (Asia), Singapore.

_____ (1980). *Malaysia: Development Pattern and Policy, 1947–1971*. University of Singapore Press, Singapore.

Rasiah, Rajah (1990). "The Electronics Industry in Malaysia". Post-graduate seminar paper, Faculty of Economics, University of Cambridge, Cambridge.

_____ (1993). "Free Trade Zones and Industrial Development in Malaysia". In Jomo, K.S. (ed.). *Industrialising Malaysia: Policy, Performance, Prospects*. Routledge, London.

_____ (1995). *Foreign Capital and Industrialisation in Malaysia*. Macmillan, London.

_____ (1996). "State Intervention, Distortionary Rents and Industrialisation in Malaysia". In John Borrego, Alejandro Alvarez Bejar, and Jomo K.S. (eds). *Capital, the State and Late Industrialisation: Comparative Perspectives on the Pacific Rim*. Westview, Boulder.

Rasiah, Rajah and Ishak Shari (1993). "The State and Economic Development Malaysia's New Economic Policy in Retrospect". Paper for the ASEAN Inter-University Seminar on Social Development, Kota Kinabalu, 12–15 November.

Ravenscraft, D.J. and F.M. Scherer (1987). *Mergers, Sell-Offs and Economic Efficiency*. Brookings Institution, Washington, D.C.

Rodan, Garry (2004). *Transparency and Authoritarian Rule in Southeast Asia: Singapore and Malaysia*. RoutledgeCurzon, London.

Rodrik, Dani (1999). "Institutions for High-Quality Growth: What They Are and How to Acquire Them". Paper delivered at the IMF Conference on "Second Generation Reforms", 14 October 1999, International Monetary Fund, Washington, DC.

Rugayah Mohamed (1995). "Public Sector". In Jomo K.S. (ed.). *Privatizing Malaysia*. Westview, Boulder.

S. Kulasingam & Others v. Commissioner of Lands, Federal Territory & Others (1982). 1, *Malayan Law Journal*: 204.

Sachs, J. and S. Radelet (1998). "The Onset of East Asian Financial Crisis". National Bureau of Economic Research Working Paper No. 6680, August.

Sadka, Emily (1968). *The Protected Malay States 1874–1895*. University of Singapore Press, Singapore.

Sakakibara, Eisuke (2001). "The East Asian Crisis — Two Years Later". *Annual World Bank Conference on Development Economics, 2000*. World Bank, Washington, DC, pp. 243–55.

Saiful Azhar Rosly (2005). *Critical Issues on Islamic Banking and Financial Markets*. Dinamas Publishing, Kuala Lumpur, Malaysia, p. 598.

Scott, James C. (1985). *Weapons of the Weak*. Yale University Press, New Haven, CT.

Securities Commission (1995). *Annual Report, 1994*. Securities Commission, Kuala Lumpur.

Selvadurai, S. (1972a). *Padi Farming in West Malaysia*. Ministry of Agriculture, Kuala Lumpur.

_____ (1972b). *Krian Padi Survey*. Ministry of Agriculture, Kuala Lumpur.

_____ (1972c). *Socio-economic Survey of Rubber Smallholdings in West Johore*. Ministry of Agriculture, Kuala Lumpur.

Senftleben, Wolfgang (1978). *Background to Agricultural Land Policy in Malaysia*. Otto Harrassowitz, Wiesbaden.

Shahari Jabbar (1985). "Malaysia Incorporated ". In Jomo K.S. (ed.). *The Sun Also Sets: Lessons in 'Looking East'*. 2nd ed. INSAN, Kuala Lumpur.

Sharom Ahmat (1970). "The Structure of the Economy of Kedah 1879–1905". *Journal of the Malayan Branch, Royal Asiatic Society* 43(2): 1–24.

Shiller, R.J. (2000). *Irrational Exuberance*. Princeton University Press, Princeton, NJ.

Shleifer, Andrei and L.H. Summers (1988). "Breach of Trust in Hostile Take-Overs". In A. Auerbach (ed.). *Corporate Take-Overs: Causes and Consequences*. University of Chicago Press, Chicago.

Shleifer, Andrei and R.W. Vishny (1997). "A Survey of Corporate Governance". *Journal of Finance*, June, 737–83.

Singh, Ajit (1992). "Corporate Takeovers". In J. Eatwell, M. Milgate, and P. Newman (eds). *The New Palgrave Dictionary of Money and Finance*. Macmillan, London, pp. 480–86.

———— (1995). "Corporate Financial Patterns in Industrializing Economies: A Comparative International Study". IFC Technical Paper 2, International Finance Corporation, Washington, DC.

———— (1997). "Financial Liberalisation, Stock Markets and Economic Development". *Economic Journal*, May: 771–82.

———— (1998). "Liberalisation, the Stock Market and the Market for Corporate Control: A Bridge too far for the Indian Economy?" In I. J. Ahluwalia and I. M.D. Little (eds). *India's Economic Reforms and Development: Essays for Manmohan Singh*. Oxford University Press, New York, pp.169–96.

———— (1999a). "Asian Capitalism and the Financial Crisis". In Jonathan Michie and John Grieve-Smith (eds). *Global Instability: The Political Economy of World Economic Governance*. Routledge, London, pp. 9–36.

———— (1999b). "Should Africa Promote Stock Market Capitalism?" *Journal of International Development* 11: 343–65.

———— (2000). "The Anglo-Saxon Market for Corporate Control: The Financial System and International Competitiveness". In C. Howes and Ajit Singh (eds). *Competitiveness Matters: Industry and Economic Performance in the US*. University of Michigan Press, Ann Arbor, pp. 89–105.

———— (2002). "Competition and Competition Policy in Emerging Markets: International and Developmental Dimensions". University of Cambridge, BSRC Centre for Business Research Working Paper No. 246.

———— (2003a). "Corporate Governance, Corporate Finance and Stock Markets in Emerging Countries". *Journal of Corporate Law* 3(1): 41–72.

———— (2003b). "Capital Account Liberalisation, Free Long-Term Capital Flows, Financial Crises and Economic Development". *Eastern Economic Journal* 29(2), Spring: 191–216.

———— (2003c). "Competition, Corporate Governance and Selection in Emerging Markets". *Economic Journal*, November: F443–F464.

Singh, Ajit and J. Hamid (1992). "Corporate Financial Structures in Developing Countries". IFC Technical Paper 1, International Finance Corporation, Washington, DC.

Singh, Ajit, Alaka Singh, and Bruce Weisse (2003). "Corporate Governance, Competition, the New Financial Architecture and Large Corporations in Emerging Markets". UNCTAD (ed.). *Management of Capital Flows: Comparative Experiences and Implications for Africa*. United Nations Conference and Trade and Development, Geneva, pp.1–70.

Singh, Ajit and Bruce Weisse (1998). "Emerging Stock Markets, Portfolio Capital Flows and Long-Term Economic Growth: Micro and Macro Perspectives". *World Development*, April: 607–22.

―――― (1999). "The Asian Model: A Crisis Foretold?" *International Social Science Journal*, June: 203–15.

Smith, Ethan and Peter Goethals (1965). "Tenancy among Padi Cultivators in Malaysia: A Study of Tenancy Conditions and Laws Affecting Landlord-Tenant Relations". Ford Foundation, Kuala Lumpur; mimeo.

South East Asia Firebricks Sendirian Berhad v. Mineral Products Manufacturing Employees Union & Others (1980). 2, *Malayan Law Journal*: 165.

Spinager, Dean (1980). *Regional Industrialization Policies in a Small Developing Country. A Case Study of West Malaysia*. Institut fur Weltwirtschaft, an der Universitat Kiel, Kiel.

Standing, Guy (1993). "Labour Flexibility in the Malaysian Manufacturing Sector". In Jomo, K.S. (ed.). *Industrialising Malaysia: Policy, Performance, Prospects*. Routledge, London.

Stein, J.C. (1989). "Efficient Stock Markets, Inefficient Firms: A Model of Myopic Corporate Behaviour". *Quarterly Journal of Economics* 104, November: 665–70.

Stiglitz, J.E. (1999). "Reforming the Global Financial Architecture: Lessons from Recent Crises". *Journal of Finance*, August: 1508–21.

Suehiro, Akira (2001). "Family Business Gone Wrong? Ownership Patterns and Corporate Performance in Thailand". ADB Institute Working Paper 19. Asian Development Bank Institute, Tokyo, May.

Suffian, Mohamed (1986). "Four Decades in the Law — Looking Back". In Mohamed Suffian, Francis A. Trindade and H.P. Lee (eds). *The Constitution of Malaysia — Further Perspectives and Developments: Essays in Honour of Tun Mohamed Suffian*. Oxford University Press, Singapore.

Summers, L.H. (2000). "International Financial Crisis: Causes, Prevention and Cures". *American Economic Review*, May: 1–16.

Supian Haji Ali (1988). "Malaysia". In Gus Edgren (ed.). *The Growing Sector: Studies in Public Sector Employment in Asia*. ILO-ARTEP, New Delhi.

Swettenham, Frank (1948). *British Malaya: An Account of the Origin and Progress of British Influence in Malaya.* Allen & Unwin, London.

Swift, Michael G. (1967). "Economic concentration and Malay peasant society". In Maurice Freedman (ed.). *Social Organization.* Frank Cass, London, pp. 241–69.

Tan Tat Wai (1982). *Income Distribution and Determination in West Malaysia.* Oxford University Press, Kuala Lumpur.

The Edge, 1 June 1998.

The Star, 10 August 2001.

The Star, 13 August 2001.

Thillainathan, R. (2000). "Malaysian Financial and Corporate Sector Under Distress – A Mid-term Assessment of Restructuring Efforts". Processed, revised version of paper originally prepared for a World Bank conference, Tokyo, Jan.

Tichy, G. (2001). "What do We Know About Success and Failure of Mergers?" *Journal of Industry, Competition and Trade* 1(4): 347–94.

Tigar, Michael E. and Madeleine R. Levy (1977). *Law and the Rise of Capitalism.* Monthly Review Press, New York.

Tirole, J. (1991). "Privatisation in Eastern Europe: Incentives and the Economics of Transition". In O.J. Blanchard and S.S. Fisher (eds). *NBER Macroeconomics Annual, 1991.* MIT Press, Cambridge, Mass.

Tobin, James (1984). "On the Efficiency of the Financial System". *Lloyds Bank Review*, July: 1–15.

Tun Datuk Haji Mohd Adnan v. Tun Haji Mustapha bin Dato Harun (1987). 1, *Malayan Law Journal*: 471.

Tybout, J. (2000). "Manufacturing Firms in Developing Countries: How Well do They Do and Why?" *Journal of Economic Literature*, March: 11–44.

U.S. Council for Economic Advisers (1998). *Economic Report of the President.* U.S. Government Printing Office, Washington, D.C.

————— (1999). *Economic Report of the President.* U.S. Government Printing Office, Washington, D.C.

Unger, Roberto Mangabeira (1998). *Democracy Realized: The Progressive Alternative.* Verso, London.

Wade, Robert and Frank Veneroso (1998). "The Asian Financial Crisis: The High Debt Model and the Unrecognized Risk of the IMF Strategy". Working Paper No. 128, Russell Sage Foundation, New York.

Warr, Peter G. (1987). "Malaysia's Industrial Enclaves: Benefits and Costs". *The Developing Economies* 25, March.

Wee, Victor Eng Lian (1997). "An Analysis of Tax Reform in Malaysia". PhD thesis, University of Bristol, Bristol.

Wheatley, Paul (1961). *The Golden Khersonese*. University of Malaya Press, Kuala Lumpur.

Whittington, G., V. Saporta, and A. Singh (1997). "The Effects of Hyper-inflation on Accounting Ratios: Financing of Corporate Growth in Industrialising Economies". IFC Technical Paper 3, Washington, D.C.

Wilkinson, R.J. (ed.) (1971). *Papers on Malay Subjects*. Oxford University Press, Kuala Lumpur.

Wilson, H. (1975). "The Evolution of Land Administration in the Malay States: A Survey of British-inspired Changes". *Journal of the Malayan Branch, Royal Asiatic Society* 48 (1): 120–33.

Wilson, T.B. (1958). *The Economics of Padi Production in North Malaya Part I: Land Tenure, Rents, Land Use and Fragmentation*. Ministry of Agriculture and Cooperatives, Kuala Lumpur.

Winstedt, Richard O. (1928). "Kedah Laws". *Journal of the Malayan Branch, Royal Asiatic Society* 6(2), June: 1–44.

Winters, S.G., Jr (1964). "Economic 'Natural Selection' and the Theory of the Firm". Yale Economic Essays, Spring.

Wix Corporation South East Asia Sendirian Berhad v. Minister of Labour and Manpower (1980). 2, *Malayan Law Journal*: 248.

Wong Sulong (1997). In *The Star*. 29 Aug.

Wong, David (1975). *Tenure and Land Dealings in the Malay States*. Singapore University Press, Singapore.

Wong Sook Ching, Jomo K.S. and Chin Kok Fay (2005). *Malaysian "Bail-Outs"? Capital Controls, Restructuring & Recovery in Malaysia*. Singapore University Press, Singapore.

Woo-Cumings, Meredith (ed.) (1999). *The Developmental State*. Cornell University Press, Ithaca.

World Bank (1980). *World Development Report*. Oxford University Press, New York.

World Bank (1983). *Malaysia: Structural Change and Stabilization*. World Bank, Washington, DC.

————— (1987). *World Development Report, 1987*. Oxford University Press, New York, for World Bank, Washington, DC.

————— (1989). *Malaysia: Matching Risks and Reward in a Mixed Economy*. World Bank, Washington, DC.

————— (1993). *The East Asian Miracle: Economic Growth and Public Policy*. Oxford University Press, New York.

————— (1998). *East Asia: The Road to Recovery*. Washington, D.C.

————— (2002). *World Development Report 2002: Building Institutions for Markets*. Oxford University Press, New York, for World Bank, Washington, DC.

Young, Kevin, Willem Bussink, and Parvez Hassan (eds) (1980). *Malaysia: Growth and Equity in a Multiracial Society*. Johns Hopkins University Press, Baltimore.

Zahara Mahmud (1970). "The Period and Nature of 'Traditional' Settlement in the Malay Peninsula". *Journal of the Malayan Branch, Royal Asiatic Society*, 43(2).

Zingales, Luigi (1998). "Corporate Governance". In P. Newman (ed.). *The New Palgrave Dictionary of Economics and the Law*. Macmillan, New York.

Index

ABF Malaysian Bond Index Fund, 117
Accountants Act (1967), 62
accounting standards, 102, 110, 228
Act of Parliament of the Federation of
    Malaya. *See* Malaysia Act (1963)
adat, 133
adat Perpateh, 20n5
adat Temenggong, 20n5
adjudicating machinery, 162, 174
administrative law, 60–1, 78n5
administrative procedures, 18, 78
agency theory, 225
agrarian reforms, 5
agriculture, 72–3
    development, 6, 24, 82
    diversification, 18, 22, 32
    land taxation, 138
    modernization, 82
    settlement 137
        pre-colonial Malay, 130–2
Agriculture Bank of Malaysia, 82
airline industry, 201, 213–4, 216–7
alienated land
    property rights, 141
Alliance phase (1957–69), 23–7
alludial rights, 133
An Act in Council of the Queen of
    England. *See* The Sabah, Sarawak and
    Singapore (State Constitutions) Order
    in Council (1963)
An Act of Parliament of the Federation
    of Malaya. *See* Parliament of the
    Federation of Malaya
An Act of Parliament of the United
    Kingdom. *See* Malaysia Act (1963)

Anglo-American
    benchmark, 228
    corporate governance, 222, 227, 229,
        235–6, 237
    financial system, 232
    framework, 232
    stock market-based economics, 229
Anti-money laundering (AML), 89
Anti-Money Laundering Act, 2001
    (AMLA), 89
Anwar Ibrahim, 50, 203–4
Arab-Malaysian Banking Group, 211
arbitration, 14, 74, 75, 157, 162, 164
Architects Act (1967), 62
aristocracy, 131
Armed Forces Fund Board (LTAT), 210
ASEAN Free Trade Agreement (AFTA),
    36, 201, 215
Asian Bond Fund 1 (ABF1), 117
Asian Bond Fund 2 (ABF2), 117
Asian Development Bank (ADB), 226
Asian financial crisis (1997), 37, 43,
    93–5, 203, 207, 213
Asian Pacific Economic Co-operation
    (APEC), 36
asset management company, 120, 204,
    206, 218, 219n2
asset market collapses, 80
asset securitization, 115
Association of Southeast Asian Nations
    (ASEAN), 201

Bai'al-'ilnah, 118
bail-outs, 43, 105, 216
Bakun Dam, 47

balance of payments, 5–6
bangsawan. See aristocracy
Bank Bumiputra Malaysia, 29, 206, 210
bank consolidation, 210, 212
Bank Islam Malaysia Berhad, 117, 123n6
bank lending, 112
bank mergers, 209–12, 219
Bank Negara Malaysia (BNM), 81, 85, 90, 113, 117, 205, 208, 209
Bank of Commerce, 209, 210
Bank of International Settlements (BIS), 234
Bank Pertanian Malaysia Act (1969), 72, 82
Bank Simpanan Nasional Act, 1974, 83
Bank Utama, 211
bank-based financial system, 239n7
Banking Act, 1973, 82, 85
Banking and Financial Institutions Act, 1989 (BAFIA), 84–5
banking industry, 63, 82, 85, 203
  and economic recession, 84
  growth, 85
  laws, 84
  performances, 88
  recapitalization, 207–8, 212
  restructuring, 206–7, 211, 212, 218
Banking Ordinance (1959), 81, 82
Bankruptcy Act (1967), 64
Bar Council, 62
Barat Daya v. Ong Gaik Kee, 60
basic legal framework, 4, 7
Berjaya Group, 216
Berle and Means-type, 227, 228
bilateral agreements, 39
Bill of Exchange Enactment Act (1934), 64
Bills of Exchange Act (1949), 16, 17
Bills of Sale Act (1950), 17, 64
Board of Commissioners of Currency, Malaya and British Borneo, 81
Bombardier Transportation (Canada), 216
bonds
  domestic, 112–7

government-guaranteed, 117, 207, 219n3
  market product range, 114
  of multiple currencies, 117
  private sector, 112–3
  public sector, 113
  tax treatment, 116 box
Borneo, 1, 3, 9, 200
Borrowings
  domestic, 86
Bretton Woods institution, 36, 80, 235
Brooke family, 3
Brunei, 3, 10
Bumiputera
  corporate ownership, 65
  corporate wealth redistribution, 184–5
  credit preference, 82
  share in wealth ownership, 39, 42
  share of corporate equity, 27–8
Bumiputera-Commerce Bank, 201
Bumiputra Malaysia Finance (BMF), 29
Bursa Saham Malaysia. *See* Kuala Lumpur Stock Exchange (KLSE)

Cahya Mata Sarawak Bhd (CMS), 211
Caine, Sir Sydney, 81
Camdessus, Michel, 222
capital controls, 86, 123n8, 218, 219
capital flight, 1, 28, 185, 218
capital inflows, 44, 80, 200
capital investment per employee (CIPE), 197
Capital Issues Committee (CIC), 96, 97, 98
Capital Market Advisory Council (CMAC), 111
Capital Market Master Plan (CMP), 110–3
capital market, 96
  and fund management industry, 103–4
  fund-raising, 111
  liquidity and diversity, 101
  regulatory and legal framework, 97–9

variety of products, 103
capital outflows, 80
capitation tax, 134
car project, 33, 183, 213, 215
cash crops, 2
casualization, 163, 171
Central Bank of Malaya Ordinance
  (1958), 81, 82–3, 121
Central Bank of Malaysia Act (1958),
  118–9, 123, 127n41
Central Bank, 7, 45, 80–1, 85
  enlarged powers, 83–4
  on capital market, 96
  powers and duties, 84
Central Depository System (CDS), 104
Central Electricity Board (CEB), 77
Central Limit Order Book (CLOB), 106,
  126–7n32, 34
Centre on Investment (COI), 190, 191
chambers of commerce, 63
chief executive officer (CEO), 108, 225
Child and Young Persons Employment
  Act (1966), 168
children, employment of, 168, 169
  Table1
China, 32, 37, 117
Chinese capitalists, 25
Chinese customary law, 20n5
civil enforcement provisions, 103
Civil Law Act (1956), 16, 65
civil procedure, 12
class relations, 129, 130, 147n4
clearing houses, 90
Code of Ethics: Guidelines on Share
  Trading, 97
Code on Takeovers and Mergers (1998),
  106, 109
collective agreements, 161, 162, 163,
  164
collective bargaining, 158, 161–4, 165,
  166, 175
Colonial Legal Service, 19n2
commercial bank, 80–3, 123n3
  crisis, 80
  domestic, 124n10

Islamic banking services, 117–8
liquidity requirements, 82
membership for, 90
commercial paper (CP), 114
Commissioner of Commodities Trading
  (CCT), 99–100
Commodities Trading Act, 1985 (CTA),
  99–100
Commodities Trading Commission
  (CTC), 99
Commodity and Monetary Exchange of
  Malaysia (COMEX), 112, 126n27
commodity futures industry, 99
commodity prices, 26, 30, 31, 34, 35, 99
Common Effective Preferential Tariff,
  215
common law principles, 15
  Anglo-American countries, 228, 230,
    236
  application in Malaysia, 64, 69, 95,
    160, 173
  English, 60, 62, 65, 70
Commonwealth Development
  Corporation, 81
Companies (Amendment) Act (1985),
  87n6
Companies (Amendment) Bill (2007),
  124n12
Companies Act (1965), 62–3, 91, 93,
  94, 124n12, 125n23
Companies Commission of Malaysia
  (CCM), 94–6, 108
Companies Commission of Malaysia Act
  (2001), 95–6
Companies Ordinance, 96
competitions law, 122–3
conciliation, 164
Confucian values, 32
conglomerates, efficiency of, 234–5, 237,
  238
Congress of Union of Employees
  in the Public and Civil Services
  (CUEPACS), 166–7
constitutional law, 61
consumer price inflation, 44

Contracts Act (1950), 17, 55, 64
Control of Rent Act (1966), 71
Controller of Foreign Exchange, 122
Convention on Settlement of Investment
    Disputes, 200
cooperation, regional, 39
co-ownership, 141, 146, 153n41, 42
Copyright Act (1911), 71
Copyright Act (1969), 71
Copyright Bill, 71
corporate bond market, 110
corporate control, market for, 231,
    232–3, 235–6
corporate debt restructuring, 205,
    212–3, 218
Corporate Debt Restructuring
    Committee (CDRC), 204, 205,
    212–3, 214, 220n12, 14–5
corporate finance, 230–2, 237
corporate governance, 107–9
    and competition, 235–6
    and corporate finance, 231–2
    best practices, 108, 223, 225, 226,
        238 box
    definition, 231
    in emerging markets, 227, 228,
        230–1
    framework, 226
    malpractices, 222
    OECD proposals, 228–30
    principles, 223–4
    problems, 226
    reforms, 226, 236, 238
    structures, 227, 235
    and takeovers, 232–3
    World Bank proposals, 228–30
Corporate Governance Survey by the
    KLSE (2002), 108
Corporate Regulation, 91–3
corporations
    income tax, 116, 183, 194–5
    listing requirements, 94–5
    performance, 225, 226, 228, 232
    private sector, 92–3
    restructuring, 205

corruption, 42, 228
corvée labour, 129, 130, 132, 135–6
counter-cyclical measures, 203
counter financing of terrorism (CFT), 89
Court of Appeal. *See* Malaysian Court of
    Appeal
Courts of Judicature Act 1964, 9, 11, 89
credit facilities, 31, 86, 179, 200, 203,
    218–9
Credit Guarantee Corporation, 83
Criminal Procedure Code, 16, 89
crisis management, 23, 43–52
crony capitalism, 44, 227, 228, 237
"crony" firm, 43
cronyism, 37, 44–5, 234
cross-subsidization, 215
currency crisis, 44–5, 222, 227
currency system, 80–1
    regional, 45
Customs Act of 1967, 196

Daim Zainuddin, 35, 80, 203, 210, 211
Daimler Chrysler, 216
Danaharta, 112, 204, 205, 206, 207,
    211, 212
Danamodal, 112, 204–5, 207–8, 211,
    220n8
Danamodal National Bhd. *See*
    Danamodal
Dato, 131
Daya Bumi project, 29
"dead land". *See tanah mati*
debentures, 94, 96, 104, 110, 115, 116
debt crisis, 36
debt markets, 112
debt restructuring, 205, 212, 213, 220.
    See also Corporate Debt Restructuring
debt-bondage, 129
decolonization, 2
deeds system, 69. *See also* Torrens land
    registration system
Demutualization Act (2004), 112
denationalization. *See* privatization
Department of Environment (DOE),
    76, 190

Department of Labour, 158
Department of Trade Unions Affairs, 165
Deposit Insurance Act (2005), 90
deposit insurance system, 90–1
deregulation measures, 38, 45
derivative exchanges, 103
developing countries
  corporations, 234, 235
  corporate governance, 236
Dewan Negara, 9
Dewan Undangan Negeri, 9
Dewan Rakyat, 9
disability, 171–2
disclosure framework, 101–2, 107,
  109–11
discount houses, 83, 123n5
discrimination, 138, 170–1
Distribution Act (1959), 70
district chiefs, 147–8n6
domestic savings, 112
domestic debt, 31, 112
domestic financial institutions, 81, 88
domestic investments, 37, 40
  private, 31, 34, 38, 185
domestic market, 4, 76, 103, 179–81,
  183, 184, 188, 191, 198, 201
double deduction for training incentive
  (DDTI), 194
Double Deduction Incentive scheme for
  Approved Training (DDIT), 197
double tax deduction, 189, 199
Draft Development Plan (DDP), 6, 7
Drainage Works Act (1954), 77
Drainage Works Ordinance (1954), 75
Drawback of Import Duty, Sales Tax and
  Excise Duty, 196

East Asia Pacific region, 117
East Asian crises, 43, 222, 233, 234,
  236–8
economic crisis, 46, 201
economic deregulation, 35, 37–9, 43,
  45, 54, 162, 163, 187
economic development
  accelerating structural change, 176

Alliance strategy, 24
  and corporatism, 175
  and economic diversification, 54
  growth, 31
  laissez-faire, 22, 23–4, 28, 177
  long-term, 237
  national programme, 10, 30
  post-colonial programme, 18, 22, 23
  and the state, 34
  successes, 32
economic infrastructure, 4, 6
economic laws, 62–5
economic liberalization, 35, 36, 48
economic measures, 25, 35, 107
Economic Planning Unit, 65
economic recession, 34–5
economic relations
  pre-colonial Malay society, 132
"economic unionism", 156
educational expenditure, 24
effective protection rate (EPR), 180
electric components, 28, 35, 163, 170,
  183, 184, 200
Electricity Act (1949), 77
Electronic Labour Exchange, 167
electronics business, 35
elite, political, 23, 227
Emergency (Essential Powers) Act
  (1979), 84
Emergency Act (1966), 57
emerging markets, 223, 227–31, 234, 236
eminent domain, 132, 133, 135,
  149n15, 150n17
Employees' Provident Fund Act (1951),
  17, 160
Employees' Provident Fund (EPF), 96,
  104, 161
Employees' Social Security Act, 1969,
  160, 171–2
employer's associations, 166
Employment Act (1955), 158, 160, 162,
  170, 173, 174, 200
Employment Injury Scheme, 160, 172
Employment Ordinance (1955), 74,
  157, 158

employment, 74–5
  annual leave, 168, 173
  casualization, 163, 171
  conditions, 158
  dismissal, 174
  employee welfare, 160
  flexibility, 163
  legislation, 160–1
  protection regulations, 163
  services, 167
  temporary, 179
  termination, 173–4
English East India Company, 2
environment, 75–6
environmental impact assessment (EIA),
  76
Environmental Quality Act (EQA), 75
Environmental Quality Council (EQC),
  75–6
EON Bank, 211
equity finance, 44, 230, 231
ersatz capitalism, 45
Essential (Protection of Depositors)
  Regulations (1986), 84
Estate Duty Enactment (1941), 68
ethnic Chinese business, 34, 183, 184
ethnic Chinese capital, 40, 192
ethnic redistribution, 22, 38, 184–6. *See*
  also inter-ethnic redistribution
exaction of a tenth, 132–5
Exchange Control Act 1953, 17–8
Exchange Control Notice (ECM), 16,
  122
Excise Act (1976), 196
Exemption from Customs Duty on
  Direct Raw Materials/Components,
  195
Exemption from Import Duty and Sales
  Tax on Spares and Consumables, 195
export allowances, 77, 181, 200
Export Credit Refinancing Scheme, 84
export-oriented industrialization (EOI),
  22, 26, 28, 38, 76, 178, 180–3, 186
export processing zones (EPZs), 29, 180,
  181–2, 202n1

export-substitution industries, 30
external aggression, 56, 57
external debt, 42

Factories and Machinery Act (1967), 75,
  172
Factories and Machinery Department,
  172–3
family, 130, 139, 143
family-controlled firms, 227, 229, 230
farm fragmentation, 142, 143
farming, 140, 141, 142
Federal Agricultural Marketing Authority
  Act, 1965 (FAMA), 72
Federal Constitution, 60
  equality of persons, 66, 70, 170–1
  executive power, 59
  importance of land, 69
  the judiciary, 58–9
  property rights, 70, 95
  state emergency powers, 56–8
Federal Court, 10–2, 55, 207
Federal government, 29, 81
  emergency powers, 56–8
Federal Industrial Development
  Authority (FIDA), 26, 76, 180–1
Federal Land Development Authority
  (FELDA), 24, 25
Federal Roads Act (1959), 77
Federal-state relations, 9–10
Federated Malay States (FMS), 2, 10,
  68–9, 71, 136, 151n29
  land laws, 136
  land tenure, 151n28
Federation of Malaya. *See* Federation of
  Malaysia
Federation of Malaysia, 2, 7–10
Federation of Public Listed Companies,
  205
females, employment of, 168–9, 171
feudal relations, 148n9
feudal rent, 132
feudalism, 138
Finance (Banking and Financial
  Institutions) Act, 84

Finance Committee on Corporate
    Governance, 95, 124n12
Finance Companies Act (1969), 82, 85
finance companies, 82, 123n3
Finance, Insurance, Real Estate and
    Business Services, 116
financial crisis, 23, 29, 39, 44–5, 67,
    86, 111–2, 124n17, 201, 203, 207,
    209–10, 213
financial liberalization, 44, 45, 80, 233,
    236, 237, 238
Financial Reporting Act (1997), 102
Financial Reporting Foundation, 102
Financial Sector Master Plan (FMSP),
    87–9, 90
financial system, 63, 82
    regulation, 80–5
    reporting, 102, 109
    structure, 81, 84, 113, 229
    supervision, 85
Fire Insurance Companies Ordinance
    (1948), 64
"fire-sale" takeovers, 233
First Five Year Plan (FFYP), 6, 7
fiscal policies
    counter-cyclical, 31
Fisheries Act (1963), 75
FMS Copyright Enactment (Cap 73), 71
FMS Land Code (1926), 69
foreign banks, 85
foreign borrowings, 30, 31, 218
foreign debt, 23
foreign direct investment (FDI), 28, 37,
    38, 180–1, 188, 200, 239n3
    in manufacturing, 184
    inflows, 186
foreign equity, 66, 188, 191, 198, 201
foreign exchange, 5, 86–7
foreign fund management companies
    (FFMCs), 104
foreign fund managers, 126n28
Foreign Investment Committee (FIC),
    65, 98, 106, 111, 199
foreign investments, 36, 80
    inflows, 24
foreign ownership, 78n7, 188

land, 70
Forest Enactment (1934), 75
fragmentation, 155n52
"fraud on a power", 95
free labour, 156
Free Trade Agreement (FTA), 201
free trade, 2, 201
Free-Trade Zones (FTZs), 29, 181, 182,
    183, 185
    tax incentives, 187–8
Free Trade Zones Act (1971), 181
front line regulators (FLRs), 102–3
fund management industry, 101, 103–4
Futures Industry Act, 1993, 90, 98, 100
Futures Industry Amendment Act, 103
futures market, 99–100

G-7, 223
gearing ratios, 234
General Agreement on Tariffs and Trade
    (GATT), 36, 186, 201
General elections, 26–7, 31, 33
Generalized System of Preferences (GSP),
    37, 192
globalization, 44
Government Investment Act (1983),
    127n40
Government Investment Certificates
    (GICs), 118
government-owned enterprises, 29
Greenspan, Alan, 222
gross domestic product, 113, 179–80,
    194, 227
*Guidelines for Islamic Real Estate
    Investment Trusts* (Guidelines), 120
Guidelines for the Regulation of
    Acquisitions of Assets, Mergers and
    Take-overs, 65
Guidelines on Securities Lending and
    Borrowing, 103
*Guidelines on the Offering of Asset-backed
    Debt Securities* (ABS Guidelines),
    114–5
*Guidelines on the Offering of Private Debt
    Securities* (PDS Guidelines), 114,
    115, 116

Guidelines on the Offering of Structured Products (Structured Products Guidelines), 115
Guidelines on Unit Trust Funds, 120

Hamid Mustapha, Tan Sri Abdul, 18n2
health and safety, 172–3
Health Department, 190
heavy industrialization, 33, 47, 183–4, 185–7
  policy, 31, 46
HICOM, 183
High Court, 9–12, 56, 59, 94
high growth with low inflation, 26
High Level Finance Committee, 108
high technology, 191, 193, 197–8
Hindu customary law, 20n5
Hire Purchase Act (1967), 65
Hong Kong, 29, 32, 117, 218
Hong Leong Bank, 210
House of Representatives. *See* Dewan Rakyat
human resource development, 195, 198
Human Resources Development Council (HRDC), 165
Human Resources Development Fund (HRDF), 194, 197, 198

ILO Conventions and Recommendations, 160
immigrant labour, 45, 163
Immigration Department, Customs and Excise Department, 190
"imperial preference" protectionism, 2
import duties, 179, 181, 190, 195, 196, 199, 201
import-substituting industrialization (ISI), 22, 25–6, 76, 178–80, 201
income disparities, 26
income tax, 68, 116, 189, 193
  corporate, 183
  exemption, 194–5
Income Tax Act (1967), 68, 194
Income Tax (Amendment) Act (1990), 122

Income Tax Ordinance (1947), 68
Income Tax Ordinance (1922), 68
incremental capital output ration (ICOR), 42
Indah Water Konsortium (IWK), 43, 67–8, 216, 217
indentured labourers, 139, 156
Indians, 3
indigenous community, 171
indigenous sources of law, 14–5
individual worker rights, 173–4
Indonesia, 30, 57, 117, 205, 218
inducing private investments, 35–43
industrial accidents, 172
Industrial Arbitration Tribunal (1965), 75, 157–8
Industrial Bank of Malaysia, 83
Industrial Building Allowance (IBA), 194, 196
Industrial Co-ordination Act (ICA), 40, 184–5, 187–8, 190, 191, 196
Industrial Court (1967), 14, 41, 74, 75, 157–8, 161–2, 164, 174
Industrial Court Ordinance, 1948, 75, 157
industrial disputes, 164
Industrial Incentives Act (1968), 26, 76–7, 181
industrial investments, 179, 199
Industrial Master Plan (IMP) (1986–95), 40, 186, 188
Industrial Relations Act 1967, 74, 75, 157–8, 160, 161–2, 164
Industrial Relations Department (IRD), 164, 174
Industrial relations, 29, 33, 74–5, 156, 157, 160, 164, 174–6
  post-colonial, 157–9
Industrial Technical Assistance Fund (ITAF), 197
industries, 6
  capital-intensive, 179
  colonial era, 177
  output growth rate, 179–80
Industry R&D Grant Scheme (IGS), 194

inequality, 26
infrastructure, 77–8
    industrial investment, 76
    law, 67
inheritance
    customary Malay (*adat*), 141, 146
    Islamic, 141, 142, 146
    laws, 70
    primogeniture, 141
in-house unions, 158, 159, 166
initial public offerings, 111
Inland Revenue Department, 122
insolvency legislation, 205
Institutional Securities Custodian
    Programme (ISCAP), 117
Insurance Act (1963), 64, 121
insurance industry, 68, 119, 121
intellectual property laws, 40
intellectual property rights, 36, 37, 71,
    191
Intensification of Research in Priority
    Area (IRPA) Fund, 197
interest rates, 30, 35, 36, 42, 96, 186,
    199, 218, 231, 234
Interest-Free Banking Unit (IFBU), 117
inter-ethnic economic disparities, 39, 65
inter-ethnic redistribution, 22–3, 40, 46,
    184, 192
Internal Security Act, 1960 (ISA), 52,
    60, 158, 159
International Tin Agreement, 1953, 73
Invalidity Pension Scheme, 160, 172
investment banks, 123n4
Investment Incentives Act, 1968, 181,
    188, 189, 196, 199
Investment Tax Allowance (ITA), 187,
    190, 193, 194, 200
investment tax credits, 77
investments
    investor, 91, 103
        protection, 101, 102–3, 228, 229
    returns of, 115
inward-oriented industries, 183
irrigated rice cultivation, 132
irrigation, 24, 72, 131, 135

Irrigation Areas Act (1953), 72
Islamic "window". *See* Interest-Free
    Banking Unit (IFBU)
Islamic Banking Act (1983), 21n6, 84,
    85, 117, 127n39
Islamic banking system, 118, 119
Islamic bond, 114
Islamic courts, 10
Islamic custom, 2
Islamic equity market, 119
Islamic financial system, 117–9
    tax treatment, 121
Islamic inter-bank money market, 118
Islamic intermediary services, 120
Islamic law, 2, 20n6, 70–1
Islamic real estate investment trusts
    (REITs), 120
Islamic Shariah law, 4
Islamic stock broking services, 120
Islamic unit trust funds, 120

Japan, 188, 190, 227, 230, 232
Japanese Occupation, 3, 6, 74, 156–7,
    177
joint-ventures, 186, 191, 196, 198
judges, 10, 58, 61
Judicial and Legal Service Commission,
    19n2
Judicial Commissioners, 10, 12
judiciary, 7, 8, 18–9n2, 50–1, 58–9
justice, administration of, 10
just-in-time (JIT), 170
juvenile Court, 13

kampung. See village
Kedah, 2
    economic structure, 13
    land systems, 135
    land-tax, 151n26
Kelantan, 2
    land systems, 135
    regional grievances, 39
kerah. See corvée labour
Keretapi Tanah Melayu (Malayan
    Railways), 77

Ketua Kampung. See local chiefs
Khazanah Holdings, 43, 198, 201
kin relations, 130
Korean Chaebol, 235
Kuala, 131
Kuala Lumpur
  regional capital market centre, 101
Kuala Lumpur City Centre (KLCC) or
  Petronas Towers, 29
Kuala Lumpur International Airport
  (KLIA), 29
Kuala Lumpur Options and Financial
  Futures Exchange (KLOFFE), 103,
  112, 126n27
Kuala Lumpur Stock Exchange (KLSE),
  63, 80, 94, 97, 98, 104, 106, 112,
  123n1
  investor protection, 103
  listed bonds, 116
  market infrastructure, 104, 105
  on stock market bubble, 80
  operations of exchange, 97–8, 106–8
  revamped listing requirements, 108,
    111, 125n23
  securities laws, 94
Kulim High-Technology Industrial Park,
  197

labour, 74–5
  discipline, 47, 74
  flexibility, 163, 175, 192, 200
  immigration, 30, 174
  productivity, 158
  reforms, 5
  relations, 156
  shortages, 37
  standards, 160, 163
Labour Court, 162, 174
Labour Department, 161, 165, 167
labour-intensive export-oriented
  industries, 26, 29, 181, 182, 191,
  200
labour laws, 29, 174, 176
  amendments, 182
  post-colonial period, 156

labour-management relations, 175
labour market, 162–3, 165, 166, 167,
  170–1, 174, 176, 192
Labour Ministry, 75, 158, 161, 164
Labour Ordinance, 200
Labour Party, 74, 157
labour unions, 74–5, 156–7, 174
Labuan International Offshore Financial
  Centre (IOFC), 44, 121–2
Labuan Offshore Business Activity Tax
  Act (1990), 122
Labuan Offshore Financial Services Act
  (1996), 122
Labuan Offshore Financial Services
  Authority (LOFSA), 122
Labuan Trust Companies Act (1990), 122
laissez faire economic development, 22,
  23–4, 28, 177
land
  accumulation, 136
  concessions, 139
  distribution inequalities, 140
  ownership, 137, 138–40, 149n14
    concentration of, 140, 142–4,
      146, 154n45
    joint, 141–2
  policy, 136, 138
  property rights, 4, 145
  rent, 129, 132–5, 139
  sales of, 142–3
  scarcity, 141
  subdivision, 141–2
  use, 132, 133, 138
Land (Group Settlement Areas) Act
  (1960), 69
Land Acquisition Act (1960), 60
Land Code (Cap 81), 70
Land Conservation Act (1960), 69, 75
land laws, 2, 4, 60, 69, 136–7, 146
  colonial period, 137, 145–6
  hinterland, 136
Land Ordinance (Cap 68), 69–70
Land Acquisition Act (1960), 70
land system
  Malacca, 134–5

land tenure, 132, 138
  colonial period, 133, 136–8, 151n28
  eminent domain, 132
  governing laws, 69–70
  pre-colonial period, 129, 133, 134
  reforms, 54, 129, 134
landlessness, 141, 146
landlord-tenant relations, 138
landlordism, 139–40, 145, 146
legal framework, 4, 9, 18
  for capital market, 97
  colonial 1, 4, 7, 15, 17–8
  to effect privatization, 66, 67, 214
  employer-employee relations, 160, 161
  governing firms, 62, 229
  history, 50
  institutions, 10–8
  models, 55
  post-colonial, 54
Legal Professions Act (1976), 62
legal system, 15, 17, 38–9, 228, 229–30, 237, 239
Lembaga Letrik Negara (LLN), 77
Lembaga Urusan dan Tabung Haji Act (1969), 82
liberalization, 40, 86
Licensed Manufacturing Warehouses (LMWs), 182, 183
Licensed Offshore Bank in Labuan, 86
Life Assurance Act (1961), 64
Life Assurance Companies Ordinance (1948), 64
light rail transit (LRT) system, 213, 214, 215, 216, 217
Lim, Kit Siang, 53n3
liquidity, 36, 103, 105, 107, 114, 117, 119, 203
  market, 112
  "providers", 123n5
Loan (Local) Act (1961), 96
Loan (Local) Ordinance, 1959, 96
local chiefs, 131
local industry, 178
Look East policy, 30, 32–4, 42, 46
Lord President, 19n2

Magistrate's Court, 13, 14
Magistrate's Courts, 10
Mahathir Mohamad
  crisis management, 43–5
  inducing private investments, 35–9
  Look East policy, 32–4
  new roles for Malaysia, 30–2
  politics of economic policy, 46–7
  in privatization, 41–3
  rule by law, 47–52
  state-business corporatism, 34–5
  transition from NEP, 39–41
Malacca sultanate, 2, 147n2
Malay business, 25, 28
Malay customary land tenure, 68–9
Malay middle class, 27–8
Malay peasant agriculture, 138–40
Malay economic/political hegemony, 27, 42
Malay society
  pre-colonial, 2, 129–30, 132, 135–6, 148n9
Malayan Industrial Development Finance (MIDF), 179
Malayan Industrial Estates Limited (MIEL), 179
Malayan Rubber Research and Development Fund Act (1958), 72
Malayan Stock Exchange, 96
Malayan Stockbrokers' Association, 96
Malayanization, 27
Malaysia, 3, 117
  administrative procedure, 18
  British colonialism, 4–7
  colonial legal heritage, 1–3, 130
  the Federation, 7–10
  laws, 14–5
  legal institutions, 10–8
  legislative procedure, 18
  statutes, 16
Malaysia Act (1963), 2, 8, 11
Malaysia Incorporated policy, 30, 33–5, 46
Malaysian Accounting Standards Board (MASB), 102

Malaysian Agricultural Research and Development Institute Act, 1969 (MARDI), 72

Malaysian Airline System Bhd (MAS), 201, 214, 216, 217

Malaysian Association of Certified Public Accountants (MACPA), 102

Malaysian Association of Certified Public Accountants, 63

Malaysian Bar, 62

Malaysian Central Depository (MCD), 106–7

Malaysian Code on Corporate Governance (2000), 108

Malaysian Court of Appeal, 10, 11–2, 55, 207

Malaysian Deposit Insurance Corporation, 124

Malaysian Derivatives Clearing House (MDCH), 103, 112

Malaysian Employers' Federation (MEF), 166

Malaysian Exchange of Securities Dealing and Automated Quotation (MESDAQ), 105, 112

Malaysian Government Securities (MGS), 117

Malaysian Industrial Development Authority (MIDA), 180, 182, 185, 190, 191, 196. *See also* Federal Industrial Development Authority (FIDA)

Malaysian Industrial Development Finance Limited, 81

Malaysian Industry Government Group for High Technology (MIGHT), 197

Malaysian Institute of Accountants (MIA), 102

Malaysian Monetary Exchange (MME), 103, 126n27

Malaysian Palm Oil Research and Development Board was established under, 73

Malaysian Resources Corporation Bhd (MRCB), 211

Malaysian Rubber Exchange (Incorporation) Act (1962), 72

Malaysian Rubber Exchange and Licensing Board Act (1972), 73

Malaysian ringgit, 44, 45
  bonds, 117
  credit facilities, 219
  depreciation, 23, 37, 38, 105, 191
  devaluation, 42
  over-valuation, 45

Malaysian Rubber Exchange and Licensing Board, 72–3

Malaysian Rubber Exchange (Incorporation) Act (1962), 72

Malaysian South-South Corporation Berhad (Masscorp), 40

Malaysian Technology Development Corporation (MTDC), 197

Malaysian Trade Union Congress (MTUC), 166

mandatory general offer (MGO), 106

Manpower and Administration Modernization and Planning Unit (MAMPU), 56

Manpower Department (MD), 165, 167

manufacturing, 76–7, 116
  colonial era, 178
  companies' licenses, 189
  investment incentives, 186–92
  output, 179

Mara, 25

marginal effective tax rate (METR), 195

maritime waterways, 130

market
  efficiency, 101
  infrastructure, 104
  microstructures, 101

market-based financial system, 239n7

mass media, 51–2

Materials Requisition Planning (MRP), 170

Maxwell, 129, 132–4, 138, 148n12, 149n15, 150n17

May 1969 racial riots, 22, 27, 57, 59, 182

Maybank, 210
medium-term note (MTN) programme, 114
Merchant banks, 83, 97, 123n4
Merdeka Constitution, 1
minimum wage, 160, 167, 200
Mining Enactment (1914), 17
mining, 73–4, 137
Minister of Labour, 162, 164
Ministry of Energy Telecommunication and Posts, 77
Ministry of Finance (MOF), 99, 100, 113, 198
Ministry of Human Resources, 164, 165, 190–1
Ministry of International and Trade and Industry (MITI), 185, 188–9, 191, 197, 198
Ministry of Trade and Industry (MTI), 27, 196
Ministry of Transport, 77
Ministry of Works, 77
minority shareholders, 91, 92, 108
Model Colonial Territories Income Tax Ordinance (1922), 68
monetary policy, 82
money laundering, 89
Moneylenders Ordinance (1951), 64
mudarabah, 199, 127n44
Mukin Gunung (Kelantan), 139
Multilateral Development Banks (MDBs), 117
Multilateral Financial Institutions (MFIs), 117
Multimedia Super Corridor (MSC), 38, 40
multinational corporations (MNCs), 86, 87, 186, 197
Multipurpose Bank, 210
Musa Hitam, 49
Muslim Courts, 20–1n6
Muslim law. See Islamic law
Muslim pilgrimage, 82

National Agricultural Policy, 31
National Bond Market Committee, 113

National Coordination Committee (NCC) to Counter Money Laundering, 89
National Development Policy (NDP), 46
National Economic Action Council (NEAC), 203
National Economic Recovery Plan, 198, 201
National Electricity Board (NEB), 77
National Front, 211
National Institute of Occupational Safety and Health, 173
National Labour Advisory Council (NLAC), 174–5
National Labour Advisory Council, 166
National Land Code (1965), 69–70
National Occupational Safety and Health Council, 173
National Operations Council (NOC), 27, 57
National Savings Bank, 83
national union, 158
National Vision Policy (NVP), 47
National Vocational Training Council (NVTC), 165
Native Courts, 14, 20n5
Negeri Sembilan, 2
nepotism, 44
New Economic Policy (NEP), 22, 27, 39, 42, 46–8, 65–6, 181
  on foreign ownership, 184
  local equity participation, 188
new industrializing economies (NIEs), 37
New International Economic Order (NIEO), 36
New Issue of Securities and the Valuation of Public Limited Companies, 97
newly industrializing country (NIC), 30, 32
non-financial public enterprises (NFPEs), 30
non-performing loans (NPLs), 204–5, 218, 219
non-resource based export industries, 183

non-tradables, 44
North Borneo, 3, 8, 10, 71
North-South Highway, 47

occupational health, 172–3
Occupational Safety and Health Act
 (OSHA), 161, 172
Occupational Safety and Health
 Department, 161, 165, 173
occupational safety, 172–3
off-budget agencies (OBAs), 30
Offshore Banking Act (1990), 121–2
Offshore Companies Act (1990), 122
Offshore Insurance Act (1990), 121–2
offshore legislation, 122
oil palm, 25, 32, 73
oil rents, 29, 74
operational headquarters (OHQs), 197
orang tebusan. See indentured labourers
Organization for Economic Cooperation
 and Development (OECD), 222–3
OTC bonds, 116
out-and-out transfer, 148n10
Outline Perspective Plan for 1971–90
 (OPP1), 27, 39, 200

Padi Cultivation Control of Rents and
 Security of Tenure Ordinance (1955),
 144–5
Padi Cultivators (Control of Rent and
 Security of Tenure) Act (1967), 72,
 145
Pahang, 2
 land systems, 135
palm oil, 35, 100, 178, 183
Palm Oil Registration and Licensing
 Authority (Incorporation) Act, 1976
 (PORLA), 73
Palm Oil Research and Development Act
 (1979), 73
Panel on Takeovers and Mergers (TOP),
 98, 99
Parliament
 constitutional provision, 9
 and the courts, 58–9

on economic laws, 62, 84
 law making power, 57
 member, 59
 passage of statutes, 19n4, 54–5, 59,
 145
 and the states, 10, 17
 two Houses, 9
Parliamentary Draftsman, Attorney-
 General's Chambers, 55
Partnership Act (1961), 62
part-time employment, 170
Payments System Act (2003), 89–90
peasant
 class structure, 139
 differentiation, 144–5, 146
 economy, 145
 rights to land, 133
pecking-order, 230
pembesar. See aristocracy
Pemungut Hasil Tanah, Daerah, 60
Penal Code, 89
Penang, 2, 69
Pengarah Tanah dan Galian Wilayah, 60
Penghulu Courts, 10, 12–3
Penghulu. See local chiefs
Peninsular Malaysia, 2, 18n1
Peninsular Malaysia. *See also* Federation
 of Malaya
Pensions Act, 66–7
peonage, 135–6
People's Republic of China, 117
pepper, 178
Perak, 2, 130
 land legislation, 138
 land rent, 135
Perbadanan Insurans Deposit Malaysia.
 See Malaysian Deposit Insurance
 Corporation
Perwira Affin Bank, 210
Perlis, 2, 15, 18
Pernas (Perbadanan Nasional Berhad),
 28
Perodua, 215
Perusahaan Otomobil Nasional Bhd
 (Proton), 213

Petroleum (Safety Measures) Act (1984), 74
Petroleum Development Act (1974), 29, 74
Petroleum Income Tax Act (1967), 68
Petroleum Mining Act (1966), 73
petroleum, 35
 exports, 178
 foreign ownership, 184–5
 legislative framework, 73
 production, 29, 73–4
 refining of, 183
 revenues, 22
Petronas, 74
Philippines, 117
Picketing, 162
Pilgrims Management and Fund Board, 82
Pioneer Industries Act (1958), 178, 181
Pioneer Industries Ordinance, 25, 76
Pioneer Investment Ordinance (1959), 199
Pioneer Status or Investment Tax Allowance, 197
Pioneer Status Tax Holidays, 187, 190, 197
plantations, 25, 139
plural society, 3
PLUS, 201
Policy Framework for the Consolidation of the Stock Broking Industry, 109–10
political patronage, 47, 216
"political unionism", 156
poll tax, 134, 150–1n22
pollution, control of, 76
portfolio investment, 200, 230n3
Pos Malaysia Berhad, 67
Post Office Savings Bank, 96
Postal Act, 67
Postal Department, 77
post-colonial period, 23–4, 37, 60
poverty
 eradication, 27, 39, 46, 49, 65
 root cause, 153n36

Price Waterhouse Coopers, 108
pricing process, 231, 237
primary commodity prices, 30
primogeniture, 141
principal dealers (PDs), 117
private banking, 44
Private Debt Securities (PDS) Guidelines, 110,113
Private Employment Agencies Act (1981), 167
private investments, 23, 28, 30, 31, 34–5, 50, 178, 185, 200
private sector
 degree of unionization, 159
privatization, 30, 33–4, 36, 41–3, 47, 52n1, 221n26
 buy-out, 228
 failures, 216
 gains from, 214
 government's policy, 18, 77
 of government projects, 200
 and legislations of laws, 66–8
 of national sewerage system, 213–4, 217
 of public transit system, 214, 217
 to re-nationalization, 213–7
Privatization Master Plan (PMP), 42
Privy Council, 10–1, 55, 58
Probate and Administration Act (1959), 70
Promotion of Investments Act, 1986 (PIA), 36, 38, 187, 188, 189–90, 192
property rights, 4, 23, 68–71, 95, 137
proprietary rights, 134, 148n12
Proprietary rights to land, 133
Proton national car project, 33, 183, 186, 201, 213, 215–6
Public Bank, 210
public expenditure, 6, 25
 counter-cyclical, 23, 30
public investments, 28, 35, 45, 178
 in human resources, 45
public sector
 degree of unionization, 159
 employment, 31

ownership of business, 28, 65
resource allocations, 65
trading of shares, 96
Putrajaya, 18n1, 29

qardhu hasan (benevolent loan), 118

racial riots. *See* May 1969 racial riots
Rahman, Tunku Abdul, 3
raja, 131
raja, right to land, 148–9n13
Rashid Hussain Bhd, 211
Razak, Tun Abdul, 27, 65, 69
Razaleigh Hamzah, Tengku, 35, 49
real economy crisis, 44
real interest rates, 36
real wages, 29–30
recapitalization process, 204
recession, 31, 80
Registrar of Businesses (ROB), 95
Registrar of Companies (ROC), 62, 63,
    93, 95, 97–8, 100, 122, 124
Registrar of Trade Unions, 182
Registration of Engineers Act (1967), 62
regulated short selling (RSS), 105
regulatory structure
    reforms, 100–1, 107
Reid Commission (1955), 1
Reinvestment Allowance (RA), 194
relationship banking, 44
re-nationalization, of business
    enterprises, 213–7
Renong Berhad, 105
Rent Control Act (1954), 17
rent exaction, 132, 133, 134
rent seeking, 44
rents, 44, 152–3n35, 217, 226
    basic types, 154–5n51
    ceiling, 144–5
Report on Corporate Governance, 108
repurchase agreements (repo), 117
research and development (R&D), 183,
    190, 193–4, 197, 198, 199, 224
*Resolutions of the Securities Commission
    Shari'a Advisory Council*, 119

resource-based industries, 182–3, 184
restructuring of society, 27, 65
RHB Bank, 210
RHB financial group, 211
Rice Production Committee, 144
Ridzuan Halim, 217
ringgit. *See* Malaysian ringgit
risk management, 109
riverine commerce
    taxation, 135
riverine *negeri*, 131
riverine waterways, 130
Road Traffic Ordinance (1958), 75
royal houses, 51
RRI of Malaya Enactment, 72
rubber, 3, 100
    agriculture, 178
    for export, 73, 183
    futures markets, 100
    industry, 72
    packing/shipping, 73
    plantation, 178
    prices, 73
    production, 142, 154n49
    replanting scheme, 6–7
    trading, 96
Rubber Export Reg. Act (1966), 72
Rubber Industry (Replanting) Fund
    Ordinance (1952), 72
Rubber Industry Smallholders
    Development Authority (RISDA), 73
Rubber Price Stabilization Act (1975),
    73
Rubber Research Institute (RRI), 72
Rubber Shipping and Packing Control
    Act (1949), 72
rural development, 5, 22, 24, 26
rural squatters, 141

Sabah, 7–8, 9
    English law, 65
    regional grievances, 39
Sabah Development Bank, 83
Sabah Land Ordinance (Cap 68), 69
Sabah, Sarawak and Singapore (State

Constitutions) Order in Council
1963, 8
safety, 172–3
sale and purchase (S&P) agreements, 210
Sale of Goods (Malay States) Ordinance
(1957), 64–5
Sales Tax Act (1972), 196
Salleh Abbas, Tun, 50
Sarawak Labour Ordinance, 200
Sarawak Land Code (Cap 81), 69
Sarawak, 3, 7–8, 9, 211
English law, 65
proclamation of emergency, 57
regional grievances, 39
Second Industrial Master Plan (IMP2),
40, 198
Second Link, 47
Second Minister of Finance, 113
Second Outline Perspective Plan
(OPP2), 46–7
securities borrowing and lending (SBL),
105
Securities Commission (SC), 45, 98–9,
100–4, 113
Securities Commission Act, 1993 (SCA),
94, 98, 99, 100, 102, 110, 113–4,
119
Securities Commission (Amendment)
Act (2000), 110, 111
Securities Industry Act, 1973 (SIA), 97
Securities Industry Act, 1983 (SIA),
97–100, 110–1, 120–1
Securities Industry Act, 1993 (SIA), 90
Securities Industry (Central Depositories)
Act (1991), 99, 100, 109
Securities Industry (Compliance with
Approved Accounting Standards)
Regulations (1999), 110
Securities
market, 96–9
public offering, 101
sedentary agriculture, 130, 134
Sedition Act, 52
Selangor, 2, 18n1, 130, 138, 151n28,
197

Senate. *See* Dewan Negara
Sessions Courts, 10, 13–4, 19, 78n2
settlement cycle, 104
sewa, 148n10
sewerage system, 43, 213, 214, 217
share ownership, 109, 216, 221, 227,
228–9, 236, 239n5
share prices, 231–2
volatility, 230
shareholders, 94–5
Shari'a Advisory Council (SAC), 118,
119, 120, 127n41
Shari'a-approved securities, 118, 120
Shari'a principles, 84, 114, 120–1
Shariah Courts, 11, 14, 20–1n6
shifting cultivation, 131–2, 134, 137–8.
See also swidden agriculture
Sime Bank, 210
non-performing loans, 206
Singapore dollar, 37
Singapore Stockbrokers' Association, 96
Singapore, 1–3, 7–8, 10–1, 28, 29, 32,
96–7, 106, 117, 199, 190, 195, 218,
227
Singapore's Central Depositary (CDP),
106
slavery, 129, 135–6
small and medium sized industries
(SMIs), 40, 83, 86, 192, 198
Small Claims Tribunals, 13
Small Estates (Distribution) Act (1955),
70
small land holdings
ownership, 142
"social corporation", 235
social relations, 132
Social Security Organization (SOCSO),
160, 172
social services, 6, 7
allocation, 24
Societies Act (1966), 60
South East Asia Firebricks case, 60
South East Asian currencies, 37
South Korea, 30, 32, 33, 194, 204–5,
215, 218

Southern Bank, 210
Special Court, 14
Specific Relief Act (1950), 17, 64
Stamp Act (1949), 68
STAR, 215
State Bar Committees, 62
state economic development corporations (SEDCs), 25, 28, 190
State of Emergency, 29, 56–8
state-owned enterprises (SOEs), 27–8, 31–2, 35–6, 41–2, 72, 228
statutory laws, 55
stewardship theory, 225
stock broking industry, 109
Stock Exchange of Malaysia and Singapore, 1965 (SEMS), 96–7
Stock Exchange of Malaysia, 96
Stock Exchange of Singapore (SES), 80, 97
Stock Exchanges of Singapore and Malaysia, 126n32
stock market
    bubble, 80, 233, 237
    capital inflows, 44
    collapses, 234
    and corporate governance, 233
    developments, 229–30, 232
    governance reforms, 226
    and Malaysia's economy, 107
    massive sell-down, 105
    new equity on, 237
    public interest in, 103 share prices, 236
    under common law legal systems, 228–9
    volatility, 231
Straits Settlements, 2, 10, 69
    colonization, 130
    land laws, 136
subdivision of landholdings, 146, 155n52, 154n43
Subordinate Courts Act (1948), 89
Subordinate Courts, 10, 12–4
substantive economic laws, 17–8
Sultan, 131

Summers, Lawrence, 222
Superior Courts, 10–2
Supplementary Income Tax Act (1967), 68
Supreme Courts, 10–1, 20–1n6, 49, 55
    English Rule, 12
    judges, 9, 50
Supreme Head of the Federation, 8
Swettenham, 129, 132, 134, 150n18
swidden agriculture, 130, 137, 145
Syarikat Pengurusan Danaharta National Bhd. *See* Danaharta
Syarikat Takaful Malaysia Sdn Bhd (1984), 118

tabarru', 119, 127n44
Taiwan, 32
Taiwanese dollar, 37
Takaful Act (1984), 118–9, 121
Takaful Act (1986), 21
takaful, 119, 127n44
takeovers, 232–3
tanah mati, 148n8
Tariff Advisory Board, 179
tariff protection, 178–9, 184, 190, 201
tax breaks, 43
tax concessions, 179, 181, 184
tax holidays, 77, 179, 181, 187, 198, 200
tax incentives, 115, 179, 182, 186–7, 189–90, 192–6, 221n25
taxation, 68
taxes, collection of, 147n5
taxes, on trade, 135–6
tax-neutral framework, 115
Taylor Woodrow and Adtranz, 216
"tea money", 145
technology enhancement, 196–9
Technology Transfer Unit, 202n2
Telecommunication Ordinance (1950), 77
Telecommunications Act, 77
Telekom Malaysia, 190
Temenggong of Johor, 2
Tenaga Nasional Berhad (TNB), 77, 190
tenancy, 139–40, 142, 143, 144–5, 146
tenurial arrangements, 154n50

Terengganu, 2
Termination and Lay-off Benefits
 Regulation (1980), 173
territorial boundaries, 130
territorial chiefs, 131
terrorism, 89
Thailand, 117
Third Outline Perspective Plan (OPP3),
 47
tin, 3, 35, 100
 exports, 72
 futures markets, 100
 industry, 152n32
 mining, 4, 25, 72, 152n32, 178
 price, 35
 production, 131
Tin Control Act (1954), 73
Tin Industry (Research and
 Development) Fund Act, 1953, 73
tin-rich Malay *negeri*, 131
toll-way operator PLUS, 201
Torrens land registration system, 2,
 69–70, 136–7
Total Quality Control (TQM), 170
trade dispute, 159
Trade Disputes Ordinance (1949), 157
trade union membership, 158
trade union movement, 157, 159
trade union, 166–7, 200
 collective bargaining, 165, 175
 colonial period, 74–5, 157
 development, 158, 159
 functions, 159, 161
 industrial action, 162
 and investments, 200
 and labour legislation, 29
 labour movement, 5, 75, 157
 laws, 156, 159
 membership, 158–9
 organization, 163, 166
 pro-active role, 176
Trade Unions Act (1959), 158, 160
Trade Unions Ordinance (1959), 74, 75,
 157
transnational corporations (TNCs), 28,

181, 201, 233. *See also* multinational
 corporations (MNCs)
Transport, Storage and Communications,
 116
treasury stocks, 94
tributes, 131, 135–6
tropical hardwoods, 178
turnkey project arrangements, 33, 191,
 196
two-tier regulatory system (TTRS), 209

UEM Berhad, 105–6
UK Copyright Act (1956), 71
UN International Convention for the
 Suppression of the Financing of
 Terrorism, 89
unalienated land
 eminent domain, 141
unemployment, 26, 29, 41, 167, 174,
 179, 192, 200
Unfederated Malay States (UMS), 2, 10
 land laws, 136
 land tenure, 151n28
unicameral legislative chamber. *See*
 Dewan Undangan Negeri
union strikes, 162
United Engineers Malaysia, 201
United Malays National Organization
 (UMNO), 26, 48, 216
 1987 party elections, 49–58
United Nations Convention on
 the elimination of all forms of
 discrimination against women
 (CEDAW, 1995), 170
Urban Development Authority (UDA), 28
urban-rural gap, 5
usufructuary rights, 133, 137
Utama Bank Group (UBG), 211

venture capital industry, 88
village, 130
Vision 2020, 30, 37, 40, 46, 47, 192

Wage Councils Act (1947), 160, 167
wage flexibility, 158, 162, 174, 176

wage labour, 139–40
wage rates, 41
Water Department, 77
Waters Enactment, 75
Watson, G.M., 81
wet-rice cultivation, 130
Wilayah Persekutuan Kuala Lumpur v. Sri Lempah Enterprises, 60
Wills Act (1959), 70
Wix Corp SEA Sdn. Bhd. v. Ministry of Labour and Manpower, 60
women
  maternity benefits, 168–9
  night shift-work, 182
won (Korea), 37
Worker Compensations Ordinance

(1952), 157
worker participation, 170
Workers' Minimum Standards of Housing and Amenities Act, 1990, 160–1
working time, 167–8
Workmen's Compensation Act (1952), 161, 171
World Bank, 36, 80, 222–3
World Trade Organization (WTO), 36, 39, 201

Yang di-Pertuan Agong, 8–9, 11, 50
  constitutional role, 59
  emergency power, 57
Yang di-Pertua Negeri, 8
yen (Japan), 37